DREAMWEAVER® MX

[inside
macromedia®]

DREAMWEAVER® MX

Julia Pryor Belinski, M.Ed.
Charles F. Belinski, Ed.D.
Scott J. Wilson, Ph.D.

[inside macromedia®]

THOMSON
™
DELMAR LEARNING

Australia Canada Mexico Singapore Spain United Kingdom United States

THOMSON

DELMAR LEARNING

Dreamweaver MX
(Inside Macromedia)
by Julia Pryor Belinski, M.Ed., Charles F. Belinski, Ed.D., Scott J. Wilson, Ph.D.

Business Unit Executive:
Alar Elken

Executive Editor:
Sandy Clark

Acquisitions Editor:
James Gish

Editorial Assistant:
Jaimie Wetzel

Executive Marketing Manager:
Maura Theriault

Marketing Coordinator:
Sarena Douglass

Channel Manager:
Fair Huntoon

Executive Production Manager:
Mary Ellen Black

Production Manager:
Larry Main

Production Editor:
Tom Stover

Cover Design:
Brucie Rosch

Editorial:
Daril Bentley

Full Production Services:
Liz Kingslien
Lizart Digital Design, Chicago, IL

NOTICE TO THE READER

DREAMWEAVER MX TABLE OF CONTENTS

CHAPTER 3

CHAPTER 4

CHAPTER 5

CHAPTER 6

CHAPTER 7

CHAPTER 8

CHAPTER 9

CHAPTER 10

CHAPTER 11

CHAPTER 12

CHAPTER 16

Application Chapter: Adding a Behavior 307

CHAPTER 17

Broaden Links with Anchors and Image Maps 313

CHAPTER 18

Working with Layers 337

CHAPTER 19

Creating Animation with Dreamweaver MX 359

CHAPTER 20

CHAPTER 21

CHAPTER 22

CHAPTER 23

CHAPTER 24

Preface

If you want to learn Macromedia's Dreamweaver MX, the Web authoring tool that has revolutionized the way Web Sites are developed, you have picked up the right book.

We know Dreamweaver MX inside and out. We have been working with and teaching Macromedia's software products as authorized Macromedia training providers for over ten years.

Our book allows you to tap into the real-world experience of successful developers in the multimedia and web development industry. Through the use of our many Tips, Shortcuts, and occasional Cautions, we will give you the benefit of this "true and tested" experience.

We designed our book from the ground up to be the essential hands-on resource for Dreamweaver MX users. We focus on what you need most, concentrate on the most frequently used features and functions, and present the information within the context of "hands-on" learning.

Those who have taken our courses are among the best trained in the industry. Why? Because our teaching method is based on a classroom-tested model of instruction. It works, whether you are learning in a classroom or on your own.

Our learning strategies are centered on the concept of "learn-by-doing." With numerous exercises and screen capture illustrations, you will build your experience base as you work through our book.

We focus on the "need-to-know" functions of Dreamweaver MX, and help you get down to the business of building leading-edge Web applications – *fast.*

We provide a "real-world" focus that reflects the development needs, project objectives, and Dreamweaver MX functionality typical of professional Web sites.

We deliver the professional experience of successful Dreamweaver MX developers – you will learn the valuable tips and shortcuts that only the experts know.

We hope you find our book valuable and have some fun along the way!

Scott J. Wilson, Ph.D.

Instructional Architect for the Thomson/Delmar Learning Inside Macromedia Series

Acknowledgments

First and foremost, we want to thank the thousands of students who have attended our classes during the past ten years. Your enthusiasm and probing questions have not only increased our enjoyment of teaching but have also helped us become better at what we do.

We would also like to thank the many people at Macromedia with whom we have worked over the years, including those in the Authorized Training Program, Authorized Developer Program, Value-Added Reseller Program, Technical Support, Marketing/Trade Events, and Development/Engineering teams.

Finally, we want to thank the many people at Thomson/Delmar Learning for their help and encouragement: Jim Gish, for helping us to better target, focus, and market the Inside Macromedia Series; Daril Bentley, whose help, guidance, encouragement, and suggestions have been greatly appreciated; Larry Main and Thomas Stover for their technical expertise and work behind the scenes; Liz Kingslien of Lizart Digital Design for her professional production work and enjoyable working relationship, and Vince Nicotina for his work on our CD-ROM.

From Julia and Chuck

We enjoy working with and teaching all of the Macromedia products, and we especially enjoy the new Studio MX series, including Dreamweaver MX. Having the opportunity to write this instructional text to share with so many others beyond our students, clients, and colleagues has been a very fulfilling experience. Thank you to our families for their support, guidance, and their toleration of us talking about "The Book." We also thank our past/present/future students, for without them we would not take as much pleasure in teaching as we do.

From Scott

Many thanks to my family, teachers, students, friends, colleagues, and fellow human beings – from whom I have learned so much along the way. God please give me the insight and strength to put into practice that which has been given. Marie-Claire, my wise and beautiful wife, thank you from the bottom of my heart for your continued support, faith, and love.

C H A P T E R   1

Getting Started

Introduction

In this first chapter you will get a quick introduction to Dreamweaver MX. You will also find information that will help you in using the book and the companion CD-ROM. The chapter concludes with a brief review of the new features in Dreamweaver MX. We hope you will find our book helpful in your quest for knowledge, and that you will find Dreamweaver MX a powerful and fun tool to use. By the end of the chapter you will be able to:

- *List skills that are frequently needed to create multimedia projects.*
- *Describe the learning strategies used in this book.*
- *Describe the icons for quick access used in this book.*
- *Execute (or drag) a file from the companion CD-ROM that will create a folder on your hard drive for saving the exercises you will work with in this book. This will also copy support files needed for these exercises.*
- *Locate necessary files on the companion CD-ROM (or those copied to your hard drive).*
- *Open the Dreamweaver MX program.*
- *List several new features of the Dreamweaver MX program.*

Overview of Dreamweaver MX

The demand for skilled web developers has continued to skyrocket over the past few years, fueled by countless businesses and organizations wanting to have an Internet "presence," combined with the dramatic increase in e-learning and e-commerce. In the ensuing search for a web authoring tool that is both powerful and easy to use, Dreamweaver has continued to catch the attention of both experienced and beginning web developers. Dreamweaver MX's visual interface dramatically reduces the initial learning curve and increases efficiency as the production effort begins.

For experienced programmers, Dreamweaver MX not only provides the capability to directly insert and modify HTML code but to also, with the use of behaviors and extensions, incorporate the use of JavaScript, XML, and other scripting languages. With the increasing need for dynamic web sites, Macromedia has incorporated the database features of Dreamweaver UltraDev into Dreamweaver MX, along with web application development tools. This combination of ease of use and functionality has made Dreamweaver MX an industry leader, and a powerful and versatile tool for both basic and advanced web developers.

Dreamweaver MX: Art and Technical Skills

Learning how to use Dreamweaver MX (or any other authoring software program) is only one aspect of what is required to create a functional and professional-looking multimedia program or web site. Generally there are many different skill sets involved. These different skills may exist within a single individual or may be represented in the composite skills of a team. These skills include the following.

- *Design and layout principles*
- *Artistic creativity and execution*
- *Writing (text and narration)*
- *Program, message, and instructional design*
- *Audio and video techniques*
- *Use of the authoring software*
- *Project management*

Although the focus of this book is to help you use the Dreamweaver MX authoring software program, the acquisition of these technical skills should be considered within the context of the additional skills that may be required. The extent to which you may need these additional skills will depend to a large extent on the type of application you are creating, its intended use, and how "professional" you want the end result to be.

We realize that many of you may not have an art background, or may just want to have fun with Dreamweaver MX for your own personal use. Therefore, the exercises included in this book do not require an art background – although they can be enhanced on your own, if you have artistic talent. If you do have artistic talent, we encourage you to take "creative license" to modify and embellish the subject matter however you wish.

Overview of the Book

The Dreamweaver MX software comes with a pretty extensive online help system. Our book focuses on presenting key points and guided practice for actually using the software in a "real-world" environment.

Chapters 1 through 24 guide you through the features and capabilities you will need the most as you develop your web projects, including other elements that add a little "punch" to your site – including Flash and other animation and interaction. The practice exercises in these chapters also include an explanation of the HTML code that is being generated (by Dreamweaver MX) behind the scenes as you create a web page using Dreamweaver MX's visual interface. Although Dreamweaver MX and its "what-you-see-is-what-you-get" (WYSIWYG) interface automatically creates the HTML needed for your web pages, we think it is still a good idea to have a basic sense of the HTML code, in case it does not do exactly what you want it to.

There is additional material we think you will find valuable as you continue to work with Dreamweaver MX. This material is located on the companion CD-ROM, within a folder named *Job Aids*. There is a document that contains a quick reference of all panels and windows in Dreamweaver MX. Additional appendix files on the companion CD-ROM include information on working with style sheets, updating templates, and understanding JavaScript. All of these documents are in a PDF format and can be printed using the Adobe Acrobat Reader, also included on the companion CD-ROM.

Instructional Approach

Because of its many features and functions, Dreamweaver MX may at first seem intimidating. We do not want to overwhelm you with a lot of details all at once, but instead will introduce the aspects of Dreamweaver MX that are the most practical and those that are most commonly used to build programs in today's workplace.

We hope to help you learn Dreamweaver MX in an intuitive way while practicing some of the techniques and shortcuts typical of the ones that web designers are using as they create Dreamweaver MX projects for real-world applications. Each chapter builds upon the last, adding new features of Dreamweaver MX to your builder's toolbox.

The chapters in our book break up the material into "learning chunks" that are suitable for most people during a single session, whether you are learning on your own or using this book within a classroom setting. The learning strategies used in these chapters are centered on the concept of "learning by doing." These learning strategies represent the synthesis of teaching multimedia software programs for over nine years as an Authorized Macromedia Training Center. Understanding the intent behind these learning strategies may help you to most effectively use what is provided here to learn and understand the Dreamweaver MX software program.

Learning Strategies

Introduction: Each chapter begins with a brief introduction to the topics to be covered, including a brief listing of learning objectives for those of you who find such things useful.

Conceptual overviews: Provide a 50,000-foot overview of the subject matter before we get into the narrowly focused details of building something.

Guided tours: Structured "walk-throughs" of how to do something or use a Dreamweaver MX feature. A guided tour is not really an exercise, but follows the notion of learning by actively "looking and doing." Many of the guided tours are followed by a practice exercise to show you how Dreamweaver MX functions "in action," and to reemphasize how to use its features as you develop.

Practice exercises: Introductory, hands-on practice in the basic skills and tools needed to develop web pages in Dreamweaver MX. The scope of an exercise is fairly narrow, focusing on the concepts and skills that have just been introduced in the current chapter. The content itself is focused on the development of web page elements and is not dependent on preexisting artistic talent. Again, if you do have artistic talent, please feel free to modify and embellish the content you find within the exercises. A practice exercise accommodates two learning environments: the classroom setting and learning on your own. Each practice exercise includes the following elements, which reflect project elements at work in the real-world development process.

- *"Description" section:* Provides a general description of the purpose of an exercise and the components that will be used within it. Generally, real-world projects include a project description, although they will typically be much more detailed than those found here.

- *"Take a Look" section:* Asks you to make use of files supplied with the book, using Dreamweaver MX to open a completed version of the exercise you are about to create. This section will ask you to pay particular attention to noted aspects of the completed exercise as you are looking at it. Where applicable, key information will be discussed, including the properties and settings of the various window palettes.

- *"Storyboard: On Screen" section:* Provides screen captures of what will be seen on screen when the exercise is completed and previewed in a browser, to serve as a printed reference. A storyboard that includes on-screen descriptions or illustrations is a vital real-world project deliverable.

- *"Storyboard: Behind the Scenes" section:* Provides screen captures displaying a sample of the completed HTML code for the exercise, to serve as a guidepost for development. Your completed HTML code may differ from ours, but the key areas (tags) should be the same. A storyboard that includes programming descriptions or notes is a vital real-world project deliverable.

- *Go Solo:* You will see this icon immediately following the storyboard sections. At this point in an exercise, you should have the information necessary to complete the exercise on your own, and we encourage you to give it a try. If you need help, however, unlike the real world you can use the step-by-step instructions that follow.

- *"Step-by-Step Instructions" section: For those who would like structured help with the details of the tasks involved in the exercise. In most instances, the numbered steps state "what" needs to be done, and the lettered substeps describe "how" to do it.*
- *"Summary" section: Each chapter concludes with a bulleted list of the major concepts and topics presented.*

Application Chapters: A Project

Each application chapter focuses on an exercise that serves as a component of a real-world application. Combined these chapters constitute a complete Dreamweaver MX application project. Each application exercise provides hands-on experience in building structures that give you an opportunity to practice the concepts and skills learned across several preceding chapters.

The companion CD-ROM contains the completed version of each application exercise. Therefore, if you choose to, you can skip over some content areas and still be able to work on other parts of the application project. Each application exercise contains the same subsections as a practice exercise — with one difference. The step-by-step instructions are not included in application exercises, so that you can master the material on your own. The application exercises do, however, include a list of the tasks you will need to perform to complete the exercise.

Icons for Quick Access

The Inside Macromedia series uses the following icons, appearing in the margin, to provide quick, visual cueing to particular types of information.

CD-ROM icon: Indicates that material from the companion CD-ROM is necessary (or available) at this point in an exercise or tour.

Tip icon: Provides additional information related to an aspect of an exercise or tour. This falls into the "nice to know but not necessary" category of information.

Shortcut icon: Provides a more efficient method as an alternative to the steps described in the text.

Caution icon: Provides helpful suggestions for avoiding actions that might result in lost time and effort.

HTML icon: Provides corresponding HTML source code for a specific Dreamweaver MX concept.

Go Solo icon: Indicates that at this point you have enough information to take control of the exercise and attempt to complete the exercise on your own.

Go Solo

DWExercises Site icon: Indicates that the site called *DWExercises* needs to be opened for the practice exercise.

DWExercises Site

DWComplete Site icon: Indicates that the site called *DWComplete* needs to be opened for the practice exercise.

DWComplete Site

The 21st Century Kitchen Site icon: Indicates that the site called *The 21st Century Kitchen* needs to be opened for the application chapter.

21st Century
KITCHEN SITE

Development Tool Only icon: Used within practice exercises and indicates that there is nothing to look at in the Document window. The exercise does not actually create anything but instead works with settings and properties in the program.

DEVELOPMENT TOOL ONLY

Using the Book on Your Own

Each book in the Inside Macromedia series has been designed for use either on your own or within a classroom setting. For those of you who will be using this book to learn Dreamweaver MX on your own, do not worry; we will guide you through the process and give you the freedom to modify what you want. Over the years, the authors have learned many software programs on our own and think that the learning strategies we are using in this book have helped us the most as learners. The following are among the "learning strategy" components in this book.

Conceptual overviews: 50,000-foot perspectives serving as introductions.

Guided tour: Actively looks at options, preferences, and so on.

Exercises: Hands-on experience with the details of how to do something.

- *"Take a Look" sections:* "Seeing" what the goal is.
- *"Storyboard" sections:* "Pre-thinking" what will be on screen and what will be necessary in terms of programming.
- *Tips: Separating the "nice to know" material from what is necessary.*

Go Solo: At this point you have enough information to complete the exercise on your own. Keep in mind that there generally is more than one way to build something. You may end up creating the exercise using different steps from those presented — and that is fine if your structure does what it needs to do.

"Step-by-Step Instructions" sections: More details for those who need or want them.

- *Numbered steps: State "what" needs to be done.*
- *Lettered substeps: Describe "how" to do what needs to be done.*

Using the Book in an Instructional Setting

As instructors for Flash, Authorware, Director, Dreamweaver MX, Fireworks (and others), the authors believe the learning strategies are equally effective (presented somewhat differently) in the instructional setting as learning on your own. In the "classroom," we use the book as a point of reference and organizational guide for the presentation of material. As a "point of reference," we do not "read" from the book – nor ask students to do so. We use the book to organize the classroom presentation. We encourage students to take notes right in the book. The elements previously outlined for self-instruction are handled in the instructional setting as follows.

Conceptual overviews: Presentation of the highlights from the book, with each instructor generally adding his or her own details or points of emphasis.

Guided tours: Using a projection device attached to the instructor's computer, as a class we "walk through" the essence of the tour.

Exercises: Again, using a projection device, as a class we "walk through" the beginning of an exercise.

- *"Take a Look" sections:* We look at the completed version of the exercise, pointing out noteworthy characteristics.

- *"Storyboard" sections:* We use the completed version to look at what is on screen and what is programmed (making reference to the screen captures in the book as well).

- *Go Solo:* We ask students at this point to try to complete the exercise on their own. If students need help, we suggest looking first at the numbered steps that state "what" needs to be done, and then trying to figure out "how" to do it on their own.

- *Instructor help:* We walk around the classroom providing help and additional information as needed.

- *Tips:* Each instructor contributes his or her own additional information based on professional experience.

Windows Versus Macintosh

Dreamweaver MX, like most of Macromedia's software, is virtually the same on both Macintosh- and Windows-based computers. The biggest variation stems from minor differences in a few keyboard keys and the absence of the right-hand button on the Macintosh mouse. Table 1-1 compares the Windows and Macintosh keyboard keys.

Table 1-1: Windows and Macintosh Keyboard Keys

Windows	**Macintosh**
Alt in combination with another key	*Opt* in combination with another key
Ctrl in combination with another key	*Cmd* in combination with another key
Right mouse button click	*Ctrl* with mouse click

Throughout the book these differences are minimized in that we most often make selections through the use of menu options, which are the same across both platforms unless otherwise noted. As we progress through the exercises, however, we will make use of Shortcut icons to provide both Macintosh and Windows versions of keyboard shortcuts.

To provide a consistent look for screen captures, most illustrations will depict the Windows version of Dreamweaver MX. When there is a major difference between Windows and Macintosh screens, Macintosh screen captures are also provided.

The companion CD-ROM contains two files listing the keyboard shortcuts for Windows and Macintosh. Look inside the folder *Job Aids* for *DWinterface_Mac.PDF* and *DWinterface_Win.PDF.*

Getting Your Computer Ready

Prerequisite Knowledge

It is assumed that you already have the skills necessary to work in the Windows or Macintosh environment prior to learning Dreamweaver MX. Specifically you should be able to:

* *Use the mouse and keyboard for basic input and selection*
* *Select and drag objects*
* *Resize windows*
* *Locate directories (folders)*
* *Locate files within directories*
* *Create directories*
* *Copy files*
* *Use the Undo command*

Preparing Your Computer's Hard Drive

Throughout this book you will be creating many Dreamweaver MX files you will want to save on your computer. When you begin working with links, files will have to be saved in order for the link to work correctly. This is also true for frames, templates, and all other linking-type files. Dreamweaver MX is very particular about the structural relationship of "saved" elements. To make it easier for you to locate these files, and easier for us to communicate to you about these files, it is strongly recommended that you save the files in a directory named *Learning_Dreamweaver* on your computer's hard drive.

Installing the Files Needed for the Practice Exercises

Windows (PC)

We recommend that you use the install program on the companion CD-ROM. This install program will create a new directory called *Learning_Dreamweaver*, and will copy to this directory all support files you will need.

- *On the companion CD-ROM, double click on the file* Install Learning.exe, *which is found in the* Windows Install *folder. Follow the directions.*
- *The default folder is* Learning_Dreamweaver. *You may change the hard drive letter where the folder will be created, but do not change the name of the folder, because this is the folder referred to in all of the exercises.*
- *A message will tell you how much space is required for the files.*
- *Files will be copied to the* Learning_Dreamweaver *folder. Subfolders are created for each chapter, and each has its own set of files. For example, Chapter 5 will have all of its files in the* ch05 *folder.*

If you do not want to copy all files to your hard drive at once (if you do not have enough room), you can just copy the files for a single chapter as needed.

- *On the root directory of your computer's hard drive (or a subfolder such as* Program Files), *create a folder named* Learning_Dreamweaver.
- *On the companion CD-ROM, find the folder* Learning_Dreamweaver *and the appropriate chapter subfolder (e.g., for Chapter 5 find* ch05). *Copy the entire chapter folder to the* Learning_Dreamweaver *folder on your hard drive.*

Macintosh

- *On the companion CD-ROM, find the folder called* Learning_Dreamweaver.
- *Drag the folder* Learning_Dreamweaver *to the Macintosh hard drive.*
- *Subfolders are copied for each chapter, and each has its own set of files. For example, Chapter 5 will have all of its files in the* ch05 *folder.*

If you do not want to copy all files to your hard drive at once (if you do not have enough room), you can just copy the files for a single chapter as needed.

- *On the root directory of your computer's hard drive, create a folder named* Learning_Dreamweaver.

• *On the companion CD-ROM, find the folder* Learning_Dreamweaver *and the appropriate chapter subfolder (e.g., for Chapter 5 find ch05). Copy the entire chapter folder to the* Learning_Dreamweaver *folder on your hard drive.*

The Companion CD-ROM

This book makes use of numerous learning activities that include preexisting HTML files, graphics, and other media elements. All of these files and elements, and a great deal more, are contained on the companion CD-ROM found at the back of the book. Place the CD-ROM into your computer's CD-ROM player. Use your computer to view the content of the CD-ROM. Figure 1-1 shows the main directory structure of the CD-ROM.

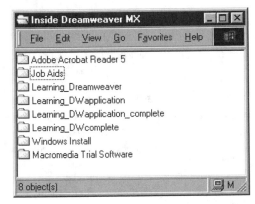

Fig. 1-1. Main directory structure of the companion CD-ROM.

Figure 1-2 shows the subfolders within the *Learning_Dreamweaver* folder.

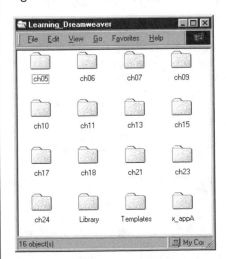

Fig. 1-2. Subfolders within the Learning_Dreamweaver *folder.*

The main folders on the companion CD-ROM are described in the following.

Windows Install: This folder contains installation programs for Windows/PC. These programs will copy to the hard drive files needed for the practice exercises and application chapters.

Learning_Dreamweaver: This folder contains subfolders for each chapter containing one or more practice exercises. The folders contain support files needed to complete a practice exercise. For Windows users, these files will be copied to your hard drive when you select the executable file *Install Learning*, found in the *Windows Install* folder on the root of the CD-ROM. For Macintosh users, this is the folder you will drag to your hard drive. This corresponds to the site that will be created, called *DWExercises.*

Learning_DWcomplete: This folder contains all completed files for the practice exercises. You will be asked to refer to these files within the "Take a Look" sections. This corresponds to the site that will be created, called *DWComplete.*

Learning_DWapplication: This folder contains files and media needed for each chapter in the book containing one or more application exercises. The folders contain support files needed to complete the application exercises. Chapter 8 provides additional information on installing this folder. This corresponds to the site that will be created, called *The 21st Century Kitchen.*

Learning_DWapplication_complete: This folder contains all completed files for the application chapters. You will be asked to refer to these files within the "Take a Look" sections.

Job Aids: This folder contains files for the Windows and Macintosh, with details on the Dreamweaver MX menus, keyboard shortcuts, panels, and windows. Additional appendix files for further learning are also included in this folder.

Adobe Acrobat Reader 5: This folder contains the installation program for Adobe Acrobat Reader 5. A version of Adobe Acrobat Reader will be needed to print the PDF files found in the *Job Aids* folder.

File Extensions and Descriptions

Note the following file type and extension names and descriptions, as they are used within this book.

- DWT (.dwt): *Dreamweaver MX template.*
- LBI (.lbi): *Dreamweaver MX library.*
- HTM and HTML (.htm and .html): *HTML documents that can be opened in Dreamweaver and browsers. These can also be opened in other HTML editing packages and word processors.*

- JPG and JPEG (.jpg and .jpeg): *Graphic file format; one of many that can be imported into HTML files.*

- SWF (.swf): *Shockwave Flash format; may contain graphics, animation, and/or sound.*

- GIF (.gif): *Graphic file format; one of many that can be imported into HTML files.*

- PNG (.png): *Graphic file format; one of many that can be imported into HTML files.*

- MNO (.mno): *Design notes; any HTML file can have associated design notes. These are located in the folder called* Notes *within the* Site *folder.*

Opening a New File in Dreamweaver MX

Windows Computer

After you have successfully installed Dreamweaver MX on your computer, you can open it like any other Windows software program.

1. From the Start menu (Windows task bar), select the *Programs* folder.

2. Open the *Macromedia Dreamweaver MX* folder. (Note that the placement of this folder in the *Programs* folder will vary, depending on where you designated placement of the shortcut.)

3. Select Dreamweaver MX. See figure 1-3.

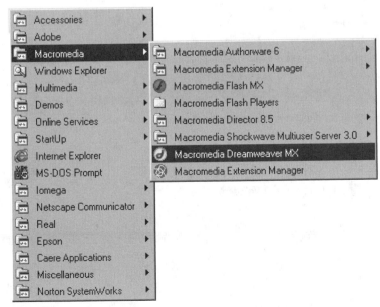

Fig. 1-3. Opening Macromedia Dreamweaver MX (Windows).

4. The first time you open Dreamweaver MX in Windows, you will be asked the type of workspace you want to use. Note the following.

   • *Dreamweaver MX Workspace is the option that specifies an integrated workspace, with the panels and work area docked in one large document. This is the workspace you will use in this book.*

   • *Dreamweaver MX Workspace, HomeSite/Coder-Style is the option that specifies the MX workspace but with the docked panels on the left side of the document and the Document window shown in Code view by default.*

   • *Dreamweaver MX Workspace is similar to the floating panels and windows in Dreamweaver MX. There are still panel groups, but they are not all docked together in one document.*

   The workspace may be changed by selecting Edit Menu | Preferences | General. This option is available in Windows only. See figure 1-4.

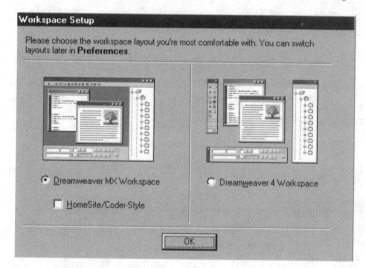

Fig. 1-4. Selecting the Dreamweaver workspace.

5. The first time Dreamweaver MX opens, you are presented with a *Welcome to Dreamweaver MX* screen. You can always redisplay this screen by selecting Help Menu | Welcome. See figure 1-5.

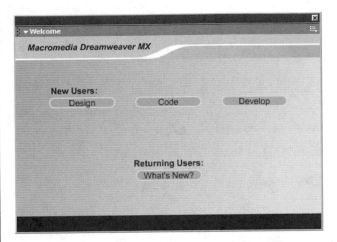

Fig. 1-5. Dreamweaver MX welcome screen (Windows).

6. A blank Document window is opened when Dreamweaver MX is launched. Many of the panels and toolbars most commonly used are opened with the Document window. We will go through these elements of Dreamweaver MX's interface in greater detail in Chapter 3. The companion CD-ROM contains files that offer a complete listing of the interface elements, in the folder called *Job Aids*. See figure 1-6.

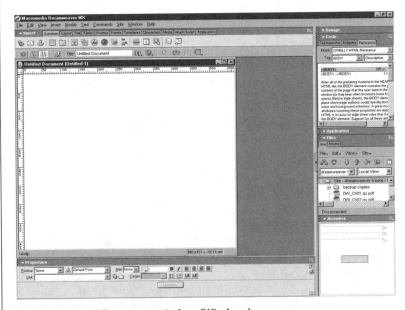

Fig. 1-6. Untitled Document window (Windows).

Macintosh Computer

After you have successfully installed Dreamweaver MX on your computer, you can open it like any other Macintosh software program, as follows.

1. Double click to open the Macintosh hard drive where you installed Dreamweaver MX.

2. Open the *Macromedia Dreamweaver MX* folder.

3. Select Dreamweaver MX. See figure 1-7.

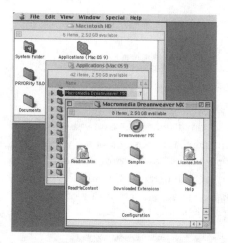

Fig. 1-7. Selecting Dreamweaver MX (Mac).

4. The first time Dreamweaver MX opens, you are presented with a welcome screen. You can always bring this screen back up by selecting Help | Welcome. See figure 1-8.

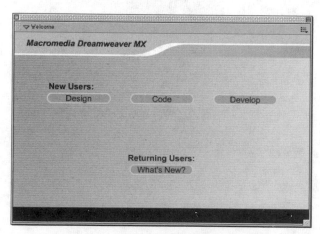

Fig. 1-8. Dreamweaver MX welcome screen (Mac).

5. A blank Document window is opened when Dreamweaver MX is launched. Many of the panels and toolbars most commonly used are opened with the Document window. We will go through these elements of Dreamweaver's interface in greater detail in Chapter 3. The companion CD-ROM contains files that offer a complete listing of the interface elements, in the folder called *Job Aids*. See figure 1-9.

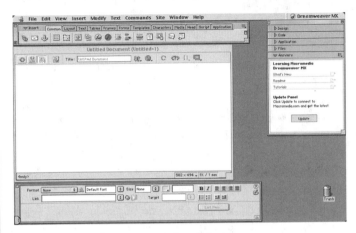

Fig. 1-9. Untitled Document window (Mac).

What's New in Dreamweaver MX?

With the new MX series of Macromedia products, the user interface has inherited a more standardized look and feel. The Macromedia MX panel management is now used in Dreamweaver MX, Flash MX, and Fireworks MX. The user interface groups collapsible, dockable panels and provides the option to collapse or expand the panels as needed. On Windows platforms, this means that the workspace windows and panels are now integrated into a single larger application window. On the Macintosh (and as an option on Windows), the same panels are floating panels in Dreamweaver MX.

In addition, Dreamweaver MX now includes all of the application development features of Dreamweaver UltraDev 4, as well as features derived from Macromedia ColdFusion Studio. New features of the Macromedia MX series of software that have been incorporated in Dreamweaver MX are described in the following.

- *A new integrated workspace layout (Microsoft Windows only) includes the option to work in Design or Homesite/Code view. Select Edit Menu | Preferences | General.*

- *Predesigned sample web page layouts to give you a head start on your designs. Select File Menu | New | Page Designs.*

- *Ability to reuse and save portions of code, called snippets. See the Snippets panel.*

- *Enhanced Dreamweaver templates now have four types of editable regions. The first is the usual editable region. The repeating region allows a content editor to copy the region and insert it into the document. The display of the optional region (i.e., an image or optional text) is up to the content editor. The editable tag attribute allows you to unlock tag attributes (i.e., the attributes of an image) in the template-based page.*

- *Templates now also have the option to set expressions. Template expressions use JavaScript functions and rules that set values in a template-based document.*

- *The Site Definition wizard fills in the required information to set up a site for the first time. It will also assist you in setting up a dynamic site. Select Site Menu | New Site.*

- *In Code view, as you type certain characters, a list appears suggesting the characters you are entering. These are called code hints. Additional attributes for a tag are also hinted at.*

- *A customizable Insert bar replaces the Dreamweaver MX Objects panels used to insert objects and behaviors in Dreamweaver MX.*

- *Using XML and JavaScript, you can now customize the Document toolbar. See "Customizing Dreamweaver" on the Dreamweaver web site.*

- *The Site panel now has its own file explorer to display not only the location of your site but the drives and folders on the entire operating system. Select Window Menu | Site.*

- *The Answers panel connects you directly with online resources from the Macromedia Support Center. You can retrieve new content at will to ensure that you always have access to the latest tips and tricks. Select Window Menu | Others | Answers.*

- *Enhanced table editing and manipulation generates better code for table edits in Layout view and Standard view. Emphasis has been placed on tables with cross-browser compatibility.*

- *Cascading JavaScript pop-up menus can now be created right in Dreamweaver MX, a capability formerly available only in Fireworks.*

- *Syntax coloring is now customizable. Select Preferences | Code Coloring.*

- *The Standard toolbar allows quick access to commonly used file commands (e.g., Open, Save, and New) and clipboard commands. Select View Menu | Toolbars | Standard.*

- *Printing from Code view now allows you to print your source code. Select File Menu | Print Code.*

- *You can now import or export a Site Definition so you don't have to recreate it on each machine accessing that site.*

Summary

- *Dreamweaver MX is one of the leading web development tools for beginning through advanced developers.*

- *The following elements used in the book are designed to accommodate different learning styles and situations.*

    Guided tour: A structured "walk-through" of how to do something (such as making menu and window selections).

    Practice exercise: An introductory, hands-on experience in learning the basic tools and skills of Dreamweaver MX.

    Application exercise: Provides hands-on experience in building structures that combine the concepts and skills learned across several chapters.

- *The Inside Macromedia series uses a number of icons, appearing in the margin, to provide quick, visual cueing to particular types of information.*

- *All work files for the exercises in this book will be saved in a folder (named Learning_Dreamweaver) on your computer's hard drive. Before beginning any of the exercises, use the Install Learning.exe file on the companion CD-ROM to copy required files for the exercises to the hard drive. On the Macintosh, drag the Learning.Dreamweaver folder from the companion CD-ROM to your hard drive.*

- *This book makes use of numerous learning activities that include preexisting Dreamweaver MX files and a variety of media elements. All of these files, elements, and a great deal more are contained on the companion CD-ROM.*

- *There are a number of new features of Dreamweaver MX, which were described in this chapter.*

The Internet Environment

Introduction

Historians may look back at this period and designate the emergence and rapid growth of the Internet as an event of equal or greater significance to the invention and use of the printing press or the telephone. The Internet can be considered to be many things, but fundamentally it is a new medium for world-wide, instantaneous communication. With the use of a personal computer or a handheld device, anyone, located anywhere, at any time, can send and/or receive information with anyone else in the world. This communication might take the form of live "chatrooms," e-mail, or posting/reading web pages.

Web sites are basically a collection of documents (web pages) that can contain text, graphics, animation, sound, navigational controls, or other elements – all organized and linked in a specific way, for a particular purpose. As with all "documents," web pages exist to communicate with readers/viewers. The purpose behind this communication might be to inform, educate, sell, persuade, motivate, entertain, or a variety of other possibilities.

As you are about to embark on your mission to "create" in this new medium of communication, you could spend long hours learning to write HTML code, and then spend many more hours writing the "code" required for your web pages. But wouldn't it be easier if there were a program where you could just type in your ideas using some sort of word processor? Where you could design and arrange the web page layout and its elements using some sort of page layout program? Where you could save your work into some type of computer file and then place this file on a computer network for all to see?

Dreamweaver MX is that program. With the use of Dreamweaver MX and its visual interface, you will soon be able to create web pages and web sites without learning HTML code. In this chapter, we will provide you with an overview of the Internet environment in order to provide a context for what you will soon be learning about Dreamweaver MX. In the following chapters, we will provide you with "hands-on" experience using various aspects of the Dreamweaver interface, as well as step-by-step practice using Dreamweaver MX functions and capabilities to create a wide variety of web page elements and to build a "real-world" web site. After you have completed this book, you will have the skills necessary to create a web site that has the potential to "communicate with the world."

Web Pages – Technically Speaking

We are going to start off looking at web pages from both a technical perspective and from an aesthetic perspective. The technical section will present an overview of some of the nuts-and-bolts aspects of web development. The aesthetic section will discuss some of the creative aspects of developing web pages and web sites.

HyperText Markup Language (HTML)

In the "old days" before Dreamweaver MX, creating web pages using HyperText Markup Language (HTML) was laborious at best. Web developers typed in all of the HTML as lines of code, similar to many programming languages of the time, and hoped it worked – with rounds of testing and debugging when it did not. Back then, including any formatting beyond one column of text and the occasional bold or underline, was difficult for anyone not trained in HTML.

HTML consists of the text you see on the web page, but it also includes a number of extra characters and symbols interwoven with the normal text. If you look closely at the HTML code that displays a web page, eventually you will "see" the text that appears on the web page, intermixed with many other symbols. See figure 2-1.

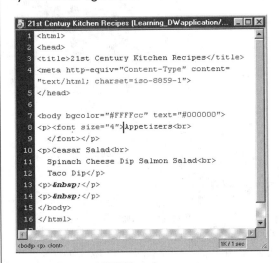

Fig. 2-1. Text and HTML code.

These additional characters in the HTML are the attribute codes for telling the web browser how to format objects on the web page and how to display the page layout. HTML has formatting codes for items such as text alignment, text color, when to start a new paragraph, and numerous other functions for which code is necessary.

HTML and other types of markup languages (e.g., XML and XHTML) consist of (1) the actual content (text and file names for media elements) within the page, and (2) predefined tags (labels) that define the structure of the page/elements. HTML continues to serve as the foundation for most web pages and web sites today.

The development of visually oriented HTML editors, such as Dreamweaver MX, has dramatically changed the way most web pages are now created. With Dreamweaver MX, web page developers are no longer obligated to know very much about HTML code. Luckily, Dreamweaver MX automatically handles the HTML coding, so that you do not have to unless you want to.

Dreamweaver MX's visual interface, menus, tools, and wizards automatically create and insert the HTML needed for displays, formatting, animation, and the like. Figure 2-2 shows Dreamweaver MX's interface.

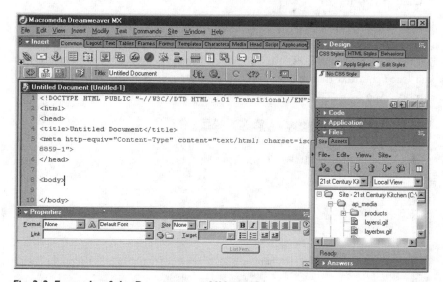

Fig. 2-2. Example of the Dreamweaver MX interface.

As you add media to your pages, modify attributes, and move elements around on the page, Dreamweaver MX automatically modifies the underlying HTML code. Some examples of these formatting characters are <b> (to turn on bold text) and </b> (to turn off bold text), and _blank to open a web link in a new blank window. Dreamweaver MX adds features to make it even easier to work with tables, layers, and frames, and to add JavaScript behaviors. We will discuss each of these features in later chapters.

Dreamweaver MX will also let you open an HTML document to view and edit within either Dreamweaver MX's WYSIWYG mode or in the native HTML code mode. This capability is known as "Round-Trip HTML," and as we continue in the following chapters you will see why this feature is so important for working with web pages and web sites.

Web Site Organization: What Your Viewer Sees

Almost from the moment of birth, we all learn to distinguish, discern, label, and "classify" things as a means of learning how to live in a world in which we are bombarded with sensory information. To a certain extent, how well we "organize" our information determines how well we get along in life.

Individuals organize information in countless ways. They are heavily influenced by their own experiences, personality traits, parental upbringing, religious convictions, political orientation, gender, nationality, and many other factors.

As a web developer and "communicator," part of your job is to organize the information you want to present in a way that will help your viewers quickly access and better understand the information they are seeking. Your organization and presentation of content, as well as means of navigation around your web site, need to accommodate the varying needs and backgrounds of your viewers, support the purpose behind the existence of your web site, and facilitate the maintenance of the site. The web content may lend itself to one of a few simple methods of organization, in which distinguishing one category from another is straightforward, as in the following.

Alphabetical order: An example here might be a web site for herbs and spices used for cooking, providing an alphabetical list in which users can click on a name to get additional information about that herb or spice.

Numerical order: An example of this organizational strategy might be a web site for replacement parts for various types of equipment, in which all parts available for a specific piece of equipment are listed by catalog number. Selecting a part number brings up detailed information on each part.

Regional/geographical order: An example might be a web site for home gardening, in which clicking on each geographical region offers different types of plants and trees appropriate for that particular area.

Chronological order: An example of this might be a web site for a state historical society, listing significant events by date.

More often than not, however, an organizational scheme is not as obvious as these. In looking at the content itself and the numerous ways users may want to access that information, there may not be obvious, clear-cut categories. The categories we create may not be as distinct or mutually exclusive as we first may have thought, resulting in the user not being sure where to look for a specific item.

In addition to concerns about how to create useful and intuitive categories, you will also need to consider the relationship among these categories, or the structure by which they are connected. You may create a web site that is linear (broad and flat), offering many categories, but each category is only a page deep. An example might be the previously mentioned web site for herbs and spices. A home page might offer a scrolling list to select from — with each selection resulting in a single page containing text, graphics, and a sound file for that herb/spice. See figure 2-3.

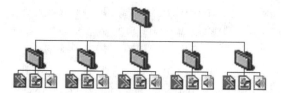

Fig. 2-3. Linear structure.

Another possibility might initially offer the viewer fewer categories to choose from, but within each category offer numerous sublevels of choices. This organizational scheme is often referred to as a hierarchical structure. You start out with a main topic (or home web page); the main page offers subtopics. Each subtopic may have additional subtopics, and so on.

The web site we will develop in this book uses a hierarchical organization scheme. Our online store has a main page that identifies the store and the purpose of the site. The home page offers the choices About Us, Products, Services, Ordering, and other sections. The Products page offers the choices Appliances, Bakeware, Cookware, and so on. Having selected Bakeware, there are additional choices for each of the specific bakeware products our online store offers. Many web sites use some type of hierarchical structure. See figure 2-4.

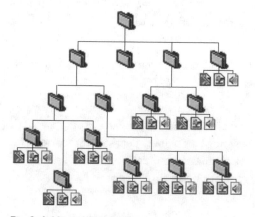

Fig. 2-4. Hierarchical structure.

There are many ways to organize and structure your web site. There will be many variables that will influence how you go about doing this. The primary motivating factor in how you organize and structure your site should be how to best communicate with your web site visitor.

Web Site Organization: File Structure on the Server

In addition to the need to organize and structure your web site from the visitor's point of view, there is also an equally important need to organize and structure the files and media elements being used to create the web site. Although the organizational scheme and structure used behind the scenes – for the files and media elements on the web server – will probably reflect the organization and structure the visitor sees on the web site, it may not be an exact reflection.

Even a relatively small web site can contain dozens, if not hundreds, of web pages and media files. To have a web site that is both fully functional and manageable, it is very important to give careful consideration to how you organize and structure these files on the web server. Dreamweaver MX can help you keep track of everything, via its Site panel (discussed in material to follow).

Dreamweaver MX (and the underlying HTML code) requires the precise name and location of the HTML documents and media elements being used to display a web page. The location or path to these files is defined by where they reside within a file/folder structure. As was the case with the interface for the user, this file/folder structure can also be organized in a variety of ways, including the flat and hierarchical structures discussed previously.

A pyramid structure is another method of organization that is very similar to the hierarchical structure; in fact, the user will probably not notice any difference. A pyramid structure organizes information by using broad categories and subcategories, as does the hierarchical. But with a pyramid structure, all information at the same level of detail or type is presented at the same level.

From a web site developer's point of view, using a pyramid structure helps to organize all of the pages and media using consistent levels. An example of a pyramid structure would be an online course with eight topic sections. Each topic of the course would have its own directory folder. Inside each of the eight topic folders would be a folder for graphic files, a folder for audio files, and so on. See figure 2-5.

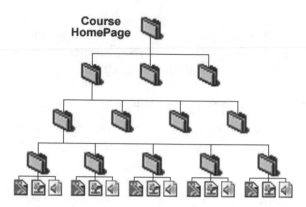

Fig. 2-5. Pyramid structure of a web site.

This pyramid structure offers a consistent method of dividing and organizing the multitude of HTML documents, graphic files, and other page elements to help you develop more efficiently, and hopefully with fewer errors. When you need to place the new graphics for a specific topic, you will know exactly where to place them, and the HTML pages will know where to find them. Regardless of what file/folder structure you end up using, what is very important is that the file/folder structure you use as you develop your web site on your local computer must also be used on the web server for posting your web site.

As you use Dreamweaver MX on your local computer and add HTML documents, graphics, and other elements to create a web page, the HTML code being created expects to locate these page elements based on the file/folder structure that exists. If this file/folder structure is not the same when the site is posted to the remote server, the elements needed for display may not be found and your web page will end up with missing content and will not function correctly.

We will go into more detail about setting up your site, and will provide you with guided practice in accomplishing this task, in Chapter 4. As a quick word of encouragement, Dreamweaver MX includes a couple of very helpful features to help you set up and manage your site.

The first feature, the Site panel, presents a "picture" of all your files and folders (directories), helping you to visually organize all files in your web site more easily. In addition, Dreamweaver MX helps you through the setup of your site, identifying where to store the various web pages and media element files. The Site panel will also automate the file transfer process of uploading the web site page and media files to the web server. Again, there will be more details about this in Chapter 4 and Chapter 23.

Delivery Considerations

Before you design and develop your web site, there are a number of factors that will affect how well your web site displays on the typical user's computer. We want to briefly touch upon a few of these factors now so that you can keep them in mind.

Ask almost anybody what their number one complaint with the Internet is and they will probably say, "It's too slow." That is, the length of time it takes to download web pages is too long. Today, we are used to instant everything, and accessing the Internet over standard phone lines does not provide the speed many of us would prefer.

Although more and more users have faster access to the Internet than a few years ago – cable modems, DSL, ADSL, and T1 and T3 connections – there is still a large population of Internet users who are still using a standard dial-up phone line with its limited capacity. To reach all users, of all capabilities, you can help visitors to your web site by carefully trying to minimize download time as you do your best to provide an interesting and professional-looking web site.

On one hand, using visual elements is an important way to add interest and appeal to your web site. On the other hand, these elements can significantly increase download time. However, there are some workable solutions. With graphics, you can significantly reduce the download time by using compression formats such as GIF and JPG, and the newer PNG. You can also add interest to and minimize download time for animations (using Macromedia's Flash) and video files by using streaming technologies such as QuickTime and RealVideo.

Another issue you will need to be concerned with is the type and version of the Internet browser your typical web site visitor might be using. All web pages do not function the same on all browsers. Also keep in mind that HTML screen text will generally display smaller on Macintosh systems than it does on Windows systems. And to make matters worse, there are some text-only web browsers out there (e.g., PDAs, Internet cell phones, and so on).

One more thing to be concerned about is what plugins are required for those extras you have added into your web site. Plugins provide web browsers with additional functionality. The plugins for Macromedia Flash and Director are already included in the 4.0 level (and above) of Internet Explorer and Netscape Navigator, but if you are using the latest versions of these programs, the user may not have the latest plugin. For updated or additional plugins, you may need to have your web site check to see what the user's browser currently has and provide access for downloading updates if necessary.

Web Pages – Aesthetically Speaking

In the previous section of this chapter we talked about some of the technical aspects of creating HTML code, web pages, and web sites. In the following section we will briefly consider the aesthetic aspects of creating web sites and the pages that make up a web site. These aesthetic issues include what visitors may want, screen design and layout, text formatting, graphics, and using other media elements such as animation, audio, and video.

The Good, the Bad, and the Ugly Web Page

As you have been surfing the Web, you more than likely have encountered a web page that has evoked the gut response of . . . yuck! It might have been the clashing circus of colors, numerous font styles, or the overall lack of design. Beginning developers in this medium commonly make the same mistake that has been made before with other media, such as printing and page layout and design. The common mistake is to use too many of the many options available. The following discusses such options.

Colors: The common mistake here is to use too many colors in the background, as part of the graphic screen treatment, or too many colors for text on screen. Some colors just do not look good together on screen. This is where some artistic talent is needed. Use a small number of colors that complement one another, and use them consistently.

Fonts: The same comments about color can be made regarding fonts. Pick a main font and perhaps one or two complementary fonts to use as accents.

Visual design: As has been the case with every "new" medium, we can learn a lot by studying what works well in an "older" medium. To start off learning about the fundamentals of visual design and page layout, you might try studying these principles in an older, well-established medium – the print medium (books, magazines, newspapers, newsletters, flyers, advertisements, and so on). We have all seen advertisements in newspapers and magazines that get our attention and create a subliminal (or overt) good feeling. This is what you are trying to accomplish with your web sites. If you want to learn more about good design and page layout, a good place to start would be to head over to the library and look at a few books about publishing and design, including page layout.

If we were to exclude content that some people disagree with or find offensive, the next largest target for criticism voiced about "bad web sites" has to do with poor visual design and/or the lack of proper functionality. Books have been written about the "do's and don'ts" of web design, but we would like to take at least a page or so to briefly address some of the more pertinent issues.

The following represent some of the more common problems found in web site design and development.

- *Slow-loading pages (due to large graphic images or animations).*
- *Web site navigation (user control) that is confusing or difficult.*
- *Web sites with an organizational structure that allows users to easily become lost.*
- *Sites with no unifying design or purpose.*
- *Content that is obviously dated or contains other telltale signs that the web master has not looked at the site in months (or years). A nonmaintained site will not give people a reason to return.*
- *Unreadable text (due to busy backgrounds, bad color combinations, and so on).*
- *Typographical errors, and poor grammar.*
- *The page is too crowded (borrowing from the "print world," there isn't enough "white space").*
- *The page is too busy (too many things going on – big graphics, animations, midi sound files, mouse trails, and so on).*
- *Sites that are misleading, and are not what they first appear to be. For example, a site professing to provide "educational information" only to find that the information is really biased or that the site is really focused on trying to sell something.*
- *Blind links that usually lead to sales and marketing sites that have nothing to do with the perceived purpose of the original site, or pop-up links that rapidly multiply and take over your browser to the point of forcing you to close your browser to stop them.*
- *Features that work on one computer system or browser, but not on another. You should check the web site's compatibility across computer platforms (Mac, Windows, and so on), browsers, browser features, and so on.*
- *Frames that do not work.*
- *Noncredible information. Web sites with "Miracle Diets from Space Aliens" might tip off most people that the content is not exactly truthful. But what about a web site with slanted, untruthful, or unsubstantiated information about a company, a health treatment or health practice, an organization, and so on. On the one hand we have "freedom of speech," and on the other hand a lot of people still think that if they read something somewhere it has to be true.*
- *Overuse of "Under Construction" signs. Every web site is a dynamic entity that is always under construction.*

There are a number of things to think about when designing a web site. A few guiding principles would suggest that you keep the look of the web site uniform – following some type of theme or style. It is also very important to keep the navigational system consistent and easy to use. These are not hard and fast rules, but general guidelines. You will have to decide how strictly or loosely you will follow them.

Perhaps the best advice is to remember to think about the viewer's perspective as you design and build your site. Look at your web site as the visitors (to the site) will see it. Perhaps ask someone to look at and "test drive" your web site, and ask them for constructive feedback. Taking the viewer's perspective should help you design and create a web site that will help viewers to more fully appreciate what your site has to offer.

Screen Design

Screen design and graphic themes are a matter of choice. Almost anything and everything is possible. Once again, think about what the visitors to your web site will want to see and what will capture their attention. There are a wide variety of books written on the topic of screen design and development of web page layouts. Go through some of these books, taking note of what you find valuable and useful.

You can also learn a lot by first-hand experience, just by browsing the Internet. Do some web research and you will be able to see a wide variety of screen designs and layouts. Look at the pages you like and think about what makes the design and layout appeal to you. There can be great value in learning from other people's good ideas. But please do not copy their design too closely, and definitely do not copy their graphics or other media elements.

Develop your own "look and feel." Get someone else to look it over and make suggestions. Keep your design clear and intuitive, and keep your visitors in mind.

Text Fonts

One of the strengths of HTML is that it can download text over the Internet very quickly. One problem, however, is that HTML can only display text using the fonts currently available on the visitor's computer and that are compatible with the web browser being used.

A common problem in using a special font is that it may look very artistic on the web page as you develop it on your computer, but if a viewer does not have that same font, what she sees will look very different from what you had intended. It could look like a disaster.

Even though you may think it is limiting, it is generally a good idea to only use fonts that are standard (or have very similar substitutes) on both Windows and Macintosh and most browsers. Dreamweaver MX offers a font selection of both serif and sans serif fonts, including Arial, Times New Roman, Courier,

Georgia, and Verdana, along with their alternate fonts as defaults. These fonts and their alternates are fairly standard on the common varieties of computer platforms and browsers, so it is a pretty safe assumption that if you use these fonts your pages should look pretty close to what you intended.

If you do want to use a fancy font, you might try placing your text in a graphic image or using the Flash text feature (Insert bar | Media). As part of a graphic, the "text" will not require fonts (because it is not really a text object anymore), and you will be guaranteed that it will look the same on all computers. The disadvantage is that graphic images take longer to download than HTML text.

There are three main uses for text on web pages: headline text, body text, and text bullets. Body text is used for the majority of text that appears on the page. Headline text is reserved for titles, headlines, and subheadings. Headline text typically uses a larger font size and serves as a quick summary of what can be found in the body text. Text bullets are generally brief phrases that abbreviate, highlight, and summarize particular information.

You might have noticed that the same font appears to be a different size when displayed on a Macintosh versus a Windows platform. Any given font will appear larger on a Windows platform. than it does on a Macintosh, because of the differences in how these two systems define how the screen is displayed. There is nothing you can do about this; just keep it in mind when you are working with your page layouts, especially when you are creating on the Mac, that potentially many of your web site's viewers may be using Windows-based computers.

Graphics

The two most popular graphic formats on the Internet are JPEG (Joint Photographic Experts Group) and GIF (Graphical Interchange Format). There are other graphic formats available, but these two formats are popular because they offer fairly good visual quality, with fairly small file sizes. Not all JPEG and GIF images use the same amount of compression or compression schemes. Be aware that some image types can be compressed more than others, depending on the amount of detail in the image.

Keep in mind when you are designing and developing your web site that graphic images take time to download. The more images you have on a page, the longer the page will require to download. The same goes for a very large graphic image you may want to use as a background (generally a bad idea on the Internet).

Many web pages use tiles to give the page a textured background. A tile is a relatively small graphic that is repeated to create a graphic pattern as the background for a web page. A small graphic image, both in size and file size, will download fast, and when repeated can cover a large area. Dreamweaver MX can automatically tile a graphic image for you. You will get practice doing this in one of our exercises later in the book. The use of tiling seems to fall in and out of favor. One month almost every page you see uses tiles, and the next month very few use tiles. If you want a solid color for the background of your web pages, simply select a background color from the Page Properties screen.

Web Safe Color Palette: If you consider the people who look at web pages, you realize that they are using computers with operating systems such as Macintosh, Windows 3.1, Windows 95/98/2000/ME/XP, Linux, and a variety of others. And let's not forget WebTV and the new handheld devices. Each of these operating systems has its own organization of colors, known as palettes. In other words, the 256 colors that Windows uses is not the same 256 colors (or even the same order) as the Macintosh. Luckily, most web browsers use the same color management scheme, consisting of 216 colors. These 216 colors are the same for the browsers no matter which computer platform they are running on. The 216 common colors are known as "browser-safe" colors. If you stick to using a web-safe color palette, the colors you use will be consistent across most browsers and most operating systems.

Navigation (User Controls)

Once again, think about the viewers of your web site. How will your viewer move from one page to another, or from one topic to another? The following are the top five things web site visitors find the most irritating.

- *Getting lost*
- *Not knowing how to move from page to page*
- *Getting lost*
- *Not being able to find what is being looked for*
- *Getting lost*

Yes, getting lost is a big sore point with most people. If visitors to your web site keep getting lost, they will not find what they are looking for, and they will probably not return.

There are two basic methods for providing navigation (user control) for web pages: (1) internal to the web page, including buttons and hot text, and (2) external to the web page; namely, the browser's Forward, Back, and Home buttons. Some standards or conventions for navigation have evolved in the computer industry and have migrated to the web environment. Examples of such standard practices follow.

- *Underlined text (using a different color than the body text) is used to indicate that the text is "hot" (i.e., hyperlinked to another web page).*

- *Action buttons (with two or more button states, such as up, down, and rollover) look like they are being depressed when clicked on by the mouse. In a nutshell, in order to simulate a button being depressed, different graphic images of buttons in a normal (or up) state, down state, and rollover state are linked to create the illusion that there is animation happening when the button is clicked. Dreamweaver MX contains a feature for easily inserting action buttons into your web pages.*

- *The cursor changes to indicate a current status. For example, the standard arrow-shaped cursor might change to a pointing hand or some other shape when the cursor is moved over a hyperlinked object or button. In other words, the cursor visually indicates that it is over something that can be clicked on to perform some action.*

The Development Process for Web Sites

Following a structured development process will not only help you create your site more efficiently but will help ensure that your site will accomplish what you have intended. Careful consideration and planning, prior to any development, is the key. The material that follows, regarding the development process, contains some guidelines for creating a web site.

Professional web developers generally follow these steps, but their process will often involve more formal steps with much more detail. You do not need to follow these steps exactly, but at least try to use the general ideas. Following a structured development process will help you significantly cut down on the amount of rework you might otherwise have to do.

Purpose and Audience

In this first development phase, you need to carefully consider what you want the site to accomplish, what audiences might be interested in it, and what types of computer systems and Internet connections will be used to view it. Consider the following.

Purpose of site: The purpose of your web site might seem obvious. However, take the time and think this through, including whatever functions and capabilities you want the site to accomplish, now and in the future. It is also a good idea to write this information down, so that you will have something to refer back to and guide your development as you get involved in the many details you will encounter.

Audience: Who do you think will be the typical visitor to your web site? What interests will she have? How much experience will she have using the Internet? What type of computer and browser will your typical visitor have? Generally you will want to design a web site to be available to the widest possible audience and range of computer platform, and the slowest Internet connection type.

Design

Next you need to consider what overall look and feel you want the site to have. How can you organize your web site to best serve its purpose and meet the needs of the typical visitor? What types of navigational controls will best serve the site? Consider the following.

Site theme/style: The next step is to think of ways to communicate the web site's message. Almost any idea, style, or theme is possible in a web site, just as long as it is consistently applied. Be creative, but try to stay with some unifying theme that will promote a sense of familiarity on the part of the viewer.

Organization: A good strategy is to create an outline of what topics will be covered in your web site and then use different colored pencils to draw lines connecting topics (indicating what areas will be linked). Remember that it is also important to take into account what organizational scheme will most easily accommodate the typical viewer's needs. If you are developing a corporate web ·site, it might contain a section for a company description, a section to explain the company's services or products, and a section highlighting contact information, with all of these areas accessible from the home page.

Prototype: Unless you are creating a very small site, it is generally a good idea to create a rough draft of the web site user interface and main structural elements before pouring in all the content. Start by creating the central graphic/visual theme for the site, and decide on your organizational structure and how you want to provide navigational controls. Put all of these elements into Dreamweaver MX and build a "bare bones" (no content) prototype of your site. The prototype will give you the opportunity to test your design and organizational ideas and make corrections before you do a lot of development work that might otherwise end up being redone.

Content Development

Text content: The next step is to collect and/or write the content that will be in the web site. Probably the easiest way to approach this is to pick up the outline you created in the design phase and then add content to fill out the outline, revising the outline with items you need to add or delete. If you already have your content, all you have to do is reorganize it for your web site.

Graphics/media elements: There are three parts to this step. The first is to identify what graphic images and media files you will need for your web site. The second is to acquire these images, animations, audio files, and video files. These files may already exist or you may need to go out and create them. Digital cameras and video camcorders are really making this task much easier. You can also create images using any of the numerous graphic and animation programs available, such as Macromedia's Fireworks or Flash. The third step is to convert the file format of these elements for use on the Internet.

Web Development

Site setup: Setting up your site involves little more than telling Dreamweaver MX where you want to save your files and providing the logon/upload information for transferring the web site files to your Internet Service Provider (ISP). The Site window in Dreamweaver MX will make it easy for you to view and organize site files.

Page layout /templates: In this step you will create the screen designs for the content area of your web pages. The look and feel of these designs should be consistent with and complement the design you have used for the web site interface and navigational controls. Using the Template tools in Dreamweaver MX, the look and feel of the site can be applied to all pages, giving the web site a unified and consistent look. You can create new pages using templates, and when you need to change the design of your pages you therefore need only change the template and all pages based on that template will be automatically updated to the new look.

Creating pages and placing content: Either by opening a new page or by using templates, you will create new pages for your web site. Then you can add the content and place the media files.

Adding hyperlinks: After you have created (or as you create) the pages in your web site, you can input the various links: links within the site and links to other sites and resources.

Adding database links: If any of the pages in your site will be "dynamic" (specific content is read from a database and displayed in a web page), you will need to set up the linkages from the web page to the database. The database contains the content (e.g., products, prices, sizes, and colors) that can be displayed in specific areas of your web pages, based on what you or the visitors to your web site want to view. The new features of Dreamweaver MX allow you to "bind" information within databases to your web pages. This basically means that you no longer have to create an individual page for each item you need to show (e.g., products) but can create one (product) page. Dreamweaver will take the (product) information from a database and put it in the correct area in your web page, effectively creating multiple pages from one page, with all of this generated in real time.

Testing, and checking for broken links: When all of your pages and linkages are completed, it is a good idea to test your site. Dreamweaver MX allows you to view each page in a browser (or multiple browsers). You can also view your entire site in a browser. If you are connected to the Internet, you can even check to see if your external links are functioning correctly. In addition, Dreamweaver MX has a menu option (Site | Check Links) to check for possible problems with links.

Web Deployment

Uploading: Once you have tested, revised, and fixed the errors in your web site, upload the site to your Internet Service Provider (ISP).

Testing: It is a good idea to test your site again after you place it on the server. It is also a good idea to test your site on a regular basis; every couple of days to every couple of weeks, depending on your situation.

Updating: One of the greatest strengths and promises of the Internet and web sites is that you can make updates to a web site and visitors can see the results as soon as you have posted the changes.

Summary

- *The Internet can be considered to be many things, but fundamentally it is a medium for worldwide communication. With the use of a personal computer or handheld device, anyone, located anywhere, at any time, can communicate (send and/or receive information) with anyone else in the world.*

- *Web sites are basically a collection of documents (HTML pages) that include text and that may include graphics, animation, sound, navigational controls, and other elements.*

- *In the past, web site developers created web pages using HyperText Markup Language (HTML). The developers had to type in the formatting code by hand, similar to many command line programming languages of the time.*

- *HTML consists of the text you see on the web page, but it also includes extra characters and symbols interwoven with the normal text. These additional characters in the HTML are the formatting and attribute codes for telling the web browser how to display objects on the web page and how to display the page layout.*

- *Dreamweaver MX's visual interface, menus, tools, and wizards automatically create and insert the HTML code needed for display, format, running of animations, and so on. Dreamweaver MX will also let you open an HTML document to view and edit within either Dreamweaver MX's WYSIWYG mode or in the native HTML code mode. This capability is known as "Round-Trip HTML."*

- *As a communicator – web developer – part of your job is to organize the information you want to present in a way that will help your viewers quickly access and better understand the information they are seeking.*

- *You may create a web site that is broad and flat, offering numerous categories, with each category being only a page deep. Another possibility might initially* offer the viewer fewer categories to choose from, but within each category offer numerous sublevels of choices.

- In addition to the need to organize and structure your web site for the user, there is also an equally important need to organize and structure the actual files and media elements being used to create the web site on the server.

- Not all of information presented in your web site needs to be typed into each page. You can use the data binding features of Dreamweaver MX to pull information from a database and place it into your web pages.

- Dreamweaver MX (and the underlying HTML code) requires the precise name and location of the HTML documents and media elements being used to display a web page.

- Before you design and develop your web site, there are a number of factors that will affect how well your web site displays on a typical user's computer. Factors include download time, type and version of browser, and necessary plugins.

- Beginning developers in this new medium commonly make the same mistake that has been made in other media; that is, if there are many options available, use them. Try to limit variations, and use what works well together (visually and functionally).

- Screen design and graphic themes are a matter of choice. Think about what the visitors to your web site will want to see and what will capture their attention.

- Even though you may think it is limiting, it is generally a good idea to only use fonts that are standard (or have very similar substitutes) on both Windows and Macintosh and most browsers. Dreamweaver MX provides a list of standard fonts.

- Keep in mind when you are designing and developing your web site that graphic images provide greater interest but also take time to download. Use a graphic format that will compress the file size and shorten download time without sacrificing too much quality.

- Foremost, think about the viewers to your web site. How will your viewer move from one page to another, from one topic to another?

- Following a structured development process will not only help you create your site more efficiently but help ensure that your site will accomplish what you have intended it to accomplish.

CHAPTER

3

The

Dreamweaver MX

Interface

Introduction

Dreamweaver MX was originally created and has been continually improved to make your tasks as a web page designer and developer easier to understand and easier to accomplish. Everything you develop in Dreamweaver MX is actually generating HTML source code. Each property and attribute you apply to an object or text is adding more HTML source code, and in some cases JavaScript. But the Dreamweaver MX interface and its many panels make this HTML generation automatic.

You do not have to spend a lot of time entering the HTML code to make a section of text bold, indented, a larger size, or a different font. This is all done through a menu or with the Property Inspector. As an example, with one step, Dreamweaver MX can create a table with four rows and two columns, and with borders, and size it to fill the Browser window. In this chapter we will take a close look at and start to work with Dreamweaver MX's interface elements. By the end of this chapter you will be able to:

- *Describe the main parts of the Dreamweaver MX workspace*
- *Describe the general functionality of each Dreamweaver MX pull-down menu*
- *Describe the use of the Insert bar, Property Inspector (Properties panel), Assets panel, Behaviors panel, Frames panel, Layers panel, History panel, Code Inspector, and Site window*

The Dreamweaver MX Workspace

The main workspace for creating and editing a document in Dreamweaver MX is called the Document window. This window has a toolbar at the top, and the Status bar at the bottom. There are two main features used to insert and modify objects in the Document window, the Property Inspector and the Insert bar. See figure 3-1. In this section, we will look at each of these elements in detail.

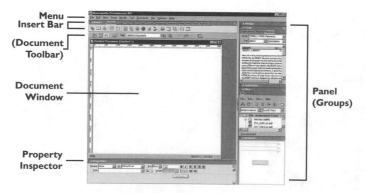

Fig. 3-1. The Dreamweaver MX workspace.

Other Workspace Elements

In addition to these interface elements, there are a variety of panels and windows that can be opened on the desktop. We will look at these panels and windows in greater detail in the next section. There are also files on the companion CD-ROM that contain much greater detail about the Dreamweaver MX interface elements. (These can be found in the Job Aids folder on the CD.)

The Document Window

The Document window displays all visible objects approximately as they will be seen when viewed in a browser. As page elements (text, graphics, forms, tables, and so on) are inserted into the Document window, HTML source code is generated behind the scenes. The Document window can be viewed in the following three view modes.

- *Design view: All visible objects are displayed as in a browser.*
- *Code view: Displays only source code (HTML, JavaScript, and other scripts).*
- *Code and Design view: Splits the Document window into two parts, showing the Design view and Code view. See figure 3-2.*

You can use the View menu or the buttons on the left-hand side of the toolbar to change to Code or Design view.

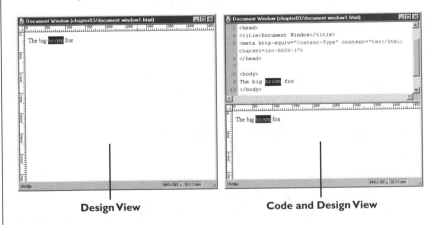

Design View **Code and Design View**

Fig. 3-2. Document window.

A document in Design view can also be displayed in two ways: Standard and Layout view. Layout view lets you insert images, text, and other media; draw tables and table cells; and design the page layout. In Standard view (the default) you cannot draw tables and cells; you can only insert them. However, you can work with layers and frames (which you cannot do in Layout view). Layout view will primarily be used when working with tables and laying out or designing the page. These options are found on the Insert bar and under the View Menu | Table View selection. See figure 3-3.

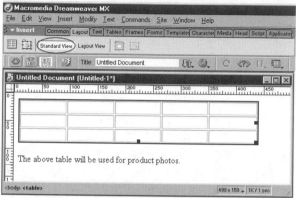

Standard View

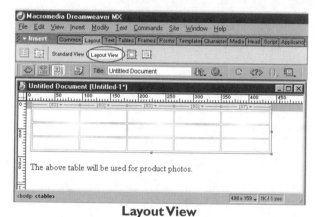

Layout View

Fig. 3-3. Document window in Standard and Layout views.

The Toolbar

Dreamweaver MX's toolbar has shortcuts to menu options for setting the way panels and windows are viewed (displayed). Figure 3-4 shows a close-up version of the toolbar. The three buttons on the left-hand side of the toolbar change the type of view in the Document window: Show Code View, Show Code and Design Views, and Show Design View. The center section in the toolbar allows the document title to be entered. This title is displayed at the top of the Browser window when the document is displayed in a browser. Continuing to the right, the File Management button contains many of the options found in the Site window.

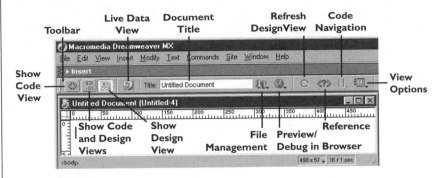

Fig. 3-4. Dreamweaver MX toolbar.

The Preview and Debug in Browser button contains options for previewing and debugging in a browser, or to edit the browser list. The next button, Refresh Design View, redisplays the Design view. The Reference button accesses the Reference panel. The Code Navigation button is used to navigate through your source (HTML) code. The last button, View Options, accesses a menu of options that is dependent on the type of view currently active. For example, in Design view the menu includes options such as Visual Aids and Frame Borders, whereas in Code view there are options such as indenting and color coding.

The Status Bar

The Status bar, located at the very bottom of the Document window while in Design view, contains three areas: the Tag Selector (on the far left), and on the far right, is the Window Information and Document Information. See figure 3-5.

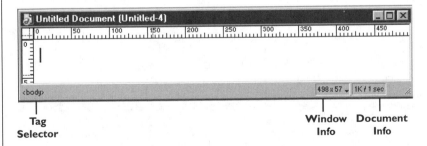

Fig. 3-5. Status bar.

The Tag Selector area displays the HTML parent tags that govern selected text or objects. If you click on a tag here, it will highlight its content in the Document window. If you click on <body>, the entire body of the document will be selected. Clicking in the Window Information area will bring up a pop-up menu in which you can resize the window to preselected dimensions, or select Edit Sizes to create a custom size.

The next area, to the right of Window Information, displays the estimated document size and download time of the current page. These estimates include all dependent files, including graphic and other media files. Options for setting window size and testing connection speed are set via the Edit Menu | Preferences | Status Bar selection.

Insert Bar

The Insert bar contains buttons for inserting many types of objects, including graphics, media, and scripting files. When an object is inserted in the page, the accompanying HTML code and scripts associated with the object are automatically inserted with the object. By default, the Insert bar is docked just below Dreamweaver's menus, but the bar can be moved and become a floating panel. If the Insert bar has been closed, reopen it by selecting Window Menu | Insert.

The buttons on the Insert bar are separated into tabbed object categories: Common, Layout, Text, Tables, Frames, Forms, Templates, Character, Media, Head, Script, and Application. In Dreamweaver, if you hold your cursor over each object in the Insert bar, a pop-up balloon will display a label with the name of the object.

Most of the objects contained on the Insert bar may also be accessed through the Insert menu. Other objects can be added to the Insert bar (and Insert menu) through Dreamweaver MX extensions (Insert Menu | Get More Objects). Figures 3-6 through 3-17 show the various categories of the Insert bar.

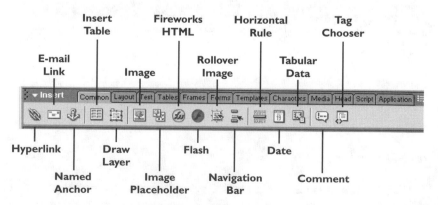

Fig. 3-6. Insert bar category Common.

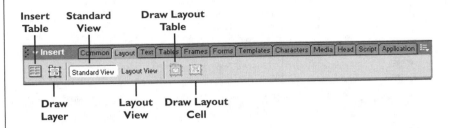

Fig. 3-7. Insert bar category Layout.

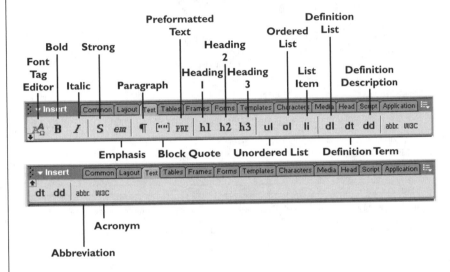

Fig. 3-8. Insert bar category Text.

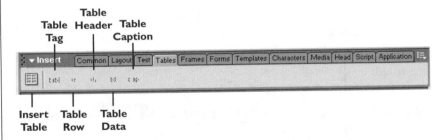

Fig. 3-9. Insert bar category Tables.

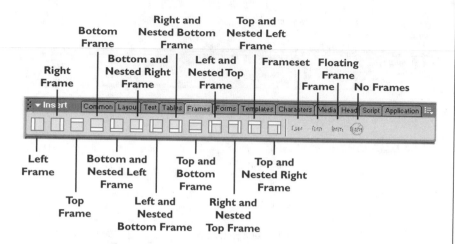

Fig. 3-10. Insert bar category Frames.

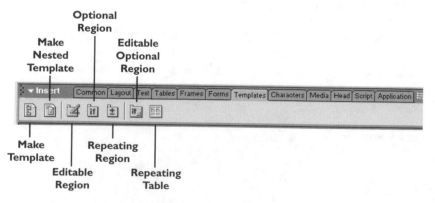

Fig. 3-11. Insert bar category Forms.

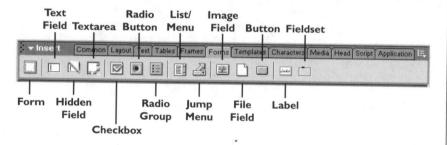

Fig. 3-12. Insert bar category Templates.

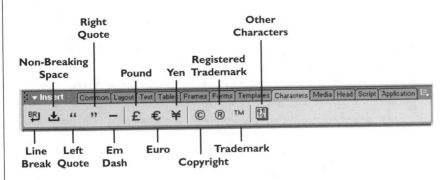

Fig. 3-13. Insert bar category Characters.

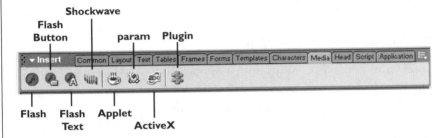

Fig. 3-14. Insert bar category Media.

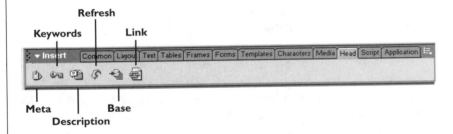

Fig. 3-15. Insert bar category Head.

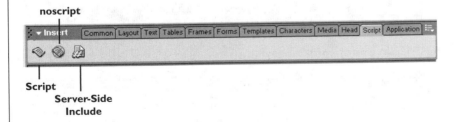

Fig. 3-16. Insert bar category Script.

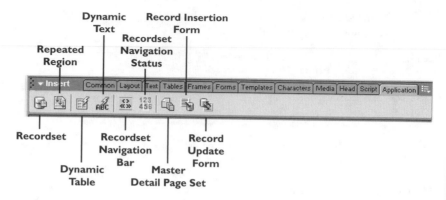

Fig. 3-17. Insert bar category *Application*.

Dreamweaver MX Menus

The Dreamweaver MX menus are similar to most Windows and Macintosh software programs. In addition, there are menus and options within menus that are particular to the needs of Dreamweaver MX. The material that follows describes the functionality of each menu, including notes on individual options. We will take a closer look at the options in each menu as they pertain to chapter concepts and when they are used in the exercises.

At the end of this section on menus, we have included a listing of the most common keyboard shortcuts for both the Macintosh and Windows. The companion CD-ROM contains two documents regarding the Dreamweaver MX interface. There is a document for the Macintosh (*DWinterface_MAC.pdf*) and a document for the Windows platform (*DWinterface_WIN.pdf*). Both are located in the folder *Job Aids* on the companion CD-ROM. You can print the appropriate file for your computer (Windows or MAC) so that you will have a detailed explanation of the Dreamweaver MX menus, keyboard shortcuts, and panels/windows. See figure 3-18.

Fig. 3-18. Dreamweaver MX's menus.

We strongly recommend that you take the time now to print the document appropriate for your computer, as it can serve as a useful learning aid as you continue through the book. You can print these files (see the following) using Adobe Acrobat Reader. Adobe Acrobat Reader 5 is included on the companion CD-ROM.

- *Macintosh: print* DWinterface_MAC.pdf
- *Windows: print* DWinterface_WIN.pdf

File Menu

The options listed in the File menu pertain to opening, saving, and testing Dreamweaver MX files. The common options include creating a new document, opening an existing document, and saving a file. When using frames, there are also the options Save Frameset and Save All Frames. Preview in Browser, which contains an option for previewing in more than one browser (Internet Explorer, Netscape, and so on), is used to test a document. In addition, the File menu contains options for locating possible problems in the pages in your site: Check Page | Check Links and Check Target Browsers. See figure 3-19.

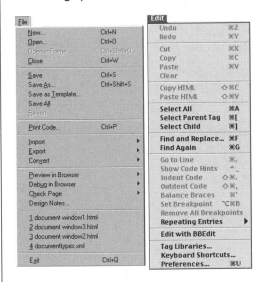

Fig. 3-19. File menu (Windows/Mac).

Edit Menu

The options listed here are the same as those found in most software packages: Cut, Copy, Paste, Select All, and of course the indispensable Undo. Find and Replace and Find Next look for text, source code, and specific tags within the current document or any document in the site. There are also several menu options related to HTML use that are only available in Code view (View | Code). They will format the lines of code and breakpoints. Set Breakpoint can be set to debug JavaScript.

The Edit menu also contains an option for setting preferences and keyboard shortcuts while working in Dreamweaver MX.

·T/P·

The Undo (Edit | Undo) feature is directly related to the History Panel (Window Menu | Others | History). Most steps are recorded in the History Panel and can be repeated (the same as using Edit Menu | Redo), or undone. The number of steps that can be recorded (and undone with Undo) is set in Edit Menu | Preferences | General. The default is 50 (undos).

New in Dreamweaver MX are tag libraries. In Code view, as you type a tag or attribute, a help list (a list of the libraries) appears, suggesting the tag or attribute you are trying to enter (so that you do not have to precisely remember syntax). The Tag Library Editor lets you add/modify/delete tags and attributes. Different scripting tags can be entered, including JSP, ASP, XML, and so on. See figure 3-20.

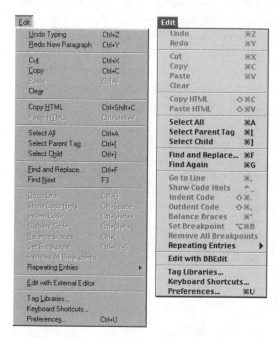

Fig. 3-20. Edit menu (Windows/Mac).

View Menu

The options listed in the View menu provide the capability to switch among views (Code, Design, and Table) in the Document window, and to turn on or off various formatting displays when the source code is displayed (Code view options). Visual Aids displays aids when working with frames, layers, tables, and image maps. Plugins lets you play/stop objects that use plugins (e.g., for Flash and Authorware), directly in the Document window. The Grid option displays a pattern of lines as the Snap to Grid option automatically aligns text or graphic objects to this pattern of lines. Shortcuts to many of these options are also found in the toolbar. See figure 3-21.

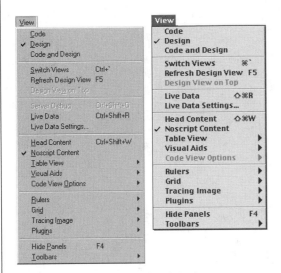

Fig. 3-21. View menu (Windows/Mac).

Insert Menu

The options listed here provide the capability to import many types of images and media elements that have been created outside Dreamweaver MX. Interactive Images inserts multiple images and animation elements created in Flash and Fireworks. This is also where elements (including tables, frames, layers and forms) can be inserted into a document. Special elements that add additional information and formatting to a document can also be inserted. Options here are Date, Horizontal Rule, and Email Links.

Some of the options listed in the Insert menu are also included in the Insert bar. Also of note are the Special Characters options, in that HTML does not accept symbols such as copyright, trademark, and quote marks. There is specific HTML source code for each of these characters. Get More Objects will link to the Macromedia Dreamweaver Exchange, from which you can download additional objects. These objects will appear in both the Insert menu and the Insert bar. See figure 3-22.

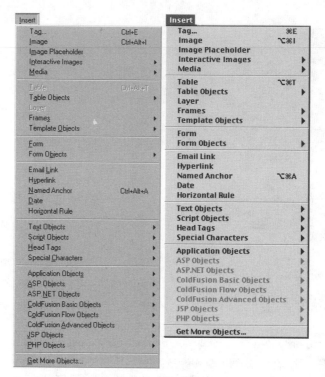

Fig. 3-22. Insert menu (Windows/Mac).

Modify Menu

The options listed under the Modify menu provide the capability to change the characteristics of page elements, work with libraries and templates, and modify animation using the Timeline feature. Page Properties contains the options for modifying the background color and background image, text color, and link colors. Template Properties is available for a template-based document. This dialog box is used to update editable tag attributes and other template parameters (such as the optional region settings).

All properties of tables – cells, columns, and rows – can be modified or added. Frameset will insert another frame into the page or modify the content of the NoFrames option. Selection Properties displays the Property Inspector (this is the same as Window | Properties). The Align option helps you select objects and line them up relative to one another. Arrange only applies to layers (Bring to Front and Send to Back) to change the arrangement of layers on top of or behind each other. Many of these options are also found in context-sensitive menus by right-clicking (Windows) or Ctrl-clicking (Macintosh) on an element in the Document window. See figure 3-23.

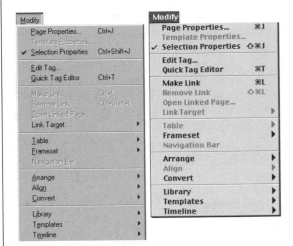

Fig. 3-23. Modify menu (Windows/Mac).

Text Menu

The following Text menu options determine or modify the attributes associated with text objects: Paragraph Format (Headings), Font, Size, Style, Alignment, and Color. The Text menu also applies to lists and includes the option Check Spelling. Most of the options found in the Text menu are also found in the Property Inspector. See figure 3-24.

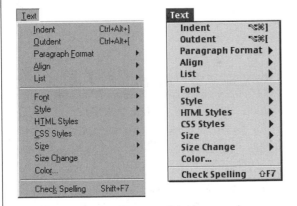

Fig. 3-24. Text menu (Windows/Mac).

Commands Menu

All options listed in the Commands menu are pertinent to working with source code. Of particular use is Clean Up HTML, especially if you are opening documents created outside Dreamweaver MX. This will remove duplicate tags and non-Dreamweaver MX comments. There are many third-party developers who are creating extensions for Dreamweaver MX that can be accessed and managed with the Edit Command list. You can record common steps using Start Recording. These steps are also found in the History panel.

If you are creating a page full of photographs, start with Create Web Photo Album to create a web page photo album complete with all required code, folders, and thumbnail images of photographs, with links to the full-size images. When working with tables, you can begin the table using Format Table, which provides predefined structures for tables that include those for colors, headings, and sorting options. See figure 3-25.

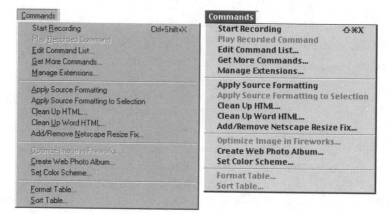

Fig. 3-25. Commands menu (Windows/Mac).

Site Menu

The options listed within the Site menu control provides options to edit, create, and open sites. Of particular importance is the option Edit Sites, which should be invoked before creating any web pages. Use Edit Sites to switch between sites that have already been defined in Dreamweaver MX. The options found in the Site menu are also found in the Site panel menus. See figure 3-26.

Note that on the Macintosh, the Site menu contains many more options than the Windows platform. The Macintosh Site menu includes options for managing files on the current site such as Check Links Sitewide and Export. On the Windows platform, these options are found in the Site panel menus.

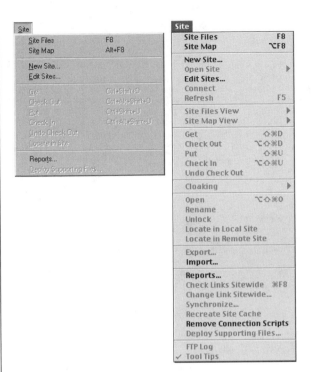

Fig. 3-26. Site menu (Windows/Mac).

Window Menu

The options listed within the Window menu control the display (or absence) of a variety of types of information windows and "dockable" floating panels. Of particular interest are the Insert bar (for inserting media elements and structures such as frames and tables) and the Properties panel (also called the Property Inspector), used to set the properties of all page elements. The Code Inspector found under Window | Others, displays the same information as the document's Code view, but in a separate window. (Code view displays source code directly in the Document window.) In Windows, if you have selected the Dreamweaver MX workspace, all panels are docked to the MX workspace, and are collected as panel groups. Otherwise, the panels are dockable as floating panels. The Launcher is customizable (Edit | Preferences | Panels) to contain shortcut buttons to many of the panels in the Window menu. The panels found here are explained in greater detail later in this chapter. See figure 3-27.

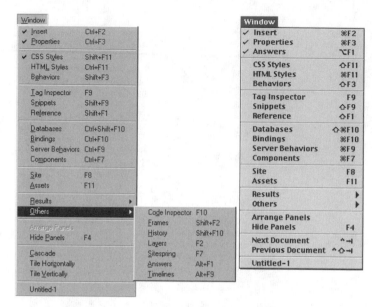

Fig. 3-27. Window menu (Windows/Mac).

Help Menu

The options listed within the Dreamweaver MX Help menu include online help (such as "Using Dreamweaver MX") and offer a variety of methods of obtaining additional information and viewing sample web pages. The Reference option displays the Reference panel (Window | Reference), containing information on HTML tags, CSS styles, JavaScript, ColdFusion, ASP, and JSP. See figure 3-28.

Fig. 3-28. Help Menu (Windows/Mac).

Common Keyboard Commands

Table 3-1 outlines common keyboard commands under the Windows and Macintosh environments.

Table 3-1: Common Windows and Macintosh Keyboard Commands

Windows Command	Macintosh Command	Function
F8	F8	Accesses site files
F10	F10	Opens the Code Inspector
F12	F12	Accesses preview in primary browser
Ctrl+F12	Cmd+F12	Accesses preview in secondary browser
Ctrl+Z	Cmd+Z	Accesses the Undo function
Ctrl+Y	Cmd+Y	Accesses the Redo function
Ctrl+J	Cmd+J	Accesses page properties
Ctrl+F2	Cmd+F2	Accesses the Insert bar function
Ctrl+F3	Cmd+F3	Opens the Property Inspector
Enter	Return	Creates a new paragraph (i.e., goes to a new line)
Shift+Enter	Shift+Return	Inserts a line break ( )
Ctrl+Shift+Space bar	Option+Space bar	Inserts a non-breaking space
Right-click	Ctrl-click	Opens context-sensitive menus

Panels and Windows

There are many panels and windows in Dreamweaver MX that contain information and options for modifying selected page elements. All of these options can be accessed and opened using the Window menu. The panels, by default, are docked by what is called a panel group. A panel group can be renamed, and any panel can be moved from group to group. See figure 3-29.

Collapse/Expand Panel group
Panel group name
Pop-Up menu

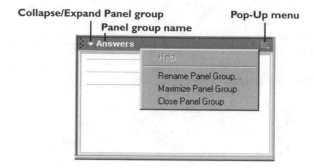

Fig. 3-29. Panel group example.

Property Inspector

Probably the most frequently used panel is the Property Inspector. The Property Inspector is opened by selecting Window Menu | Properties. This panel lets you view and edit the properties for the currently selected page element. The options shown on this panel will vary, depending on what type of element is currently selected (e.g., graphic, text, and frame). You can select an object either in the Document window or in the Code Inspector. Many of these options are also found in the Text menu and Modify menu. Figures 3-30 through 3-38 show the options listed for the most frequently used objects. In Dreamweaver MX, if you roll your cursor over each object in the panel, a pop-up balloon will display a label describing that object.

Fig. 3-30. Property Inspector - Text.

Fig. 3-31. Property Inspector - Table.

Fig. 3-32. Property Inspector - Image.

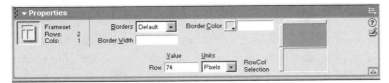

Fig. 3-33. Property Inspector - Frameset.

Fig. 3-34. Property Inspector - Frame.

Fig. 3-35. Property Inspector - Layer.

Fig. 3-36. Property Inspector - Library.

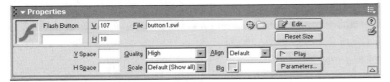

Fig. 3-37. Property Inspector - Flash.

Fig. 3-38. Property Inspector - Form.

Assets Panel

The Assets panel includes listings and options for Dreamweaver MX's library and templates, in addition to external media such as video, images, and scripts. The Assets panel is in the Files panel group and is opened by selecting Window Menu | Assets. Dreamweaver MX provides the convenience of being able to simply drag an item from the Assets panel to the page. You can also drag more than one object at a time. The Assets panel lists all objects in your site, across all pages. Links can be created from page elements in the Document window to files listed in the Assets window. See figure 3-39.

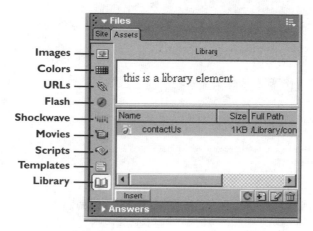

Fig. 3-39. Assets panel.

Behaviors Panel

You can use the Behaviors panel to attach behaviors to page elements and to modify previously attached behaviors. The Behaviors panel is in the Design panel group and is opened by selecting Window Menu | Behaviors. We will cover behaviors in much more detail later in the book. A behavior is a combination of an event and the action that results based on that event. The visual change as you move your cursor over a button, the ability to control sound, and many other HTML functions require the use of a behavior.

When a behavior is attached to a page element (actually to an HTML tag), Dreamweaver MX generates the JavaScript required for that behavior. Many of the extensions to Dreamweaver MX are actually behaviors providing even more functions to Dreamweaver MX. Behaviors are also categorized by browser version and type, in that all behaviors do not work in all browsers, or at least do not work the same way. Figure 3-40 shows an example of a behavior that will play a sound when the page is loaded.

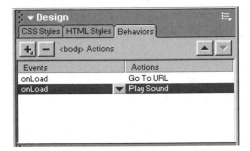

Fig. 3-40. Behaviors panel.

Frames Panel

The Frames panel displays the names of individual frames. By default, the Frames panel does not appear when opening Dreamweaver MX. The Frames panel will appear in the Advanced Layout panel group when selected via Window Menu | Others | Frames. This panel provides the easiest means of selecting a frame or frameset so that its properties can be modified in the Property Inspector. See figure 3-41.

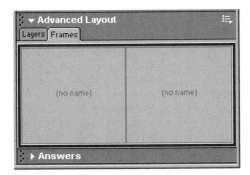

Fig. 3-41. Frames panel.

Layers Panel

The Layers panel lists all layers in the document. Like the Frames panel, by default the Layers panel does not appear when opening Dreamweaver. The

Layers panel will appear in the Advanced Layout panel group when selected via Window Menu | Others | Layers. There are options for changing layer names, for ordering layers via Z-index (arranges layers relative to other layers), and for adjusting layer visibility. This panel provides the best means of listing all of a layer's properties in a page at one time. See figure 3-42.

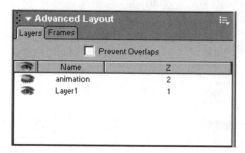

Fig. 3-42. Layers panel.

History Panel

The History panel will list most of the recent steps that have been executed for the current document. The History panel is opened by selecting Window Menu | Others | History. The number of steps that can be saved is set in Dreamweaver MX Preferences (Edit Menu | Preferences | General). The default number of steps that will be saved is 50. This is also the same number of Undos (Edit Menu | Undo) that are available in Dreamweaver MX. Steps can be deleted, replayed, and changed within the History panel. This is very useful when you make a lot of changes and need to replay the steps to see how a problem occurred. See figure 3-43.

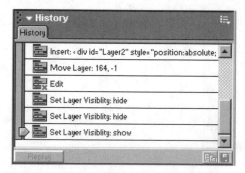

Fig. 3-43. History panel.

Code Inspector

The Code Inspector opens the HTML source code in a separate window from the Document window. The Code Inspector is opened by selecting Window Menu | Others | Code Inspector. The Code Inspector allows you to view and edit the HTML code and JavaScript that has been created by Dreamweaver MX. With this window, you can modify the HTML, insert new HTML, or insert JavaScript and other types of script (such as XML). The Code Inspector contains the same information and options as are available in Code view in the Document window. With Dreamweaver MX, you really do not need to know the complexities of HTML code. However, the Code Inspector provides the opportunity to view the HTML code so that you can use it to learn HTML. See figure 3-44.

Fig. 3-44. Code Inspector.

Site Panel and Site Window

The Site panel helps you organize your web site files and upload them to the hosting server. The Site panel has its own file explorer to display not only the location of your site but also the drives and folders on the entire operating system. By default on the Windows platform, the Site panel is integrated into the Dreamweaver MX workspace, but can be expanded to a full window. To open and close the Site panel, select Window | Site.

Selecting a different Site view (Site Files or Site Map) from the Site menu can also open the Site panel. Site Files lists all files on the local site and remote site. The Site Map option displays the relationships among files on the local site (like a flow chart or organizational chart).

The Site panel has buttons (in expanded view) and pull-down menus (in collapsed view) to move back and forth between the Site Files (remote and local), Site Map, and Testing Server options. The Site panel also has its own set of menus for managing a site, including checking links sitewide. Use the Site

·T*i*P·

The Site window on the Macintosh can only be displayed in expanded view and is always a separate window from the Design Document.

panel to post files to a remote site, to obtain files from a remote site and place them on the local site, and to rename files. Another great feature of the Site panel is that if you rename, move, or delete a file, Dreamweaver MX will update all links to that file automatically. This can be a real time saver, and minimizer of errors on your site.

If more than one person will be working on a single site, be sure to use the Check In/Check Out feature in the Site window. When a file is opened, the developer's name will be displayed next to the file on the server, so that someone else knows not to work on the same file at the same time. Think of the Site panel as a mini Windows Explorer or Macintosh Finder whereby you can organize and maintain all of your files. Various aspects of the Site panel are shown in figures 3-45 through 3-49.

Fig. 3-45. Site panel as dockable panel (Windows).

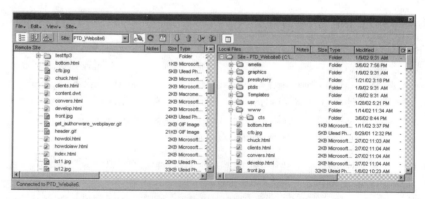

Fig. 3-46. Site panel expanded per Site Files view (Windows).

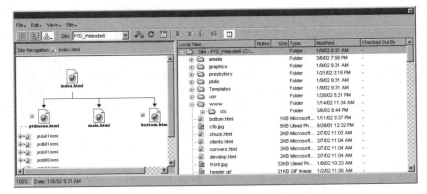

Fig. 3-47. Site panel expanded per Site Map view (Windows).

Fig. 3-48. Site panel expanded per Site Files view (Macintosh).

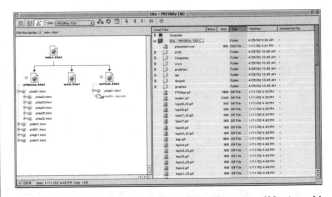

Fig. 3-49. Site panel expanded per Site Map view (Macintosh).

Summary

• *The Dreamweaver MX workspace consists of the Document window, Insert bar, toolbar, Status bar, and Property Inspector.*

• *The Dreamweaver MX menus and many of the options found within the menus are consistent in organization and function with the menus in many Windows- and Macintosh-based software programs. Dreamweaver MX's menus include File, Edit, View, Insert, Modify, Text, Commands, Site, Window, and Help.*

• *Dreamweaver MX's toolbar has shortcuts to the more common menu options, such as for setting the way panels and windows are viewed.*

• *The Document window is the main work area for Dreamweaver MX. The Document window is where you will place all page elements, such as text, graphics, forms, and tables.*

• *The Status bar contains three different areas: the Tag Selector (on the far left), Window Information, and Document Information.*

• *There are many panels and windows in Dreamweaver MX that enhance the development of web pages. If you have selected the Dreamweaver MX work-space (Windows option only), the panels are dockable so that they can be combined into one panel, with tabs for the separate sections. Commonly used panels are the Property Inspector, the Assets panel, the Behaviors panel, the Frames panel, the Layers panel, the History panel, the Code Inspector, and the Site panel.*

• *Many of the menu options are also found in the Dreamweaver MX panels and windows.*

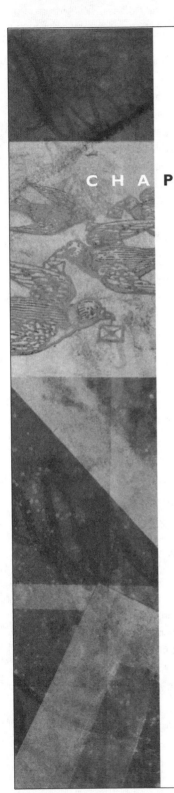

CHAPTER 4

Setting Up a Site

Introduction

You will find as you use Dreamweaver MX more and more that not only is it a software package that helps you easily and quickly create web pages but guard against functional errors. You have probably been to a web site in which when you click a hot link you are taken to a page telling you that the page no longer exists. You have probably also had the experience of rolling your cursor over a graphic and receiving a JavaScript error. Dreamweaver MX can help you prevent these types of errors with the use of functions that check your links, warn you when renaming or moving a file will break a link, and prevent two people from working on the same file at the same time.

Before you begin to create web pages using Dreamweaver MX, you should organize all of your files relative to a site structure. Defining your site and its structure is the foundation of creating links between files, storing media files for graphics and sound, and placing your web pages on a server. This chapter explores these issues. By the end of this chapter you will be able to:

* *Create a new local site*
* *Modify a local site*
* *Use the Site panel to view site files and site maps*
* *Describe the importance of setting up a site before creating HTML documents*

Web Site Overview

Before we dive into the details of Dreamweaver MX, it is important that you become familiar with the concepts and terminology that will be used throughout the rest of the book. These are terms used in the real world of web development. After this brief overview, we will start working with Dreamweaver MX.

What is a web site? To the Internet user who sees what appears on the screen, a web site is a collection of web pages that may contain text, photographs, graphics, sound, and animation. To the web site developer, a web site is also what is behind the scenes, on the web server. What is behind the scenes should exist as a well-defined directory and file structure, with each page and media element having a specific path location and file name. With a well-organized site, the developer will not only locate files easily and quickly but be able to minimize functional errors.

Whenever you want to create a link to another page, another web site, or particular spot on a specific page, Dreamweaver MX needs to know the position of the page relative to the linking item. This ensures that when you place the files on the Web the links will still work correctly.

In Chapter 23, you will see how to define a site location (called a remote site) on the Web itself. You will be creating your web pages on a hard drive, or local computer, known as the local site. When the structure of the folders within these two sites mirror each other, moving elements to and from the local site to the remote site becomes much easier, with less possibility of errors such as deleting or losing files. See figure 4-1.

Fig. 4-1. Site panel: Mirror of the local and remote sites.

Site Definition

At a minimum you should set up the location where the files will be stored on the local computer (your computer). The site definition will specify the directories (or folders) in which files will reside, including HTML pages and all graphics, sound, animation, and other external media being used. The definition of a site (the setup) includes the following.

- *Local Info: Defines the location for files on the local computer (local site).*
- *Remote Info: Defines the location of files on the remote computer (remote site, or Internet server).*
- *Testing Server: Defines the testing server to process dynamic pages in Dreamweaver MX. This can be the local computer, a development server, a staging server, or a production server. The local and remote information must be set before defining the testing server.*
- *Cloaking: Excludes files with specified extensions from any site operations.*
- *Design Notes: Developer notes about a file, such as whether it is a draft, what media elements still needed to be created, and so on.*
- *Site Map Layout: Layout of the map for the local site (local computer).*
- *File View Columns: Defines the "look" of Site Files listing in the Site panel. Columns can be added, deleted, renamed, and moved.*

To define a new site, select New Site from the Site menu. You can also create a new site or modify an existing site by selecting Site | Edit Sites while in the Document window or Site window, or by selecting Edit Sites from the pull-down menu in the Site panel. The Edit Sites option will also allow you to export/import a site's settings to use to define a site on another computer. See figure 4-2.

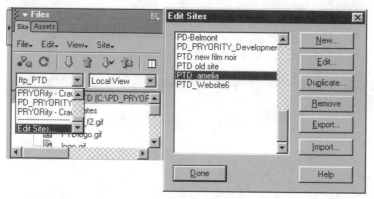

Fig. 4-2. Site panel pull-down menu and Edit Sites dialog box.

A new feature in Dreamweaver MX is the Site Definition wizard. The wizard will ask specific questions about your site to fill in the information needed to define the local, remote, and testing servers, as well as all categories found in the Site Definition window. To access the wizard, select the Basic tab found in the Site Definition window. See figure 4-3.

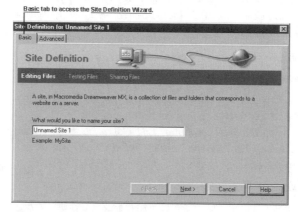

Fig. 4-3. Site Definition wizard.

Site Definition: Local Info

The Local Info option defines the location of the files on your local hard drive. See figure 4-4. Instead of developing on the Internet, Dreamweaver MX provides the means to develop on your local computer and after most of the development and testing is complete to copy or upload the files from your local computer to the remote site or web server connected to the Internet.

·T/P·

Define a site for each web site you are creating. You may also want to define a site for each subdivision of a web site (i.e., just for the marketing or products section of a site).

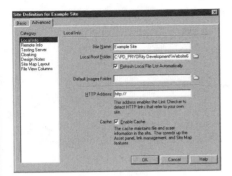

Fig. 4-4. Site Definition: Local Info category.

Site Definition: Remote Info

The Remote Info option provides specific information about the remote site Dreamweaver MX will need when you are ready to copy or upload the files from your local computer (defined in Local Info) to the remote site or web server. See figure 4-5.

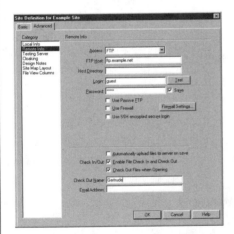

Fig. 4-5. Site Definition: Remote Info category.

Generally, the FTP (File Transfer Protocol) access will be used to send files to a server. To use FTP, you will need the FTP address of your server, a user log-in, and a password. Your web master or Internet provider should be able to provide you with this information.

Pay particular attention to the Enable File Check In and Check Out feature of the remote site. This should be used if more than one person could be working on a site. Figure 4-5 shows the additional options available when this option is selected.

More details of remote information are found in Appendix E in the *Job Aids* folder on the companion CD-ROM. When you are ready to copy your files to the server, refer to that section for guidelines on posting to the remote site using Dreamweaver MX.

Site Definition: Testing Server

A new feature in Dreamweaver MX, the Testing Server option, defines a location for dynamic content (see Chapter 24). This location will default to the location of the remote site if one has been defined. See figure 4-6.

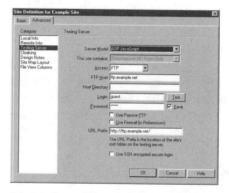

Fig. 4-6. Site Definition: Testing Server category.

Site Definition: Cloaking

Another new feature in Dreamweaver MX, the Cloaking option, excludes files with a specified extension from all site operations. Any files with the extension will be displayed in a disabled color and have a red line through the icon. See figure 4-7.

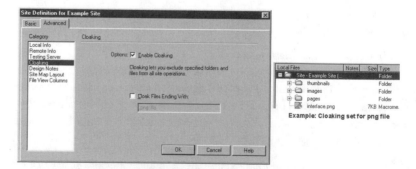

Fig. 4-7. Site Definition: Cloaking category.

Site Definition: Design Notes

Design notes are strictly for development purposes. These notes are attached to a file so that anytime a file is opened, or listed in the Site panel, the design notes are available to view and edit. The options listed on this page pertain to how these notes can be used. See figure 4-8.

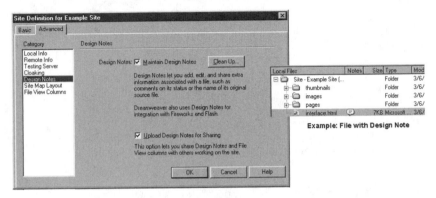

Fig. 4-8. Site Definition: Design Notes category.

You can use design notes to record any comments you may want for yourself or other members of a team — about issues with media elements, JavaScript notes, unfinished work, and so on. The options Maintain Design Notes and Upload Design Notes for Sharing are (by default) automatically checked for a new site.

Pressing the Clean Up button (within Define Sites | Design Notes) will delete any design notes no longer associated with a file. This may occur when you delete, rename, or move a file while outside the Dreamweaver MX application.

Design notes inherit the same name as the HTML page, with an additional extension of *.mno*. These are saved in a folder called *_notes* within the folder of the current document. For example, when design notes are entered for the file *index.html*, the notes are saved in a file called *index.html.mno*.

Figure 4-9 shows an example of design notes. These design notes are accessed via File Menu | Design Notes. Remember that these notes are for you and the others who may be working with the same file or web site. You have the option of setting the status of the file by selecting *draft, revision 1, revision 2, revision 3, alpha, beta, final,* or *needs attention.* There is also a button for inserting the current date in the notes.

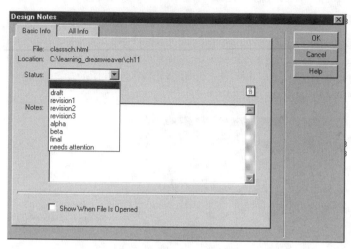

Fig. 4-9. Design Notes window.

Site Definition: Site Map Layout

The options listed on the Site Map Layout page define the structure of the site map. See figure 4-10. The options under Number of Columns, Column Width, and Icon Labels will determine the basic appearance of the site map. Selecting Display Files Marked as Hidden will show hidden pages and links in italics. Dependent files, those files that are external to an HTML document such as images and sounds, can also be listed by selecting Display Dependent Files in the Site Map Layout. This would help you see a quick list of all media elements being used for a single file.

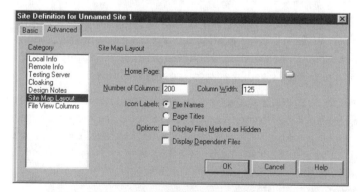

Fig. 4-10. Site Definition: Site Map Layout category.

Site Definition: File View Columns

The options listed on the File View Columns page allow you to add, delete, or modify the columns displayed in the site map. See figure 4-11.

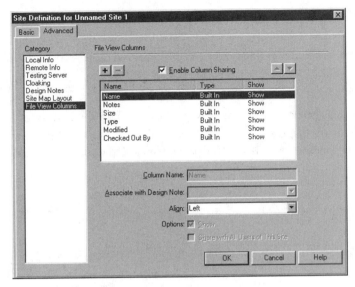

Fig. 4-11. Site Definition: File View Columns category.

Site Panel

Once a site has been defined using the Site Definition wizard, the Site panel becomes the primary Dreamweaver MX tool for working and managing your local and remote sites. The Site panel will allow you to perform the following.

- *Define the location of your files on the local computer (Edit Sites| Local Info).*

- *Define the location of your files on the Web (Edit Sites | Remote Info).*

- *View a listing of files on the local site and remote site (Site files view).*

- *View a diagram of the pages and how they link to each other, including all media elements on a page (Site map view).*

- *Define and view files on the testing server (Site panel toolbar | Testing Server button).*

In addition, the Site panel provides elements for managing your web site. While in Dreamweaver MX, whenever you rename, move, or cut a file on your local site, Dreamweaver MX will update any links to the file. When a file is deleted or cut from the local site, Dreamweaver MX will warn you if the file is linked to other files. The following are some of the management tool abilities of Dreamweaver MX.

- *Rename a file and automatically relink pages to the renamed file (File Menu | Rename).*

- *Move files and automatically relink pages to the new location of the file (drag the file to a new location in Site Files).*

·T/P·

The home page can be changed (or set) directly in the Site panel. Select a file in the site files for the Local site. Right mouse click (Windows) or Control+mouse click (Macintosh) to see a context menu for the file. Select *Set as Home Page*. This new page will now appear at the top of the site map.

- *Create folders within the local site (File Menu | New Folder).*
- *Turn off the Read Only option for a file (File Menu | Turn off Read Only).*
- *View the name of the person who is currently working on a file (select Check Out, and you must be connected to the remote site).*
- *Reset the home page (File Menu | Set as Home Page).*

Use the Site panel toolbar to select the type of view. When the Site panel is collapsed (Windows only), you can select Local, Remote, Testing Server, or Map files. When the Site panel is expanded, the panel is split into two panels and you can select more than one view. See figure 4-12.

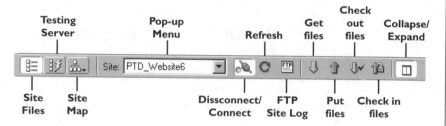

Fig. 4-12. Site panel toolbar.

Site Map

Within the Site panel you have the option to list files in the local site and/or display the local site files as a map. The Site Map view provides the tools for manipulating the local site to:

- *Link to a new file. This inserts a hot text link in the file. (Drag the Point To File icon from the site map to the site files.) See figure 4-13.*
- *Remove and change links between files. (Use the Context menu or Site menu in the Site panel.) See figure 4-14.*
- *View broken links. (Use the context menu or select File Menu | Check Links.)*

Site Map   **Point to File**

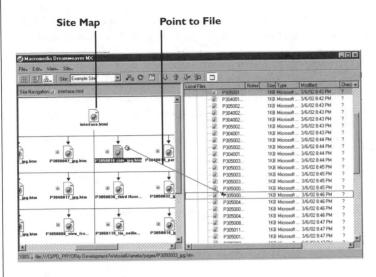

Fig. 4-13. Site map with Point To File option.

Fig. 4-14. Site map Context menu.

Practice Exercise 4-1: Creating a New Site

Description

The very first thing you should do before you begin to create web pages for a site is to define the site. Defining a site provides Dreamweaver MX with the background information about the site, such as the working directory on the

Shortcut

There are many options available from the context menu for each file in the Site Map. Select a file or folder and right mouse click (Windows) or Control+mouse click (Macintosh) to access the context menu.

computer, Internet addresses, and Internet and FTP access passwords. After you define the site, you can then save and link files, and place media elements relative to that site's organization.

In this exercise you will create a new site that will be used for the practice exercises in this book. We will also create the home page for the site on your local computer. We will not connect to a server at this time.

Take a Look and Storyboard: On Screen

DEVELOPMENT TOOL ONLY

In this particular exercise, nothing is actually created for the user to see. You will not be able to open the exercise until you have completed this exercise yourself. This heading has been placed here to maintain the consistency of the practice exercises.

Storyboard: Behind the Scenes

Figure 4-15 illustrates how your Site panel will look after you have defined your site in this exercise. The left side of the Site panel is the Site map. Notice the Target button next to *index.html* (this file will be created in the practice exercise). Dragging this Target button to another file, either in the site map or File list, would create an automatic link to that file from *index.html*.

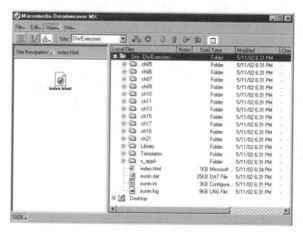

*Fig. 4-15. Site panel for **DWExercises**.*

Step-by-Step Instructions

Go Solo

1. We are going to define the location and properties for accessing files on the local site. We must first open the Site Definition dialog window.

    a) Open Dreamweaver MX.

b) Select Site Menu | New Site. The Site Definition dialog window will open, with Local Info selected. This menu option can be selected from the Document or Site panel.

2. We are going to create a local site for use in the rest of this book. We will use the Site Definition wizard to define our new site.

a) In the Site Definition window, select the Basic tab at the top of the window.

b) Question 1: What would you like to name your site? Type in *DWExercises*. Click on the Next button.

c) Editing Files, Part 2: We will not be using a testing server. Select the radio box for "No, I do not want to use a server technology." Click on the Next button.

d) Editing Files, Part 3: We want to edit files on our local machine. The folder that will be used to store your files has already been copied to your hard drive if you followed the steps in Chapter 1. Refer to that chapter now to create this folder. The work you do in all of the exercises in this book will be stored in this folder. Select the radio box for "Edit local copies on my machine, then upload to server when ready."

e) To browse for the local folder, select the icon that looks like a folder. This icon allows you to browse for a file. Click on the Folder icon.

f) Use the Scroll window to locate the directory *Learning_ Dreamweaver* on your computer. The location of this folder will probably be on your root folder or in program files (Windows). (If you do not find this folder on your local computer, follow the directions found in Chapter 1.) Click on Select. Click on the Next button to go to the next wizard screen.

g) Sharing Files: We will not be connecting to a remote server at this time. To the question "How do you connect to your remote server?," select None from the pop-up menu. Click on the Next button.

h) Summary Screen: The Summary screen displays the settings you have just selected on the previous screens. Your window information should look like the Local Info view shown in figure 4-16. The only exception may be the drive letter or name for the *Local Root* folder (i.e., C:\ might be D:\ on a Windows system, or Macintosh HD on a Macintosh system). You have now defined the local information and the location where your Dreamweaver files will be stored on your local drive. By default, all links in your web pages will be set relative to this location while you are working on the local drive.

CAUTION

The site named *DWExercises* that you will create in this exercise will be the same site used in all practice exercises in this book. In each of the practice exercises from this point forward, we will assume that you have created the *DWExercises* site as indicated here. We will give you periodic reminders to this effect.

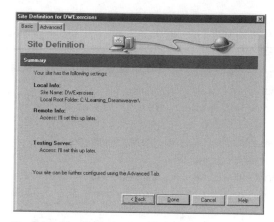

Fig. 4-16. Site Definition wizard Summary.

3. Now let's set the remaining elements in the site definition. This is done in the Advanced tab.

   a) Select the Advanced tab (in the Site Definition window).

   b) Select the category Local Info. You will see the folder that you selected in the wizard as your local root folder. New in Dreamweaver MX is the option of defining the *Default Images* folder where images will be saved. As an example, if you drag an image from the desktop to your HTML file, the images will be automatically saved in this default folder. We will leave this field blank.

   c) Make sure there is a check mark next to Enable Cache. The cache file contains a list of all files in the local site and will speed up the link management, Assets panel accessibility, and site map features. This must be created if you are planning to use the Assets panel. See figure 4-17.

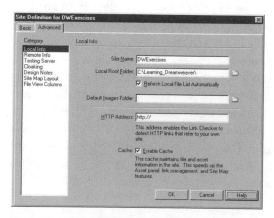

Fig. 4-17. Site Definition: Local Info category.

4. While still in the Site Definition window, click on the Design Notes category on the left-hand side of the dialog box. Once again, design notes are text notes attached to a file. If you do not intend to use design notes, you should uncheck the options in this category to save space on your local hard drive and remote site. We will not change anything in the Design Notes area, as we do want to maintain design notes.

5. Click on the Site Map Layout category on the left-hand side of the dialog box. The Site Map Layout will display a tree diagram of the files in your local site. The branches (rows and columns) of the tree are the links between HTML documents and media files.

    a) In the Home Page field, type in *index.html*. This is going to be the main (or first) page users see when they enter this site. This file does not exist yet, but as soon as you leave this screen Dreamweaver will try to create it for you on the local site.

    b) The Number of Columns and Column Width options will affect the way the site map is displayed. Type in *10* in the Number of Columns option. The number of columns relates to the number of files that will be listed in a row in the site map. You can experiment with this number later to see how it affects the look of your site map. See figure 4-18.

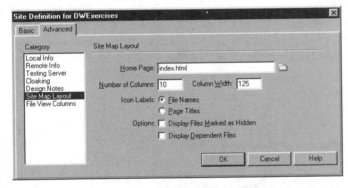

Fig. 4-18. Site Definition: Site Map Layout category.

6. Select the category File View Columns on the left-hand side of the Site Definition window. You will receive a message that tells you "File index.html does not exist. Would you like to create it?" Click on Yes. You just created an empty page called *index.html* on your local site (the home page you entered in the Site Map Layout option). You can type any file name you want in this box, or browse for an existing page. Just remember that when you are entering the name of a file that does not exist you should include the extension *.html* (or *.htm*). Otherwise, Dreamweaver MX will create the file without an extension.

7. Look at the options for the File View Columns selection. This is used to change the structure of site files in the Site panel.

8. Your site has now been defined. Click on the OK button at the bottom of the Site Definition window to complete this exercise. We will take a quick look at what we just created. The Site panel for the site you just created is going to try to open.

9. Because we selected Enable Cache (under Local Info), you will see the message "The initial site cache will now be created." This scans the files in your site and starts tracking links as you change them. When the site cache is finished being created, the Site panel is displayed.

   a) The right-hand side of the Site panel will display a folder named *Learning_Dreamweaver* on your hard drive, and a file within it called *index.html*. This empty file was created when you entered *index.html* as the home page in the Site Map Layout information.

   b) The left-hand side of the Site panel will show the list of files for your remote site when you are connected to the site. Because we are not connected, this side of the window is initially blank.

The file you define as the home page may be changed at any time by selecting the file and selecting Site | Set as Home Page.

10. In the upper left-hand corner of the Site panel, click on the button named Site Map (it is the third button from the left, see figure 4-19). This will display the site map in the left-hand side of the Site panel. *index.html* will be the only file listed, and the only reason it is displayed in the site map is because it was set as the home page. The *Home Page* file will always display at the top of the site map, with any files it links to being displayed as branches.

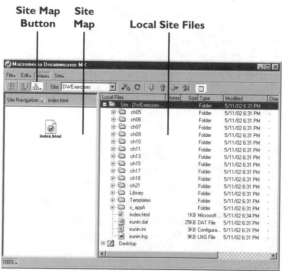

Fig. 4-19. Site panel for DWExercises site.

Summary

- *Before creating a web page for a site, the first step in using Dreamweaver MX is to define the site where the page will reside. The site structure determines the location and relative linking between pages each time you save or move a file/page.*

- *Create a site structure on your local computer that will mirror the site structure on the remote site (Internet server). This minimizes errors in linking between files, and in linking pages to their media elements when they are posted to the remote site.*

- *Be sure to check out the features in the Site panel that help you to manage your site. There is further discussion in the last chapter of this book on how to manage your site. Also see Appendix D and Appendix E in the Job Aids folder on the companion CD-ROM.*

- *A site has now been created called DWExercises, which will be used in further practice exercises in this book.*

C H A P T E R

5

Creating an

HTML Page –

Starting with Text

Introduction

As you begin to create your web pages, there are some fundamental formatting issues you should be aware of. For instance, you might ask if you can modify the font, style, and color of text. Can the background color of a page be changed? Are there "style" formats in HTML similar to the "style" formats found in many word processing packages? Actually, the answer to all of these questions is yes.

Whether you are creating a simple, straightforward site that informs the public about your company, or a site that is full of animation and graphics, you will probably use text and will want to control the text and page attributes. This chapter explores these issues. By the end of this chapter you will be able to:

- *Set the background color and title for a page*
- *Insert a graphic into the background*
- *Add text to a page*
- *Modify the format of text*
- *Add a heading to a page*
- *Modify a text style*

Page Properties

The very first step you should make when starting a new HTML page is to set the page properties. By default, a new page will have a solid white background, no title, and black text. These properties can be changed by selecting Modify Menu | Page Properties. See figure 5-1.

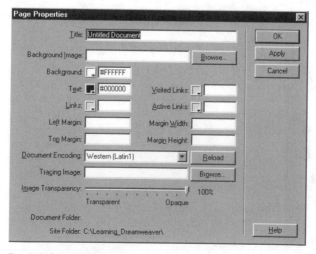

Fig. 5-1. Page properties.

General Properties

The following options in the Page Property window set general properties. See figure 5-1.

Title: Title is the name of the page when viewed inside a browser window. The default title is "Untitled Document." You can use this Title option to provide the visitor with information such as the purpose of the page, the name of the site or company, and so on. Do not confuse the page title with the file name. The file name is the name you give the page when you save it, and it is the file name that will display at the top of a Document window while you are editing the file in Dreamweaver MX. This title is what will display in the Title bar at the top of an HTML page when it is viewed from a browser. The title can also be set in the Dreamweaver MX toolbar.

Background color: Dreamweaver MX provides a web-safe palette to select the background color for the entire page.

Text: The Text box will be blank when you first open the Page Properties option. This means that the default color (black) will be used for the color of all text in the current page. Use this Text option to change the default color of the text that will appear in the current document. This is also the border color for images.

Color of Links

In addition to the previously discussed general attributes, you can use the Page Properties options to set the color of links. Any links you create on a page will use a default color unless you change it.

Links (or hyperlinks): The default color is blue. Hyperlinks are words or phrases that when clicked on with the mouse cause some action to occur, such as jumping to another page, displaying a hot tip, or modifying a graphic. Note that a hyperlink can also be attached to a graphic and thus the links color also applies to the border color of a graphic if the graphic border width is greater than zero.

Visited links: The default color is purple. Visited links are hyperlinks that have already been selected. This provides a visual cue that the link and the page associated with the link has already been visited. Again, this also applies to the border on graphics.

Active links: The default color is red. Active links are hyperlinks that are currently in the process of being selected or clicked. You will find that this color is not always seen because the action of the hyperlink occurs so quickly – such as jumping to a new page.

·T*i*P·

If you want to save a color to reuse for text, background colors, and tiles, add the color to the Assets panel. For example, to add the background color to Favorites, right mouse click on the background color and select Add to Color Favorites. To access the color, select Assets | Favorites | Colors. Use the Eyedropper tool to select the color.

·T*i*P·

When the color boxes (Text, Links, Visited Links, and Active Links) in the Page Properties box are blank, the default colors will be used.

Many Internet users are accustomed to the default link colors of blue, purple, and red. Therefore, to maintain consistency of use, we suggest that you use the default link colors unless they are aesthetically or functionally not appropriate for a page. Most importantly, these colors should be consistent within your site.

Background Image

The Page Properties window also provides the option to import a graphic to display in the background of a page. The following tips may help you in using a graphic as the background.

- *If the graphic is smaller than the page dimensions, the graphic will repeat, or tile. See figure 5-2.*

- *Keep the background graphic small. Background graphics that have large file sizes are one of the primary culprits of slow page downloads.*

- *If you want a graphic pattern to fill the entire page (no matter what size it is), try to use a tile graphic. The graphic can be as small as one pixel in height and width.*

- *Sometimes the background image is the last thing to display. Set a background color that can display until the background image downloads.*

**Original Tile
60 x 60**

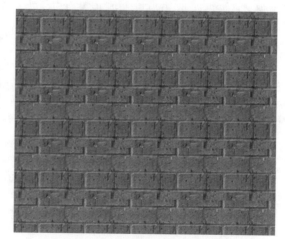

Tile repeated to create the background image

Fig. 5-2. Sample tile graphic pattern for backgrounds.

To summarize, the following are the main options you will probably want to change under Page Properties.

- *The title for the page. It looks unprofessional to leave it as "Untitled Document."*

- *The background color for the current page.*

- *The text and link colors, if the colors do not work well on your site.*

Practice Exercise 5-1: Defining a Site (A Review)

Description

In Chapter 4, you defined a site that is going to be used to save all files created in the practice exercises throughout this book. Each practice exercise also has a section (called "Take a Look") that lets you look at the completed version of the exercises that reside on the companion CD-ROM. To make it easier to access the files used in the "Take a Look" sections, we will create a new site called *DWComplete*, referenced throughout this book.

Take a Look and Storyboard: On Screen

In this particular exercise, nothing is actually created for the user to see. You will not be able to open the exercise until you have completed this exercise yourself. These headings have been placed here to maintain the consistency of the practice exercises.

Storyboard: Behind the Scenes

Figure 5-3 illustrates the Local Info setting for this new site.

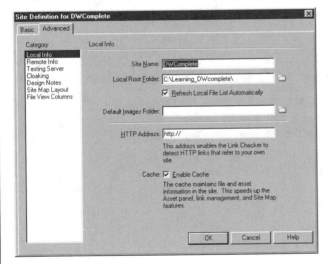

*Fig. 5-3. Site Definition Local Info setting for the **DWComplete** site.*

Go Solo

CAUTION

The site named *DWComplete* that you will create in this exercise will be the same site used in the "Take A Look" sections in this book. In each of the practice exercises from this point forward, we will assume that you have created the *DWComplete* site as indicated here. We will give you periodic reminders to this effect.

Step-by-Step Instructions

1. We are going to define the location and properties for accessing files on the local site. To create a new site, from the Document window or Site panel, select Site Menu | New Site. The Site Definition dialog window will open, with Local Info selected.

2. We are going to create a local site for use in the rest of this book, in the "Take a Look" sections of practice exercises. The remote site information will not be entered.
    a) In the Site Name field, type *DWComplete*.
    b) Next to the *Local Root* folder, select the *Browse* folder icon.
    c) Select the companion CD-ROM and find the folder called *Learning_ DWcomplete*. Click on Select.
    d) The HTTP address will not be changed. This is usually changed only if you are linking to absolute paths within your site. Absolute paths contain the complete file path on your hard drive (e.g., C://). This path might not be the same as your web site viewer's hard drive information.
    e) Click to place a check mark next to Enable Cache.
    f) Your window information should look like the Local Info view shown in figure 5-3. The only exception may be the drive letter for the CD-ROM.

3. We will not change the Remote Info or Design Notes category.

4. Click on the OK button at the bottom of the Site Definition window to complete this exercise. We will take a quick look at what we just created.

5. Because we selected Enable Cache (Local Info), you will see the message "The initial site cache will now be created." When the Site Cache is finished being created, the Site panel is displayed.
    a) The right-hand side (the local site) of the Site panel will display a folder named *Learning_DWcomplete*.

Practice Exercise 5-2: Placing Text on a Page

Description

We are going to start with the basics in this exercise. In this exercise you will:

- *Set page properties, including background color and page title*
- *Preview pages in the browser*
- *Copy and paste text outside Dreamweaver MX*
- *Set the text and line spacing*
- *Insert a horizontal rule*
- *Check spelling*

Take a Look

Before beginning the exercise, let's take a look at the exercise in its completed state so that you can clearly see what it is you are about to build.

1. Make sure you are working with the site *DWComplete*. (If you do not have this site created, follow the directions in the previous practice exercise.) You can confirm that you have already created the site by selecting the Site panel and selecting *DWComplete* from the Site pop-up menu.

2. Using the Site panel, find the subfolder *ch05*. Locate and open the file named *dw05ex1.html* by double clicking on it.

3. The file *dw05ex1.html* should now appear in your copy of Dreamweaver MX. Note the following properties of this completed exercise.

   - *The title of the page and the background color*
   - *There is a horizontal line between sections of text*
   - *Some paragraphs have a blank line between them*

Storyboard: On Screen

Figure 5-4 shows you how the finished page will look when viewed through a browser. Notice that the name of the page (*American History*) appears at the very top, in the browser's Title bar.

CAUTION

Before starting this exercise, it is important that you have previously set up your site according to the instructions found in Chapter 4. Remember that each time you insert graphics or link files, Dreamweaver MX uses the site definition to set the address or relative link to the file. If this is not set up, an absolute link will be set. Using absolute links will generally cause a problem when you place the page on the remote site, because it will not be able to find the dependent or linked files. This is because these files are pointing to your local computer hard drive.

CD-ROM

DWComplete Site

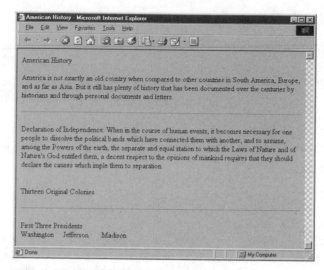

Fig. 5-4. Finished page in browser.

Storyboard: Behind the Scenes

In figure 5-5, the bottom section illustrates the Dreamweaver MX Document window, whereas the top section shows the HTML code created by Dreamweaver for the text and formatting. Notice the correspondence between the highlighted HTML code and what you see in the Document window.

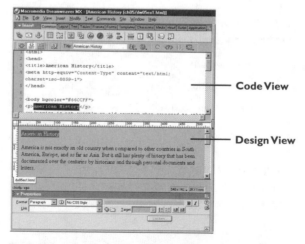

Fig. 5-5. Document window (bottom) and HTML window (top).

To access the HTML code, select View Menu | Code and Design, or select the Show Code and Design Views button at the upper left of the Design window.

Step-by-Step Instructions

Go Solo

DWExercises Site

1. Let's start by making sure you are working with the site we created in Chapter 4. You can confirm this by selecting Site panel | Site pop-up menu | *DWExercises*.

2. We are going to start with a new document.
    a) Select File Menu | New to open a new blank document.
    b) The New Document dialog appears. This dialog box allows you to select many types of files that can be created and modified in Dreamweaver.
    c) With the General tab selected, select the category Basic Page to create an HTML document.
    d) Click on Create. (You can also double click on the item or press the Enter key).
    e) A new document appears in the Document window. See figure 5-6.

CAUTION

Make sure the Save In window shows *Learning_ Dreamweaver*. This is the folder the page will be saved in and should match the folder defined in our site definition (Chapter 4). If *Learning_ Dreamweaver* is not displayed, use the pull-down menu to locate the folder *Learning_Dreamweaver*.

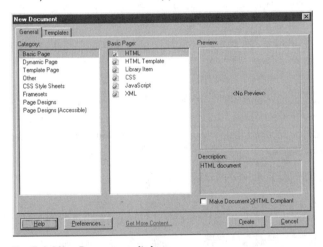

Fig. 5-6. New Document dialog.

·T/P·

It is generally a good idea to always enter a page title for every document you create. If you do not, the HTML page will display "Untitled Document" at the top of the window when displayed in a browser. Everyone visiting your site will see the page labeled as "Untitled Document."

f) Select File Menu | Save (you can also use the Save As command, in that this file has never been saved).
g) Browse or use the Explorer Window to locate the *Learning_ Dreamweaver* folder and subfolder *ch05* on your computer.
h) In the File Name field, type *dw05ex1.html*. Select Save. See figure 5-7.

Dreamweaver MX will automatically add an *.htm* or *.html* extension based on the preferences set in Dreamweaver MX (Edit menu), but we suggest you type in the full *.html* extension. The *.html* extension is applicable to both the Windows and Macintosh platforms (in addition to some other platforms) and is more widely used across the Web. If you want to be sure your web pages can be viewed through the widest possible assortment of platforms and browsers, make sure you use the complete extension, *.html*.

Also, use only lower-case letters in the naming of your files, and stay away from spaces and special characters. This is because at some point you will probably end up using JavaScript, which is case sensitive. Some operating systems, such as UNIX, are also case sensitive and there are still a lot of web servers based on UNIX.

```
folder: Learning_Dreamweaver
 └─ folder: ch05
        └─ dw05ex1.html
```

Fig. 5-7. File structure for exercise.

If you are often creating the same type of file (e.g., HTML document or page design), you can set up the default document type to open without the New Document dialog box appearing. Select Edit Menu | Preferences or Dreamweaver Preferences (MaxOS X), and select the New Document category. Under Default Document Type, select the document type for all new documents to be based on (i.e., HTML document).

3. Let's change the page properties.
    a) Select Modify Menu | Page Properties, or right mouse click on the document and select Page Properties.
    b) The top entry field is for the page title. This is the information that will be displayed along the top of the web page window in the browser. Type in *American History*.

4. Now let's set the background color, in the third entry field from the top of the Page Properties window. You can either type in the six-character HTML color code or select a color from the Color palette. Let's use the Color palette, which is a lot more user-friendly. See figure 5-8.

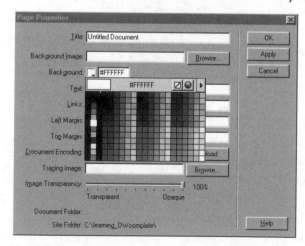

Fig. 5-8. Color palette.

a) Mouse click on the square to the right of the word *Background*. (It is the square that has the little down arrow in the lower right-hand corner.)

b) Move the cursor (which is now an Eyedropper icon) around the palette. You will notice that the color viewer in the lower left-hand corner of the screen will show what color the Eyedropper is over. Also note that the HTML code for this color is displayed in the lower center of the Palette window.

c) Click the Eyedropper on a light color (from the top row) of your choice. Once you click on a color, the Color palette will disappear and the color shade and HTML code will show up in the Page Properties window. You can also use the Eyedropper to pick up a color from a graphic already in the document.

d) Click on the Apply button to preview your changes, and then click on the OK button.

5. This is a good time to check your work.
   a) Look at your document. You should now see a color as the background of your page.
   b) Look at the top of the Document window. You should see the name of this page, *American History*, in the pop-up menu in the toolbar, and in Dreamweaver's Title bar.

6. Let's save our work. Select File Menu | Save to save our latest changes. We have previously saved the file as *dw05ex1.html*.

7. Now let's preview your work in a browser. It is a good idea to periodically view your web pages in the browsers while you are creating. It is also a good idea to view your page in more than one browser.
   a) Select File Menu | Preview in Browser, and select the name of a browser (you might have only one browser listed at this point).
   b) Your web browser will open, and you should see your colored background and the page name in the Title bar. Close the Browser window.
   c) To add another browser to the list of browsers, select File Menu | Preview in Browser | Edit Browser List. This option takes you into the Preview in Browser Category of Preferences. This window will let you select the primary browser and secondary browser to use when previewing a page. To add another browser, select the plus (+) symbol (do this only if you know another browser is installed on your computer). You will need to browse for the executable file for the browser. These files are usually located in the *Windows/System* folder. Those of you using a Macintosh can use Sherlock to locate the files. See figure 5-9.

·T/P·

As you are previewing your work in different browsers, you should look for any differences in alignment, positioning, and functionality of your HTML page. Browsers can differ in the way they display media and interact with the page properties. It is better to ascertain these differences early in the development process (and adjust for the differences), rather than finding them after you have finished.

You may decide to make it a requirement that the user must have at least a specific version of a browser (such as Version 4, so that you can use layers) to narrow the browser compatibility issues. You can also check a user's browser version and display a note to the user such as "This site requires browser Version 4 or above." Later in this book, you will use a behavior that will check the user's browser version.

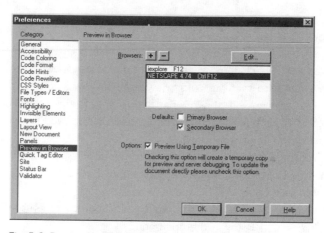

Fig. 5-9. Preview in Browser option under Preferences.

8. Now for some practice adding and deleting text on a page. When you open a new page in Dreamweaver MX, the cursor will be blinking in the upper left-hand corner, just like a word processor. Do not worry about formatting just yet. You will do that later.

   a) Type *American History* at the top of the page.

   b) Press the Enter/Return key.

   c) Your cursor now looks as though it is two lines below the line you just typed in. On this new line, type a short paragraph of text. Type anything you want, but make sure to type enough text that Dreamweaver MX automatically "word wraps" your sentence to continue the paragraph to the next line. For this text, do not use the Enter/Return key to move the text to the next line. Let Dreamweaver MX "wrap" the text for you.

   d) Now you should really be able to see that there is a blank line (double line break) between the first paragraph you typed (*American History*) and the second paragraph you typed.

   e) Whenever you press the Enter/Return key after a line of text, it will automatically insert one blank line. This is how you create a new paragraph.

9. Now for some more text.

   a) Press the Enter/Return key after the last line of text you just typed in the paragraph.

   b) Now you will type some new text, but this time the text will be separated by single line breaks. You can create a single-line break by simultaneously pressing the Shift key and Enter/Return key. Type in the following.

Thirteen Original Colonies (Shift Key & Enter/Return Key)

First Three Presidents (Shift Key & Enter/Return Key)

Washington Jefferson Madison (Shift Key & Enter/Return Key)

c) We need to enter some spacing between the three presidents' names we just typed. Place your cursor between Washington and Jefferson. Press the space bar. Nothing happened, did it? You cannot enter more than one space in an HTML file using the space bar. To enter more than one space, you need to insert what is called a non-breaking space. Select the Non-Breaking Space option from the Insert menu. To insert more spaces, keep selecting Insert Menu | Non-Breaking Space. See figure 5-10.

NOTE: The Insert bar contains many shortcuts to items found in the Insert menu. To insert the non-breaking space, from the Insert bar select Characters tab | Non-Breaking Space. If the Insert bar is not displaying, select Window Menu | Insert.

Insert Bar

Insert Non-Breaking Space

Fig. 5-10. Insert bar and Non-Breaking Space option.

10. Save the file on your hard drive by selecting File Menu | Save.

11. Let's look at another way to get text into Dreamweaver MX – by copying and pasting. We will use the Site panel to access an RTF (Rich-Text Format) file.

a) Select Site Menu | Open Site | *DWExercises*.

b) Find the *ch05* folder. Locate and double click on (open) the file *dw05a.rtf*. This file should open in your computer's default word processor or notepad.

c) If your file opens in a word processor, you should notice that the file contains some words that are in bold. (If the RTF file opens in Notepad (Windows) or SimpleText (Macintosh), bold or other formatting styles will not be displayed. These programs only support basic text formatting. This does not matter, as described in the following steps.)

d) Highlight all of the text in the file and select Edit Menu | Copy (in your word processor) to copy the text to your computer's clipboard. Close the RTF file (and the word processor). See figure 5-11.

Shortcut

It will probably be faster to enter non-breaking spaces by using the keyboard shortcut Ctrl + Shift + space bar (Windows) or Cmd + Shift + space bar (Macintosh).

Instead of typing text directly into Dreamweaver, you can copy and paste text from other documents. The caution here is to watch out for formatting (visible or hidden) that already exists in the text you are about to copy. Existing formatting can create havoc in your web pages, and you may not understand why the text is doing strange things (additional line breaks, tabbing, spacing, strange characters, and so on). The easiest way to get around the existing formatting is to save your text as a *.txt* file.

Declaration of Independence: When in the course of human events, it becomes necessary for one people to dissolve the political bands which have connected them with another, and to assume, among the Powers of the earth, the separate and equal station to which the Laws of Nature and of Nature's God entitled them, a decent respect to the opinions of mankind requires that they should declare the causes which imple them to separation.

*Fig. 5-11. Text within the **dw05a.rtf** file.*

12. Return to Dreamweaver MX and the file *dw05ex1.html*.

13. In Dreamweaver MX, position the cursor on the blank line above the line *Thirteen Original Colonies* and press the Return/Enter key to insert a new line. The cursor should now be positioned on the new line.

14. Select Edit Menu | Paste to paste the text from the RTF file into your document. Dreamweaver's paste option will preserve the line breaks from the original file. It does not preserve any other formatting, such as bold or italic styles.

15. Press the Enter/Return key again. Now let's try something a little different. Select Edit | Paste HTML. Note that in using this option the original line breaks (margins) do not remain within the text. However, if there were any HTML tags within the text, they would be recognized and the text would be displayed per the HTML tags (i.e., via the *<b>* tag to make it bold).

16. Dreamweaver MX has a nice spell checking option built into the program. Let's take a quick look.
    a) Select Text Menu | Check Spelling. You can add words to your Personal Dictionary if you want to.
    b) Click on the Close button when the spell check is finished.

17. Now let's take a look at the horizontal rules that divide a page into sections.
    a) Position the cursor on the blank line above the *Declaration of Independence* paragraph.
    b) Select Insert Menu | Horizontal Rule, or Insert bar | Common | Horizontal Rule.
    c) You can change the alignment and size, and remove the shadow on the horizontal rule using the Property Inspector. Select the horizontal rule with your cursor. Select Window | Properties. Change whatever attributes of the horizontal rule you wish.

18. To clean up the file, delete the first *Declaration of Independence* paragraph that did not keep the line breaks. Insert an additional horizontal rule between *Thirteen Original Colonies* and *First Three Presidents*. See figure 5-4 for an example of what your page should now look like.

·T/P·

Edit | Paste will preserve the original line breaks in the text copied from another software program. However, no other formatting is preserved. If you need to copy a lot of text from another program, you might try saving the file in your word processor as an HTML file. Then open the file in Dreamweaver MX. If the file was created in Microsoft Word, a lot of extra HTML tags are included that are not necessary. In Dreamweaver, select Commands Menu | Clean Up Word HTML to get the file back to a "native" document.

Shortcut

You can also use the shortcut keys Shift + F7 (Windows and Macintosh) to check spelling.

19. Save your work by selecting File Menu | Save.

20. Close the current document by selecting File | Close, or by right mouse clicking on the tab of the file at the bottom of the Document window (Windows only). See figure 5-12.

Fig. 5-12. Document window showing Document pop-up menu (Windows only).

HTML: A Brief Overview

HTML, like other types of markup languages (e.g., SML and XML), consists of predefined tags (labels) that define the structure of the page and its elements. Every web page that resides on the Internet and is viewable through a web browser consists of HTML. As you use Dreamweaver MX to add media to your HTML pages, modify attributes, and move elements around on the page, Dreamweaver MX actually modifies the HTML code.

In the "old days," programmers had to type in all of the HTML code as lines of code, similar to many programming languages of the time. With the development of visually-oriented HTML editors such as Dreamweaver MX, web page developers no longer need to know very many of the HTML codes. Dreamweaver MX's interface, menus, tools, and wizards create and insert the HTML needed for displays, formatting, animation, and many other functions.

Even though Dreamweaver MX creates and edits most of the HTML you will need for your web page, it is still a good idea to understand the basic concepts and design of HTML. Knowing the basics about HTML will allow you to correct errors you may inadvertently create when you add, modify, or delete elements in a page. As you become more proficient with web page development, you may want to add extra HTML and JavaScript functions that are not included in Dreamweaver MX. Figure 5-13 shows an example of the standard HTML in a web page – also called a document.

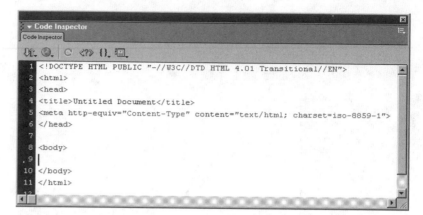

Fig. 5-13. HTML as seen in the Code Inspector (Window Menu | Others).

HTML

Note the following basics in regard to HTML.

- *Tags represent instructions for the formatting, appearance, and function of elements on a web page. The tags are names surrounded by the less than (<) symbol and the greater than (>) symbol. There is generally a start tag (at the beginning of an instruction) and an end tag (at the end of the instruction) for each name. The end tag will have a slash before the name. <Head> and </Head> are the start and end tags, respectively, for the Head instruction.*

- *The HTML document is divided into two sections: the head and the body.*

- *<Head> defines general properties of the document, such as the title and content information (called the meta tag).*

- *<Body> contains the elements displayed on the page. This will include much of the formatting: text, graphics, animation, video, sound, buttons, and so on.*

- *Some tags have attributes that further describe the element. For instance, to define the color and font size for some text, only the <font> tag is used, but it has two attributes: one for color, and one for size.*

  <font color="#CCCCCC" size="1">this is some text</font>

As we move forward in this book, we will look at the HTML code that is automatically created (behind the scenes) by Dreamweaver MX as we create an exercise. This should help you gain a better understanding of what happens to the HTML code each time you modify attributes, add media, and create hyperlinks. This broader understanding should help you correct problems you may encounter with the HTML code later on.

Setting Text Properties

Before we modify the attributes of the text on our page, there are some important things you will need to understand about what makes text on an HTML page a little bit different from text in a word processor document. Let's start with a few things about HTML font typefaces and font sizes.

Font (Typeface)

The default font for HTML pages is defined in each user's browser preferences. Generally if the user has not changed these preferences, the default font is Times New Roman. One way to modify the font for a single character or entire page is to use the Property Inspector or by selecting Text Menu | Font.

In one sense, for the web pages you create, you can use any font you want to. However, from a practical standpoint, if a user's computer does not have the font you selected, the text will be displayed according to the preferences set in the user's browser. To help preserve the appearance of a web page with the text displaying as close to the original design as possible, you can use font lists. A font list will provide alternatives for the display of text on the user's computer. For example, you might create a font list that has three fonts: Garamond, Arial, and Times. The user's browser will display the text on your web page using the first font on the list that is also installed on the computer. If none of the fonts in the font list are installed on the user's computer, the browser's preferences will be used.

You will probably want to create font lists that include five fonts or fewer. To create a font list in Dreamweaver MX, select Text Menu | Font | Edit Font List. See figure 5-14.

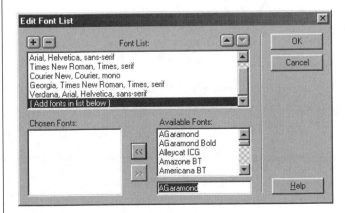

Fig. 5-14. Font list.

·T/P·

If you want to insert text that has a specific font that is probably not on a user's machine, an alternative to creating a graphic is creating a Flash file with the text. From the Insert menu, select Interactive Images | Flash Text. You will be asked the typeface, font, size, and color of the text. You can also make the text interactive and give it a rollover color and link. A shocked Flash file will then be created (.*swf* extension) on your site, with the text in it and the font embedded in the Flash file.

Font Size

In HTML pages, font size is normally referenced in terms of either an absolute or relative size.

Absolute Font Size

Absolute font sizes include values from 1 to 7, with 3 being equal to the default size specified in the user's preferences.

Relative Font Size

Relative font sizes are indicated by a plus or minus symbol and are relative to the default font size (3), unless that default size has been changed through the use of an HTML tag, <basefont>. The relative sizes are in increments of 20%. A size of +1 is 20% larger than the default size. A size of -1 is 20% smaller than the default size. See figure 5-15.

absolute value	7	6	5	4	3	2	1
relative value	+4	+3	+2	+1	none	-1	-2
	word	word	word	word	word	word	word

Fig. 5-15. Font size range.

Font sizes can only be in the range of 1 to 7 (like absolute font size). Therefore, a relative size of +5 (which equals a size of 8 if the default size is 3) will only display at the maximum size of 7. The default font size is generally comparable to 12-point size if the user has not changed his browser preferences.

Setting the Default Size

To force the default size and thus override the browser's preferences set by the user, you can use the <basefont> tag. Although Dreamweaver MX does not have an insert for this tag (yet), you can type the tag in yourself using the HTML Code view.

To change the default size for the entire page, place the <basefont> tag immediately after the opening <body> tag. All succeeding text will then pick up the font setting. Figure 5-16 shows an example of the HTML code for the <basefont> tag. Note that the new size set with the <basefont> tag only shows while previewing the document in a browser window. You will not see the effect of the <basefont> tag in the Dreamweaver MX Document window.

HTML

The following two lines of HTML code will display text using the same font size (as long as the default is still 3):

<Font size="5"> word</Font>

<Font size="+2"> word</Font>

```
<html>
<head>
<title>Untitled Document</title>
<meta http-equiv="Content-Type" content="text/html;
charset=iso-8859-1">

</head>
<body bgcolor="#FFFFFF">
<basefont size = 4>
This is some line of text.
</body>
</html>
```

Fig. 5-16. HTML for <basefont> tag.

HTML Formatting Versus CSS Formatting

Text can be formatted with HTML or cascading style sheet (CSS) formatting. HTML formatting has options such as font, size, bold, and italic. CSS formatting applies a CSS class style to the selected text (or other element) and has many properties that cannot be controlled using just HTML. A class style is a rule that describes how a page element should be displayed. This style can set more than one attribute at a time. CSS styles are not recognized by IE 3.0 or Netscape 4.0. See figure 5-17.

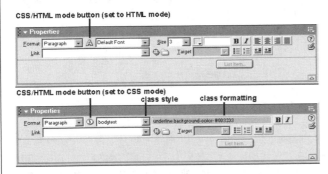

Fig. 5-17. Property Inspector for a text object.

Setting a CSS Style

If you want to set a style for a block of text, an entire page, or an entire site, you may want to use CSS styles. CSS are very similar to the styles set inside a word processing program. Each style has a name, and each style has a set of specific attributes that can be applied to a block of text or page. CSS styles can also be created in an external file that can be linked to multiple pages, so that every page has access to the same formatting (like templates in a word processing package). For instance, a CSS style can be created (call it *.style1*) to set the font to Helvetica, the text color to #CCCC99, and the size to 14. Any

HTML

You can also set the default color and font face using the HTML *<basefont>* tag, but these are only displayed correctly in Internet Explorer. This *<basefont>* tag sets the size, font face, and color for the text, as follows.

<basefont size = 4 face = "Verdana" color="#0000FF">

time this style is applied to a block of text, that text will become Helvetica, size 14, color #CCCC99.

When a CSS style is created, HTML code is inserted in the *<head>* tag of the document. The following is the HTML generated for this style example.

```
<head>
<title>American History</title>
<meta http-equiv="Content-Type" content="text/html;
charset=iso-8859-1">
<style type="text/css">
<!--
.style1 { font-family: Helvetica; font-size: 14px; color:
#CCCC99}
-->
</style>
</head>
```

CSS styles also have other categories besides just formatting text. The categories are Type, Background, Block, Box, Border, List, Positioning, and Extensions. Access the CSS styles by selecting Window Menu | CSS Styles. You can also select the HTML/CSS Mode button in the Property Inspector to select, create, and edit a CSS style for a selected text. CSS styles are further discussed in Appendix B, in the folder *Job Aids* on the companion CD-ROM.

Practice Exercise 5-3: Enhanced Text

Description

Although some of the pages you see on the Internet at the present time are full of animation, graphics, and a lot of fancy effects, most pages are still going to have plenty of plain text. But it does not have to be plain. It can have color, or be of various sizes and styles, and these text attributes will add value to your page when used appropriately. In this exercise you will:

- *Create a font combination, or font list*
- *Set the font color, font size, and alignment for text*
- *Create lists: bulleted, numbered, and indented*
- *Use text styles and modify styles*
- *Check spelling*

Take a Look

Before beginning the exercise, let's take a look at the exercise in its completed state so that you can clearly see what it is you are about to build.

CD-ROM

DWComplete Site

1. Make sure you are working with the site *DWComplete*. (If you do not have this site created, follow the directions in the first practice exercise in this chapter.) You can confirm this by selecting Site panel | Site pop-up menu | *DWComplete*.

2. Using the Site panel, find the subfolder *ch05*. Locate and open the file named *dw05ex2.html* (by double clicking on it).

3. Select File Menu | Preview in Browser | your browser, or press the F12 key to launch the default browser. The file *dw05ex2.html* should now appear in your browser. Note the following properties of this completed exercise.

    •*The font attributes of the text, including color, size, font type, and bold style*

    • *The center alignment of the text*

    • *The bulleted lists and numbered lists*

    • *Page properties: title and background color*

    • *The horizontal bar separating content in the page*

Storyboard: On Screen

Figure 5-18 shows how the HTML document should look when you are finished with this exercise.

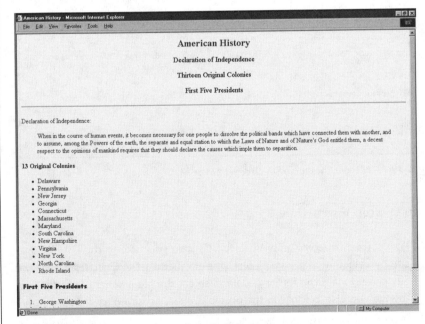

Fig. 5-18. Completed screen viewed through browser.

Storyboard: Behind the Scenes

When you are finished with this exercise, your HTML document should look similar to what is illustrated in figure 5-19, when viewed within Dreamweaver MX.

```
<html>
<head>
<title>American History</title>
<meta http-equiv="Content-Type" content="text/html; charset=iso-8859-1">
</head>

<body bgcolor="#CCFFFF">
<h2 align="center"><b><font color="#000066">American History</font></b></h2>
<p align="center"><font size="+1">Declaration of Independence</font></p>
<p align="center"><font size="+1">Thirteen Original Colonies</font></p>
<p align="center"><font size="+1">First Five Presidents</font></p>
<hr>
<p>Declaration of Independence: </p>
<blockquote>
  <p> When in the course of human events, it becomes necessary for one people
     to dissolve the political bands which have connected them with another, and
     to assume, among the Powers of the earth, the separate and equal station to
     which the Laws of Nature and of Nature's God entitled them, a decent respect
     to the opinions of mankind requires that they should declare the causes which
     imple them to separation. </p>
</blockquote>
<p> <b>13 Original Colonies</b></p>
<ul>
  <li>Delaware </li>
  <li>Pennsylvania </li>
  <li>New Jersey </li>
  <li>Georgia </li>
  <li>Connecticut </li>
  <li>Massachusetts </li>
  <li>Maryland </li>
  <li>South Carolina </li>
  <li>New Hampshire </li>
  <li>Virginia </li>
  <li>New York </li>
  <li>North Carolina </li>
  <li>Rhode Island </li>
</ul>
<p> <font face="Comic Sans MS, Arial, Times New Roman"><b>First Five Presidents
  </b> </font></p>
<ol>
  <li>George Washington </li>
  <li>John Adams </li>
  <li>Thomas Jefferson</li>
  <li>James Madison </li>
  <li>James Monroe </li>
</ol>
</body>
</html>
```

Fig. 5-19. HTML document within Dreamweaver MX.

Step-by-Step Instructions

Go Solo

DWExercises Site

1. Let's start by opening an existing file. Change your site to the *DWExercises* site by selecting Site panel | Site pop-up menu | *DWExercises*. Using the Site panel, locate the folder *ch05* and select the file *amerhis1.html*. (Part of this file was also created in the previous exercise, saved as *dw05ex1.html*.)

2. We are now going to change the font of some of the text in this file. Select Text Menu | Font | Edit Font List. See figure 5-20.

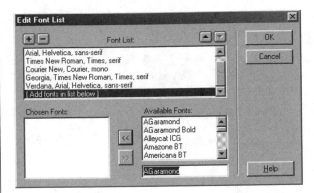

Fig. 5-20. Edit Font List window.

3. Within the Edit Font List window is a list of available fonts installed on your computer. We are going to select three fonts from the Available Fonts list the browser will use to display text. It generally is a good idea to select three fonts: the preferred font and two alternates. It is also a good idea to include at least one "standard" font (such as Times or Arial) in your font list. In this part of the exercise, if you do not have one of the fonts we are selecting installed on your computer, select another font from the list.

    a) Select Comic Sans by selecting the font in the Available Fonts list, and then click on the double left Arrow button between the Chosen Fonts box and Available Fonts box. This will copy the font to the Chosen Fonts list.

    b) Select Arial by clicking on the font to highlight it, and then click on the double left Arrow button to copy the font to the Chosen Fonts list.

    c) Select Times New Roman by clicking on the font to highlight it, and then click on the double left Arrow button to copy the font to the Chosen Fonts list.

    d) The fonts will be used in the order you select them. The first font will be used whenever possible. If it is not possible, the second or third font will be applied to the text. See figure 5-21.

·T/P·

To add font lists, click on the Plus (+) button in the upper left corner of the Edit Font List window. To remove font lists, click on the Minus (–) button in the upper left corner of the Edit Font List window.

Because you can have more than one font list, for ease of use, you may want to put the most commonly used font list at the top of the list of font lists. Select the font list and press the Up arrow until the list moves to the top.

CAUTION

The font lists are only available on the computer in which the font list was created.

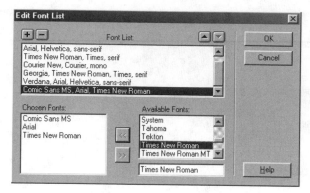

Fig. 5-21. Font list.

    e)   Click on the OK button to save your font list.

4.   To apply a font list to text, we will use the Property Inspector (Window | Properties).

    a)   Make sure you are seeing the the Property Inspector.

    b)   To view all properties, click on the Expander Arrow icon in the lower right corner until the arrow points upward.

    c)   Select the text *13 Original Colonies*.

    d)   From the Property Inspector, select the pull-down menu for the default font. This menu lists any font combinations created using the Edit Font List command. Select the font combination we just created. The text on screen now changes to the new font in our font list. Note that the font combinations are listed in the order in which they were added to the Edit Font list. To move a font combination (primary font and alternate fonts) you use most often to the top of the list, go back into Edit Font List (under Text Menu | Font) and drag the selected font combination to the top of the list. See figure 5-22.

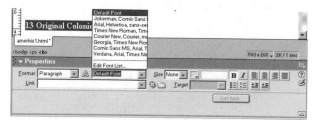

Fig. 5-22. Property Inspector and font.

5.   Now let's use the Property Inspector to set color and size.

    a)   Highlight the text *American History* on the top line of the page.

b) Make sure the Property Inspector window is active (Window Menu | Properties). If there is already a check mark next to the Properties menu, the inspector is already open.

c) In the Properties window, you can modify the text's format, font type, size, and color, in addition to style (bold, italic) and alignment. Click on the Bold button.

d) In the Property Inspector, from the Format pop-up menu, select Heading 2. The headings are the HTML tags H1 through H6. These tags have default size and styles to apply to text. H1 applies the largest font size by default, and H6 the smallest. See figure 5-23.

Format pop-up menu

Fig. 5-23. Property Inspector format selection.

e) Select the Color Swatch option (the little colored square to the right of the Font Size window).

f) The Color Picker will open, showing the 216 colors common to both the PC and the Macintosh.

g) Using the Eyedropper, select a color. It is best to go for a darker color. When you select a color, the Color Picker window will close and your text will be in the new color.

h) Notice in the Properties window that the Color Swatch option now shows your selected color and the HTML code for that color.

i) Let's make the other headings a larger size. At the top of the document, highlight *Declaration of Independence* ... through *First Five Presidents*. In the Property Inspector, select Size | +1. This will make these headings one size larger relative to the default size.

6. Next let's get some practice aligning text using the menus.
   a) Highlight the top line of text (*American History*).
   b) Select Text Menu | Alignment.
   c) Left, Center, or Right alignment is listed. For this exercise, select Center.

7. Now practice aligning text using the Property Inspector.
   a) Highlight the next three lines of text (*Declaration of Independence* to *First Three Presidents*).

b) In the Property Inspector, select the Left Align button on the upper right-hand area of the window (next to the Bold and Italic buttons).

c) You can also use the keyboard shortcut. See the Shortcut at left.

8. Let's create a bulleted list of the states.

a) Highlight the list of states (*Delaware* to *Rhode Island*).

b) Select the Bullet List button. This is also known as the Unordered List button. Notice that the list is now single spaced. See figure 5-24.

You can also create a bulleted list by selecting Text Menu | List | Unordered List.

Unordered List (Bullet List)

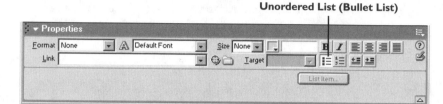

Fig. 5-24. Property Inspector showing Unordered List button.

Insert Bar: The Insert bar | Text category also has most of the formatting we are doing from the Property Inspector, including format (h1,h2,h3) and lists.

9. The formatting needs some improvement.

a) Highlight the heading *13 Original States*.

b) From the Property Inspector, select the Bold button.

10. To create a numbered list, highlight the list of the first five presidents, *Georgia Washington* to *James Monroe*. See figure 5-25.

Ordered List (Numbered List)

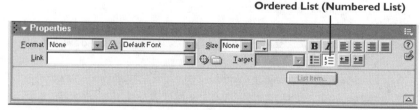

Fig. 5-25. Property Inspector showing Ordered List button.

a) Select the Numbered List button (also known as the Ordered List button).

b) You could also create a numbered list by selecting Text Menu | List | Ordered List. Notice that the numbered list is single spaced.

11. Next, let's look at indenting text. Indenting text is done by selecting the Text Indent/Text Outdent buttons found in the Property Inspector.

a) First, let's separate the title from the first line of text. Place the cursor to the left of the word *When* at the beginning of the *Declaration of Independence* paragraph. Press Enter/Return to insert a blank line. See figure 5-26.

Text Outdent   **Text Indent**

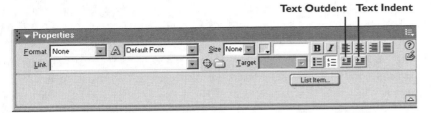

Fig. 5-26. Property Inspector showing Text Outdent/Text Indent buttons.

·T/P·

Note that lists apply to paragraphs. If we had only inserted a single-space line (Shift + Return/Enter) instead of a new paragraph line (Return/Enter), *both* the title and paragraph would have indented.

b) Let's indent the first paragraph (the opening of the Declaration of Independence). Place the cursor anywhere in the *Declaration of Independence* paragraph.

c) In the Property Inspector, locate and click twice on the Text Indent button. The paragraph's left margin should have moved to the right twice – about an inch in all.

d) This is perhaps one indent too far. Click on the Outdent button once to move the paragraph margin to the left.

12. Let's look at the HTML code Dreamweaver MX has created.

a) Select the menu option Window | Others | Code Inspector. Look through the code to begin to get familiar with it.

b) Close the Code Inspector by clicking on the Close box in the upper corner of the Code Inspector window.

 Shortcut

Code Inspector: F10 (Mac and Windows)

Summary

• *Use the Page Properties option to set the title and background color of a page. These properties also set the default color of text and links.*

• *Use the formatting features in Dreamweaver MX to set text font, font size, color, and other attributes.*

• *You can create bulleted (Unordered) lists, numbered (Ordered) lists, and indented text in Dreamweaver MX.*

• *Whenever you press the space bar, Dreamweaver MX will only enter a maximum of one space. To insert more spaces, insert a non-breaking space. The HTML code for this is <nbsp>.*

• *When you reach the end of a line and continue to type, the text automatically wraps to the next line, with a single line break.*

• *Whenever you are in Text Editing mode and you press the Enter (Windows) or Return (Macintosh) key, you will receive a double line break, not the normal single line break as in word processing programs. This defines a paragraph and has the tags <p> and </p>.*

- To start a new line of text without the double line break, hold down the Shift key when you press the Enter/Return key. This is called a line break, and has the tag <br> without an end tag.

- The Property Inspector provides a shortcut to the same features found in the Dreamweaver MX menus and Insert bar: alignment, text attributes, color, size, and so on.

- Do not forget that every word you type, and font and color you set, is backed up by the HTML code. Use the HTML window to view and learn the HTML code.

- Preview a page in different browsers often to check for inconsistencies across versions and browsers.

- Use the Spell Check function to check text.

C H A P T E R

6

Importing

Graphics

Introduction

Often the reason someone has found your web site is that they made use of a search engine. Once at your site, your job has just begun. You will need to grab the user's attention and interest him in looking deeper into your site and viewing the information you have to offer. One way to capture attention is through the use of visuals: animation, photos, custom graphics, simple line drawings, and clip art.

Although you cannot create or modify graphic images in Dreamweaver MX (other than changing image size), we thought it was important to discuss the development of graphics for the Web, because they have a big impact on the effectiveness and performance (download time) of web pages. In this regard, Dreamweaver MX does allow you to control the way images are displayed in terms of their location, borders, and interactivity. From within Dreamweaver, you can also link directly to graphic editing software (such as Fireworks) by simply double clicking on the graphic to modify it. By the end of the chapter you will be able to:

- *Describe the basic guidelines for using graphics in web pages, including graphic formats*
- *Insert a graphic and set its location relative to the rest of the site*
- *Place a graphic image on a web page in relationship to other elements on the page*
- *Modify property settings for graphics, including alignment, border, width, height, and spacing*
- *Use the <Alt> tag to display an alternate image or text*

An Overview of Graphics in HTML Pages

All graphics are not created equal; that is, they are just not all the same. Not only are they different in the way they look, but also in the way they are formatted and displayed. Various graphic formats differ in the way they compress and store information about a graphic. On the Internet, this is very important, because the greater the compression, the smaller the file, and the faster the download time.

If you reduce the number of colors used in your image, this will help to reduce the file size. But you must balance possible file size reduction with how much quality you are willing to give up in an image. Generally, as you decrease the number of colors, you also decrease the quality of the graphic. Try it for yourself and see.

The next section presents a brief summary of graphic formats commonly used on the Web. We have listed some characteristics for each format. You might try saving an image in more than one format and then checking its file size and quality to determine the format you want to use for a particular image.

JPEG/JPG (Joint Photographic Experts Group)

When to use: Best for photorealistic images (as opposed to line drawings). Use for images that require more than 256 colors and scanned photographs.

Advantages:

- *Supports up to millions of colors.*
- *You can adjust the compression ratio for the graphic. The more you compress an image, the smaller the resulting file size. Usually a graphic compressed to 80% or so of its original size will look just about the same as 100%, but will be smaller in file size so that it will download much faster. Compressing even further will reduce file size more but may produce a noticeable loss of fidelity.*
- *Has the option for progressive download. This is when the image loads gradually so that it looks like it is "building up" on the page.*

Disadvantage:

- *Compressed images will have smaller file sizes, but using higher percentages of compression will cause the image quality to degrade rapidly. Image quality is based on the amount of compression and level of detail in the image.*

GIF (Graphics Interchange Format – CompuServe)

When to use: Images with repetitive areas of solid color compress best when exported as GIF. This is probably the best choice for nonphotographic images, such as black-and-white and grayscale photographs and graphics, cartoon-like graphics, logos, graphics with transparent areas, and animations.

Advantages:

- *Recognized by most graphic software packages*
- *Can set transparent colors*
- *Very small file size and therefore download very quickly*

Disadvantages:

- *Only supports 256 colors (8 bit or lower)*
- *CompuServe (creators and owners of the GIF format) royalty fee for commercial distribution of images in the GIF format*

·T**i**P·

Use three-letter extensions (jpg, not jpeg) on file names. Also, try to use all lowercase naming, because some systems (such as UNIX) are case sensitive.

PNG (Portable Network Graphic)

When to use: The PNG format was created as a cross-platform file format. It is a lossless compression, meaning that no quality loss occurs when the image is saved in the PNG format. It internally contains the characteristics for the authoring system so that viewing software (like browsers) can display the image correctly.

Often developers will create and save the original graphics in the PNG format because PNG permits layers. However, they then need to export them into a different format for use on the Web, in that all browsers do not recognize the PNG format.

Advantages:

- *Supports 8-bit, 16-bit, or 32-bit color*
- *Allows transparency using alpha channel*
- *Allows indexed graphics, grayscale, and true color*
- *Can be progressive (such as JPEG)*
- *Contains layers*

Disadvantages:

- *Not all graphic software packages recognize*
- *Not all browsers (especially older ones) recognize*

Additional Guidelines for Using Graphics on the Web

The following are some additional guidelines for creating and using graphics on the Web to minimize download time.

- *Split a large image into multiple files so that it will download faster. You can accomplish this "splicing" within your graphics software program.*
- *Preload images whenever possible, especially graphics being used for the various button states (up, over, and down images).*
- *Reuse the same graphic when possible. Once a graphic has downloaded the first time, it will display quickly with each successive display.*
- *Compress the images and use fewer colors to decrease the size of the image.*
- *If you can use layers (see the chapter on layers):*
  - *Display a large image that covers the entire screen until all other images are available, and then hide the layer with the large graphic.*
  - *Use hidden layers to preload an image for later use. This is especially useful when creating quizzes that display feedback based on the user's response.*

Graphics Terminology

There are some common terms you may encounter while working with the Web or other multimedia delivery. Understanding these terms will help you get the maximum benefit from using the tools found in most graphics packages, such as Fireworks and Photoshop.

Compression: On the Web, the smaller the graphic file size, the shorter the download time. Compression removes assumed redundant information from a file, such as some of the color information. With higher compression you will have a smaller file, but there may be a loss in quality. File formats with "lossy compression" means that the image will have some loss of quality. PNG is a "lossless" format where quality loss does not occur (as much).

Dither: This process combines two or more colors to create a color that does not exist in the current color palette. This option is available when going from a higher bit depth, such as millions of colors, to a lower bit depth (such as 256 colors).

Try to avoid dithering if possible, because dithering will make the graphic file larger. Only use this option if the graphic quality is otherwise unacceptable. For example, photographs often need to be dithered when compressing to a smaller bit depth.

Transparency: Transparency makes specific colors in an image transparent so that anything (e.g., text or companion graphic images) behind the image will show through the transparent areas of the image. This technique is useful when displaying irregularly shaped images over colored or patterned backgrounds.

You can also make something seem as though it is transparent by making the background color of the image the same color as the web page background. Transparency is available for PNG and GIF formats.

Web-safe color: The Web-safe Color palette consists of 216 colors. These colors will appear correctly when viewed on Macintosh or Windows platforms as long as the user's monitor is set to 256-color resolution or higher.

Splicing: Splicing cuts an image into two or more pieces (images). These multiple images can then be positioned in a web page to look as though one image is being displayed. The advantage of splicing is that the smaller images will download faster than one large image.

Smoothing: Available for JPEG files, this blurs the image to decrease the number of colors needed for the graphic.

Loss: Loss of color. The higher the number, the higher the loss. This reduces file size but also reduces image quality.

Interlace Images option: Displays an image at low resolution when it first downloads, and then slowly displays 100% resolution. Transparency is available for GIF and PNG.

Inserting Graphics Using Dreamweaver MX

The Common tab of the Insert bar contains the following six icon buttons for inserting various types of graphic images and files (see figure 6-1).

- Image: *The most common. Use this icon for inserting a graphic image.*

- Image Placeholder: *For inserting a placeholder when the final graphic is not yet available.*

- Fireworks HTML: *For inserting graphics and HTML code created in Fireworks.*

- Flash: *For inserting a Flash movie.*

- Rollover Image: *For inserting a rollover image. This icon brings up the dialog box for entering the original and rollover images, the alt text, and the link information.*

- Navigation Bar: *Click on this icon to open the dialog box for entering information about a button to be placed in a navigation bar. This is like the rollover image except that more than one button object can be created at a time. You can select to create a vertical or horizontal navigation bar.*

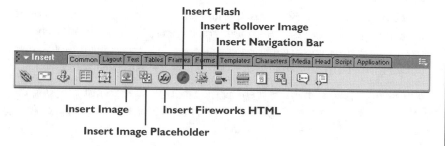

Fig. 6-1. Insert bar showing the Common tab.

You can also add graphic images to your web page by using the options under Insert Menu | Interactive Images. Insert options available are Rollover Image, Navigation Bar, Flash Button, Flash Text, and Fireworks HTML. The Flash Button option contains dozens of ready-made buttons, complete with rollover states that are ready for you to enter the label information. The Flash Text option allows you to create text buttons using many more font types than are normally available in an HTML environment.

Graphic Properties

Before we begin an exercise that inserts graphics into a web page, we will briefly explain some of the main properties concerning graphics. All of these properties are found in the Property Inspector when a graphic is selected on the screen. We will start in the upper left-hand section of the Property Inspector (with a graphic selected), and proceed to the right, looking at all options in the top row. We will then start in the bottom left and proceed again to the right. See figure 6-2.

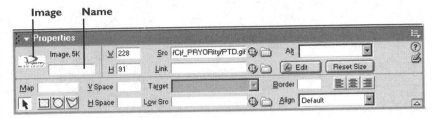

Fig. 6-2. Property Inspector with image selected.

NOTE: The image object needs to be selected to see its properties in the Property Inspector.

Image information: In the upper left, you will find a small version of the selected image, along with its file size.

Name field: You can type a name into this field so that you can refer to the image with a scripting language such as JavaScript.

Width and Height (W and H fields): The width and height of the original dimensions, in pixels, of the image is displayed here by default when it is inserted in a page. To change the dimensions of the image, type in a new value in the width and height boxes, or use the drag boxes at the corners and sides of the image. To keep the same proportions, hold down the Shift key as you resize the image. To restore the image to its original size, click on the W and H field labels in the Property Inspector. See figure 6-3.

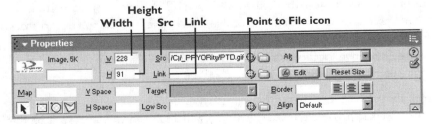

Fig. 6-3. Width and Height example (pixels).

You can also specify the width and height in the following measurement units by typing labeled values next to the number value: pc (picas), pt (points), in (inches), mm (millimeters), and cm (centimeters).

Src (source): Src is the file name and path to the image inserted in a web page. There is a Browse Folder icon next to this option to allow you to search for the image. When you click on this icon to browse for the image file, a dialog box will appear, allowing you to search for the image to insert (see figure 6-4).

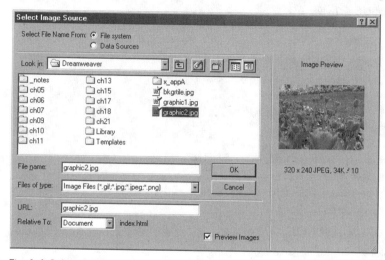

Fig. 6-4. Select Image Source dialog box.

Link: This field is used to specify a hyperlink for the image. The Point-to-File next to the Link file can be dragged to the Assets panel to link to a page or media element.

By default, the location of the image file is relative to the document that calls it. This means that when you place the document on the remote site, the HTML code will look for these images in the folder or subfolder within the folder the HTML document is in. Relative to Document is the preferable setting for location of images, in that you do not need to worry about the name of the root folder, just the folders of the web site. If you use absolute locations (as opposed to relative), the links will have the complete directory address of the computer (your computer) that created the link. In other words, a relative location is relative to the HTML file and can be moved from computer to computer and server to server.

An absolute location is the full directory listing (e.g., *c:/hard drive/my documents/work in progress/company x/project y/website z*) and will only work on the computer that created the web site. In addition, it cannot be moved from the original computer without the links being broken. You will probably only select

Relative To | Site Root when you are trying to reference an image being used across multiple sites relative to the site root. Let's look at a couple of examples. The following are examples of "relative to document."

- *The SRC (source) is a file within the current folder* image1.jpg.
- *The SRC (source) is a file within a subfolder (graphics) of the current folder* subfolder/image1.jpg.

The following are examples of "relative to site root."

- *The SRC (source) is a file within the current folder* image1.jpg.
- *The SRC (source) is a file within a subfolder (graphics) of the current folder* . . . subfolder/image1.jpg.

When you insert an image and have selected *Relative To | Document*, Dreamweaver MX determines the relative location of the image file to the web page document. If the web page document has not yet been saved, Dreamweaver MX cannot determine the relative location. You will receive an error message to the effect that the path to the image cannot be determined until the document has been saved (see figure 6-5). As soon as you save the document, the relative path is determined.

Fig. 6-5. "Insert image" error message.

If you have not saved your document and insert an image that is in a subfolder, and then select Relative To | Site Root, you will see a broken link icon in your document (see figure 6-6). Once the document is saved, the image will appear in place of the broken icon. You must save your Dreamweaver MX file so that relative locations can be assigned.

Fig. 6-6. Broken link.

Align: The Align property aligns the image relative to the text and other media on the same line. It is not used to align the image on the page. To align images on the page, use the Align tools (Align Left, Align Center, Align Right). See figure 6-7.

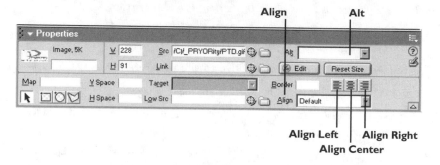

Fig. 6-7. Align property versus Align Left/Center/Right.

The Align options are as follows. See figure 6-8 for examples of these Align options.

- Browser Default: *This is based on the browser. It is usually the same as Baseline.*

- Baseline and Bottom: *Aligns the bottom of the text (the text baseline) to the bottom of the object/image.*

- Absolute Bottom: *Aligns the absolute bottom of the text, including descenders (as in the letter g), with the bottom of the object/image.*

- Top: *Aligns the tallest text character to the top of the object.*

- Middle: *Aligns the text baseline with the middle of the object.*

- Absolute Middle: *Aligns the middle of the object with the middle of the text.*

- Left: *Positions the object/image on the left margin. Text on the same line will begin before the object and will generally force the object to the next line. The rest of the text paragraph will wrap around and to the right of the object.*

- Right: *Positions the object/image on the right margin. Text on the same line will begin before the object and will generally force the object to the next line. The rest of the text paragraph will wrap around and to the left of the object.*

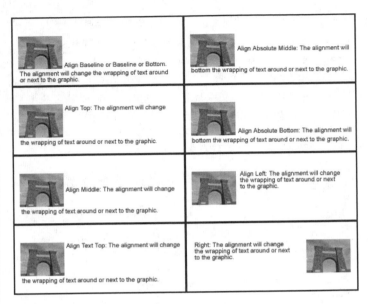

Fig. 6-8. Align options examples.

Alt (alternate text): The Alt box is expecting a text entry. Alt will display the text when a user's browser is set to download images manually and for text-only browsers. When a speech synthesizer in text-only browsers is used for visually impaired users, the text is spoken out loud.

In most browsers, the Alt box will display alternate text (on top of an image) when the cursor or pointer is rolled over the image. Like hot tips, this can be used for cueing the user to what the image is for (such as a catalog), where the image will link to, or a description of the image. See figure 6-9.

Fig. 6-9. Image with Alt text.

Map Name field: This field allows you to create client-side image maps.

Vertical and Horizontal space (V Space and H Space fields): These fields are used to insert blank space above and below (vertical space) or to the left and right side (horizontal space) of an image, measured in the number of pixels for spacing. Use these Property Inspector options to manipulate vertical and horizontal space in separating images from text, other images, and the edges of a page. To remove the spacing, delete the number in the space box, enter *0*, or click on the V and H field labels. See figure 6-10.

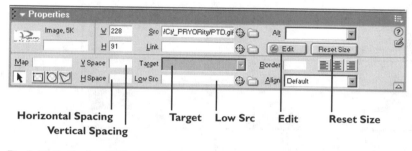

Horizontal Spacing   **Target**   **Low Src**   **Edit**   **Reset Size**
Vertical Spacing

Fig. 6-10. Vertical and Horizontal spacing.

Target: This field specifies the frame or window in which the linked page should load. This option will be grayed out (not available) if there is no link on the image.

Low Src: This field specifies the image that should load before the main image. You can load a black-and-white version of the image quickly, giving users an idea of what color image to expect.

Border width: The Border option will draw a box around the perimeter of an image. Enter a number greater than 0 to set the border in pixels. Enter 0 or leave the box blank for no border. See figure 6-11.

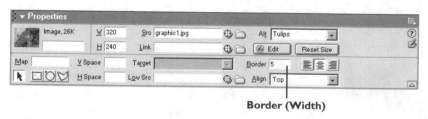

Border (Width)

Fig. 6-11. Border (width).

CAUTION

The image border color is overridden by link colors when the image has a link attached to it. This is not apparent in the Document window, only when viewed in a browser.

The Border option is primarily used for images that are hyperlinked. Clicking on the image takes the user to a new page or new position in the current file. (Note, however, that a border can be used for linked or unlinked graphics.) The border color is based on the text color (set in Page Properties). You can set the border color to a different color using the menu option Text | Color.

If the image has a link, the border color is set by the link colors, also set in Page Properties.

Edit: This button launches the image editor you have specified in the External Editors option and will open the selected graphic in that image editor. Double clicking on the graphic image in the Document window will also open the graphic in your image editor (for example, Fireworks). When you have completed your edits, click on the Done button and Fireworks will close and you will be returned to Dreamweaver MX.

Reset Size: This button resets the W (width) and H (height) values back to the original size of the image.

Image placeholders: If you do not have the final graphics available when you are creating your web page, use an image placeholder. You can set the size (height and width), color, and the Alternate text setting (Alt) for the placeholder graphic. You can also add a name to the placeholder graphic to help remind you what graphic needs to be inserted. The placeholder graphic will display with the name, size, and color you specified in the dialog box when in Editing mode. When you preview your page in your browser, you will not see the name, size, and color information; you will only see a graphic placeholder space with a missing graphic indicator and the alternate text.

Dreamweaver MX and Fireworks

Chances are that when you purchased Dreamweaver MX, Macromedia Fireworks was bundled with it. This is just one indication of how closely the two products are related. Not only do they have a similar interface but a set of integrated features that allows you to work with files from the other application.

Because all graphic files are external to an HTML document, if you modify a graphic file, the updated version will appear in the web page the next time you open the page. If you create HTML code in Fireworks and import the graphic into Dreamweaver MX, the HTML code is also imported.

Dreamweaver MX's Round-Trip Graphics Editing feature allows you to open, edit, and optimize graphics in Fireworks from Dreamweaver MX. From the Site window, you can open graphic files in Fireworks by just double clicking on the graphic file (as long as the Preferences option External Editors is set to Fireworks). You can also open Fireworks to edit a graphic by selecting a graphic image in the Design window and selecting Edit in the Properties panel. See figure 6-12.

·TIP·

Image Placeholders: Hold an empty place in your page for future graphics. Insert | Image Placeholder or Insert bar | Common.

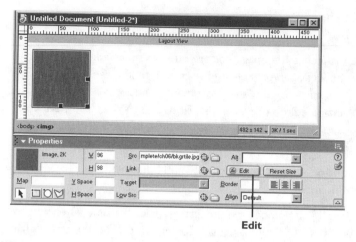

Fig. 6-12. Property Inspector showing Edit option.

Fireworks will open with all available windows and menus. When you click on Done, the file will be saved to the location from which you opened it. See figure 6-13.

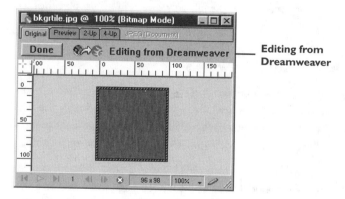

Fig. 6-13. Dreamweaver MX transitioned to editing in Fireworks.

Fireworks graphics (as well as other graphics) are imported into Dreamweaver MX using the Insert Image option from the Insert Bar | Common tab selection or by selecting Insert Menu | Image item. You can also use the mouse to drag a graphic from the Assets panel directly to a page.

Image maps are another time-saving device that can be created in both Fireworks and Dreamweaver MX. An image map is a single graphic image that has hot spots over designated areas of the image. The areas act as hot spots for the user to click on. For example, think of a menu bar. Instead of having to create a number of graphics, one for each menu item, you can create one graphic image for the entire menu. You can then divide the menu graphic into hot spots corresponding to each menu item and assign each menu item (hot spot) a behavior, such as calling another URL.

Some designers and web developers prefer to create the visual layout of their entire web page within Fireworks. What makes this truly possible and a great time saver is that Fireworks, although being able to develop and "slice" graphic images for use on the Web, can also create HTML code allowing for rollover images and link information. Using Fireworks, you can create the look-and-feel and the navigation for your web site and export it all to Dreamweaver MX. Once in Dreamweaver MX, you can add the content for each page. The following are the steps for importing Fireworks HTML into a Dreamweaver MX page.

1. Create a graphic (or set of graphics) in Fireworks that contains HTML code. For example, you could create buttons with URL links already programmed in, image maps with slices and coding, JavaScript, and many other possibilities.

2. In Dreamweaver MX, open a new file (or existing file) and save it.

3. Place the cursor in the desired position where you want to place the image.

4. Select Insert Fireworks HTML from Insert Bar | Common tab or select Insert Menu | Interactive Images | Fireworks HTML.

5. Click on OK to import the graphic image along with its HTML code or its JavaScript and image slices. See figure 6-14.

Insert Fireworks HTML

Fig. 6-14. Insert bar | Common | Insert Fireworks HTML selection.

Practice Exercise 6-1: Adding Graphics to a Page

Description

In this exercise we will insert images into a web page and modify the properties so that a graphic displays with a border and is aligned with the text and other graphics on the page. Note the following elements covered in this exercise.

*   *Using the Insert bar*
*   *Inserting an image relative to the current document*
*   *Image alignment relative to the text*
*   *Setting a border around an image*

- *Vertical and horizontal spacing around images*
- *Using the <Alt> tag for graphics*

Take a Look

CD-ROM

DWComplete Site

Before beginning the exercise, let's take a look at the exercise in its completed state so that you can clearly see what it is you are about to build.

1. Make sure you are working with the *DWComplete* site. You can confirm this by selecting Site panel | Site pop-up menu | *DWComplete*.

2. Locate the *ch06* folder and the file named *dw06ex1.html*. Double click on *dw06ex1.html* to open the file.

3. The file *dw06ex1.html* should now appear in your copy of Dreamweaver MX. Note the following properties of this completed exercise.

    - *Select one of the images on screen and select Window Menu | Properties to bring up the Property Inspector. Look at the properties that are set, including Src and Border.*

    - *The position of the first graphic relative to the text.*

    - *The size of the border around the graphic.*

    - *The vertical and horizontal spacing around the second graphic.*

    - *Roll your mouse over one of the graphics and notice the text that appears over the graphic. This is set in the <Alt> tag.*

Storyboard: On Screen

Figure 6-15 shows you what the finished page will look like when viewed through a browser.

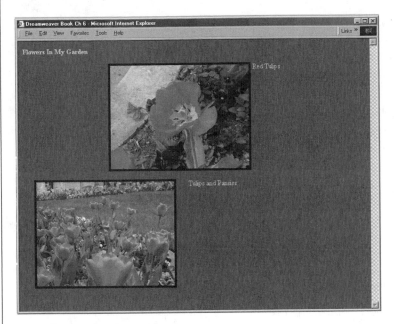

Fig. 6-15. Completed exercise.

Storyboard: Behind the Scenes

Figure 6-16 shows the HTML code behind the text and graphic formatting set through Dreamweaver MX.

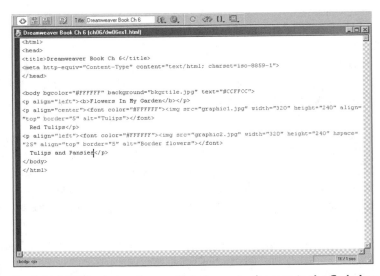

Fig. 6-16. HTML window for completed exercise (as seen in the Code Inspector).

Step-by-Step Instructions

Go Solo

DWExercises Site

1. Make sure you are working with the site *DWExercises*, which we have been using in previous chapters. In the Site panel, select *DWExercises* from the Site pop-up menu.

2. We are going to start with a new document. We have normally been using the File menu to open a new window (or document). You can also use the Site panel to open a new file. The advantage of doing it this way is that you do not have to search for the correct folder in which to save a file. You actually see the entire file structure at one time.

    a) Select the folder *ch06*. In the Site panel, select File Menu | New File. A new file icon appears in the Site panel under the *ch06* folder, with the file name highlighted.

    b) Type the file name *dw06ex1.html* in the File Name box. Press Enter/Return. A new empty HTML document has just been created.

    c) Double click on the file *dw06ex1.html* to open it.

3. Now let's enter some text.

    a) Type *Flowers In My Garden* on the first line of the page.

    b) Highlight the text and set it to size 6 using the Property Inspector or Text Menu | Size.

    c) Place the cursor at the end of *Flowers In My Garden* and press the Enter/Return key to add a blank line after the text.

4. Now let's insert an image.

    a) Select the Image icon from the Common tab of the Insert bar. You can also use the Image selection under the Insert menu or the Ctrl+Alt+I keyboard command.

    b) The Select Image Source dialog box now appears. Notice that the Select Image Source dialog box has an Image Preview area on the right-hand side of the window.

    c) Use the scroll bar to find the folder *ch06* (within the *Learning_Dreamweaver* folder). Select the file *graphic1.jpg*. Before leaving this window, set the Relative To Document option. Generally you will use Relative To Document not Relative To Site Root when selecting objects within the same folder or subfolder of the current folder. You can either single click on the file name and then click on Select or double click on the image name to open the file.

Shortcut

Insert bar Insert Image shortcut:

Ctrl+Alt+I (Windows)

Cmd+Opt+I (Macintosh)

d) If the graphic image is not already in the same folder or a subfolder of the local site folder, you will be prompted to save a copy of the file in the root folder of your web site (see figure 6-17). It is highly recommended that you do this; if not, the HTML file will not be able to find the required graphic images when the file is run on the Internet. You would select Yes to copy the graphic file to the site folder. You will not receive this message if you have already copied the exercise files to your hard drive.

·T/P·

As a suggestion, copy all images to your site before inserting them into your web pages.

Fig. 6-17. Prompt to copy a file during Insert Image operation.

e) Your imported graphic should now appear on your Dreamweaver MX page. Notice that there are sizing handles on the graphic, with which you can resize the graphic image if necessary.

5. Add an extra line after the graphic by pressing the Enter/Return key.

6. We are going to add another graphic to the current document but use the Insert bar this time.
   a) Click on the Image icon on the Common tab of the Insert bar.
   b) Use the scroll bar to find the folder *ch06*. Select *graphic2.jpg*. You can either single click on the file name and then click on Select or double click on the image name to open the file.

7. Your document should now have a line of text at the top of the document, followed by two graphics. See figure 6-18. Let's add some descriptive text.
   a) Move your cursor just to the right of the first graphic image of the flowers.
   b) Type in *Red Tulips*.

CAUTION

If you begin to insert an image in an HTML document and select Cancel before selecting Save, a broken link icon will appear in your document window.

Simply delete the icon. If this same icon ever appears later in your document, it means that the file cannot be found. Usually this is because the graphic file or HTML document has been moved, or renamed outside Dreamweaver MX. To fix the broken link, double click on the icon and select the graphic file that should be displayed.

Fig. 6-18. The exercise at this point.

8. Notice that the text you just typed is aligned with the bottom of the graphic. The positioning of text relative to a graphic is set by the alignment properties of the graphic – not the alignment properties of the text. Let's change this alignment.

Shortcut

Property Inspector shortcut is:
Ctrl + F3 (Windows)
Cmd + F3 (Macintosh)

a) Select the first graphic and look at the Property Inspector (Window Menu | Properties). The alignment for the graphic is set at Browser Default, which is generally the same as Baseline or Bottom.

b) We want our text to be aligned with the top of the graphic. Select the Align pull-down menu in the lower right-hand corner of the Property Inspector. Select Top. The text will move to the top of the graphic, aligning the top of the graphic with the top of the text. See figure 6-19.

T/P

The Align for Images control does not align text. It aligns the image relative to the text following (after) the image.

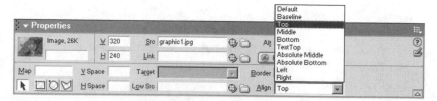

Fig. 6-19. Property Inspector showing Align pull-down menu.

c) We also want our graphic/text combination to be centered on the page. Make sure you have your cursor somewhere on the line with the graphic and the text (or have the graphic selected), and then click on the Align Center icon on the right-hand side of the Property Inspector. This icon is on the bottom half of the Property Inspector. You may have to click on the Expand arrow (Down arrow), located in the lower right, to view the entire window. See figure 6-20.

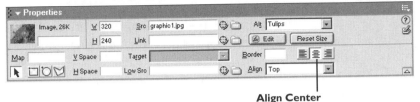

Align Center

Fig. 6-20. Property Inspector showing Align Center icon.

9. Let's type a text caption on the right-hand side of the second graphic.
    a) Move your cursor just to the right of the second graphic image of the blue and red flowers.
    b) Type in *Tulips and Pansies*.
    c) Align this text also at the top of the graphic. Select the second graphic and select the Align pull-down menu in the lower right-hand corner of the Property Inspector. Select Top. The text will move to the top of the graphic, aligning the top of the graphic with the top of the text.
    d) We will leave the graphic/text aligned on the left side of the page.

10. Select File Menu | Save to save your file.

11. Preview the file by pressing the F12 key. This is the shortcut key for File | Preview in Browser | default browser.

12. Now for a border.
    a) Let's add a border around both of the graphic images.
    b) Select the first graphic to highlight it.
    c) In the Property Inspector, locate the Border entry box. It is on the bottom half of the Property Inspector. You may have to click on the Expand arrow (Down arrow) to view the entire window. See figure 6-21.

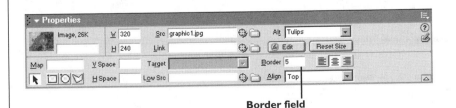

Border field

Fig. 6-21. Property Inspector showing Border entry box.

·T*i*P·

Do not confuse the two alignment functions in Dreamweaver. When a graphic is selected, the Property Inspector has an Alignment pull-down menu. These options align the graphic relative to any other elements (text and graphics) positioned on the same line or paragraph. The second function – the Align icons (Align Left, Align Center, Align Right) – sets the alignment for the entire line (paragraph).

d) The default border is no border (i.e., the Border box is empty). The number 0 in the box also indicates no border. Type *1* in the Border box and press the Enter/Return key. This will create a border of 1 pixel width. (The larger the number, the wider the border.)

e) Try experimenting with various border widths. Try pixel widths of 1 to 5, to give you a nice thin border. A large number such as 85 pixels will give you a picture frame type of border. For this exercise, let's use something smaller.

f) Type in *5* for the border size of the second graphic. Press the Enter/Return key.

13. We will now set an alternate text to display on top of an image when the cursor is rolled over that image.
a) Select the first graphic (the tulips).
b) In the Alt box of the Property Inspector, type *Tulips*.
c) Select the second graphic (the various flowers).
d) In the Alt box of the Property Inspector, type *Border Flowers*.

14. Preview the file. Select File | Preview in Browser | Default Browser.

Shortcut

Preview in Browser shortcut is F12.

15. Notice how the text next to the two graphic images is flush with the graphic. Let's add some space around the graphic.
a) Select the second graphic that is still on the left-hand side of the page.
b) In the left-hand side of the lower half of the Property Inspector there are two spacing entries: V Space for vertical spacing and H Space for horizontal spacing. Let's add a little space to the left- and right-hand (horizontal sides) of the graphic. Type *25* in the H Space option to place a 25-pixel spacing on each side of the graphic.
c) Press the Enter/Return key. Note that the text moves further away from the graphic and the graphic moves away from the left-hand side of the page. See figure 6-22.

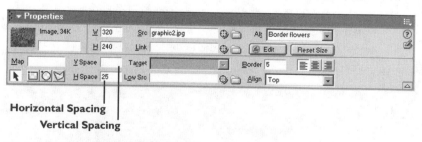

Horizontal Spacing
Vertical Spacing

Fig. 6-22. Horizontal and Vertical spacing.

16. Select File | Save to save your file.

17. While we are dealing with graphics, let's add a graphic to the background on the page. This will display behind all elements on the page.
    a) Select Modify Menu | Page Properties.
    b) Next, click on the Browse button to locate the background graphic image. Use the scroll bar to find the folder *ch06*. Select *bkgrtile.jpg*. You can either single click on the file name and then click on Select or double click on the image name to open it.
    c) The graphic will automatically be "tiled" in the background.
    d) Click on OK to exit Page Properties.

18. Select File | Save to save your file.

19. Preview the file. Select File Menu | Preview in Browser | Default Browser.

20. The text on top of the dark background graphic is difficult to read now. Do you know how to change the color of all text at one time? Let's see.
    a) Select Modify Menu | Page Properties.
    b) Click on the Color box next to Text. Select a light color for the text. Click on OK.

21. Now let's look at the HTML code Dreamweaver MX has created.
    a) Select View Menu | Code and Design. (Or select the Code and Design View button in the toolbar.)
    b) Highlight the image and/or text in the Design view to automatically highlight the HTML code around the objects.
    c) Look at the HTML tags surrounding the images and the text. Pay particular attention to the following.

    `<body bgcolor="#FFFFFF" background="background-tile.jpg">`: *Image for the background set in Page Properties*

    `<p> <p/>`: *Paragraph that is set any time you press the Enter/Return key*

    `<p align="center">`: *To align, a paragraph is set via Text | Alignment or Property Inspector | Align icon*

    `<img src="graphic2.jpg" width="320" height="240" hspace ="25" align="top" border="5">`: *Set in Property Inspector*

    d) Close the HTML Source window by clicking on the Close box in the upper corner.

·T**i**P·

Whatever the size of the background graphic, it will try to fill the entire browser window by automatically being "tiled" in the background. This will allow you to use a smaller size (image and file) graphic and still cover the entire screen. Try to avoid using large graphic images, as they take a relatively long time to download and your viewers may not want to wait.

·T**i**P·

You can also look at the HTML code in the Code Inspector. The code opens in its own window. Press the F10 key to open the Code Inspector.

  HTML

Summary

- *Select the format for images to display on the Internet based on the type of image (drawing, clip art, photograph). Try to find a good compromise between quality and file size (which will affect the download time of an image).*

- *The Property Inspector provides many properties for images, including alignment to other images, alignment on the page, border, spacing around the image, and alternate text (rollover text).*

- *Continue to increase your knowledge of HTML by looking at the HTML code generated by Dreamweaver MX that is used to display your images. Try to associate the HTML tags with the Dreamweaver MX tool used to generate the tag.*

- *You will be prompted to copy inserted images to the current site folder that do not already reside there. As a suggestion, copy all images to your site before inserting them into your web pages.*

- *Background images will tile to fit the size of a browser window. Use small images to decrease the download time to display the background and decrease the amount of time required to redraw other graphics on top of the background image.*

CHAPTER **7**

Why Reinvent

the Wheel? —

Using Templates

Introduction

In previous chapters we discussed the importance of designing your web site. It is important to take the time to think about the purpose of your web site. After you have this purpose established and have designed the look and feel of the web site, you can structure the content around that purpose. This process will result in a much more consistent, functional, and focused web site. Consistency in design is especially important. Think in terms of user navigation. The user should not have to look all over a page to figure out how to get back to the home page.

In this chapter you will learn the enormous benefits of developing Dreamweaver MX templates to create your web pages. Not only do templates provide the basic guidelines to ensure consistency in your pages but dramatically shorten your development time because they provide the basic framework or structure for your pages. By the end of the chapter you will be able to:

- *Describe the basics of Dreamweaver MX templates, including the six types of editable regions*

- *Create a template from an existing document*

- *Modify a template and update pages linked to the template*

- *Create a document based on a template*

- *Describe what cannot be included in a template*

An Overview of Dreamweaver MX Templates

Once you have thought about the visual design of your web site and the pages that will exist within it, you will often find that the page structure (or design) will be the same across multiple pages. For instance, you may decide to place your company logo in the upper left-hand corner of each page. You may decide to use the same graphic elements in the background of each page. The user control (navigation) buttons may always be on the top, to the right of the logo. This consistent look and feel of your web pages will help promote a more professional image, as well as help the user quickly figure out how to get around your site. Dreamweaver MX templates provide an essential tool for creating basic formatting and consistency for your web site.

Dreamweaver MX templates are documents that have areas on the page that are predefined or locked (such as the logo area in the previous example) and areas that can vary across pages (editable regions for text content). Think of a Dreamweaver MX template as a blueprint that defines the areas of a page as to where to place your text, buttons, graphics, and so on.

·T/P·

Appendix A in the Job Aids folder on the accompanying CD-ROM discusses the process of Modifying Templates.

When you apply a template to a web page, that page picks up the placement of its media elements from the template. If you then change the position of media elements in a template, any pages linked to that template pick up that new media position. Dreamweaver MX will update all pages based on the template automatically. In figure 7-1, the only thing that changes is the text. The template has set and displayed the heading and navigation buttons.

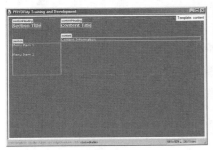

Template

**Document Window –
Document linked to template**

Fig. 7-1. Template, and document linked to template.

Using Dreamweaver MX Templates

In the practice exercises later in this chapter, you will learn how to create a template from an existing document, how to modify a template, and how to update the pages linked to that template. The following are the general steps necessary for using templates.

1. Create a new document or have an existing document open.

2. Insert and place common media elements, such as logos, background graphic, frames for graphics, and navigation buttons. These should be consistent across pages (e.g., home, site map, and contact).

3. Insert and place temporary media elements. These elements may change across pages. Such elements include text, graphics, additional navigation, sound, video, animation, Flash files, and so on. You can also simply insert an empty square area (or table) as a placeholder.

4. Save the document as a template (File | Save as Template). The template will be saved with the extension *.dwt* in a folder called *Templates* on the local web site.

5. With the template open, define the editable regions (by default, everything in a template is locked, or uneditable).

6. Define the page properties for the template. By default, pages created (or linked) to a template inherit the page properties of the template except for the page title.

7. Save the file (template). The original document will be updated with any changes you may have made to the template.

Template Preferences

Templates have their own preferences that set the color of the editable and locked regions. Select Edit Menu | Preferences, and then select the category Highlighting.

- *When the template is open, the editable regions are highlighted in the Document window and the HTML window. You will not see the locked regions highlighted. Graphics that are editable are not highlighted in the Document window, but their code is highlighted in the HTML window.*

- *When a page linked to a template is open, the locked regions are highlighted in the Document window and the HTML window. You will not see the editable regions highlighted. Graphics that are locked are not highlighted in the Document window, but their code is highlighted in the HTML window.*

Creating Editable Regions in Templates

Dreamweaver MX has four types of editable regions for templates. A template is not very useful if there are no areas within the page, created from a template, in which you can edit content. The regions are Editable Region, Repeating Region, Optional Region, and Editable Tag Attribute. A description of each region follows.

Editable Region

This is the most commonly used function within templates. Any type of media can be placed in an editable region, including text, graphics, animations, an entire table, or one cell of a table. It is a good idea to have an editable region for each type of media that will be modified on individual pages (i.e., a text region for text, a graphic region for photos, and so on). This way you can control alignment and some of the formatting characteristics of individual pages. Do not make it an editable region if the object (and/or its characteristics) does not differ from the template.

Repeating Region

Repeating Region is used to allow some additional formatting to be applied when adding content. One use of the Repeating Region feature is for allowing web page content developers to add rows to a table without being able to modify the format of the table. There are two types of repeating regions: a repeating region and a repeating table. To edit an editable region in a document based on a template, options are found in the Modify | Templates menu and the Edit | Repeating Entries menu selections. See figure 7-2.

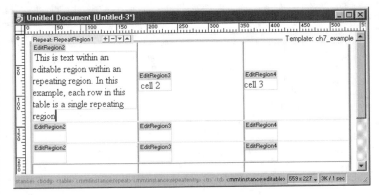

Fig. 7-2. Repeating table example as seen in Dreamweaver.

Optional Region

The Optional Region feature is used for content that may or may not be displayed when the page is viewed in a browser. An example of an optional region is a New Item graphic on the product pages of an online catalog. The option to show or not show is based on a conditional statement. An optional region can also be an editable optional region, which means that a region that is optional can also be edited in the template-based document.

To create the editable, optional, or repeating region, highlight an object or place the cursor in an empty area, and then make one of the following selections.

Insert Bar | Templates | applicable button

Insert Menu | Template Objects

Context menu (right click object) | Templates | type of region

In creating a repeating table region, do not have an object selected in the document but simply place the insertion point (cursor) in an empty area of the document.

To insert a region into a Template use the Insert Menu | Template Objects or Insert bar | Templates.

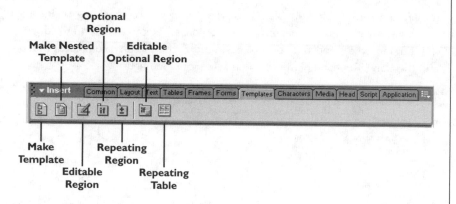

Fig. 7-3. Insert bar showing Templates category.

To remove any of the regions from a template, select the editable region (or tag) and select Modify Menu | Templates | Remove Template Markup.

Editable Tag Attributes

The editable tag attributes can be used just like the optional region, but the web content developer has the ability to unlock a tag in the page attached to a template. An example of an application of this is a fixed image in the template, with a page attached to the template being able to modify an attribute of the image (such as its size). This gives more flexibility for individual pages (such as making more room on the page for other content). To define an editable tag attribute, highlight the object you want to create an editable tag for (e.g., image or text) and then perform one of the following.

- *Select Modify Menu | Templates | Make Attribute Editable.*
- *In the Editable Tag Attributes dialog box, select (or add) the attribute to make editable.*
- *Check the box Make Attribute Editable.*
- *Fill in the (default) values for the attribute.*

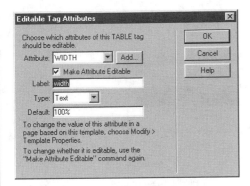

Fig. 7-4. Editable Tag Attributes dialog box.

To modify an optional region or editable tag attribute in a document based on a template, select Modify Menu | Template Properties. From the list of available attributes, select the attribute to modify for this page and then enter the new value.

To delete an editable tag attribute from a template, select Modify Menu | Templates | Make Attribute Editable. For each attribute that should *not* be made editable, select the attribute and uncheck the Make Attribute Editable option.

Creating a Document Based on a Template

After creating a template, new documents can be created based on the template. Select File Menu | New. In the New Document dialog box, select the Templates tab. All sites defined on your computer will be listed by name. Select the site you are currently working in, and then select the template. Click on OK. A new HTML document is created, with all default attributes and objects (and regions) the template has.

Apply a Template to an Existing Document

Open an existing HTML document. Select Modify Menu | Templates | Apply Template to Page.

HTML in Templates

Dreamweaver MX templates will not be recognized by other software packages, including some template features created with earlier versions of Dreamweaver. The template file is just seen as another HTML page. Notice the <!— *TemplateBeginEditable name = somename* —> and <!— *TemplateEndEditable* —> tags throughout the file in figure 7-5. A tag with the symbols <!— is generally translated as a comment. Dreamweaver MX, however, recognizes these specific comments and translates them into areas of the file that are locked or

There are predefined page layouts you can base templates (or new HTML documents) on. These layouts contain many of the features of a web site, including tables, headers, footers, CSS styles, and accessibility options. Select File Menu | New | Page Layouts.

HTML

editable. Also notice the highlighting around the editable regions (and the region name) in figure 7-5.

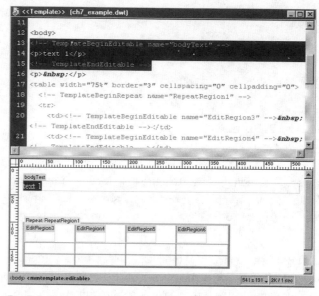

Fig. 7-5. Code and Design views for a Dreamweaver MX template.

In this example, the name of the editable region is *bodyText*. The curly brackets around it indicate that an empty area was defined for the region by placing the cursor in a blank area of the Document window and selecting the Editable Region button from the Templates tab of the Insert bar.

When you apply a template to a page in Dreamweaver MX, a special comment is inserted after the *<html>* tag. Any editable regions are also defined by comments. When Dreamweaver MX opens a page with the following comment, it knows to go to the named template file to get the formatting for the page. You will not be able to access the locked regions.

```
<!–#BeginTemplate>
```

If you open a document linked to a Dreamweaver MX template in any software package other than Dreamweaver MX (such as a word processing software or other HTML editing package), the template comment *<!—#BeginTemplate>* is strictly seen as a comment and you can modify anything in the document you want to, including the locked regions. If you do modify something in the locked regions and then reopen the page in Dreamweaver MX, you may have irregular displays because the locked regions may no longer match the template. If the template is changed, it will replace

HTML ◀▶

HTML ◀▶

the areas of the document with the locked regions, and you will lose anything you changed in the locked regions while outside Dreamweaver MX.

Nested Templates

You can also create a template within a template. For example, you have a layout for your web site (including the header information for your company), and this is stored in a template. You want to create a template for all products you carry, but you want the header of this new template to use the same header information contained in the main template, on which all other pages in the site are based. First create a page using the main template, add the editable regions for the product information, and save as a nested template.

This will come in handy when your boss asks you to change all pages in the web site to reflect the new logo in the header (the one in the upper left-hand corner that now needs to be in the upper right-hand corner). Because you used Nested Templates, you only have to modify the main template and in doing so all pages in the web site are updated, including the product pages based on the nested template (itself based on the main template).

Special Elements That Can Be Included in a Template

- *Tables*
- *Hyperlinks*
- *Baseline font (default font)*
- *Custom styles (must be in an editable region)*
- *Behaviors*
- *Timelines (must be in an editable region)*
- *Any media elements (images, sounds, video, animations)*

Special Elements That Cannot Be Included in a Template

- *Frames, because a frameset is actually a compilation of two or more pages*

Useful Tips When Using Templates

- *When naming editable regions, use generic names that describe the general content of what will be in the region, so that you and other members of the team can more easily identify what goes in each area. Use simple names such as Heading, Bullets, Main paragraph, and so on.*
- *Templates do not need to be placed on the remote site. All of the HTML code needed for a page linked to a template is inside the actual document. The template simply provides a linking mechanism to update multiple pages at one time. We suggest, however, that if a team is working on the same web site, the*

templates be placed on the remote site or network so that they are accessible to the entire team for development purposes. Remember to be careful about the process of how templates are modified, and by whom.

Practice Exercise 7-1: Creating a Template from an Existing File

Description

There are actually two ways to create a template, as follows.

- *Create a new template based on an existing document or template*
- *Start with a blank template and build it within the template Document window*

In this exercise you will open an existing HTML file and convert it to a template file. One of the main steps in creating a template is setting which areas of the template will be editable. The following elements are covered in this exercise.

- *Saving a document as a template*
- *Setting editable regions in a template*
- *Reviewing HTML code for a template file*

Take a Look

CD-ROM

DWComplete Site

Before beginning the exercise, let's take a look at the exercise in its completed state so you can clearly see what you are about to build.

1. It is important for the exercises in this chapter that you have already copied files from the companion CD-ROM to your hard drive. These instructions are found in Chapter 1.

2. You should be in the *DWComplete* site. In the Site panel, locate the folder named *Templates* and the file named *homegard.dwt*. Double click on *home-gard.dwt* to open the file.

3. The file *homegard.dwt* should now appear in your copy of Dreamweaver MX. Note the following properties of this completed exercise.

    - *The Title bar will contain the word Template as a cue that you are working in a template file. All menus are still the same (and available), as if you were working in a regular HTML document.*

    - *Some areas of the page have a blue border (or some other color if the preferences for highlighting have been modified). These are the editable regions of the template.*

- Select *Modify Menu | Templates* and notice the names of items at the bottom of the submenu. These are names of editable regions. Select *Product Description*. Everything within that editable region is highlighted on the page.

- Select *Window Menu | Others | Code Inspector* to open the HTML code. Notice the *<!— >* tags throughout the code. Dreamweaver MX uses these comment tags to identify the editable regions of the file. Notice that these editable regions in the HTML code are also highlighted in the light blue color, as they are in the Document window.

4. Close the file (File | Close).

Storyboard: On Screen

Figure 7-6 shows you how the finished template will look.

Fig. 7-6. Completed template in the Document window.

Storyboard: Behind the Scenes

Figure 7-7 illustrates the HTML code for the Dreamweaver MX template we are going to create. Notice that the highlighted HTML code is always between the *<!— #BeginEditable —>* and *<!— #EndEditable —>* tags.

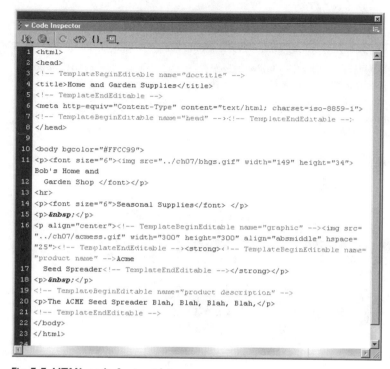

Fig. 7-7. HTML code for template.

Step-by-Step Instructions

1. We are going to open an existing document that has been copied to your hard drive when you installed the chapter exercises in Chapter 1.

   a) You should be in the *DWExercises* site. In the Site panel, locate the *ch07* folder and in it the file named *homegard.html*. Double click on *homegard.html* to open the file.

   b) The file *homegard.html* should now appear in your copy of Dreamweaver MX.

2. Select File Menu | Save as Template.

   a) In the Save as Template dialog box, the name of the document you are saving is the default name for the template. The document's name was *homegard*, so by default the template would be named *homegard*. But we are going to change the name of the template.

   b) In the Save As field, type *mainpage*. Select Save. See figure 7-8.

You may see some other templates already listed. In Chapter 2, these were copied to the site when you copied the files from the companion CD-ROM.

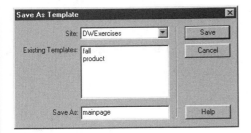

Fig. 7-8. Save as Template dialog.

3. The template is now open in Dreamweaver MX. When you selected Save, Dreamweaver MX took the name of the template and automatically added the *.dwt* extension. The file was then saved in a folder called *Templates* on the root folder of the current site. If the folder *Templates* did not exist, Dreamweaver MX would have created it on the site root folder.

4. You can tell you are in the template by looking at the Title bar and seeing <<Template>>. The name of the template, *mainpage.dwt*, will appear in the Title bar.

    a) Do you see any difference on the page? You should not, because we have not yet set up any editable regions.

    b) When they are set, they will be highlighted in a color that has been set in Preferences | Highlighting.

5. Select File | Close to close the template. You should receive the warning "This template doesn't have any editable regions. Are you sure you want to continue?" If you do not set any editable regions, all pages attached to this template would look exactly the same. In the next exercise we will set the editable regions. For now, click on OK.

6. Back in the Site panel, look for the folder called *Templates*. See figure 7-9. If the folder *Templates* did not already exist when you selected Save as Template, Dreamweaver would have automatically created it. You should also see the file *mainpage.dwt* that we just created in the *Templates* folder.

The name you assign to a template should be a unique name. It is also used as the file name for the template. Dreamweaver MX automatically adds the *.dwt* extension to the end of the name. Because the name is also the file name, use the rules for naming files, just like you would in any application. Template names can include spaces but cannot include special characters. The following characters are "illegal" for use in file names: question mark (?), double quote ("), single quote ('), and left and right angle brackets (< and >).

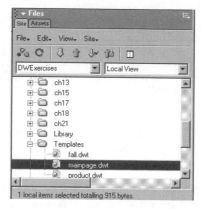

Fig. 7-9. Site panel with Templates folder.

7. Now we are going to reopen the file to set the editable regions.

   a) From the Site panel, double click on *mainpage.dwt* in the *Templates* folder to open it.

   b) Click to select the *ACME Lawn Spreader* graphic.

   c) Select the Editable Region button from the Templates tab of the Insert bar. See figure 7-10.

Editable Region

Fig. 7-10. Insert bar showing Templates tab.

Use the Site panel or Assets | Templates to access (and create) templates.

   d) Type in *graphic* to name the region, and then click on OK. See figure 7-11.

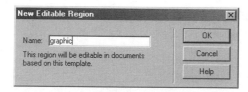

Fig. 7-11. New editable region.

   e) Highlight the entire product name (*Acme Seed Spreader*) to the right of the graphic.

   f) To make the product name editable, select Insert bar | Templates | Editable Region and name it by typing in *product name*. Click on OK.

g) Without moving the cursor away from the text you just set to be "editable," select Text | Style | Bold. Open the Code Inspector (F10 key) to see what you just set to Bold. You will see the *<!— TemplateBeginEditable name="product name" —>* and *<!— TemplateEndEditable —>* tags. This means that the bold style will always apply to the text no matter what the text itself is changed to in a linked document. If the bold tags were inside the editable tags, it could be turned off in a linked document. Close the Code Inspector window.

h) Select the product description *The ACME Seed Spreader*, and then select New Editable Region and type in *product description* to name it. Click on OK.

i) Save the file using the Save option in the File menu.

j) The following prompt will appear: "You have changed a template. Do you want to update?" Select Yes, and then click on Close.

k) You should now have three editable regions: *graphic*, *product name*, and *product description*.

8. Preview the file in a browser by pressing the F12 key. Even though this is a template, it is also an HTML document and you view it just like any other file.

9. Close the Browser window to return to Dreamweaver MX and the template.

10. Let's look at the HTML code Dreamweaver MX has created.

a) Press the F10 key to open the Code Inspector.

b) Look at the HTML that is highlighted. These are the editable regions in the template.

The first insert for the template is around the *<title>* tag, which is automatically (and always) an editable region in a template.

```
<!— TemplateBeginEditable name="doctitle" —>
<title>Home and Garden Supplies</title>
<!— TemplateEndEditable —>
```

<!— TemplateBeginEditable name="graphic" —> identifies the image SRC as editable. The name of the editable region is graphic.

<!— TemplateBeginEditable name="product name" —> identifies the text as editable. The name of the editable region is product name.

<!— TemplateBeginEditable name="product description" —> identifies the text as editable. The name of the editable region is product description.

11. Close the Code Inspector window.

Shortcut

The F10 key is the keyboard shortcut for Window | Others | Code Inspector.

·T/P·

When saving a template after creating editable regions, you may receive a warning about a region being set inside a <P> tag (the paragraph tag). This prevents an individual page from adding additional paragraphs to the region.

HTML

12. Select File | Save to save your file. A prompt box will appear, asking you to update pages. Select Yes, and then click on Close.

13. Close the template using File | Close.

Practice Exercise 7-2: Creating a New HTML Page Based on a Template

Description

Here is a common scenario: You want to add new product pages to your supply catalog. Because you want the "look and feel" to be consistent across all of the pages, you will want to create each page from a template. You will also see how using templates can save development time. The following elements are covered in this exercise.

- *Creating a new page based on a template*
- *Modifying a page linked to a template*
- *The Templates panel*

Take a Look

CD-ROM

Before beginning the exercise, let's take a look at the exercise in its completed state so that you can clearly see what it is you are about to build.

DWComplete Site

1. Change the site to the *DWComplete* site.

2. Locate the folder named *ch07* and the file named *dw07ex2.html*. Double click on *dw07ex2.html* to open the file.

3. The file *dw07ex2.html* should now appear in your copy of Dreamweaver MX. Note the following properties of this completed exercise.

- *This page has the same structure (format) as the previous exercise, but notice the product graphic and name are different.*
- *The product description is an actual paragraph of text that is going to be copied from a text file.*
- *The highlighted (colored) areas of the page. These are editable regions.*
- *The name of the template (in the upper right-hand corner of the page to which the template is attached).*

Storyboard: On Screen

Figure 7-12 shows you what the finished HTML document will look like.

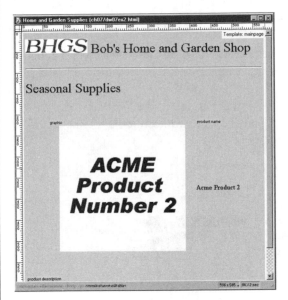

Fig. 7-12. Completed exercise in the Document window.

Storyboard: Behind the Scenes

Figure 7-13 shows the HTML code for the Dreamweaver MX template we are going to create. Notice that the highlighted HTML code is always between the *<!— #BeginEditable —>* and *<!— #EndEditable —>* tags.

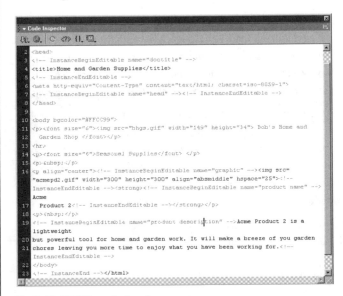

Fig. 7-13. HTML code for document.

Go Solo

DWExercises Site

CAUTION

When creating a file based on a template using File | New, all defined sites are listed. We suggest that you only create new HTML pages based on templates in the current site. If you want to use a template from a different site, copy that template using Assets | Template panel.

·T/P·

Another way to create a template-based document is to create a new blank HTML document, and then via the Assets | Templates panel, select the template and click on the Apply button.

Step-by-Step Instructions

1. Change to the *DWExercises* site by using the Site panel. We are going to create a new page in this site, based on the template created in the previous exercise.

   a) Select Window Menu | Assets and select the Template button. Right click (Windows) or Control click (Macintosh) on the template called *mainpage*. See figure 7-14.

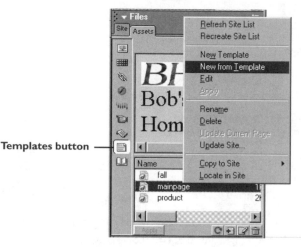

Fig. 7-14. Assets | Templates | New From Template.

   b) From the context menu, select New From Template.
   c) Notice that certain regions of the page are highlighted. The highlight identifies which regions are editable and which regions are not.
   d) Save your new HTML page. Select File Menu | Save and locate the folder *Learning_Dreamweaver*, subfolder *ch07*. Save as *prod2.html*.

2. Now let's select a new graphic in a file created from a template.

   a) Double click on the *product* graphic to open it so that we can select a new source file. (You could also select a new source file by using the Property Inspector and selecting the Browse Folder icon next to Src.)
   b) Select the file *acmepd2.gif* in *ch07*. The new graphic will replace the original product graphic.

3. Next, let's modify text in a file created from a template.

   a) Select (highlight) the text *Acme Seed Spreader*, next to the *product* graphic.
   b) Type in *Acme Product 2*.

4. To change another editable region, in this case the text for product description, we are going to use the menu option to make sure we have selected the entire editable region for modification.

   a) Select Modify Menu | Template | Product Description. *Product description* is the name of the editable region we want to modify. See figure 7-15.

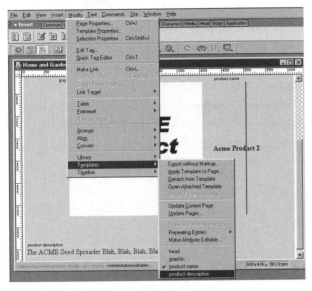

Fig. 7-15. Modify Menu | Template.

   b) To copy text from an external file, select the Site panel and the site *DWExercises*.

   c) Double click on the text file *prod2.txt* in *ch07* to open this file in Dreamweaver MX.

   d) Select all of the text and copy the text into the clipboard.

   e) Close the text file.

   f) Go back to *prod2.html* (you can do this by selecting Window Menu | *prod2.html*). The product description should still be highlighted.

   g) Select Edit | Paste (in Dreamweaver MX) to paste the text from your computer's clipboard, replacing the original product description.

5. Preview the file in a browser by pressing the F12 key.

6. Close the Browser window to return to Dreamweaver MX.

7. You have just created a new HTML document based on a template. The original graphic and text were changed for the specific HTML document. The document still has the locked regions that included the logo, header, and title. It also picked up the page properties from the template – primarily the title and the background color. The title is editable, but the

background color is not. The background color and other options in the page properties are set in the template.

Summary

• *Create one or more Dreamweaver MX templates to use as the basic structure for HTML documents.*

• *Dreamweaver MX templates decrease the amount of development time when like elements are positioned and functions are set in a template.*

• *Dreamweaver MX's template functionality is not recognized outside Dreamweaver MX but is seen as comments by other HTML editors.*

• *Create placeholders in templates for graphics, text, and sound that will vary across pages. Set a common height and width for a graphic placeholder.*

• *Look at Appendix B, Modifying Templates, on the accompanying CD-ROM for further study.*

·T*i*P·

Use Editable Tag Attributes to make attributes (i.e., text styles) editable from page to page but locked if the page should match the template.

CHAPTER **8**

Application Chapter: Creating the "Look and Feel" of the Web Site and Templates

Introduction

In this first application chapter, we will set up a new site and begin to create a group of pages that, when completed at the end of the book, will be linked together to form a fully functioning web site. Many of the features and options we have been discussing in previous chapters will be included in the pages we create in this chapter.

Application Exercise Objectives

By the end of this chapter you will:

- *Set up a new web site for storing the web site files and media elements for the application chapters*
- *Create an HTML page for displaying project information*
- *Incorporate text and graphics into the HTML page*
- *Create a template*
- *Create a page from a template*

Application Project Overview

Throughout this book you will find a number of application chapters. These chapters differ from the instructional chapters in that they will challenge you to combine the knowledge and techniques acquired from several previous chapters and apply your newly developed skill to create part of a "real-world" web site.

Each application chapter focuses on creating one of six application exercises that when combined will make up a fully functioning application project, an online store with the name *The 21st Century Kitchen*. Each application exercise is a separate and distinct element of the overall application project. Each exercise can be found in its completed form on the companion CD-ROM. In this way you can choose to complete a few application exercises on your own and integrate your work with the other completed exercises we supply. Alternatively, you can complete all of the application exercises on your own. The choice is yours.

We have designed the overall application project, *The 21st Century Kitchen*, and all component exercises found in each of the application chapters to reflect the types of structures and project objectives you are likely to find if you worked for a firm or department responsible for creating web sites. After you have completed the entire application project, you will have a "portfolio project" typical of the thousands of HTML-based web sites in existence.

Application Chapters

Chapter 8: Creating the "Look and Feel" of the Web Site and Templates

In this application chapter, you will set up the Online Store web site and create the layout for the product pages. One of the features of the product pages will be "rollover" buttons (Previous Item and Next Item). In this exercise, you will also create a template from the product page and use it to create additional product pages. Our template will include a navigation bar (expanded in later chapters) and the title graphic to create a similar look for each page.

The product pages will contain descriptions and photographs of the various products *The 21st Century Kitchen* offers. Visitors to this web site will be able to browse through and read about the products before making a purchase.

Chapter 12: Creating the Main Menu Page and Linking It to Product Pages

In this application chapter, you will create a main menu (home) page for the web site, as well as links to the various product pages. This main menu page will contain a navigation bar using items from a library. The main menu page in *The 21st Century Kitchen* web site will be the first page the visitor sees. This page has three purposes: to let the visitor know the name of the store, to describe the store and the web site, and to provide a way to navigate to the other pages in the site.

Chapter 14: Using Frames

In this application chapter, you will use frames to create a directory listing of recipes. The user will be able to select from a category of recipes and then a specific recipe to view instructions for preparing the dish.

Chapter 16: Adding a Behavior

In this application chapter, the home page will now check the browser version to send versions 3.0 and below to an alternate URL. Additional behaviors will be added in later chapters.

Chapter 20: Working with Layers

In this application chapter, a guide of the products available at *The 21st Century Kitchen* will be created. The interactive guide will be created with the use of image maps and layers.

Chapter 22: Adding a Form

Every online store needs an order form. In this application chapter, you will create an information and order form for the web site for *The 21st Century Kitchen*.

Preparing Your Computer for the Application Project

Before starting the application chapters, we recommend that you copy the support files (images and other media) from the companion CD-ROM to your computer's hard drive.

Windows (PC)

We recommend that you use the install program on the companion CD-ROM. This install program will create a new directory called *Learning_DWapplication* and will copy all support files to this directory.

- *On the companion CD-ROM, double click on the file* Install Application.exe, *found in the folder* Windows Install. *Follow the directions.*
- *The default folder is* Learning_DWapplication. *You may change the hard drive letter (or name) where the folder will be created, but do not change the name of the folder, because this is the folder referred to in all of the exercises.*
- *A message will tell you how much space is required for the files.*
- *Files will be copied to the* Learning_DWapplication *folder. This includes a sub-folder called* ap_media, *which contains the external media needed for the application exercises.*

Catchup files for Application Chapters

- *If you choose to start an application chapter without completing the previous application exercise, we have included starting folders for each chapter. These can be copied from the folder called* Application_Chapters_catchup *on the companion CD-ROM. For example,* starting_ch12 *folder contains a completed version of Application Chapter 8's work, and so on for the rest of the chapters. Copy the* Application_Chapters_catchup *folder directly to your hard drive..*

Macintosh

- *On the companion CD-ROM, find the folder called* Learning_DWapplication.
- *Drag the folder* Learning_DWapplication *to the Macintosh HD.*
- *The external media needed for the application exercises are located in the sub-folder called* ap_media.

Application Exercise 8-1: Creating the "Look and Feel" of the Web Site and Templates

Description

The main purpose of the product pages is to present information to the user on specific products. Users will be looking at this web site because they want to learn about a product and (hopefully) purchase it. The information presented on the web page (product description and possibly a photograph) will help the user make an educated decision about the purchase.

In this first application exercise, you will learn a number of techniques useful to the creation of a product information page. You will first set up the site, including creating the directory structure that will be used for storing the HTML, graphic, template, and note files that will be created throughout the application exercises. In the second activity in this exercise, you will create an HTML page for displaying product information. In the third activity, you will create a template from the product information page that can be reused to create other project pages, so that all product pages will have the same look and feel.

Take a Look

Let's take a look at how the finished exercise will look. Open Dreamweaver MX and select File Menu | Open to locate the companion CD-ROM. Locate the folder *Learning_DWapplication_complete* and select the file *ap08.html*. Preview the file (*ap08.html*) in a browser by pressing the F12 key. Note the following properties as you complete this exercise.

 CD-ROM

- *Layout of the page, noting graphic and text areas*
- *The graphic banner at the top of the page*
- *Main Menu button*
- *While in the Document window, the highlighted areas representing template regions*

You will be dealing with the following Dreamweaver MX concepts in the exercise.

- *Defining a site*
- *Page properties*
- *Property Inspector for text and images*
- *Templates and editable and locked regions*
- *Insert Rollover Image (Insert menu | Interactive Images)*
- *Preview in browser*
- *Indenting text*

Storyboard: Browser View

Figure 8-1 shows how the product web page will look in a web browser when the exercise is completed.

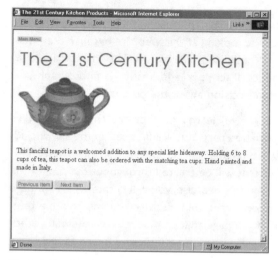

Fig. 8-1. Product page in browser.

Storyboard: Dreamweaver MX View

Figure 8-2 shows how the template for the product web page will look in Dreamweaver MX when the exercise is completed.

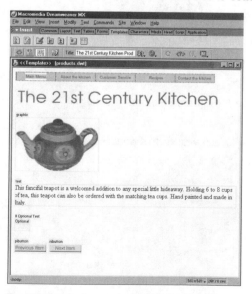

Fig. 8-2. Product page in Dreamweaver MX.

Application Project Steps

Complete this exercise on your own, guided by the general steps that follow. You can always refer back to the completed example you viewed in the "Take a Look" section of this exercise. The following steps are intended as a guide. This is your project, so feel free to make whatever variations you like.

1. Open Dreamweaver MX and define a new site named *The 21st Century Kitchen*. For the local root folder, browse for the folder *Learning_ DWapplication* on your hard drive. If you did not install (copy) this folder from the companion CD-ROM, create this folder now. This folder will be used in all application chapters. See figure 8-3.

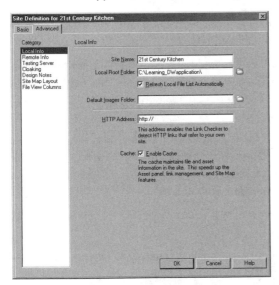

Fig. 8-3. Site defined for application chapters.

2. Create a new HTML file and set the page properties. Title the page *The 21st Century Kitchen Products*. Set a background color if you wish. We recommend a beige: #FFFFCC. We will use this color as a background for all pages in the web site.

3. Save your file as a template by selecting File Menu | Save as Template. Name the template *products* and be sure the file is saved in the folder called *Learning_DWapplication*.

4. At the top of the page, insert a rollover image using the Rollover Image icon on the Insert bar's Common tab. Name it *mainMenu* and use the graphic image *21main.jpg* for the original image and *21maino.jpg* for the rollover image (in the *ap_media* subfolder). All of the buttons in the appli-

cation chapters have two states. The additional (o) in the file name is for the *rollOver* state graphic.

5. On the next line, below the Main Menu button, insert the banner graphic *21ckbnr.jpg* found in the *ap_media* subfolder.

6. On the next line, import the photograph of the teapot, *tea.jpg*, found in the *ap_media/products* subfolders.

7. On the next line, type in some product information about the teapot. Add a few extra lines (Enter or Return key) after the text. You will need the extra lines later.

8. Create an editable region for graphic images (where the teapot is) and name it graphic.

9. Highlight the text of the product description and create an editable region for text information named *text*.

10. Below the editable region you created for the product description, add an editable optional region. Name this region *Optional*. This section can be used if the page for a product needs an additional area for text or possibly another graphic.

11. Create an editable region for the Previous Item and Next Item buttons. (Insert Menu | Template Objects | Editable Region). Creating an editable region will allow the links for the buttons to change across pages. Name the editable regions *pibutton* and *nibutton*.

12. Save the template. (Do not worry if you receive a <p> tag warning. If you do, click on OK.)

13. Create a new page based on this template (*products*). Name the new page *teapot.html* and make sure it is saved in the folder *Learning_ DWapplication*.

14. Preview your product web page in your browser.

Summary

You have accomplished three things in this exercise: you have set up the web site folder (the place to store all of the web site HTML, graphics, and other files), you have created a web page for product information, and you have created a template. In the next application exercises, you will modify the product page template, create additional pages from this template, and add links to the pages.

CHAPTER **9**

Links

Introduction

In this chapter we are going to focus on one of the main capabilities of the Web: being able to link between pages within a single web site and then from one web site to another. How cumbersome it would be if you had to type in the address for every single page you wanted to look at, including the pages within a single site. The Web would not be what it is today without the dynamic capabilities of links. By the end of the chapter you will be able to:

- *Describe the properties associated with links, such as colors, custom cursors, underlined text, and graphic borders*

- *Create a link between pages in the same site and across web sites*

- *Use techniques to jump to a new page, including opening a new browser window*

- *Manage and troubleshoot links*

Link Basics

Two things are needed to create a link: an object initiating the link, and a destination.

Link object: Text and graphics are the most common types of objects that can serve as links. You can also have e-mail links, links to databases, and links to other applications. Graphic images may have multiple links (hot spots) using image maps. A linked object can even be an animated object moving across the screen. The bottom line is, if you can see an object on the screen, it can be turned into a link. Think of a link as something that is "hot" (i.e., can be interacted with by the user).

Link destination: Having one HTML document link to another is the most common type of link. If you are linking to another HTML document, the destination is the file name of the HTML document. If the document you are linking to is not in the current folder, the link destination will also need to include the location of the document, known as its path. You can also link to a specific position on a page using anchors.

Chapter 17 covers the special links related to anchors and image maps.

Summary of Steps for Creating a Link

- *Highlight the text or object the user will click on to initiate or execute the link.*

- *Using the Property Inspector, in the Link field, perform one or both of the following.*

  - *Enter the file name of the HTML document to link to. The path to the destination is also required if the file is in a different folder/directory than the calling document.*

- *Enter the anchor name for the position to link to on the page. Anchors are entered with a # (pound sign) in front of them. The anchor generally is inserted into a spot on the page before setting the link (Insert | Named Anchor). You can also use the Point To File icon to link to an anchor.*

• *Preview the page in a browser to test the link.*

Deleting a Link

• *Delete the reference in the Link field in the Property Inspector, or use Modify Menu | Remove Link. See figure 9-1.*

Link Field

Fig. 9-1. Property Inspector showing Link field.

Page Properties and Link Colors

When you enter an anchor or file name in the Link field of the Property Inspector, the linked object inherits the default link colors from the page properties. We recommend that you do not change these colors, because they are the colors users are most familiar with on the Web and they are easily identifiable. However, sometimes these default colors may not work well with the design colors of your backgrounds and other text colors, so you may need to change them. The following are the types of color links set in Page Properties.

Links: The color of text and the border of a graphic image (if the graphic has a border) to which a link is attached. The default link color is blue.

Visited links: Linked objects the user has already selected (visited). The default color for visited links is a light purple.

Active links: The color of linked objects as they are being selected. Sometimes the user will not even see this color because the link happens so quickly as the browser jumps to its new destination. The default color for active links is red. See figure 9-2.

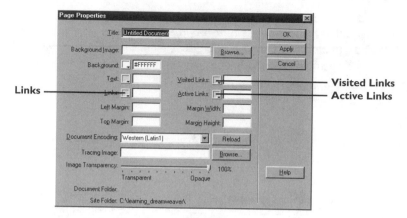

Fig. 9-2. Page Properties option showing link colors.

A link attached to text can have its own link color (different from the default link color for every other link on the page) by inserting the *<font>* tag between the link (anchor) and tag *(<a>* and *</a>)*. Using Dreamweaver MX, simply select the linked object and using the Property Inspector select the color in the Text Color box (next to the Size box).

You cannot set a specific link color for a single linked graphic. It will always pick up the page's default color for links defined in the page properties. You also cannot set a unique color for a single item for the visited and active link colors, whether the item is a graphic or text. All visited links will have the same color, and all active links will have the same color per page.

Miscellaneous Notes on Links

- *You must preview a document in a browser to test the links. Links are not active in the Dreamweaver MX Document window.*

- *When an object has a link assigned to it, you will see the following changes.*

  - *The cursor becomes a custom cursor when rolling over an object with a link assigned to it. The type of custom cursor used can be changed through the Styles settings.*

  - *Linked text will automatically be underlined. (But there is a way to remove the underlining if you really do not want it, as described in material to follow.)*

The underlining of hypertext links can be removed by redefining the style for the *<a>* tag. However, this changes the tag for the entire document, so that none of the hypertext links in the current document will be underlined. For example, when creating quizzes and tests in an HTML document, you may not want the questions' possible answers (links to feedback) to be underlined. To modify the *<a>* tag and remove the underline for hypertext, you would perform the following.

1. Select the hypertext (text with a link attached to it).

2. Select Window | CSS Styles to bring up the Styles panel.

3. Select the New CSS Style icon at the bottom of the Styles panel.

4. In the New Style dialog window, select Redefine HTML Tag. If *a* is not displayed as the tag to redefine, select *a* from the tag pull-down menu (*a* is the tag for links).

5. For the Define In option, select the radio button for This Document Only. Click on OK.

6. Select the category Type in the Style Definition dialog window. Check the box next to None under Decoration.

7. You have just added a new style for the <*a*> tag. If you need to edit the style, select the radio button for Edit Styles, and then select the style to modify and the Edit Style Sheet icon at the bottom of the Styles panel (instead of the New Style icon).

Target Links

There is an additional option that can be set for a link and that involves how (or where) the linked page opens. There are two choices. First, the linked page can open in the current browser window, replacing the current page in the window. Second, the link can open in its own browser window, leaving the previous page open in the original browser window. There is no right or wrong choice here; it is a matter of personal choice.

However, as you may have noticed while using links from one web site to another, it is fairly easy to forget the page or address from where you started and to where you may want to return. Selecting the Back button in the browser may or may not get you back to where you started. If you are concerned about users selecting a link to leave your site and you do not want them to lose their way back to your site, you may want to have the new link page open in its own browser window. This way your web site will remain on screen in its own browser window behind the new browser window.

You can make this choice with the use of the Property Inspector's Targets for Links. The target (_blank and _self) refers to the window in which the linked page should load. The target also can refer to the frame in which the linked page will open (see Chapter 13). The following are the available targets.

• _blank: *loads the linked file in a new browser window.*

• _self: *loads the linked file in the current frame or window (same as the Link window). This is the default target.*

- _top: *loads the linked file in the current browser window. The difference in this Target option from _self is that when there are frames, all frames are removed and the linked file replaces the entire browser window. _self only replaces the current frame (not the entire window).*

- _parent: *loads the linked file in the parent frameset or window of the frame that contains the link. If the current frame is not nested inside another frame, the linked file loads into the full browser window, thus acting like the target _top. See figure 9-3.*

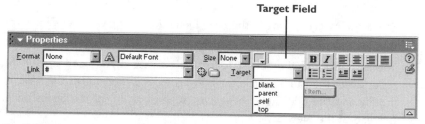

Fig. 9-3. Property Inspector showing Target options for links.

HTML Code for Links

HTML

The anchor tag designated in HTML is *<a>*, which is the primary tag used to designate a link. This tag provides the custom cursor when rolling over the link, underlines text, and changes the color of the links. Whenever an object has a link to a URL, the object will be surrounded by a beginning tag *<a>* and end tag *</a>*.

One attribute for the anchor tag is the hypertext reference designated as *<href>*. This attribute defines what to link to. The HTML code is written as follows.

```
<a href="menu2.html"> contact me </a>
```

Here, *contact me* is the hypertext phrase and *menu2.html* is the HTML document to which to link. If linking to an anchor on the current page, the HTML would look as follows.

```
<a href="#contact">contact me</a>
```

Here, there is an anchor somewhere on the current page called *contact*. If linking to an anchor in a separate page, the HTML would look as follows.

```
<a href="menu2.html#contact"> contact me </a>
```

Here, the hypertext *contact me* is linked to the anchor named *contact* in the HTML document called *menu2.html*. If the target were set to anything other than the default (*_self*), the HTML would look as follows.

```
<a href="menu2.html" Target="_blank">contact me</a>
```

Here, the document *menu2.html* will be opened in a new browser window when *contact me* is clicked on.

E-mail Links

E-mail links provide an easy way for a user to send you e-mail from within your web site. The recipient's address (your address) can be automatically filled in for the user, along with the subject of the e-mail. This type of link can be useful when you want feedback or want to give the user an easy way to contact you for additional information.

As with all links, the linking information is enclosed within the anchor tag (*<a>*). The following are examples of e-mail links and the parameters you can include. The HTML for an e-mail link will look as follows.

```
<a href="mailto:sales@yourname.xyz">
```

HTML

Here, the *href* attribute points to the e-mail address. All e-mail links begin with *mailto:*, followed by the e-mail address. There are no spaces within the *href*. In Dreamweaver MX, when using the Link field in the Property Inspector, just start the link in the form *mailto:[address]*. Do not include quote marks. The question mark (?) separates additional parameters to add to the e-mail. To insert a subject for the e-mail, you would use the following form.

```
mailto:sales@yourname.xyz?subject=Send a catalog
```

Here, the text *Send a catalog* will display in the subject (RE:) box. There are other parameters that can be included for e-mails, but they do not work for all e-mail programs. If you know what e-mail program the user will use, you can try some of the other parameters. Each parameter is separated by the ampersand (&). Examples follow.

```
mailto:sales@yourname.xyz?subject=Send a
_catalog&cc=dan@yourname.xyz
```

Here, the text *cc* inserts a name for the carbon copy. In the following, the text *bcc* inserts a name for the blind carbon copy.

```
mailto:sales@yourname.xyz?subject=Send
a_catalog&cc=dan@yourname.xyz&bcc=susie@abc.xyz
```

In the following, the text *body* inserts text into the body of the e-mail.

```
mailto:sales@yourname.xyz?subject=Send a catalog&cc=Dan
_Denver&body=This is the body
```

CAUTION

When referring to the names of our fictitious web sites and e-mail addresses, we will frequently use the extension *.xyz* instead of *.com* to emphasize that the references are fictitious.

Changing the Status Bar Text Pertaining to a Link

When you are viewing a page in the browser and you roll your mouse over the top of the link, by default the path to the page it will link to will be displayed in the browser's Status bar. However, you can use a behavior to change the text displayed in the Status bar for a link. This can be changed by inserting an additional attribute on the link tag (*<a>*). Dreamweaver MX provides an option to do this within the Behavior window, per the following.

* *Select the linked item (it should already have the link set in the Link field).*
* *Select Window | Behaviors. A new Window panel will be displayed, with the tab Behaviors selected.*
* *Select the + key at the upper left-hand corner. While holding the mouse down, select the option Set Text | Set Text of Status Bar.*
* *Type the text you want displayed in the Status bar when rolling the mouse over the linked item while viewing the page in the browser.*
* *Preview in the browser to test the text in the Status bar.*

Managing Links

The concept and practice of managing your links not only refers to the links between HTML pages but links from the HTML page to media (sound, graphics, video, animation, Flash, and so on). In Dreamweaver MX, you must also consider the link from HTML pages to a template or library object.

Dreamweaver MX has built-in mechanisms for helping you keep your links updated as you modify pages and elements in your web site. However, if you delete pages or elements or inadvertently forget to download an updated file with a link from the remote site, you may encounter broken links. To avoid this and other problems, let's take a look at some options to help you manage your links.

Managing Links in the Site Panel

When you have many pages that are linked, it is often very useful to get the big picture of the relationships among the files. Dreamweaver MX's Site Map feature can provide this "big picture." See figure 9-4. A site map displays the files by icon, shows the links between the files with the use of connector lines, and includes the option to display all media (dependent files) used within a page.

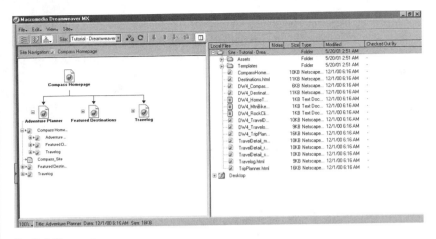

Fig. 9-4. Site map.

·T/P·

Window's users: You might want to expand the Site panel when using the site map, so that you get a bigger picture (as in figure 9-4).

Site Maps and the Home Page

A site map is driven by the home page you set for the site. The home page can have any file name, but if you want the user to be able to just type in the URL for your site without a file name, you should name your home page *index*, *home*, or *default* (with either the *.htm* or *.html* extension). These three file names are automatically recognized by browsers as the default page with which to open a site, if a file name is not entered. For instance, if your home page is called *home.html* and your web site address is *www.yourname.xyz*, the user need simply type in the following (in most browsers these days, it might be as simple as *yourname.xyz*).

http://www.yourname.xyz

If your home page (or the page you want your site to open with) is called *page1.html*, the user would type in the following.

http://www.yourname.xyz/page1.html

To view the site map, define a home page by selecting an existing HTML page (in the Site panel) and use one of the following methods.

- *On a PC, right mouse click (Mac, Ctrl + click) on an HTML file in the Site panel and select Set as Home Page.*

- *Select Site panel | Site Menu | Set as Home Page.*

- *When defining the site, use the Site Menu | Edit Sites selection and select the category Site Map Layout. Then enter the name of the home page (with the extension) or browse for an existing file. If you enter the name of a file that does not exist, Dreamweaver MX will create a blank HTML file in the site root folder for you. Be sure to include the extension for the file.*

Site Map Layout

Because the site map shows the links between files, and between files and external media, there can be a lot of information displayed in the site map you may not want to see all the time. There are options you can set within your site definition that will change the layout of the site map. See figure 9-5. These options are accessed via Site Menu | Edit Sites | Site Map Layout, or while in the Site panel by selecting View Menu | Layout.

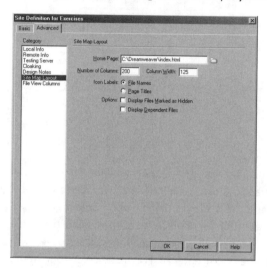

Fig. 9-5. Site Map Layout options.

Number of Columns: Number of icons that will be displayed, from left to right, in the site map.

Icon Labels/File Names: Will display the name of the file under an icon in the site map. Icon Labels | Page Titles displays the page title under the icon. If you do not have unique names for all your pages, it is probably not a good idea to display the icons with the page titles. This option may also be accessed via View Menu | Show Page Titles. This turns the titles on (page titles displayed) or off (file names displayed).

Display Files Marked as Hidden: Will list those HTML pages that have been marked within Dreamweaver MX to be hidden from view. This option may also be accessed with the menu option View | Show Files Marked as Hidden.

- *A file is set to be hidden/shown in the site map by selecting the file and then View | Show/Hide link. Hiding a link file cuts down on the number of files displayed in the site map and may make it easier to work with.*

- *For the hidden file to be shown, you will need to select View | Show Files Marked as Hidden. All hidden files will then show in the site map.*

- *To force a file to show all the time in the site map, select the file and then select View | Show/Hide link. To reset more than one file at a time to show, select multiple files using the Shift key, or use the mouse to select multiple files within the site map.*

Display Dependent Files will list all dependent files (media and external links) for all linked pages. If there are a lot of dependent files in one HTML document, this site map could become very crowded and difficult to decipher. Under most circumstances, you will probably not want to show dependent files in the site map layout. An example of a dependent file would be any image that has been inserted into a file.

Changing the Name of a File Linked to Other Files

What if you wanted to change the name of a file (media or HTML) that is linked more than once in the site? While in the Site panel, select the file you want to rename (either in the site map or Site Files list). To edit the file name, select the menu option File | Rename, press the F2 key, or single click on the file and single click on the name. As soon as you change the name, you will receive the option to update all pages linked to this file. Instead of needing to open each file linked to another page or element you are renaming, you can use this feature and save a lot of time.

Practice Exercise 9-1: Link to a New Page

Description

Most of the links created on a web page are links to a new page within the same web site. There may also be references to other sites, including a business partner's site, additional information on other sites, sites to download plug-ins, and so on. The new page that is opened can be opened in the current browser window or in its own browser window. This second option is useful when you do not want the user to leave your page (or site) and get lost in the "web" of pages that can be opened. The following elements are covered in this exercise.

- *Create hypertext by attaching a link to a word or phrase in an HTML document*
- *Link to a new page within the current site*
- *Open a new page in its own browser window*
- *Set the size of the new browser window that is opened*
- *Open a browser window without its menu bar*
- *Use the Site panel to create a new file and link*
- *Manage the links to check for broken links*
- *Attach an e-mail link to the page*

·T/P·

Be sure you do not change the name of a linked file outside Dreamweaver MX. This will create a broken link within your site. If you do change names outside Dreamweaver MX and then need to fix any links to the new file, use the Site panel's Site Menu | Change Link Sitewide option and type the name of the old file in the Change All Links To field.

CD-ROM

DWComplete Site

Take a Look

Before beginning the exercise, let's take a look at the exercise in its completed state so that you can clearly see what it is you are about to build.

1. Make sure you are working with the site *DWComplete*. You can confirm this by selecting the site name from the Site pop-up menu in the Site panel.

2. Locate the folder *ch09* and within it the file named *dw09ex1.html*. Double click on *dw09ex1.html* to open the file.

3. The file *dw09ex1.html* should now appear in your copy of Dreamweaver MX. Note the following properties of this completed exercise.

   • *The underlined/blue text in the page is the hypertext. When it is viewed in Dreamweaver MX, the links are not active. (Roll your mouse over one of the words and nothing happens.)*

   • *Select (single click on) the underlined title My Self at the top of the bulleted list and look at the Property Inspector. In the Link field is the name of an HTML page. This is the page that will be opened when My Self is selected.*

   • *At the bottom of the page, the link for the text Museum of Digital Art shows mailto:, which indicates an e-mail link.*

   • *Notice the following additional formatting on the page.*

      The font on the text is set to Garamond, Arial, sans serif. The text will display in the first available font listed in the default font choices.

      The first paragraph is indented.

      The bulleted list is indented.

      The horizontal rule.

4. Close *dw09ex1.html*.

5. Locate the *ch09* folder and within it the file named *myself.html*. Double click on *myself.html* to open the file.

6. This is the page that will open when selecting *My Self* from the previous document. Note the following properties of this completed exercise.

   • *Under the picture is an interactive (Back button) image that will return to the previous page (or the home page, in this case). Look at the Property Inspector to see the link.*

   • *The text www.mda.xyz is underlined and is linked to the URL www.mda.xyz. Again, the text Museum of Digital Art is an e-mail link.*

Storyboard: On Screen

Figure 9-6 shows you what the finished page will look like when viewed through a browser.

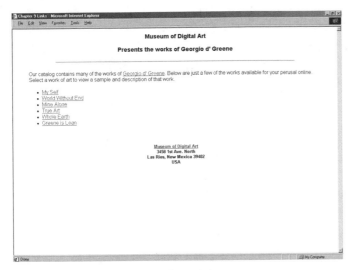

Fig. 9-6. Completed exercise within a browser.

Storyboard: Behind the Scenes

Figure 9-7 shows some of the key HTML code behind links.

Link opens a new Browser window at a specific size.

```
Our catalog contains many of the works of <a href="#"
onMouseDown="MM_openBrWindow('about_georgio.html',",'width=300,height=400')">
Georgio d' Greene</a>.
```

Link opens a page in the current Browser window.

```
<a href="myself.html">My Self </a>
```

HTML for a rollover image that links to a page when the image is clicked.

```
<a href="ch10exer1.html" onMouseOut="MM_swapImgRestore()"
onMouseOver="MM_swapImage('button_back',",'back_button_f02.gif',1)">
<img name="button_back" border="0" src="back_button_f01.gif" width="44" height="19">
</a>
```

Link to a external site.

```
<a href="http://www.mda.com">www.mda.com</a>
```

An e-mail link

```
<a href="mailto:director@mda.com">Museum of Digital Art</a>
```

Fig. 9-7. HTML window for completed exercise.

Step-by-Step Instructions

1. We are going to open an existing document that was copied to your hard drive when you installed the chapter exercises in Chapter 1.

   a) Change to the *DWExercises* site. Use the Site panel to locate the *ch09* folder and within it the file named *digital.html*. Double click on *digital.html* to open the file.

   b) The file *digital.html* should now appear in your Dreamweaver MX window.

2. Now to create the first link to an individual page describing and displaying artwork.

   a) Select the text *My Self*. Using the Property Inspector, select the Browse for File button next to the Link field.

   b) Search for the file *myself.html* in the *ch09* folder, within the *Learning_Dreamweaver* folder. Before selecting the file, make sure that *Relative to* is set to Document. See figure 9-8.

If Relative to Site Root is selected, the file must actually be saved to the Web server before it can be previewed. This option will be used when linking to folders between sites. You typically use Relative to Document when linking to files within the current site.

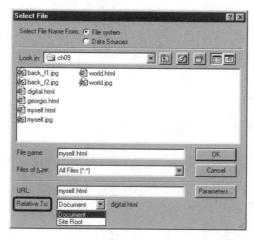

Fig. 9-8. Link to File | Select File dialog window.

You can also link to a file by using the Point to File tool (next to the Link field). Drag the Point to File icon to a file in the Site panel.

   c) Select *myself.html* by double clicking on the file or by clicking on the Select button.

   d) The text *My Self* should now be underlined and be blue in color. The Link field in the Property Inspector contains the name of the file, *myself.html*.

   e) Save the file.

   f) Preview the file in a browser by pressing the F12 key. Move the cursor over *My Self* and click on this text. The new page appears in the browser window, with the artwork *My Self*.

   g) Close the browser window to return to Dreamweaver MX.

3. There is another page that has some biographical information about the artist. As we link to this new page, we will open the page in its own window, with the browser's menu bar turned off. The size of the window when it opens will also be set as we link to the page. We will use a behavior to set the window attributes. The behavior also has the option to set the URL to which to jump. We will get into more detail about behaviors in a later chapter. Behaviors are primarily precoded JavaScript that gives your HTML pages more functionality.

    a) In the line of text *contains many of the works of Georgio d' Greene,* highlight the words *Georgio d' Greene.*

    b) Select Window Menu | Behaviors. The Behaviors panel now opens.

    c) Click on the plus (+) icon in the top left of the window to view the Behaviors pull-down menu. Notice that very few menu options are available. To be able to select the behavior we want, there needs to be an anchor tag (<*a*>) in the hypertext. (The available behaviors depend on the type of media that is selected: text, image, body of the page, and so on.)

        Click somewhere in the Behaviors window to deselect the pull-down menu.

    d) To set the anchor tag without actually setting a link, type in a pound sign (#) in the Link field while *Georgio d' Greene* is highlighted. Press the Enter/Return key to set the tag. The text is now an underlined and colored link.

    e) Go back to the Behaviors panel and select the plus (+) icon. Now there are a lot of menu options available. Select Open Browser Window.

    f) Insert the following information in the Open Browser window.

        URL: Browse for the file *georgio.html* in the *ch09* folder. Before selecting the file, make sure that the *Relative to* is set to Document.

        Window Width/Height: Set Window Width to 300 and Window Height to 400.

        We do not want any of the menu options displayed, so leave everything else unchecked.

        The title of the linked page has already been set in the document, so we do not need to enter the window name. See figure 9-9 for the completed entries in the Behaviors window.

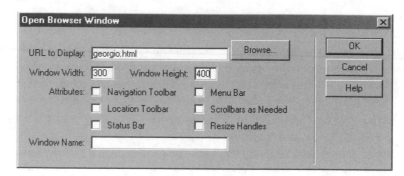

Fig. 9-9. Behaviors | Open Browser Window.

g) Click on OK.

h) Save the file.

i) There may be some cleaning up to do for the link to work the way we want it to. This depends on whether you have used the behaviors before in Dreamweaver MX. Listed in the Behaviors window should be an event starting with the word *on*, such as *onMouseOver* or *onClick*. A downward-pointing arrow and the behavior Open Browser Window will follow the event. We want the browser to open when we click down on the text; therefore, the event we want is *onClick*. To change the event, perform the following.

Click on the downward-pointing arrow. A list of available events for the browser version is displayed. We are going to want our users to be using the browser of version 4.0 or above, so select the menu option *Show Events For | 4.0 and Later Browsers*.

Click on the downward-pointing arrow again and the events available for browsers under version 4.0 and above are listed. Select *onClick*. See figure 9-10.

Fig. 9-10. Behavior window event and behavior.

j) To have the link page (*georgio.html*) open in its own browser window, select *_blank* in the Target pull-down menu in the Property Inspector.

·TiP·

The difference between *onMouseDown* and *onClick* is that *onMouseDown* happens immediately. The user cannot change his mind and move the mouse away from the hypertext. On the other hand, the mouse has to stay over the hypertext as the mouse button is clicked and let up in order for the *onClick* event to execute.

k) Save the file.

l) Preview the page to see how the _blank target opens a new browser window, and to see the size of the window as it opens.

m) Close both browser windows and return to Dreamweaver MX.

4. Now we want to add something so that the user will be able to contact the art museum via e-mail.

a) At the bottom of the page is the name and address of the art center. Highlight the text *Museum of Digital Art*.

b) In the Link field of the Property Inspector, type in *mailto:director@youre-mail.xyz*. There are no spaces in the address, including on either side of the colon (:). To test this, replace *director@youremail.xyz* with your own e-mail address. See figure 9-11.

Fig. 9-11. E-mail link.

c) Save the file.

d) Preview the page and click on the link *Museum of Digital Art* to send an e-mail. Your default e-mail software (if you have set one up on your computer) will open with the e-mail address in the address box.

5. Close the browser window.

6. Close the file *digital.html*.

7. Now we want to make some changes to the *myself* page by adding a Back button to return to the main or previous page, and insert a link to the museum's home page.

a) In the Site panel, locate the *ch09* folder and within it the file named *myself.html*. Double click on *myself.html* to open the file.

b) Currently, this page does not contain linked items. To add a Back button that will return to *digital.html*, move your cursor to the right-hand side of the picture and press the Enter/Return key to move to a new line.

c) On the new line, we will insert an image for the link. We could use Modify | Insert to insert the image and then insert the name of the URL to which to link. Instead, let's create an interactive Rollover button that changes appearance when the mouse rolls over the button. Dreamweaver MX provides a quick method of doing this.

d) Select Insert | Interactive Images | Rollover Image. Fill in the following.

Image Name: Type in *button_back*. JavaScript will use this name.

Original Image: Select Browse and search for the file *back_f1.jpg* in the *ch09* folder. This image is displayed in the normal, or up, state of the button.

Rollover Image: Select Browse and search for the file *back_f2.jpg* in the *ch09* folder. The image is displayed when you roll the cursor over the button

Preload Rollover Image: Should be checked to preload to the user's hard drive as the page is loading. Then the button is ready to change images as soon as the user rolls the mouse over the button.

When Clicked, Go To URL: Select Browse and search for the file *digital.html* in the *ch09* folder. Now when the user clicks the button, the browser displays *digital.html* in the browser window.

Click on OK. See figure 9-12.

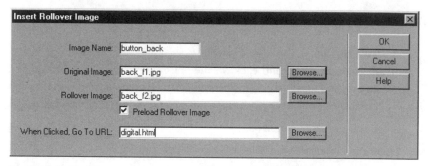

Fig. 9-12. Insert | Interactive Images | Rollover Image completed for exercise.

   e)   To display a tool tip when the user rolls the mouse over your button while the Back button is selected, in the Alt box in the Property Inspector type in *Back*.

8. To place the Back button in the middle of the page, perform one of the following.

   Select the Back button image and then Text Menu | Align | Center

   Select the Back button image and in the Property Inspector click on the Align Center button.

9. Preview the file in a browser by pressing the F12 key. Move the cursor over the *Back* button image and click on the button. The browser opens *digital.html* in the browser window.

10. Close the browser window to return to Dreamweaver MX.

11. Now we need to add what is necessary for the user to be able to jump directly to another site, in this case the site for the art museum.

    a) In the line of text *visit the Museum of Digital Art home page*, highlight the text *www.mda.xyz*. In the Property Inspector, in the Link field, type the complete URL for the site to jump to; in this case, *http://www.mda.xyz*. (This site does not actually exist; so if you would like to test this link, you can use any other valid address.)

    b) To have the link (to page *www.mda.xyz*) open in its own browser window, select *_blank* in the Target pull-down menu.

    c) Preview the page to see how the *_blank* target opens a new browser window with all of its default menu options available.

12. Save the file.

13. Close the file *myself.html*.

14. The Site panel can also create links between files without ever opening the file itself. We will use the Site panel to insert a link to go to the next work of art in the list after *My Self*. It is called *World Without End*, and the HTML file is called *world.html*.

    a) We want to use a site map to view the links between files in *ch09*, so we need to set a file in *ch09* as the home page. Macintosh user, switch your view to the Site panel (Window | Site). On a Windows system, select the Expand button on the Site panel.

    b) In the Site panel, select *digital.html*. Select Site Menu | Set as Home Page.

    c) Select Window Menu | Site Map, or select the Site Map button in the toolbar of the Site panel.

    d) The files linked to *digital.html* are shown in the site map. Select *myself.html* in the site map (not in the file list).

    e) Click the Point to File icon next the the file *digital.html* and while still holding down the mouse on the icon, drag the mouse to the file called *world.html* in the file list (in *ch09*) on the right-hand side of the Site panel. See figure 9-13.

Shortcut

Windows: right click on the file *digital.html* and select Set as Home Page.

Macintosh: Ctrl+click on the file *digital.html* and select Set as Home Page.

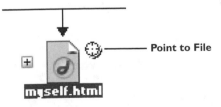

Fig. 9-13. Point to File icon.

f) Open *myself.html*. Notice the text *world.html* at the bottom of the page. It is underlined and colored, indicating that it is a hyperlink. When using the Point to File icon, a hyperlink is inserted in the file. The name of the file you pointed to becomes the text of the hyperlink. This is a quick way to insert links to a lot of files. You can then change the text and its position.

g) Change the text *world.html* to *Next Artwork*.

h) Save the file.

i) Close *myself.html*.

15. On your own site, now would be a good time to select File Menu | Check Links (in the Site panel). Any items linked to external URLs should show up in External Links. Links with just the anchor tag (*<a>*) but no URL (a # sign is in the Link field) will also show in Broken Links. These are actually okay. Any other links should be checked. Chapter 23 goes into more detail about checking links on a site.

Summary

- *Files can be linked to one another and to media assets such as images, video, sounds, and animation.*

- *The properties of links may be changed using the Page Properties option for the default colors and the Property Inspector to change individual links.*

- *Links can be removed and created using the Site panel.*

- *A linked file may replace the file in the current browser window. Alternately, you can set the target to _blank to open the linked file in its own window. Behaviors can be attached to the link to open the new window without menus and at a specific size.*

- *When you rename a file in the Site panel, any links to that file with the new name can be updated automatically by Dreamweaver MX to minimize broken links. Refrain from renaming files outside Dreamweaver MX, because Dreamweaver MX will not be able to track the changes and the links will be broken.*

- *Did you notice that the pages on the Works of Art have the same format? They are good examples of pages created based on a template. In the DWcomplete site, the remaining "works of art" pages are based on a template.*

CHAPTER

10

Working with Tables

Introduction

Trying to design and creatively place graphics and text on your web pages without the use of tables can sometimes be frustrating. Without tables and the alignment tools tables provide, all elements (text, graphics, and so on) are limited to being lined up left to right, top to bottom. The arrangement is systematic but generally not very interesting to view.

Tables provide the means to creatively position elements in a nonlinear fashion and to control the layout of web pages. The format (columns and rows) of a table is similar to the format of a spreadsheet program. With the use of tables, you can lay out a web page much like you would design a document for a newsletter. HTML tables have many of the same properties as other software programs that use tables.

A cell is defined by the intersection of a row and a column. Cells can be merged or split. Tables can be nested within one another and can have borders. Tables can also be sorted and contain row or column headers. In addition, background images can be placed within a cell or within the entire table. By the end of the chapter you will be able to:

- Insert a table into an HTML page
- Select a table and table cells, rows, and columns
- Use the following formatting capabilities and properties associated with tables:
  - Borders
  - Background images
  - Width and height size
  - Vertical and horizontal alignment of content in cells
  - Cell pad and cell space
- Split and merge cells
- Set cell and row headers
- Sort tables
- Use the Table view (Layout and Standard views) to draw a table or cell on a page and modify areas of the table
- Use the options in the Property Inspector and menus for tables
- Recognize HTML for tables

Tables Overview

In Chapter 18 you will be introduced to layers. A layer is another HTML feature that allows you to freely position elements on a web page, including placing elements on top of each other. But viewing web pages with layers is limited to those using newer versions of the most popular browsers – and there are still a significant number of users out there using older-version browsers. In addition, layers are a little more temperamental than tables and can sometimes become difficult to work in combination with other elements on your page.

The alternative to layers (and a very efficient alternative at that) is using tables. The majority of web pages on the Internet use one or more tables. Tables are not sensitive to browser type and version, and they are virtually invisible to the average Internet user. Figure 10-1 shows a page that has a table in it as viewed in the Dreamweaver MX Document window and as viewed in a browser. With borders turned off, the user will not see the lines separating the rows and columns, although they are there for you to use while creating the web page.

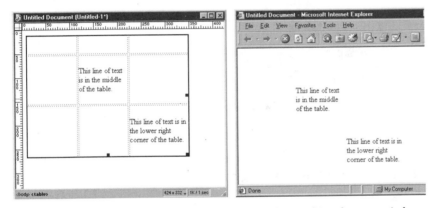

Fig. 10-1. HTML page with table in a Document window and in a browser window.

Creating a Table

A page can contain one or more tables, and tables can be nested inside each other. Tables consist of rows, columns, and cells – all with their own set of properties, including background color, alignment, and width. There are three ways to create tables in Dreamweaver MX, as follows.

- *Using the Insert menu*
- *Selecting Insert bar | Tables*
- *Drawing a table with the Layout Table tool*

Insert | Table and Insert Bar

This is the standard way of creating tables. To use these options, you must be in the Standard view. To select Standard view, you can select View Menu | Table

View | Standard View or use the Insert bar and select Layout | Standard View. See figure 10-2.

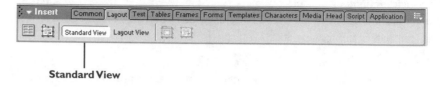

Standard View

Fig. 10-2. Insert bar | Common | Standard View.

Place the cursor where you want the table and then select Insert Menu | Table or Insert Bar | Tables | Insert Table. When you select Insert Table, you will be prompted for the number of rows and columns for the table. See figure 10-3.

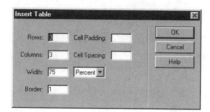

Fig. 10-3. Insert Table prompt.

There are additional properties to set when inserting a table. They are the spacing between cells (cell padding and cell spacing), table width, and border width.

Space Between Cells

Cell padding: Number of pixels between the edge (border) of the cell and the cell's content. This is especially useful if you are using borders in your table and do not want the content too close to the border. Default value is one (1) pixel. Note that a null (or blank) cell padding actually defaults to one (1) pixel. Enter zero (0) for no cell padding.

Cell spacing: Number of pixels between table cells. Default value is one (1) pixel. Note that a null (or blank) cell padding actually defaults to one (1) pixel. Enter zero (0) for no cell spacing.

Width: Width of the entire table in pixels or percentage of the browser window. If you want a fixed width that does not change with the size of the browser window, enter the width in pixels. To let the table expand with the size of the browser window (or size of the user's monitor resolution), enter a percentage in the Width box. If you want the table to fill the width of the window, set the width to 90%, not 100%, to compensate for task bars and other floating panels on users' machines.

Border: Width (number of pixels) of the border around the table and its cells. The default value is one (1). Enter zero (0) for no border. After the table has been created, use the Property Inspector to set the color of the border.

Draw Layout Table/Cell

Probably the easiest way to lay out areas of your page for text and graphics and other visible elements is to draw a table and its cells with the Draw Layout tools. While in the Layout view, the Draw Layout Table tool lets you draw a table with your mouse. When you first draw the table, it will not contain any cells and will be gray in color. You can then draw cells anywhere within the table using the Draw Layout Cell tool. You can access the Layout view and Draw Layout tools from Insert bar | Layout. See figure 10-4.

Draw Layout Table

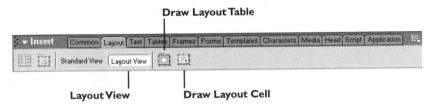

Layout View   **Draw Layout Cell**

Fig. 10-4. Insert bar | Layout view.

Summary Steps to Create Table and Cells in Layout View

1. Change to Layout view by selecting View | Table View | Layout View or by using the Insert bar and selecting Layout | Layout View.

2. Select Draw Layout Table in the Insert bar.

3. Move the cursor to where you want to begin the table. Hold down the mouse as you draw a rectangle for the table. The mouse cursor (pointer) turns into a plus (+) symbol to let you know that the Draw tool is selected and that the area you are creating the table in is valid. At first, if you have difficulty drawing the table, move the cursor until the plus (+) symbol appears – then draw.

4. To create a cell within a table, select the Draw Layout Cell tool in the Insert bar.

5. Move the cursor to the area on the screen where you want the cell and hold down the mouse while you draw a rectangular area for the cell. If you draw a cell outside a table, another table is automatically created around the cell.

·T/P·

Note that you cannot draw a table next to another table or inside an existing paragraph (*<p>* tag), even if it is a blank line.

When you draw cells, a grid of rows and columns is created in the table. The cells can span several rows and columns. If cells are drawn close to other cells, they will automatically snap to the existing cells. New cells will also automatically snap to the side of the table or page if they are drawn close to the edge. Figure 10-5 shows a table with many cells that span columns and rows. The gray areas do not contain cells and cannot contain content.

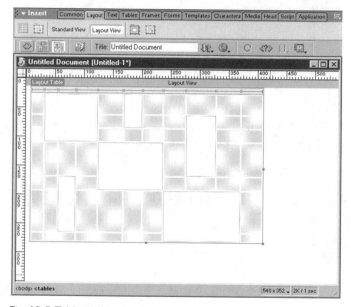

Fig. 10-5. Table in Layout view.

Selecting Tables, Cells, Rows, and Columns

To set the properties for a table, you must first select the table or a portion of the table. You can select a table either in Standard view or in Layout view.

Selecting Tables in Standard View

Selecting an entire table: To select an entire table, perform one of the following.

- *Click on a row or column border, or the top left, bottom, or right edge of the table.*

- *Place the cursor in one of the cells in the table. Select Modify Menu | Table | Select Table. The shortcut key is Control/Command + A.*

- *Right mouse click (Mac, Opt + click) on one of the cells and select Table | Select Table.*

- *Place the cursor in one of the cells in the table. Use the Status bar and select the last <Table> tag.*

Selecting rows and columns in Standard view: Selecting rows and columns in Standard view is much like selecting them in a spreadsheet application. Move the cursor to just above the top cell of a column until the cursor turns into a downward-pointing arrow and then click. The entire column should now be selected.

A row can be selected the same way as a column, except that you must move the cursor to the left-hand side of the table at the edge of a row until a right arrow appears – then click. The entire row should now be selected. You may find that an easier way to select a row is to place the cursor in a cell within the row you want to select and select the row *<tr>* tag in the Document Status bar. See figure 10-6.

‹body› ‹table› ‹tr› **‹td›**		510 x 351 ⌄	1K / 1 sec

Fig. 10-6. Status Bar with Table Tags in the document.

Selecting a cell: To select a cell in Standard view, place the cursor in the cell, and in the Document Status bar, select the last cell *<td>* tag you see.

Selecting multiple adjacent cells: To select multiple adjacent cells in Standard view, drag the cursor to highlight the cells. Alternatively, select a cell and hold down the Shift key and select another cell. All cells between the two selected cells will also be selected.

Selecting multiple cells – not adjacent: To select one or more cells that are not adjacent to each other, use the Control/Command key to select/deselect each cell.

Selecting Tables in Layout View

Selecting an entire table: To select an entire table in Layout view, perform one of the following.

• *Click on the Table tab at the top of the table.*
• *Click in an empty (non-layout) area of the table.*
• *Use the Status bar and select the <Table> tag after the cursor is placed in a table cell.*

Selecting rows and columns: A row can only be selected in Layout view by selecting the row *<tr>* tag in the Status bar. Columns cannot be selected in Layout view.

Selecting a cell: To select a cell in Layout view, hold down the Control/Command key and click on the cell, or click on the border (edge of a cell), or select the cell *<td>* tag in the Status bar. A selected cell will be outlined in blue. This color can be modified in Preferences | Layout View.

·T/P·

Use the Status bar to select a table row. The *<tr>* tag represents a row.

·T/P·

The *<td>* tag can be selected in the Status bar to select a table cell.

·T/P·

To select an entire table cell in Layout view, hold down the Control/Command key and click on the cell.

Selecting multiple cells: Multiple cells cannot be selected in Layout view unless they are in the same row – and then you have to select the entire row.

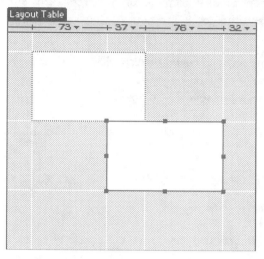

Fig. 10-7. A selected cell in Layout view.

Formatting a Table

Tables can be formatted and modified while in Standard or Layout view. Standard view has the options for formatting the look of the cells and selecting entire rows and columns. Layout view gives you the option to work with individual cells.

·T*i*P·

Layout view lets you move a table cell by just dragging it.

While in Layout view, cells can be moved to another location within the same table by selecting the edge of the cell and dragging the cell to its new position. The table will automatically add, delete, and resize rows and columns to accommodate the cell.

A cell can also be resized in Layout view by dragging the selection handles around the cell after the cell has been selected. This is quicker than typing a specific number in the Property Inspector, but may not be as accurate if you are trying to lay out your table according to the sizes of images and other elements on the page.

Table Tab

The Property Inspector is the primary tool for modifying and viewing properties of a table. In Layout view, you can also see the width of columns in the Table tab and set some properties that are not available in the Property Inspector. The Table tab appears at the top of all tables while in Layout view.

These tabs can be turned off in Edit | Preferences | Layout View. The width of the column is also shown in the Table tab. Let's take a closer look at the Table tab. See figure 10-8.

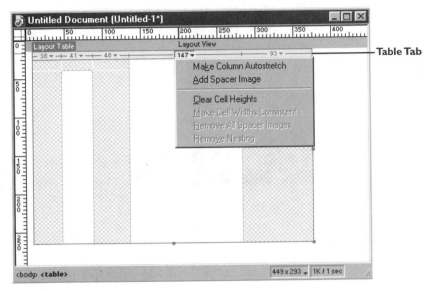

Fig. 10-8. Table tab and Column Header menu.

Autostretch

If there is a squiggly line in the Table tab, that means the column has been set to Autostretch (resize) with the size of the browser window. See figure 10-9 for an example. Autostretch will "stretch" a table to fill a specified percentage of the browser window. This is especially useful if you want a column to automatically widen to fill a browser window so that there will not be a lot of blank space to the side of the cell. But there are times when you may not want to use the Autostretch feature. For example, if a block of text is set to align with the edges of a graphic, you may not want the width of the cell with the text in it to change (widen) so that the text expands past the width of the graphic.

·T*i*P·

You can also set a column to Autostretch in the Property Inspector by first selecting the column and then selecting Autostretch.

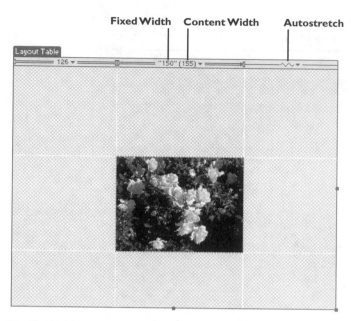

Fig. 10-9. Table tab with column widths, actual and set width.

To set a column to Autostretch, click on the Column Header menu at the top of the column and select Make Column Autostretch. Only one column per table can be set to Autostretch. If the table contains any nested tables within or spanning this column, they are automatically set to Autostretch. To create the autostretch, Dreamweaver MX sets the width of the column to 100%. This forces the column to stretch across any area of the browser window not taken up by another column. In Standard view, setting the column or table width to 100% will also set Autostretch.

Spacer Image

The Table tab also has the Add Spacer Image option. This option is not available for columns set to Autostretch. The spacer image is a transparent (GIF) image named *spacer.gif*. It is placed on your hard drive when you install Dreamweaver MX. If you choose Add Spacer Image, you are prompted to copy *spacer.gif* to your site or select your own spacer image. Unless you have an image of a specific size or appearance that you want to use, use the default image. The original size of *spacer.gif* is 1 pixel, but this can be reset within Dreamweaver MX to any size you need to force a column's width and height.

The advantage to inserting spacer images is that they lock in the minimum width of a column or height of a row. If you do not use spacer images and a column does not have content and does not have a fixed width, the column will disappear when viewed in the browser. Rows will disappear without content and a fixed height. Spacers are also used so that a column/row has a minimum size that will not change no matter how small a browser window is. This keeps blocks of text from becoming too narrow.

Other Table Options

Clear Cell Heights (Table tab) and Clear Cell Widths (Modify | Table) remove the pixel and percentage value of all cells in the table. These functions are useful when you have added new content or replaced images/animation and the previous height and width settings (usually when they were larger) do not work well in terms of the alignment and layout.

Clear Row Heights and Clear Column Widths (Property Inspector) remove the pixel and percentage value of all rows/columns in the table. This is the same as Clear Cell Heights and Clear Cell Widths, respectively. These features, along with the Make Cell Widths Consistent, allow you to quickly add uniformity to your table layout.

Make Cell Widths Consistent (Table tab) sets the width of all cells to match the content in that cell. If you have set the width of a cell/column to a fixed width and then insert content that is wider than the fixed width, two numbers appear in the Table tab (Layout view). The actual size of the content appears in parentheses and the fixed size you set appears in quote marks. Make Cell Widths Consistent sets the fixed width to the actual size of the content. Only one number (the actual or content width) then appears in the Table tab.

Property Inspector for a Table

The Property Inspector has different options for a table, depending upon whether you are in Layout or Standard view. Let's take a closer look at these properties and how they affect how a table is viewed in a browser – and how different browsers display tables. See figure 10-10.

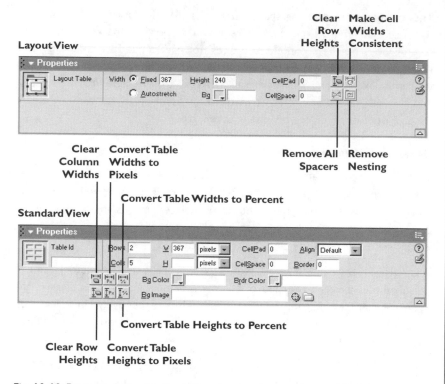

Fig. 10-10. Property Inspector for tables showing Layout view and Standard view.

Table | Rows and Columns: Displays the number of rows and columns in the selected table. Enter larger numbers to add rows at the bottom of the table or columns to the right of it. Enter smaller numbers to remove rows from the bottom of the table or columns from its right side.

Table | Bg Image: Sets a background image for the entire table. If the image is not as wide as the table, the image will begin to repeat (tile) itself behind the entire table in Internet Explorer 3.0 and higher. In Netscape 4.0, the image tiles itself between each individual column that has content in it. If the column does not have content, the background image will not be displayed in that column. Notice in figure 10-11 that the background image is not smooth in Netscape as it tiles from column to column. To remove the background image, delete the file name in the Bg Image box of the Property Inspector.

·TIP·

Placing a layout cell in every column of a table forces the background image to tile the width of the table.

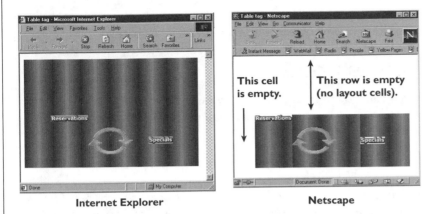

Internet Explorer   **Netscape**

Fig. 10-11. Background image set for a table.

Table/Cell/Row/Column | Bg | Background URL of Cell: Sets a background image for a cell. If an entire row or column is selected, this image tiles in each cell and restarts the tile from column to column within Netscape (just like the background image for the table). Internet Explorer does not support background images for rows. Instead, the background image would need to be set for every cell in the row.

Table/Cell/Row/Column | Bg | Background Color: Sets the color of a table/cell/row/column. Setting the background color of a cell will override the color set in the row or table.

Table/Cell/Row/Column | Brdr | Border Color: Only sets the border color if the border is a number greater than zero (0). If the table also has a border color set, the cell border color will display inside the table border color. Although table border color is supported in Netscape, cell border color is not supported.

Cell/Row/Column | Merge and Splitting Cells | Span: To make a cell larger within a table, the cell is merged with other cells while in Standard view. This is also called spanning rows or columns. You only have to select a single cell to span to the next row or column by selecting Modify Menu | Table | Increase Row/Column Span. You cannot span a cell past the width of a table. To merge cells, you select two or more cells and then select Modify | Table | Merge Cells, or use Property Inspector | Merge Selected Cells.

To split a single cell into one or more rows or columns, select the cell and then select Modify Menu | Table | Split Cell, or use Property Inspector | Split Cells Tool. Any cell can be split. Decrease Row | Column Span is used for a single cell and can only be applied to cells that have been merged or had their span increased.

Cell/Row/Column | Header: Sets the selected row or column as the table header. The content in table headers is centered and bold by default.

Working with Tables

Creating and modifying tables in Dreamweaver MX is easy and relatively quick to do. However, there are a few things you need to remember when working with tables.

* *Tables cannot be next to each other unless the two (or more) tables are nested inside the same table.*

* *Borders apply to the entire table. You cannot have borders turned on/off for just a cell. However, you can insert a table inside a table to make it look as though a single cell has borders.*

* *The width of the first row in a table sets the rest of the cells in the column.*

* *The height of the first column in a table sets the rest of the cells in the row.*

HTML for Tables

HTML ◁▷

It would be a good idea to become familiar with the HTML code for tables, as they will take up a large area of your HTML code. Each cell has its own tag area, as does each row and entire table. Dreamweaver MX does not automatically insert column tags. All column properties are applied to each cell within each column.

```
<table width="422" border="4" cellpadding="0" cellspacing="0" height="262" bordercolor="#FFCC66">
  <tr>
    <td width="58" height="69"></td>
    <td width="91"></td>
    <td width="140" background="tile.png" bgcolor="#CC00FF"></td>
    <td width="117" bgcolor="#FF6699"></td>
  </tr>
  <tr>
    <td height="55" width="58" bgcolor="#009900"></td>
    <td valign="top" width="91" bgcolor="#009900"><img src="text.png" width="91" height="15"></td>
    <td bgcolor="#009900" width="140"><img src="box.gif" width="107" height="64"></td>
    <td bordercolor="#CC0066" bgcolor="#FF6699"><img src="text.png" width="59" height="17"></td>
  </tr>
</table>
```

Fig. 10-12. Example of HTML for a table containing two rows, four columns, and eight cells.

The following is an example of HTML code for a simple table.

```
<table width="500" border="0">
```

This code defines the start of the table and specifies that the table be 500 pixels in width with a border width of zero pixels (no border). The following code further defines the table.

```
<tr>
  <td> </td>
  <td width="50"> </td>
  <td> </td>
</tr>
```

This code defines the table as follows.

- *The <tr> tag defines the beginning of a row.*
- *The </tr> tag defines the end of the row. Everything between the <tr> and </tr> tags is within the same row.*
- *The <td> and </td> tags define a cell. These tags will always be inside the <tr> begin and end tags (for the row). The   is a nonbreaking space in the cell and nothing else.*
- *The defined cell is 50 pixels in width. This sets the column width. However, the 50-pixel width will be overridden if another cell in the same column has a larger width.*
- *The three <td> tags inside the <tr> and </tr> tags signify that there are three cells (or columns) in this row.*

Each of the previous cells has a height of 50 pixels, which sets the height of the row, as follows.

```
<tr>
  <td height="50"> </td>
  <td height="50"> </td>
  <td height="50"> </td>
```

The following is the end of the table.

```
  </tr>
</table>
```

Menu Options for Tables

Sort Table

Tables are sorted by column. To sort a table, select the table or place the cursor somewhere within the table and select Commands Menu | Sort Table. You will be prompted for the number of columns to sort and the sort order: numerically or alphabetically, and ascending or descending. The option Keep TR Attributes With Sorted Row keeps the properties of sorted rows with individual cells. TR is the row tag.

Format Table

Dreamweaver MX provides preset formats for tables, including sorting, text formatting, and color schemes. Select Commands Menu | Format Table. You can always use Format Table as a starting point for your table and then change any of the attributes after the initial table has been formatted. This is especially useful if rows alternate colors or text styles. See figure 10-13.

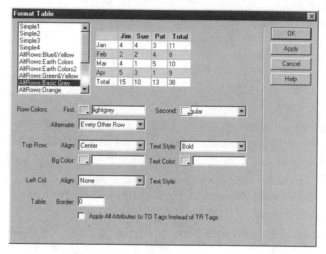

Fig. 10-13. Format Table menu option.

Practice Exercise 10-1: Building a Table

Description

The Internet Training Company wants to list a schedule of the classes they offer. The company wants to include the names of the courses, the days each course is taught, and the hours the classes are held. The page should also include the name of the company, the company's logo, and some contact information. The graphics for the header, logo, and contact information have already been created for you.

In addition, the company would like the major burgundy color that appears in all graphics to extend the width of the browser window, no matter what size the window is. This color should appear in the header and footer, where the contact information is displayed. The following elements are covered in this exercise.

• *Creating tables using the Standard view and Layout view*

• *Nesting tables*

- *Selecting a table and its cells, rows, and columns*
- *Formatting a table's width and height*
- *Setting the table properties for borders, colors, and table headers*
- *Using the Layout view to add a table and cells*

Take a Look

Before beginning this exercise, let's take a look at the exercise in its completed state so that you can clearly see what it is you are about to build.

 CD-ROM

 DWComplete Site

1. Select the site *DWComplete*.

2. Locate the *ch10* folder and within it the file named *dw10ex1.html*. Double click on *dw10ex1.html* to open the file.

3. The file *dw10ex1.html* should now appear in your copy of Dreamweaver. This web page lists the classes at Internet Training, Inc.

    a) Make sure you are in Standard view by selecting View Menu | Table View | Standard View or by selecting Insert bar | Layout | Standard View.

    b) There are two tables on this page. The outermost table contains the interface for the page: a header graphic, a left tab graphic, and a bottom graphic with contact information. This table does not have borders. The contact for the page is inside another table, which does have borders.

    c) Select the outermost table by clicking on the right-hand edge of the table with the mouse. In the Property Inspector, the table width is set to 100% and the border is set to 0 (zero, or no border). There are four rows and three columns. You probably cannot even tell that there is a fourth row because it is only one pixel in height and is at the bottom of the table. For this table, the last row forces the fixed widths of the columns and the percentage width for an Autostretch column.

    d) Place the cursor in the upper right-hand cell. This cell looks like it has a burgundy graphic in it. In the Property Inspector, the Bg (Background URL of cell) box contains a URL. There is no image in this cell. The lower right-hand cell (in burgundy) has the same settings.

    e) Select the graphic with the *Internet Training, Inc.* title in it. Notice that it does not fill the cell, yet the cell still has a burgundy image in the entire cell. The Property Inspector shows a background image in that cell. This is also the same for the cell with the image for the contact information.

f) Select the innermost table with the list of classes by clicking on one of the borders of the table. Open the Property Inspector (Window | Properties) and notice that the border is set to 1 (one). Select a cell or column in this table and notice the fixed amount.

g) Change to Layout view by selecting View | Table View | Layout View.

h) Two Table tabs should be displayed on screen. Make sure View | Table View | Show Layout Table Tabs is checked.

i) By looking at the Table tabs you can tell how many columns are in each table. There are three columns in the outermost table. There are three columns in the *list of classes* table.

j) The large table also has a squiggly line at the top of one of the columns in the Table tab. This means that the column is set to Autostretch. Autostretch sets each cell in the Autostretch column to have a width of 100%. This column will expand/retract to force the table to fill 100% of the browser window, no matter what its size. (You may need to widen the Document window to see the third column.)

k) Close the current document (*dw10ex1.html*).

Storyboard: On Screen

Figure 10-14 shows you how the finished page will look when viewed through a browser.

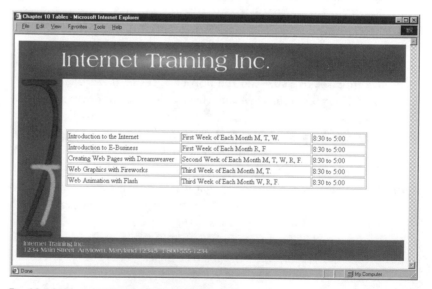

Fig. 10-14. Completed exercise within a browser.

Storyboard: Behind the Scenes

Figure 10-15 shows some of the key HTML code behind the tables.

```
<table border="0" cellpadding="0" cellspacing="0" width="100%">
  <tr>
    <td background="tile.jpg" height="86" valign="top" colspan="2"><img src="itinc.jpg"
width="680" height="86"></td>
    <td width="100%" background="tile.jpg" valign="top"> </td>
  </tr>
  <tr>
    <td height="360" width="110" valign="top"><img src="itlogo.jpg" width="100"
height="360"></td>
    <td width="702">
    <table border="1">
      <tr>
        <td width="255">Introduction to the Internet</td>
        <td width="295">First Week of Each Month M, T, W.</td>
        <td width="119">8:30 to 5:00</td>
      </tr>
      <tr>
        <td width="255">Introduction to E-Business</td>
        <td width="295">First Week of Each Month R, F</td>
        <td width="119">8:30 to 5:00</td>
      </tr>
      <tr>
        <td width="255">Creating Web Pages with Dreamweaver</td>
        <td width="295">Second Week of Each Month M, T, W, R, F.</td>
        <td width="119">8:30 to 5:00</td>
      </tr>
      <tr>
        <td width="255">Web Graphics with Fireworks</td>
        <td width="295">Third Week of Each Month M, T.</td>
        <td width="119">8:30 to 5:00</td>
      </tr>
      <tr>
        <td width="255">Web Animation with Flash</td>
        <td width="295">Third Week of Each Month W, R, F.</td>
        <td width="119">8:30 to 5:00</td>
      </tr>
    </table>
    </td>
    <td></td>
  </tr>
  <tr>
    <td height="47" colspan="2" valign="top" background="tile.jpg"><img src="itaddr.jpg"
width="680" height="47"></td>
    <td background="tile.jpg"></td>
  </tr>
  <tr>
    <td height="1"><img height="1" width="110" src="/ch10/spacer.gif"></td>
    <td><img height="1" width="702" src="/ch10/spacer.gif"></td>
    <td></td>
  </tr>
</table>
```

Fig. 10-15. HTML for completed exercise.

Step-by-Step Instructions

1. We are going to start with a new file.

    a) Make sure you are in the *DWExercises* site. Use the Site panel to select the *ch10* folder.

    b) While the *ch10* folder is selected/highlighted, using the menus in the Site panel, select File Menu | New File.

    c) Type in the name of the file, *classsch.html*. Be sure to type in the extension *.html*, as Dreamweaver MX will not automatically add the extension when files are created this way with the File menu. You should now have a file called *classsch.html* in the *ch10* folder of the site *DWExercises*.

Go Solo

DWExercises Site

·T/P·

For this exercise, make sure your monitor resolution is set to at least 800 x 600 pixels.

2. Double click on the file *classsch.html* to open it.

3. We will use a table for the class schedule. Because this main table will have borders, another table will be needed for the header, logo, and contact information that will surround the class schedule. We will create the main table first – in Layout view, so that we can draw the cells freeform anywhere on the page.

    a) To change to Layout view, select View Menu | Table View | Layout View, or select the Layout View button in the Insert bar. See figure 10-16.

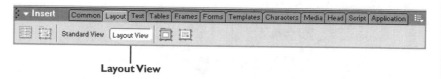

Layout View

Fig. 10-16. Insert bar | Layout | Layout View button.

    b) Within Insert bar | Layout, select the Draw Layout Cell button. See figure 10-17. The cursor will change to a plus (+) to indicate you are ready to draw a cell.

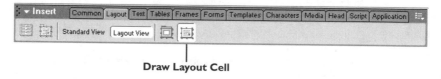

Draw Layout Cell

Fig. 10-17. Draw Layout Cell button in Insert bar.

    c) We are going to draw three cells, one right after the other: one for the header at the top of the screen, one for the logo underneath the cell but tall and narrow on the left side of the screen, and one at the bottom of the screen for the contact information.

Let's draw the header cell. The Draw Layout Cell button should be still selected. Hold down the mouse and draw a rectangle from the upper left-hand corner to the middle of the page. As soon as you let go of the mouse, the cell is created within a table. Do not worry if a column is created to the left of the cell. This just means you did not start drawing the cell all the way over to the edge of the page. You can select Undo (Control/Command + Z) to redraw the cell. To make the cell you have created align with the left-hand side of the table, select the edge of the cell with your cursor and drag one of the left selection tools to the left-hand side of the table to resize the cell. The table should only have two columns and two rows when you have drawn this first cell. See figure 10-18.

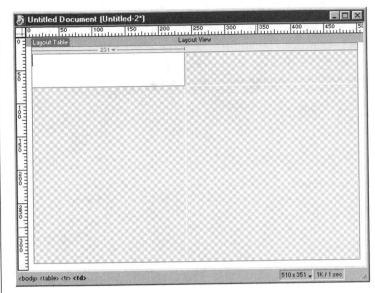

Fig. 10-18. Table with header cell only.

Let's draw the cell for the logo. Select the Draw Layout Cell button again, but this time as you draw the cell hold down the Control/Command key as you draw each cell so that you do not have to keep selecting the Draw Layout Cell button. Draw the tall narrow cell starting on the left-hand side of the table under the header cell and down to about the middle of the table. See figure 10-19.

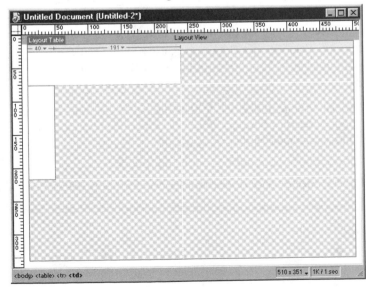

Fig. 10-19. Table with header and logo cells.

Let's now draw the cell for the contact information. Draw a cell on the left-hand side of the table, under the logo cell and the same width as the header cell. The bottom of the table has a gray area without cells. See figure 10-20.

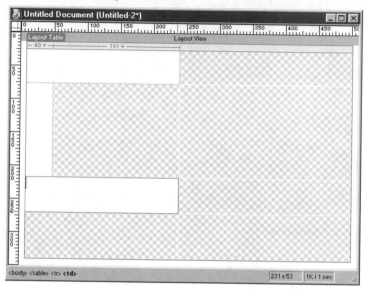

Fig. 10-20. Table with header, logo, and contact information cells.

4. Now let's check the table in Standard view. Select View Menu | Table View | Standard View. To select the table, click on the right-hand edge of the table. The table should have three rows and two columns. Use the Property Inspector to check the number of rows and columns. If your table does not look like that shown in figure 10-20 and has the wrong number of rows and columns, change back to Layout view and perform one of the following.

- *To remove any columns, resize cells to span the column you want to delete. Resize a cell by selecting the edge of the cell with your cursor and dragging one of the selection tools on the side of the cell.*

- *To get rid of a row, resize a cell to span the row you do not want.*

- *To add a row, resize a cell to make it smaller and a new row will be created. See figure 10-21.*

Fig. 10-21. Table in Standard view with header, logo, and contact information cells created.

5. Save the file.

6. Now we have to create the table for the list of classes. It will go into the cell in row 2, column 2. Because the table is a straightforward tabular table, we will use the Insert menu to create it.

   a) Place your cursor in the cell in row 2, column 2. Select Insert Menu | Table.

   b) You will be prompted for the number of rows and columns. Type in *3* for columns, *5* for rows, *100* for percent width, and *1* for border. Cell spacing and cell padding should be empty (blank).

   c) A table should now be displayed in the middle cell. The table fills the cell (100% width) and has borders.

7. Save the file.

8. Preview the file in a browser by pressing the F12 key. There is no content, but you should see a table with borders somewhere in the middle of the screen.

9. Close the browser window to return to Dreamweaver MX.

10. Now you are ready to place the content. The header, logo, and contact information are all images. The images were copied to the *ch10* folder when the files were copied to your hard drive in the first chapter.

    a) To insert the header image, place the cursor in the top cell and select Insert Menu | Image or Insert bar | Common | Insert Image button. If the image was not already located in the local site, you would receive a pop-up window asking if you want to save the image in the site folder.

b) Locate and select the file *itinc.jpg* in the *ch10* folder within the *Learning_Dreamweaver* folder on your hard drive.

c) For the logo, place the cursor in the cell in row 2, column 1, and select the Insert Image button from the Insert bar. Locate and select the file *itlogo.jpg* in the *ch10* folder within the *Learning_Dreamweaver* folder.

d) For the contact information graphic, we will insert the image another way. In your Site panel, with the *DWExercises* site open, open the folder *ch10*. Drag the file called *itaddr.jpg* from the Site panel to the bottom row of the table.

e) Save the file and preview it. Notice if there are any white spaces between the graphics. We will clean up the table later in the exercise. Exit the browser window.

Shortcut

To insert an image, drag an image from the Assets panel.

Fig. 10-22. Table with images and nested table.

11. Before we start cleaning up the table, let's put the entries in the class schedule table. When you get ready to enter the first information into the third column, it may have become too small for you to place the cursor. You can resize the columns in the table by dragging the border between columns. See figure 10-23.

a) Type the following entries in row 1 of the Class Schedule table.

Column 1: Introduction to the Internet

Column 2: First Week of Each Month M, T, W.

Column 3: 8:30 to 5:00

b)   Type the following entries in row 2 of the Class Schedule table.

    Column 1: Introduction to E-Business

    Column 2: First Week of Each Month R, F.

    Column 3: 8:30 to 5:00

c)   Type the following entries in row 3 of the Class Schedule table.

    Column 1: Creating Web Pages with Dreamweaver MX

    Column 2: Second Week of Each Month M, T, W, R, F.

    Column 3: 8:30 to 5:00

d)   Type the following entries in row 4 of the Class Schedule table.

    Column 1: Web Graphics with Fireworks

    Column 2: Third Week of Each Month M, T.

    Column 3: 8:30 to 5:00

e)   Type the following entries in row 5 of the Class Schedule table.

    Column 1: Web Animation with Flash

    Column 2: Third Week of Each Month W, R, F.

    Column 3: 8:30 to 5:00

Introduction to the Internet	First Week of Each Month M, T, W.	8:30 to 5:00
Introduction to E-Business	First Week of Each Month R, F	8:30 to 5:00
Creating Web Pages with Dreamweaver	Second Week of Each Month M, T, W, R, F.	8:30 to 5:00
Web Graphics with Fireworks	Third Week of Each Month M, T.	8:30 to 5:00
Web Animation with Flash	Third Week of Each Month W, R, F.	8:30 to 5:00

Fig. 10-23. Class Schedule table.

f)   Save the file.

12. Let's clean up the tables.

13. To remove space between cells so that graphics will display next to each other, the cell padding and cell spacing need to be set to zero (0). This is probably needed for the graphics, the header image, logo/side image, and contact information. Select the entire table the images are in and make sure the Cell Space and Cell Pad options are set to 0. The easiest way to select the entire table is to click on a column divider or select the *<table>* tag in the Dreamweaver MX Status bar.

14. We do not want the content in the Class Schedule table to wrap within a cell. Therefore, the table will have to be wider. To allow the table to get wider, the main table it is nested in will also need to be widened.

a) Select the main table with the images in it by clicking on one of the cell dividers in the table.

b) Drag the selection handles to the right to widen the outer table. Widen the columns in the inside (nested) table until the text in the class list does not wrap. You can also use the Property Inspector and enter the new width for each column. The table should have a width of about 775 pixels.

15. There needs to be some space between the logo image and the Class Schedule table. The width of the logo image is 100 pixels (you can find that information by selecting the image and looking at the Property Inspector). We will put an extra 10 pixels to the right of the image by setting the column width to 110.

a) Place the cursor in the cell with the logo and select the cell *<td>* tag in the Status bar (at the bottom of the Document window) to make sure you have the cell selected and not the image.

b) In the Property Inspector, type *110* in the width (W) box. If the cell width does not change, you may need to widen the main table to give the column room to grow.

16. The last row is probably larger than it needs to be. It only needs to be as tall as the contact image.

a) Select the last row of the table by placing the cursor in the last row and selecting the row *<tr>* tag in the Status bar. The contact image has a height of 47 pixels.

b) In the Property Inspector, type 47 in the height (H) box. See figure 10-24.

·T/P·

When changing a table's width from pixels to percent, delete the width (W) number first, and then change to pixels or percent. Alternatively, select Convert Table Widths to Pixels/ Percent in the Property Inspector.

·T/P·

For background images to tile correctly from cell to cell, the tag for the background image should be within each cell tag (<td>). It does not work correctly for all browsers if the property is inside the row tag (<tr>).

Introduction to the Internet	First Week of Each Month M, T, W.	8:30 to 5:00
Introduction to E-Business	First Week of Each Month R, F	8:30 to 5:00
Creating Web Pages with Dreamweaver	Second Week of Each Month M, T, W, R, F.	8:30 to 5:00
Web Graphics with Fireworks	Third Week of Each Month M, T.	8:30 to 5:00
Web Animation with Flash	Third Week of Each Month W, R, F.	8:30 to 5:00

Internet Training Inc.
1234 Main Street Anytown, Maryland 12345 1-800-555-1234

Fig. 10-24. Table after changing the width of the outer table.

17. Save the file and preview it. This would be a good time to preview the page in Netscape and in Internet Explorer, because the two browsers display tables differently, depending on what is in the table. This will become an issue later, when we place a background image in the cells. Exit the browser.

18. The company wanted the burgundy in the header and contact images to extend the width of the table. To do that we will set the cell's background image to a small image that is only 40 x 40 pixels. To display the background image seamlessly from cell to cell, we will set each cell in the row to have a background image.

    a) Place the cursor in the rightmost cell of the top row. This cell is empty. To select all cells in the current row, click on the row *<tr>* tag in the Status bar. The Property Inspector will now reference the row.

    b) In the Property Inspector, next to the Bg (background image for row), select the Browse button. Locate and select the file *tile.jpg* in the *ch10* folder. The right-hand cell in the top row now is filled with the burgundy tile.

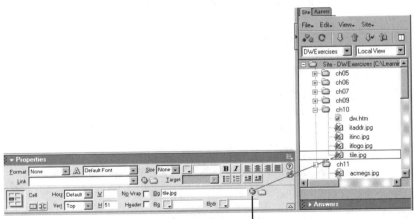

Cell and Point to File Button

Fig. 10-25. Property Inspector | Table Cell (and Point to File).

·T/P·

Another way to place a background image in the cell is to use the Point to File icon on the Property Inspector and drag it to the image to use in the Site panel. See figure 10-25.

    c) Save the file and preview in Internet Explorer. The top cell extends its burgundy color past the right-hand edge of the class schedule. Exit the browser.

    d) Preview in Netscape. If you do not have Netscape set up as a browser, select File Menu | Preview in Browser | Edit Browser List and add Netscape to the list of browsers. (It is included on your Dreamweaver MX software CD.) When previewed in Netscape, the background image will not display unless there is content in the cell.

We will fix this by placing layout cells in the last column of the table. Exit the browser.

19. We will force the background image to tile the full width of the table, but keep a fixed width on the first two columns so that the class list schedule table does not change size with the browser window size.

In our exercise, our table has three columns. We want the third column to actually extend to the edge of the page. We want to extend the background image as well. We can accomplish this by placing a layout cell in the third column.

a) Change the Table view to Layout view (Insert bar | Layout | Layout View).
b) Select the Draw Layout Cell button in the Insert bar.
c) Draw a cell in the top row, column 3. Also draw a cell in the bottom row, column 3 (in the row with the address bar).
d) Save the file and preview it in Netscape. The background image now extends. Resize the browser window to be smaller and the page does not shrink with the window. It looks as though the table has a fixed width instead of a percentage of the browser. Exit the browser.
e) While still in Layout view, to change the table for a width equal to the percentage of the window, select the entire table by selecting a border of the table. Select Autostretch in the Property Inspector. See figure 10-26.

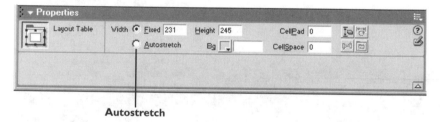

Autostretch

Fig. 10-26. Property Inspector for table Autostretch.

f) Save and preview the page. The table should now stretch and retract with the size of the browser window whether you preview in Netscape or Internet Explorer.

20. The bottom row also needs a background image to extend the width of the browser window.

a) Change back to Standard view (Insert bar | Layout | Standard View).
b) Place the cursor in the rightmost cell of the bottom row. This cell is empty. To select all cells in the current row, click on the row *<tr>* tag in the Status bar. The Property Inspector will now reference the row.

c) In the Property Inspector, next to the Bg, select the Browse button. Locate and select the file *tile.jpg* in the *ch10* folder. The right-hand cell in the bottom row is now filled with the burgundy tile.

d) Save the file and preview it. The bottom row extends its burgundy color to the edge of the window. Exit the browser.

e) Change to Layout view and look at the top of the last column. A squiggly line is displayed to show that the column is set to Autostretch. Only one column can be set to Autostretch and when we selected Autostretch for the entire table, Dreamweaver MX automatically set the last column to Autostretch. For the HTML, this means that each cell in the last column now has a width of 100%.

f) At the top of the Document window (in the toolbar), select the Show Code and Design Views button. The HTML code appears in its own window in the top portion of the window. The document displays in the bottom half of the window.

HTML

g) In the HTML code, look for the code *<td width="100%"> </td>*. When you find it, highlight this cell tag and notice in the Document window which cell is highlighted. It will be one of the cells in the last column. The width of 100% will make this column stretch/retract so that the table fills a percentage of the window. The percentage the table will fill is set in the width percentage for the entire table.

21. There is one more thing to clean up. The Class Schedule table needs to be a fixed width so that there is less spacing between the columns.
   a) Select the Class Schedule table by clicking on its right-hand edge.
   b) In the Property Inspector, click on the button Convert Table Widths to Pixels and then delete the number in the Width column.
   c) If the table still has too much spacing, resize the columns by dragging the column border.
   d) Save and preview the file in both Internet Explorer and Netscape to make sure the table still looks correct.

Summary

- *Tables lay out elements on a page through the use of cells, rows, and columns.*

- *Tables work in all browsers but have some differences in the way some of the properties are processed and displayed. Be sure to always preview pages with tables in Netscape and Internet Explorer.*

- *Tables can have many properties, including borders, colors, and background images.*

- *Use the Table Cell Space and Table Cell Pad options in the Property Inspector to move images closer together or farther apart.*

- *The Layout view lets you draw cells virtually anywhere on a page. A table is automatically created to surround the cell.*

- *Use the Standard view to access most of the properties pertaining to tables and to resize columns and rows. Use the Layout view to resize and move cells.*

- *Autostretch will stretch/retract a column until the table fills a set percentage of the browser window.*

- *Spacers prevent a column or row from deflating (becoming smaller to an almost 0 x 0 dimension) when the column or row does not contain content.*

CHAPTER

11

Still Recreating?

Using a Library

Introduction

Have you taken some time to get on the Internet and look at the design of the some of the web sites? Notice that within a single site the same navigation buttons, headers, and logos — maybe even the same sounds — occur on most, if not all, of the pages within the site. In Dreamweaver MX, these recurring elements are best created in a library. A Dreamweaver MX library is a file with one or more elements that are linked to multiple HTML documents. When the library item is modified, all pages linked to that library item are updated with the changes. You no longer have to change twenty web pages because your boss came in and decided that all navigation buttons should be vertical instead of horizontal. By the end of the chapter you will be able to:

- *Describe what a Dreamweaver MX library is, and how to use it*
- *Create a library item*
- *Add a library item to a page*
- *Modify a library item and update pages linked to the library item*
- *Detach a document from a library*

An Overview of the Dreamweaver MX Library

As you remember from an earlier chapter, a Dreamweaver MX template is a document (with a *.dwt* extension) that formats a page and sets the properties of the elements on the page. You use a Dreamweaver MX template when you primarily want to reuse a design, format, and structure. The template provides a means of creating consistent web pages in design, format, and structure.

A library, on the other hand, can be used most effectively when you want to reuse media elements on different pages. If you change an element in the library, it is easily updated wherever it may appear in the web site. An example may help.

Let's say you want to have the same four navigation buttons on each page of your web site. You want the buttons to always be right next to each other. You also want each button to always have the same functions so that when you roll the cursor over the button it changes to a glowing button, and when you click on a button it always jumps to the same page.

Let's also say you have five different page formats (templates) you are using in your web site. This makes a difference in our current discussion because if there were only one template, you could just as easily set up the buttons and their actions in the template and would not need a library item. Figure 11-1 shows two different pages that use different templates for their design but have the same navigation bar. The navigation bar is a library item.

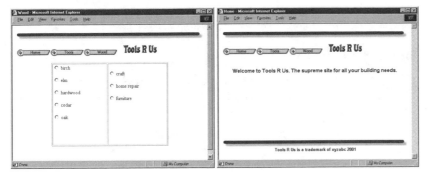

Fig. 11-1. Example of a web page with a library item.

But what about a company logo? Should it go into a library if it is used across all your web pages? The answer depends on whether it is a simple graphic (one state) or has a second state (such as a rollover image) associated with it. If the logo is a single graphic image, to change the logo all you need to do is open the original graphic file in a graphics program, change the logo image, and save it back to the same location, using the same file name. Dreamweaver MX will pick up the new logo and display it wherever the old logo appeared.

However, if the logo has an alternate image attached to it so that when you roll the mouse over the logo a second image displays or an animation plays, these images would probably be best placed in a library. In this situation, you would have two associated graphic elements and an action (the rollover) that all need to stay together. Placing these items in a library will make it much easier to make changes in the future. If you wanted to change the action from a rollover to a mouse click, you would only need to change it in the library and it would be updated wherever it appears.

Using a Dreamweaver MX Library

Creating Library Items

- *A library item is a file containing content and HTML tags, which does not include the <Body> or <Head> tags.*

- *Select Window Menu | Assets and select the Library icon to open the library panel and create a library item. When a library item is opened, a window will open with <<Library Item>> in the title bar. The window background is gray, not white, like the Document window. Most of the same menu options are available for a library item as are available for a document.*

- *You can also create a new library by selecting File Menu | New | Library Item.*

- *The library item will be saved with the extension .lbi, in a folder called* Library *on the local web site.*

- *When you save a library item, any pages linked to the library will be updated (an Update Library Items dialog window will appear).*

Library Preferences

- *Library items have their own preferences that set the color of the library item inserted in a document. Select Edit Menu | Preferences, and then select the category Highlighting.*

- *When a page linked to a library item is open, the library item is highlighted in the Document window in the color set in Preferences.*

HTML for a Library Item Within a Document

A Dreamweaver MX library item will not be recognized by other software packages. When you place a library item in a Dreamweaver MX document, a special comment is inserted at the insertion point. When Dreamweaver MX opens a page with this comment, *<!—##BeginLibraryItem>*, it knows to go to the named library file to get the elements from the library. You will not be able to modify the library item within the document but must open the library to edit the item. Figure 11-2 shows the complete HTML for a document linked to a library called *chlib.lbi*. The *BeginLibraryItem* tag has been highlighted for you.

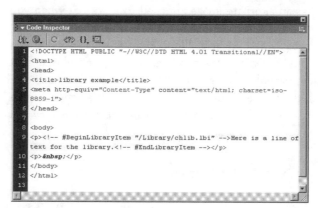

Fig. 11-2. HTML for a library item.

If you open the document in any software package outside Dreamweaver MX, the library tag is strictly seen as a comment, and you can modify anything in the document you want to – including the elements referenced by the library item. If you do modify the elements within the library item and then reopen the page in Dreamweaver MX, the changes will be ignored because Dreamweaver MX will retrieve the library item and reset the elements back to the settings in the library. In this example, the name of the library item is *copyright* and it just contains some text about the copyright.

```
<body bgcolor="#FFFFFF">
<p><!— #BeginLibraryItem "/Library/copyright.lbi" _
—>copyright © 1998 <!— #EndLibraryItem —>
</body>
</html>
```

Library Options

Detach from Original: This unlinks a page from a library item. It does not remove the HTML code referencing the library. This option is available in the Property Inspector when the library item is highlighted.

Update Pages: Available from Modify Menu | Library, this updates all pages (or selected pages) with any modifications that were made to the library. A Status window is displayed to show how many pages were updated successfully. This window is just like the window for templates, but the Library Items option is checked to update pages linked to this library. See figure 11-3.

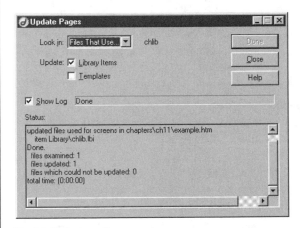

Fig. 11-3. Update Pages option.

Once a library has been created, you can perform the following.

- *Insert the library into documents in the same site as the library item.*
- *Modify the library. Any pages linked to the library item are updated with the changes.*
- *Copy the library item to use on another site.*

Special Elements That Can Be Included in a Library

The following items are commonly placed in a library. The key is that they are recurring or reused within or across pages.

- *Navigation bar*

·T/P·

To copy a library item to another site, right click on the library in the Assets | Library panel and select Copy to Site from the context menu.

- *Text that is reused across pages*
- *Any recurring media (such as images, text, and sound) that have actions (called behaviors)*
- *Tables*
- *Forms*

Special Elements That Cannot Be Included in a Library

Library items can only be inserted into the body section of an HTML document. The following cannot be in a library item because they insert HTML code into the head section.

- *Timelines*
- *Style sheets*

Tips for Using a Dreamweaver MX Library

- *When naming a library item (file), use generic names that reference what will be in the library so that you and other members of the team will have some idea of what the library is for when it is listed in the Library panel. Use simple names such as nav bar, exit sound, copyright, and so on. The library item is saved in a folder called Library in the site and given the same file name as the library item.*

- *If you rename a library file name in the Site panel, it also wants to change any links to the library. A dialog window will appear to update pages linked to this library.*

- *Library items do not need to be placed on the remote site. All HTML code needed for a page linked to a library is inside the actual document. The library just provides a linking mechanism to update multiple pages at one time.*

  We suggest, however, that if a team is working on the same web site, the libraries be placed on the remote site (or network) so that they are accessible to the entire team for development purposes. Again, permission to update and distribute new libraries should be carefully monitored.

- *If you are making major changes to the library item and need to really see what the items look like in reference to other elements on the page, it is sometimes easier to detach a page from a library, modify the page, and then recreate the library.*

- *If you delete a library from your local web site, the comments (HTML code) referencing that library are not removed from any pages that were linked to the library. This will not cause any problems unless you create another library item with the same name. In this case, the page will link to the new library when you update pages. (This is one way to totally change a library item, or copy a library from another user and have the existing pages link to the new file.) To change the HTML code and thus get rid of all references to the deleted library, detach*

CAUTION

Behaviors can reside in a library item, but they must be added while the library item is editable. Insert the library item in a document, add the behavior, delete the original library item (in the Library panel, making note of the exact name), and then save (recreate) the library with the original name.

the page from the library (Modify | Library | Detach from Library) before deleting the library.

- *You can link multiple library items to one page.*
- *You cannot insert behaviors while in the library, but you can create a library item that has elements with behaviors already attached to it. To add behaviors to an existing library item, detach the library from a document, add the behavior, and then recreate the library and name the library the same name as the original library. It is case sensitive, so be sure to name it exactly the same way.*

Practice Exercise 11-1: Creating a Library Item

Description

A good example of a use for a Library object is copyright information you want to use on multiple pages. This type of information is typically text, and may also include a graphic image. We do not want to use a template because we are going to place the copyright information in different areas on the page. We do not want to include all text information as part of a graphic image because it is not necessary and we want to cut down on download time. The following elements are covered in this exercise.

- *Creating a Dreamweaver MX library*
- *The Assets | Library panel*
- *HTML code for a Dreamweaver MX library*
- *Aligning images with text*

Take a Look

Before beginning the exercise, let's take a look at the exercise in its completed state so you can clearly see what you are about to build.

1. It is important for the exercises in this chapter that you have already copied files from the companion CD-ROM to your hard drive. These instructions are found in Chapter 1.

2. You should be in the *DWComplete* site. Locate the folder called *Library* and then the file named *ch11copy.lbi*. Double click on *ch11copy.lbi* to open the file.

3. The file *ch11copy.lbi* should now appear in your copy of Dreamweaver MX. Note the following properties of this completed exercise.

 CD-ROM

 DWComplete Site

- *Look in the title bar for <<Library Item>>, as a cue that you are working in a library file. All menus are still the same (and available), as if you were working in a regular HTML document.*

- *The background color of the page is gray. Modify | Page Properties is not available for a library.*

- *Select Window Menu | HTML to open the HTML code. Notice that the basic HTML tags are not included (<head>, <body>, and <html>)*

- *Close the file (File | Close).*

- *Notice the Library folder. This folder is where all Dreamweaver MX libraries will be stored.*

- *The extension on the library we just opened is .lbi.*

- *The graphic is aligned with the text in the copyright.*

- *Close the file ch11copy.lbi.*

Storyboard: On Screen

Figure 11-4 shows you what the finished library will look like.

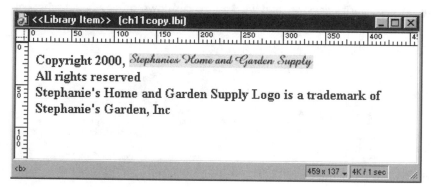

Fig. 11-4. Completed Dreamweaver MX library.

Storyboard: Behind the Scenes

Figure 11-5 illustrates the HTML code for the Dreamweaver MX library we are going to create. Notice the only HTML tags are the *<div>* for the alignment center and *<b>* (bold) tags. There are no *<html>* or *<body>* tags.

Fig. 11-5. HTML code for library.

Step-by-Step Instructions

1. You should be in the *DWExercises* site. Select File Menu | New to open a blank HTML document.

2. Type the following four lines. There is a line break between each line (Insert Menu | Line Break, or Shift + Enter/Return).

   Copyright 2000
   All rights reserved
   Stephanie's Home and Garden Supply Logo is a trademark of
   Stephanie's Garden, Inc.

3. Highlight the text you just typed and set it to Bold using the Property Inspector.

4. While in the Property Inspector, set the text to Align Center.

5. Now let's insert a graphic next to *Copyright 2000.*
   a) Place the cursor after *Copyright 2000*. Press the space bar once to enter a space.
   b) Insert the image called *coname.jpg* found in the *ch11* folder in the *Learning_Dreamweaver* folder.
   c) Change the Align Property option of the graphic to absolute middle so that the text *Copyright 2000* is centered to the middle of the image.

6. Highlight all of the text and the graphic, and select Modify Menu | Library | Add Object to Library.

7. The Library portion of the Assets panel will open. Notice the Library icon highlighted on the left-hand side of the Assets panel. See figure 11-6.

DWExercises Site

Go Solo

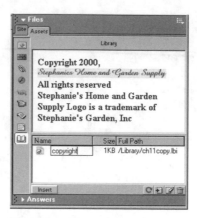

Fig. 11-6. Library panel with new library object being created.

8. In the highlighted name box, erase the name *Untitled* and type in *copyright*. (Make sure to use all lowercase letters, as this is also going to be the file name for the library.)

9. Press Enter/Return to save the new library name.

10. Returning to the Document window, click somewhere on the background. Notice that the new Library object (the text you typed) is now highlighted.

11. In the Library panel (select Window | Assets and select the library icon (if the panel is not still open), double click on the Library object *copyright* to open it.

12. *copyright.lbi* opens in the Library Document window. <<*Library Item*>> is in the title bar to tell you that you are now in the library. The gray background color is another visual cue that you are in a library.

13. Close the library (File | Close).

14. Close the untitled document into which you typed the copyright text. Select No under Save. We just used this document to type the text into and create the Library object; we do not want to save it.

15. Look in the Site panel and notice that the *Library* folder now has the file named *copyright.lbi*. When you created the Library object, Dreamweaver MX automatically saved a file with the same name of the Library object (*copyright*) and added the extension *.lbi*. The file is saved in the *Library* folder in the site root folder. If the *Library* folder does not exist, Dreamweaver MX will create it.

Practice Exercise 11-2: Adding a Library Element to an Existing Page

Description

You have created the copyright information you want to place on each page of *Stephanie's Home and Garden* web site. Let's go through the steps to add the Library object *copyright* to one of the web pages. The following elements are covered in this exercise.

- *Inserting a Library object into a document*
- *Reviewing HTML code for a document with a library*
- *The Library panel*

Take a Look

Before beginning the exercise, let's take a look at the exercise in its completed state so you can clearly see what you are about to build.

 CD-ROM

 DWComplete Site

1. It is important for the exercises in this chapter that you have already copied files from the companion CD-ROM to your hard drive. These instructions are found in Chapter 1.

2. You should be in the *DWComplete* site. Locate the *ch11* folder and locate the file named *dw11ex2.html*. Double click on *dw11ex2.html* to open the file.

3. The file *dw11ex2.html* should now appear in your copy of Dreamweaver MX. Note the following properties of this completed exercise.

   - *At the bottom of the document you will see some copyright information highlighted with a light tan (or some other color if the preferences for highlighting have been modified).*

   - *You cannot change or even highlight the copyright (highlighted) text in that area. Go ahead and try. This is a Library object.*

   - *Select Window Menu | HTML to open the HTML code. Notice the <!—#BeginLibraryItem —> tags toward the bottom of the page. Dreamweaver MX uses this tag to identify the library file to which to link the Library object. Notice that these Library objects in the HTML code are not highlighted, as they are in the Document window.*

   - *Close the file (File | Close).*

Storyboard: On Screen

Figure 11-7 shows how the completed HTML page will look.

Fig. 11-7. Completed exercise within browser.

Storyboard: Behind the Scenes

Figure 11-8 illustrates the HTML code for the Dreamweaver MX library we are going to insert. Notice the highlighted HTML code between the <!—#BeginLibraryItem —> and <!— #EndLibraryItem —> tags.

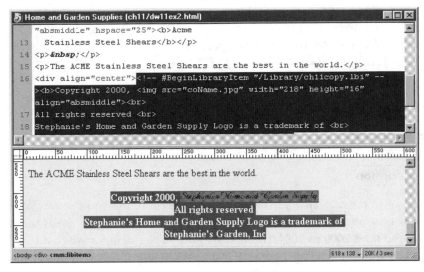

Fig. 11-8. HTML code for the library as seen in Code view.

Step-by-Step Instructions

1. We are going to open an existing document that has been copied to your hard drive when you installed the chapter exercises in Chapter 1.

   a) You should be in the *DWExercises* site. Locate the *ch11* folder and within it the file named *homegard.html*. Double click on *homegard.html* to open the file.

   b) Move the cursor to the last line of the page after the text *in the world*. Press Enter/Return to move the cursor to a new line.

   c) Open the Assets | Library panel (Window | Assets).

   d) Select (single click on) the *copyright* Library object.

   e) Select the Insert button at the lower left corner of the Library panel.

   f) The Library object's information (the copyright details) will appear in your HTML document where the cursor was positioned. The object is highlighted and cannot be modified.

   g) To make the copyright information centered, select Text Menu | Align | Center.

2. Preview the file in a browser by pressing the F12 key. Notice that the Library object looks like a regular text item (i.e., no longer highlighted).

3. Close the Browser window to return to Dreamweaver MX and the library.

4. Now let's look at the HTML code Dreamweaver MX has created.

DWExercises Site

Go Solo

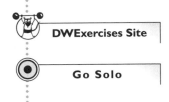

CAUTION

Be careful not to double click on a Library object in the Library panel, as that will open the Library object, not insert it.

·T/P·

Another way to insert a Library object is to drag the Library object from the Library panel directly to where you want it in the Document window.

a) Press the F10 key. This is the shortcut key for Windows | Code Inspector.

b) At the bottom of the page is the *<!— #BeginLibraryItem "/Library/copyright.lbi" —>* tag.

5. Save your document.

6. Close the document.

Practice Exercise 11-3: Modifying a Library Item

Description

As is often the case, after you have uploaded the entire site, you discover your client now wants to change the copyright information. The year needs to be changed from 2000 to 2001. This is a "real-world" scenario for which it really pays to know how to use Library objects. Let's modify the Library object and let Dreamweaver MX modify all pages that use this Library object. The following elements are covered in this exercise.

- *Modifying a Library object*
- *Updating pages linked to a library*
- *Property Inspector for a Library object*
- *The Library panel*

Take a Look

Before beginning the exercise, let's take a look at the exercise in its completed state so you can clearly see what you are about to build.

DWComplete Site

1. Change to the *DWComplete* site.

2. Locate the *Library* folder and in it the file named *ch11cpy2.lbi*. Double click on *ch11cpy2.lbi* to open the file.

3. The file *ch11cpy2.lbi* should now appear in your copy of Dreamweaver MX. Note the following properties of this completed exercise.

    • *This Library object has the same content as the previous exercise.*

    • *Notice the different year, which is now 2002.*

Storyboard: On Screen

Figure 11-9 shows you what the finished HTML document will look like.

TIP

When is a file saved? You can tell a file has not been saved by looking in the title bar with the document file name. There will be an asterisk (*) next to the file name when it has *not* been saved.

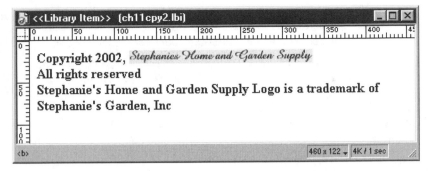

Fig. 11-9. Completed library.

Storyboard: Behind the Scenes

The HTML code is not any different in this exercise from previous exercises, so we will just start the step-by-step instructions.

Step-by-Step Instructions

1. First we will open a document, and a Dreamweaver MX library, and then modify a Library object.

    a) In the Site panel for the *DWExercises* site, locate the *ch11* folder and within it the file *homegard.html*. Double click on *homegard.html* to open it.

    b) Because this page has the Library object we want to modify linked to it, we will open the Library object in the document. Locate the copyright information at the bottom of the page. Double click on the copyright information and the Property Inspector for the Library object opens. See figure 11-10.

Fig. 11-10. Property Inspector for the Library object.

    c) Select Open in the Property Inspector (for the library item). There are other ways to open a library object:

        • *Open the library directly from the Site panel under the* Library *folder by double clicking on it.*

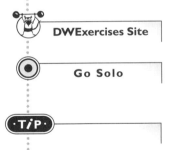

DWExercises Site

Go Solo

·T/P·

If you did not complete the last exercise, start with *homegard2.html*, found in the *ch11* folder.

- *Open a new document and then select Window Menu | Assets | Library icon. Double click on the Library object or single click on the Library object and select the Edit icon at the bottom of the Library panel.*

- *Open a document linked to a Library object. Double click on the Library object in the Document window. The Property Inspector opens. Select Open.*

2. The Library Object window will now open with the Library object's content. Notice that the background is gray. The different color of background helps you realize that you are in the Library object editing screen, as does the *<<Library Item>>* in the title bar.

3. Now let's make some changes to the Library object.
    a) Modify the year (2000) to be 2002. The copyright information should look as follows.

        Copyright 2002,

    b) After you have made the correction, close the library file by selecting File | Close.
    c) A confirmation dialog window will appear asking if you want to save changes to *copyright.lbi*. Click on the Yes button. See figure 11-11.

Fig. 11-11. Save Library Dialog window after changes.

    d) The Update Library Items confirmation dialog window will now appear, telling you that you have changed a library item, and asking if you want to update all of the pages in the local site that use this item. Select the Update button. See figure 11-12.

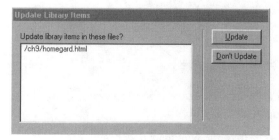

Fig. 11-12. Update Library Items confirmation dialog window.

e) One more dialog window will appear. It will show you the progress of the updating of the pages in the local site with the revised copyright information. See figure 11-13.

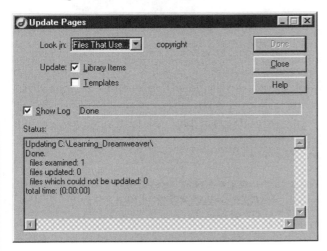

Fig. 11-13. Update Pages progress dialog window.

f) After you have made sure the correct number of files was updated in the status area of the Update Pages dialog window, click on the Close button in the upper right-hand corner of the window.

4. Save the file *homegard.html*.

5. We have not previewed this file for a while. Press F12.

6. Close the file.

Summary

- *A Dreamweaver MX library provides the means to share text and media combinations across HTML documents (and templates).*

- *A Library object is identified in Dreamweaver MX by a comment <<BeginLibraryItem>>.*

- *The Library object cannot be modified in a document. To open the Library object to modify it, select Property Inspector | Assets | Library panel or Site panel.*

- *Libraries do not need to be uploaded to the remote site for documents linked to the library to work correctly. This is because the HTML code needed for the elements in the library is actually inserted into the HTML documents. Do upload the library to the remote site if other team members need access to the library.*

- *Library objects are saved in a folder called Library in the Site folder. Dreamweaver will not look for Library objects outside the Library folder.*

·T/P·

You do not have to worry about saving the new Library object information for each page that uses the object; Dreamweaver MX automatically saves the Library object information in each file that uses that specific Library object. There is one exception: if you have a page open in Dreamweaver while you are editing the Library object, Dreamweaver MX will update (insert) the content of the new changed library but will not save it. You will need to save that file in the normal way. Dreamweaver will not automatically save the Library object information in a file that is currently open.

12

Application Chapter: Creating the Main Menu Page and Linking It to the Product Pages

Introduction

Most web sites have one page that users see when they first enter a site. This page is usually known as the index, home, or main menu page. In this exercise, you will create a front page for *The 21st Century Kitchen*. A good front page does three things: it tells the user what the site is or to whom it belongs (name of business, organization, and so on), describes the function of the site or business/organization, and provides a way to navigate to the other pages in the site.

Application Exercise Objectives

By the end of this chapter, you will create:

- *A main menu page*
- *Additional product pages from a template*
- *Links between the product pages and the menu page*
- *A Library object with the menu buttons*

Application Exercise 12-1: Creating the Main Menu Page and Linking It to the Product Pages

Description

In this application chapter, we will create the home page of our web site. On this home page we will create the beginning of a menu bar that will occupy the left-hand side of each page in our web site. We will also create some additional product pages using the template we created in Chapter 8. Finally, we will create some links between the home page and the various product pages. The menu bar will be displayed in each page, and therefore needs to be placed in a library. The library can then be inserted in all templates for the site that require the menu.

Take a Look

CD-ROM

Let's take a look at what the finished exercise will look like. Open Dreamweaver MX and use the menu option File Menu | Open to locate the companion CD-ROM. Locate the folder *Learning_ DWapplication_complete* and select the file *ap12.html*. Look at the layout of the web page, noticing the graphic and text areas. Take a look at the file and the HTML code in Dreamweaver MX. You will be using the following Dreamweaver MX concepts in the exercise.

- *Placing images*
- *Creating tables*
- *Rollover image*
- *Creating a Library object*
- *Creating pages from a template*
- *Linking pages*

Storyboard: Browser View

Figure 12-1 shows how the product web page will look in a web browser when the exercise is completed.

Fig. 12-1. Completed exercise within browser.

Storyboard: Dreamweaver MX View

Figure 12-2 shows how the product web page will look in Dreamweaver MX when the exercise is completed.

Fig. 12-2. Dreamweaver MX view of completed exercise.

Application Project Steps

Complete this exercise on your own, guided by the following general steps. You can always refer back to the completed example that you viewed in the "Take a Look" section of this exercise.

NOTE: The following steps are intended as a guide. This is your project, so feel free to make whatever variations you like.

21st Century KITCHEN SITE

1. Create a new HTML file in Dreamweaver MX.

2. Title the page *The 21st Century Kitchen*.

3. Save the new page as *home.html*.

4. At the top of the document, insert the banner graphic *21ckbnr.jpg* found in the *ap_media* subfolder.

5. Under the banner graphic, create a one-row, two-column table (make sure you are in Standard view), width at 90 percent, 0 border. When the table appears, drag the divider bar to make the left-hand column narrower than the right.

6. Create the menu bar on the left-hand side of the screen by adding the following buttons: Appliances, Bakeware, Cookware, Specialty Items, and Place Order. Using the Insert Rollover Image feature, create the buttons using the graphic images (found in the *ap_media* subfolder) *21app.jpg* and *21appo.jpg*, *21bake.jpg* and *21bakeo.jpg*, *21cook.jpg* and *21cooko.jpg*,

21spec.jpg and *21speco.jpg*, and *21po.jpg* and *21poo.jpg*. Use the Enter/Return key to add a line between each button. Save your work. Do not worry about adding the link for each button; we will do this later.

7. If the table divider has not resized to the width of the buttons, drag the divider so that width of the left-hand column is just slightly more than the width of the buttons. In the right-hand column, insert the graphic *homegr.jpg*.

8. Preview your work in your web browser just to make sure the rollover states of the buttons are active. When you roll the mouse over each button, the text on the button should change.

9. Select the five buttons you just inserted and drag them onto the Library panel. Alternatively, you can select the buttons and then select Library Menu | Modify | Add Object to Library. Name the new Library object *NavBar*.

10. Just for fun, open a new HTML document and drag the *NavBar* Library object to the new page. All of the buttons should have been copied to the new page, so check in your browser to see if the rollover state works. Close the file; you will not need to save it.

11. Create product pages for the breadboard and the garlic baker using the template you created in Chapter 8 (the template name was *products.dwt*). Name these files *bread.html* and *garlic.html*, respectively. Notice that you can only edit in the editable regions you set up in Chapter 8. All other areas are locked.

12. Link the Speciality Items button on the home page (*home.html*) to the Teapot product page (*teapot.html*). You will have to open the library item to add the link. (Double click on the NavBar library object, click on Open in the Properties panel, select Specialty Items in the Property Inspector panel, and enter *teapot.html* in the Link window. Close the Library (*NavBar*) window and click on Yes to save, updating any files that need to be updated.

13. Open the *teapot.html* page and link the Next Item button to the *bread.html* page.

14. On the *bread.html* page, link the Previous Item button to the *teapot.html* page and the Next Item button to the *garlic.html* page.

15. On the *garlic.html* page, link the Previous Item button to the *bread.html* page.

16. Save each page and preview your work in a web browser. You should have made changes to the following files: *home.html*, *teapot.html*, *bread.html*, and *garlic.html*.

17. The *home.html* page (and the others) needs a navigation bar that is displayed at the top of every page. It includes the Main Menu, About the Kitchen, and Contact the Kitchen buttons, among other buttons.

a) Insert a blank line above the banner graphic.

b) Insert a table with one row and five columns.

c) There will a different button in each column. Insert rollover images in each column per the following.

	Graphic Images	Object Name
Button 1	21main.jpg and 21maino.jpg	mainMenu
Button 2	21about.jpg and 21abouto.jpg	about
Button 3	21cust.jpg and 21custo.jpg	service
Button 4	21rec.jpg and 21reco.jpg	recipes
Button 5	21contact.jpg and 21contacto.jpg	contact

d) Change the background color of the table to match the background color of the buttons (#CCCC99).

e) Change the size of the table to match the width of the other table on the page with the buttons in it.

f) Set the size of the each column in the table to be the same width, and center all buttons in their cells.

g) Set the link for the Main Menu button to point to the file *home.html*.

18. Now add the table you just created to the library, and name it *mainNav*.

19. Change the page background color of the *home.html* page to match the one that is being used for the product pages (#FFFFCC).

20. Name the page *21st Century Kitchen Home Page*.

21. Save and preview. Check that all rollover buttons are working.

22. Close the *home.html* file and open the template you created in Chapter 8, called *products.dwt*.

a) Delete the Menu button at the top of the page.

b) Add the new library object you just created – called *mainNav* – in place of the Main Menu button that is already above the banner graphics.

c) Save the template and click on Yes to update all pages. Check some of the product pages to see that they now have a main navigation bar on them.

d) Preview in your browser, checking the Main Menu, Specialty Items, and Previous/Next buttons.

Summary

You have accomplished four things in this exercise: you have created a home page for your web site, you have created a Library object, you have updated and used the Product template to create two additional product pages, and you have created links between the various pages.

CHAPTER 13

Working

with Frames

Introduction

Think of frames as a way to divide (visually and functionally) an HTML page into two or more areas. Frames give you the ability to change one or more of these areas within the page without having to redisplay (download) the entire page. For example, visualize an area across the top of the page for a banner or title (you might put the company or site name here). On the left side visualize an area for a menu or listing of the site's content sections. Finally, visualize a third area on the page where the content completely changes to correspond to the menu button that was just selected.

With frames, as a user selects a new menu item, the entire page does not need be redisplayed. Only the frame with the content for the menu item needs to be changed (downloaded). The banner frame and menu frame are unchanged. Frames provide a more efficient method of organizing and displaying content, as well as generally improving the performance of displaying pages (decreasing the amount of time required).

If web pages with frames did not have the limitation of requiring newer browser versions (3.0 and above), a lot more web sites would use frames. Frames are very useful when you want some information to remain on screen all the time, such as a table of contents, indexes, a glossary list, or submenus. By the end of this chapter you will be able to:

- *Describe why and where to use frames*
- *Create a frame set and associated frames*
- *Describe the limitations associated with using frames*
- *Use Dreamweaver MX to check for browser compatibility with frames*
- *Use the Dreamweaver MX tools for frames*
- *Work with HTML code for frames*

Frames Overview

Although most people commonly use the word *frame*, what they are usually referring to is actually a web page called a frame set, which consists of two or more separate pages called frames. Figure 13-1 shows a web page using frames and the Dreamweaver MX Frames panel. Each rectangular area is a frame that is linked to an HTML page that can be swapped with any other HTML page. Surrounding the frames is a frame set that defines the layout of the entire page by defining (1) the name of each frame (see the Frames panel) and (2) the location of each frame in the frame set. In the example in figure 13-1, a menu will be displayed in the left frame, and will remain on screen as long as the frame set is on screen. As each menu item is selected, only the content frame on the right (*contact.html*) will change. It will be updated to reflect the most recent menu choice.

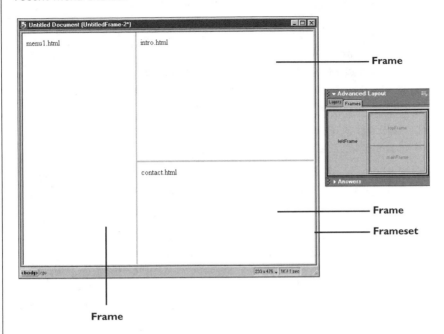

Fig. 13-1. Web page with frames and corresponding Dreamweaver MX Frames panel.

Basic Concepts Involving the Use of Frames

Working with frames can be a little tricky at first. Later in this chapter we will help you get started working with frames through the use of guided tours and exercises that will give you hands-on experience with frames. However, as a brief introduction, the basic concepts that follow might help you get oriented.

- A "frame" web page will contain a frame set of two or more related frames.
- The frame set is an HTML page and each related frame is an HTML page.
- You will need to save the frame set and each frame.
- Name each frame. These names will be needed to set the links between frames.
- Set the properties of each frame in terms of borders and scrolling.
- Set the page properties for each HTML page, including the frame set. These properties include page title, background color, and text/link colors.
- When creating links between frames, make sure the correct target is set in the Property Inspector.

Frame Terminology

Frame set: An HTML page that contains two or more frames.

Frame: A single HTML page inside a frame set.

Parent: The frame set of the current frame. Because there can be more than one frame set in a Document window, there can be multiple parents. A frame set can also have a parent frame set. JavaScript can be programmed to access the parent.

Child: Each frame within a frame set. Each child is numbered. JavaScript can be programmed to access a child.

Target: The frame (or window) in which the linked content (text, graphic, HTML page, and so on) will open. This option is found in the Property Inspector. The target can be set to _blank, _parent, _self, or a frame name.

Because each frame in the frame set is actually an HTML page, each frame has its own page properties: title, background color, and text/link colors. In addition, each frame has properties defining whether or not the frame will have borders or scroll bars. The Src (source) of the frame is the HTML page to which the frame is linked. These properties are set in the Property Inspector for the frame. See figure 13-2.

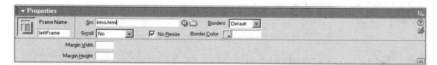

Fig. 13-2. Property Inspector for frames.

The thing to remember about frames, however, is that they are only compatible with version 3.0 browsers and above. There are also text-based browsers that do not support frames, including some of the new PDAs. There are still users out there who have not updated their browsers for any number of reasons, including the fact that their computers cannot handle the requirements of the later versions. You will need to decide for yourself whether the use of frames will significantly limit the number of users who will have access to your site.

If you cannot use frames, you can still use tables to lay out your information in a grid-like fashion on the screen. Tables are not as versatile in swapping areas of content as frames are. With the use of tables, updating requires that the browser replace the entire HTML page instead of just the part that needs updating — as is the case with frames.

•TIP•

The target is related to the link option. When a link is activated, the target defines how the link (URL) will open in the current window, new window, or frame.

Suggested Uses for Frames

The following are some examples of when you might want to use frames.

Menu: Each time a menu or topic item is selected on the left side of the page, the content on the right side of the page changes to reflect a new page pertaining to the menu (or topic) item selected. This new topic page may be a single page or contain multiple pages, with page navigation to go forward and back among these topic pages. Going from one page to another within a "topic" takes place within the current frame, replacing only the content within this frame. The menu stays on the screen the entire time (and does not have to be reloaded and redisplayed).

Other Elements of the Web Site Interface: You may want one frame in the frame set to continuously display something, such as a Flash animation of your company logo. You may want to designate another frame to contain information that needs to be updated frequently – something like *Today's News Highlights.* In this case, isolating the small *News* frame will make updating easier and faster.

Help list: The Dreamweaver MX Help uses frames. Press F1 in Dreamweaver MX to view the help.

Glossary, references, index, table of contents, or other types of lists: Each time a list item is selected, the list stays on the screen and only the content frame changes pertaining to the list item selected.

Test questions with feedback: Place the question stem and multiple-choice answers in one frame. When the user selects one of the answers, the question and answers remain on screen, as the feedback associated with the selected answer is displayed in a second frame. The feedback frame is blank until the user selects one of the possible answers.

Tips for Working with Frames

Compensation for Nonaccessibility to Frames

These days most web users are probably using newer versions of browsers, which provide frame support. However, you may determine that to meet the broadest base of potential visitors to your site you need to consider users who cannot access frame-based web pages. You may need to compensate for those users who are still using an old browser version or text-based browsers.

Using the noFrames *Tag*

There is a built-in alternative to allow nonframe-supported browsers to access your site. The solution actually involves using frames, but isolating information for those browsers that do not support frames and placing it in an area with a *<noFrames>* tag. The *<noFrames>* tag surrounds the HTML code for the content that will not be displayed inside frames.

Dreamweaver MX will provide you with a window to create the "no frames" content when you select Modify Menu | Frameset | Edit NoFrames Content. You can place whatever elements in this window you would like, including text, images, sound, and animation. Any tags required for these elements are placed inside the *<noFrames>* tag of the frame set. When a nonframe-supporting browser loads the page, it will execute the code inside the *<noFrames>* area. See figure 13-3. To exit the *noFrames* content window, select Modify Menu | Frameset | Edit NoFrames Content again.

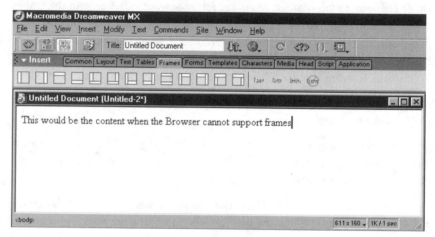

Fig. 13-3. Edit NoFrames content.

Two Versions of the Web Site

One method of compensating for the fact that users cannot use frames is to create two versions of your web site: one version using frames and the second using a "no frames" option. You can then include HTML code that will check for which type of browser is being used and provide an automatic selection to go to a specific page, based on the browser version detected.

Checking for Browser Version: An Example

Although we have worked with some simple behaviors in previous practice exercises, we have not gone into any depth yet with behaviors. We get to these details a little later, in the chapter on behaviors. However, within the context of this chapter, we did want to show you that Dreamweaver MX does include a behavior that will help you check for frame compatibility. This behavior will check a user's browser version to see if it will support frames. You will want to place this behavior on the first page, as it is loaded into the browser window.

At this point, you know that a behavior is a combination of an "event" and a "task." An event is the action that triggers the execution of the task. An event could be when the mouse is clicked (*onClick* or *onMouseDown*), or it might be when the cursor rolls over an image (*onRollOver* or *OnMouseOver*). With our current situation, we need to check for something as soon as a page loads, before anything else is displayed or executed. The event needed here is *onLoad*. We will use the *onLoad* event to check for browser version. To create a page that checks for browser version and then jumps to a page based on the version, you would perform the following.

1. Starting with a new document, in the Document Status bar, select the *<body>* tag.

2. In the Behaviors panel, select the plus (+) Button, and select the behavior Check Browser.

3. When the Check Browser dialog box first appears, version 4 and above browsers are being checked. Because frames will work with version 3 and above, we will check for 3.0 instead. See figure 13-4.

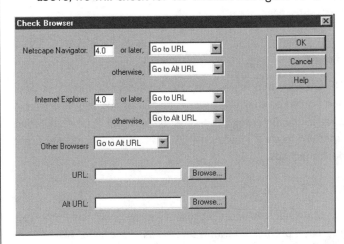

Fig. 13-4. Behavior | Check Browser.

4. You are now prompted to select what page to go to when the browser is Netscape 3.0 and above or Internet Explorer 3.0 and above, and all other frame-supporting browsers. The options are to stay on the current page, jump to the Alt URL, or jump to the URL.

5. The URL should be the URL for the page with frames. In most cases, you can have Netscape (V3) and Internet Explore (V3) go to the same page.

6. The Alt URL should be the URL for the page without frames. This would be for browsers that are older than version 3.

We would suggest that the page that contains the behavior to check the browser version should not have any content on it, and should only be used as a router (e.g., *home.html*). This being the case, you will have a page structure similar to that shown in figure 13-5. You can also use the router page to check for other things, such as whether the user needs a plugin or for determining the resolution of the monitor.

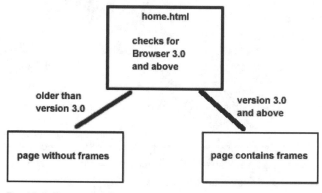

Fig. 13-5. Structure of router page.

Creating Frames

Dreamweaver MX provides two ways to create frames. They can be created by using predefined frames or they can be designed using the mouse. We suggest initially creating frames by using predefined frames and then if you wish, using the mouse method to create additional frames or split a frame. Let's take a quick look at both methods.

Using Predefined Frames

When the Frames tab is selected, icon representations of various frame sets are displayed. These same predefined frame sets are also available with the use of Insert Menu | Frames. Using predefined frames is probably the easiest way to create frames and it is a good starting point for creating more complicated frame sets. See figure 13-6.

·T/P·

To create and/or split frames, use a combination of the predefined frames (Insert Menu | Frames or Insert bar | Frames) and the mouse to create additional frames.

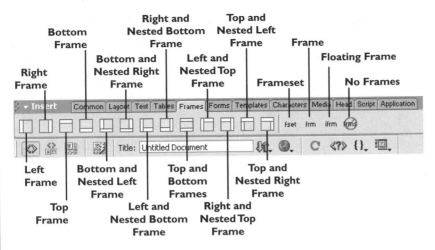

Fig. 13-6. Insert bar | Frames.

Using the Mouse to Create Frames

1. To use the mouse to create or delete frames, the frame borders need to be displayed. They are displayed automatically when frames are created with Modify Menu | Frameset or with the Insert bar | Frameset. Frame borders can also be displayed by selecting View Menu | Visual Aids | Frame Borders. The borders look a little like a picture frame around the page.

2. To add a frame with the mouse, hold down the Alt/Option key and drag a frame border in the direction of where you want the frames. For example, if a frame is to be split vertically, drag the left or right border inward. If a frame is to be split horizontally, drag the top or bottom border inward.

3. To split a frame into four frames, drag one of the corner borders (note the four-arrow cursor as you enter a corner) inward.

4. If the document already has frames and you want to split a single frame into two frames, use the Frames panel to select the frame you want to split. Then hold down the Alt/Option key and drag a border within the selected frame to create the split you want.

Figure 13-7 shows an example of using the combination of the Frames panel and the mouse to split the middle frame into two horizontal frames. First, the frame was selected in the Frames panel (notice the dotted outline in the frame in the Document window to indicate it is highlighted). Then holding down the Alt/Option key, the top border of that frame was pulled down to split the existing frame into two frames.

Shortcut

To select a single frame, select the frame in the Frames panel or hold down the Alt key (Windows) or Option+Shift (Macintosh) and click inside a frame.

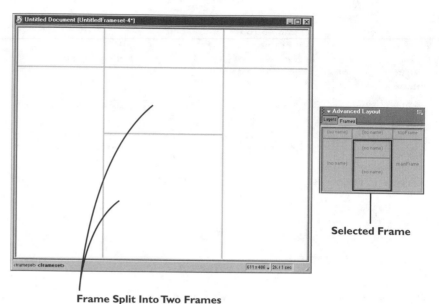

Selected Frame

Frame Split Into Two Frames

Fig. 13-7. Splitting frames using the mouse.

Designing and Creating Frames

The following are tips and shortcuts you may find helpful if you need to modify a predefined frame set or find that you need a more complicated structure and want to create the frame set yourself.

- *Turn on frame borders to see the working area of your frame set. You can do this by selecting View Menu | Visual Aids | Frame Borders. Note that if you create a predefined frame set, the frame borders are automatically displayed.*

- *Bring up the Frames panel so that you can watch the frames being created and can select an individual frame or frame set. Select Window Menu | Frames.*

- *To create a frame, drag a frame border in the direction in which you want the frame. For instance, if you want to split the window vertically, drag the frame border from the left or right side. If you want to split the window horizontally, drag the frame border from the top or bottom.*

- *To delete a frame, drag the frame border to the edge of the frame border or off the page.*

- *To resize a frame, just drag a border.*

·T/P·

To see frame borders, select View Menu | Visual Aids | Frame Borders.

- *To split a single frame into two frames, select the frame in the Frames panel. A dotted line will encircle the frame in the Document window. Hold down the Alt/Option key as you drag the frame border (of the current frame). You can also split a single frame by placing the cursor in the frame and then selecting Modify Menu | Frameset | Split Frame Left, Right, Up, Down. You can also use one of the predefined frame sets under Insert bar | Frames. Whenever a single frame is split, a new frame set is created. These are called nested frame sets. See figure 13-8.*

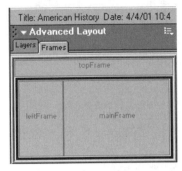

Fig. 13-8. Nested frame sets (as shown in the Frames panel).

Selecting Frames and Frame Sets

Remember that frames and frame sets are individual HTML pages. When a frame set is opened, the pages linked to each frame within the frame set are opened in the frame set. To change the HTML page a frame is linked to, or to change any of the other properties of the frame, you must first be able to select the frame.

Selecting a Frame

In the Document window, hold down the Alt (Windows) key or Option + Shift (Macintosh) keys and click inside a frame, or in the Frames panel (Window Menu | Frames), click inside the frame.

Selecting a Frame Set

In the Document window, click on a frame border, or in the Frames panel (Window | Frames), click on the border of the frame set. The frame set has the very wide border. You can also click on a frame and then hold down the Ctrl/Cmd key and press the Up arrow key on your keyboard to select the frame set of the frame. This is called selecting the parent frame set of the frame. When a frame set is selected, you can press the Ctrl/Cmd key plus the Down arrow key on your keyboard. This is called selecting the child frame.

Shortcut

To select a single frame: Alt/Opt + shift and click inside a frame.

You can tell when a frame is selected. It will have a dotted line around the perimeter of the frame.

Guided Tour 13A: Frame Set Versus Frame

Before we actually begin creating pages with frames, let's take a quick look at creating frames and frame sets and working with the Frames panel.

1. Open the site *DWExercises* by selecting the site in the Site panel.

2. If you have any document windows open, be sure to close them at this point. This includes any untitled documents that may have opened with Dreamweaver MX.

3. Let's create a new file. Select File Menu | New | Basic Page | HTML. A new blank Document window should now be open.

4. We will use the predefined frames first.

    a) From the Insert bar, select the Frames category. See figure 13-9.

Fig. 13-9. Insert bar | Frames category selected.

    b) Notice the predefined frame sets and how they are represented by various icons. Each icon depicts the number and position of each frame for that predefined frame set. These frame sets are also available by selecting Insert Menu | Frames.

    c) We will create a frame set that has four panels of approximately equal size. Experiment with the various frame presets, arranging the borders until you have four frames (two-by-two).

5. There are now actually five HTML pages in this Document window. Each of the four frames is its own HTML page, and there is the frame set, which is also an HTML document.

6. Let's take a look at these five HTML pages in the window by using the Frames panel. Select Window Menu | Frames. See figure 13-10.

The Frames panel is within the Advanced Layout panel group.

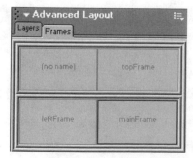

Fig. 13-10. Frames panel.

7. The Frames panel shows the four frames. To select a particular frame, click on the frame in the Frames panel. Let's select the frame called *cornerFrame*.

   a) Select Window | Properties. The Property Inspector shows the properties for the selected frame, *cornerFrame*. See figure 13-11. Look in the Src box and notice that there is a URL already there. Whether frames are created with predefined frames or created from scratch, whenever the frame is created in Dreamweaver MX, a default file name is given to the frame. The file name always starts with *UntitledFrame*, followed by a number assigned by Dreamweaver MX. The path to the source file is the *Site* folder.

Fig. 13-11. Property Inspector | Frame.

   b) Also note in the Property Inspector that the Borders option is set to default (which is No) and that Scroll is also set to default (which is No).

8. In the Frames panel, select the lower left frame.

   a) If this frame contained a list of items – for a menu for example – we might need to make this frame scroll. In this case you would use the Property Inspector to set Scroll to Auto. A scroll bar would then appear only if the content in this frame did not fit in the visible area.

   b) But let's continue with another property. Select the No Resize box so that the user cannot resize the current frame.

9. One at a time, select each of the other two frames (*topFrame* and *mainFrame*) and look at the Property Inspector. Notice that these frames also already have an *Src* file linked to the frame.

10. Let's look at the properties associated with frames. These are all found in the Property Inspector when a single frame is selected. (Note that there are different properties for frames and frame sets.)

   • Name: *Name of the frame. It is very important to enter a name here, as the name is used for hyperlinking and for scripting purposes. The name should be a single word, although you can include the underscore character (_). Do not include special characters in the name, and do not include spaces.*

   • Src: *URL source for the frame.*

- Borders: *The default will let the user's browser determine if borders are displayed. Possible options are default, Yes, and No. This overrides frame set settings.*

- Scroll: *Places a scroll bar on the right side of this frame (not the entire page). The default for most browsers is Auto, which means the scroll bar only appears if the content does not fit in the frame.*

- NoResize: *Sets a fixed size for the frame. If NoResize is checked, the user will not be able to resize the frame by selecting the frame's borders.*

- Border Color: *Sets the color of the borders adjacent to the frame. This overrides frame set settings.*

- Margin Width: *Sets the width of the left and right margins. The margins are the area between the frame border and the content in the frame.*

- Margin Height: *Sets the width on the top and bottom margins.*

11. Let's look at the frame set. To select the frame set, perform one of the following.

    - *In the Frames panel, click just outside the frames, where the thick frame border is shown.*

    - *In the Document window, click on one of the frame borders.*

    a) You can verify that you have the frame set selected by looking at the Property Inspector. It will say *frameset* where the name is usually displayed. It also shows the number of columns and rows associated with the frame set. See figure 13-12.

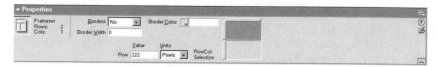

Fig. 13-12. Property Inspector | Frameset.

    b) Frame sets (like frames) also have an *Src* file, but it is not shown in the Property Inspector.

    c) In the right-hand corner of the Frameset Property Inspector, you will see a small diagram of the frame set (the RowCol Selection area), with "buttons" for selecting the left column, right column, top row, and bottom row.

    d) To set the size of the frames in the right column to be a percentage of the browser window, use the RowCol diagram, selecting the right column "button" and then selecting a percentage in the Units pull-down menu. In the Value field, type *80*. With these settings, the right column (which is two frames) will stretch to fill 80% of a browser's window.

e) Now select the left column "button." Notice that its value is a relative value. The column will be allocated space in the Browser window after all other frames have been displayed. In this example, the right column will take up 80% of the browser's window. The left column will take the remainder of the space (20%).

12. Let's look at the properties associated with a frame set.

- Borders: *The default will let the user's browser determine if borders are displayed. Possible settings are default, Yes, and No.*

- Border Color: *Sets the color of all borders.*

- Border Width: *Sets a fixed size for the frame. If NoResize is checked for a single frame, the user will not be able to resize the frame by selecting the frame's borders.*

- Row/Column size: *Sets the size of rows and columns. This measurement can be in pixels or percentage of Browser window.*

13. Let's add another frame to this frame set. We will split the upper right frame into two frames that are horizontal to each other.

a) Using the Frames panel, select the frame called *topFrame*. In the Document window, a dotted line surrounds this frame to show that it is selected.

b) Hold down the Alt/Option key and in the Document window drag the border between the two right frames upward into *topFrame*.

c) You should now see another frame called *(no name)*.

d) Select the frame *(no name)* and in the Property Inspector, in the Frame Name field, type *midFrame*. The new name now appears in the Frames panel.

14. When *topFrame* was split into two frames, a new frame set was also created. You can see this new frame set in the Frames panel. Frame sets are displayed with a thick border (like a picture frame). See figure 13-13.

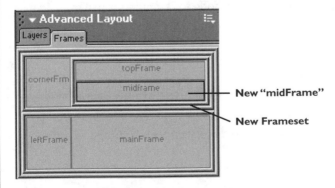

Fig. 13-13. Frames Panel showing two frame sets.

·T i P·

When you are saving files the first time for frame sets and frames, we suggest that you save the frame set first, and then select each frame individually and save until all frames have been saved. When previewing a page with a frame set, make sure that all frames and the frame set have been saved at least once so they have a name you have assigned them. Then select File | Save All before you preview in a browser.

15. At this point, nothing has been saved. Select File | Save. The Save As dialog window asks you where to save the file and what to name the file. The file name is defaulting to the default name assigned by Dreamweaver MX when the frame set and frames were created. The name shows up as *UntitledFrame* and a number.

    But how do you know what is being saved at this point? The answer is, the frame that is currently selected at the time you select File | Save. Select Cancel so that you do not save the frame. We will look at another selection instead.

16. Select File | Save Frameset As. Only one frame set is saved for a page, even though there may be nested frame sets. The file name for a frame set follows the same naming conventions as any other HTML page (we are using lowercase, no spaces, *.html* extension). For this tour we will not actually save anything, so click on Cancel.

17. If we were actually saving all frames (and frame sets), you would save the frame sets (File | Save Frameset), then save each frame, one at a time. Select each frame (simply place the cursor in a frame) and select File | Save. Place the cursor in the next frame and save, and so on, for each frame.

18. On your own, add some more frames. Delete a frame or two by dragging a frame border off the page.

19. Close the Document window. You will be asked if you want to save the frame set. Select No. Because the frame set is not being saved, you will not be asked to save the frames.

20. Now let's try it for real.

HTML and Behaviors for Frames

HTML for a Frame Set

HTML

Figure 13-14 shows the HTML source code for a frame set with four frames. One frame has been split into two frames.

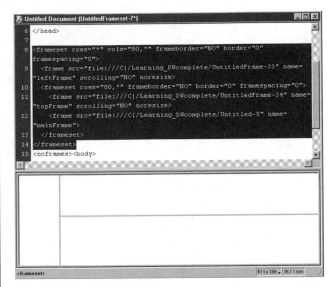

Fig. 13-14. Sample HTML source code for a frame set with four frames.

The key areas of the HTML source code for frames and frame sets are explained in the following examples. The following defines the first frame set and the frames. In this example, the frame set has 1 row and 2 columns. The frame set tag takes the place of the *<body>* tag in the file for the frame set.

```
<Frameset rows="525" cols="315,341">
```

In the following, the frame called *Menu* is linked to the URL *Menu1.html*.

```
<Frame src="Menu1.html" name="Menu">
```

The following is a frame set nested within the first frame set that was created when one of the frames was split. It has two rows.

```
<Frameset rows="263,262">
```

In the following, the frame called *heading* is linked to the URL *heading.html*.

```
<Frame src="heading.html" name="heading">
```

In the following, the frame called *content* is linked to the URL *contact.html*.

```
<Frame src="page1.html" name="content">
```

The following ends the nested frame set.

```
</Frameset>
```

The following ends the main frame set.

```
</Frameset>
```

The following defines the content to display when the browser cannot support frames.

```
<noFrames><body bgcolor="#FFFFFF" text="#000000">
</body></noframes>
```

Behaviors for Frames

To illustrate the versatility of frames, the following describe some of the additional behaviors that can only be used with frames.

- Set Text of Frame: *Replaces the text in a specific frame with new text. This is a great feature for giving feedback on a test or displaying tool tips and descriptions when the user rolls the cursor over an image.*

- Go to URL: *This behavior can actually be used without frames. However, without frames, the URL replaces the entire page or opens in a new window. With frames, only the specified frame changes (goes to) the new URL. You can actually have more than one frame go to a new URL with a single interaction.*

- Insert Jump Menu: *This behavior inserts a list of URLs from which the user can choose. The URL replaces the current frame. This is a Form object, so a form must be created first, or you can use Insert | Form Objects | Jump Menu.*

- *In addition to these behaviors, Insert Menu | Navigation Bar inserts images with up and down states, and the URLs to link to. It includes an option for specifying the frame to place the URL in.*

Practice Exercise 13-1: Setting Up a Frames Page

Description

In this exercise you will create a home page for a fictional company called Bikes R Us. The home page will be made up of different frames: a menu in one frame, a selection of bikes in another frame, and miscellaneous content in other frames. In addition, there will be a frame at the bottom of the page with navigational buttons for home, contact, and references. The following elements are covered in this exercise.

- *Creating a frame set and frames*
- *Adding a frame*
- *Selecting frame sets and frames*
- *Setting the size of frames*
- *Saving a frame set and frames*
- *Setting the title of the HTML file linked to the frame*

DWComplete Site

CD-ROM

Take a Look

Before beginning the exercise, let's take a look at the exercise in its completed state so that you can clearly see what it is you are about to build.

1. Make sure you are working with the site *DWComplete*, which we have been using in previous chapters. You can confirm this by selecting the site in the Site panel.

2. Find the subfolder *ch13* and locate the file named *dw13ex1.html*. Double click on *dw13ex1.html* to open the file.

3. The file *dw13ex1.html* should now appear in your copy of Dreamweaver MX. Note the following properties of this completed exercise.

   • *The page may look as though it is empty. Select View Menu | Visual Aids | Frame Borders.*

   • *Notice the five frames. Click inside a few of the frames and notice that each frame is linked to an HTML document and that it has its own title (look at the title bar of the Document window to see the title and file name).*

   • *Select Window Menu | Others | Frames to see all frame names and the frame set. There are actually three nested frame sets.*

   • *Select one of the frame sets. They have the thick frame borders in the Frames panel. Click on one of the frame set borders to select it. In the Property Inspector for the frame set, look at the value for a frame. Some of the frames are set to pixels (fixed size), and some to relative size.*

Storyboard: On Screen

When this exercise is viewed through the browser, there will only be a blank window; therefore, there is no illustration to show here.

Storyboard: Behind the Scenes

Figure 13-15 shows the HTML code generated behind the frame set.

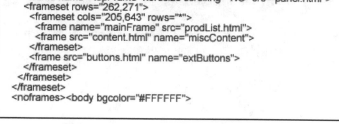

```
<frameset rows="*" cols="156,851*" frameborder="NO" border="0" framespacing="0">
  <frame name="leftFrame" scrolling="NO" noresize src="menu.html">
  <frameset rows="80,*" frameborder="NO" border="0" framespacing="0">
   <frame name="topFrame" noresize scrolling="NO" src="panel.html">
   <frameset rows="262,271">
     <frameset cols="205,643" rows="*">
      <frame name="mainFrame" src="prodList.html">
      <frame src="content.html" name="miscContent">
     </frameset>
     <frame src="buttons.html" name="extButtons">
   </frameset>
  </frameset>
</frameset>
<noframes><body bgcolor="#FFFFFF">
```

Fig. 13-15. HTML source code for the completed frame set.

Step-by-Step Instructions

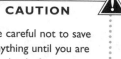
DWExercises Site

Go Solo

1. Make sure you are working with the site *DWExercises*.

2. We are going to start with a new document.
   a) Make sure all document windows are closed, including any untitled documents.
   b) Select File Menu | New | HTML Basic Page. A new empty Document window opens.
   c) This first file is going to be our frame set. Select the File menu and notice that the frame set cannot be saved yet (Save Frameset is not available). This is because there are no frames yet.

3. Now let's create the frames. Figure 13-16 shows a diagram of the frame set we will create. We can start with a predefined frame set and then modify the frame set to add another frame.

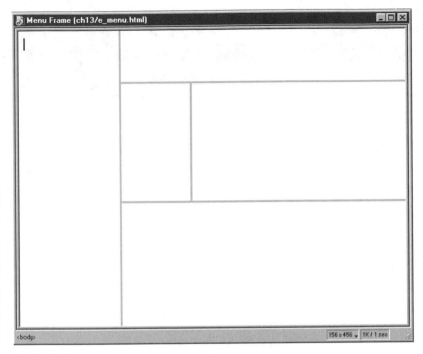

Fig. 13-16. The frame set you are about to create.

a)   Select the Frames tab. The Insert bar | Frames contains graphic icons of the most commonly used frame layouts.

b)   You will see thirteen Frame objects in Insert bar | Frames. The Frame object closest to the frame structure we want is Insert Left and Nested Top Frame (this icon is tenth from the left). This Frame object already has the two columns we need, with two rows in the second column. In the second column, we will add a third row and then split it into columns.

Select the Insert Left and Nested Top Frame frame set. See figure 13-17. As soon as you make your selection, the frame border displays (around the outside of the Document window) and there are now three frames in the window.

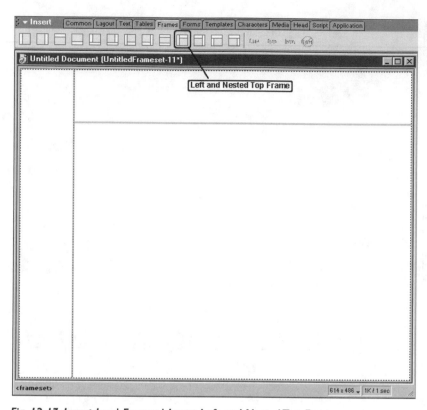

Fig. 13-17. Insert bar | Frames | Insert Left and Nested Top Frames.

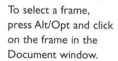
c) Now let's prepare to add another row in the second column. In the Frames panel (Window Menu | Frames), select the frame called *mainFrame*. You may have to click away from the Frames panel and then back on the frame called *mainFrame*. You know the frame is selected when there is a dotted line around the frame in the Document window and the Property Inspector references the frame.

d) To add the row, hold down the Alt/Option key as you drag the bottom border of the *mainFrame* frame in the Document window up to about the middle of this frame. You should now have three rows. The new frame does not have a name. It shows up as *(no name)* in the Frames panel.

e) Let's name the new frame you just created. Select the frame called *(no name)* in the Frames panel. Locate the Property Inspector and in the Frame Name field, type *extButtons*.

f) The frame (*mainFrame*) in the right column, middle row, now needs to be split into two columns. Select this frame (*mainFrame*) in the Frames panel. While holding down the Alt/Option key, in the

Document window, drag the right border of the frame to the left until the border is in the middle of the frame. Two frames should now be in this middle row: *mainFrame* and *(no name)*.

g) We need to name the new frame you just created. Select the frame called *(no name)* in the Frames panel and in the floating Properties panel, in the Frame Name field, type *miscContent*.

h) Take a look at the Frames panel. There are now multiple frame sets. This occurred when we created additional rows and columns. Figure 13-16 illustrates what the Document window should look like now. The size of the frames may not be the same. We will fix that next.

4. Some of the frames may need to be resized. Select the outermost frame set by clicking on any of the outer edges of the frame border (surrounding the Document window). We will use the Property Inspector to set the size of each frame in the frame set.

a) To make sure the leftmost frame is wide enough for a menu, in the Property Inspector for the frame set, select the left column in the RowCol Selection diagram. In the Column Value field, type *150*. The units should be set to pixels. See figure 13-18.

Fig. 13-18. Property Inspector | Frameset.

b) The frame called *topFrame* is in another frame set. Select the *topFrame* frame in the Frames panel. Hold down the Ctrl/Option key as you press the Up arrow to select the frame set for this frame. (You may have to click somewhere in the Document window first before going back through this selection process.)

c) Once the frame set for *topFrame* has been selected, select the top row in the RowCol Selection diagram. In the Row Value field, type *80*. Units should be set to Pixels.

d) The frames called *mainFrame* and *miscContent* are in still another frame set. Select the *mainFrame* frame in the Frames panel. Hold down the Ctrl/Option key as you press the Up arrow to select the frame set for this frame.

e) Once the frame set for *mainFrame* has been selected, select the left column in the RowCol Selection diagram. In the Row Value field, type *205*. Units should be set to Pixels.

f) The frames we have not set to a fixed size will all have a relative size. This means that they will take up any space left over after the fixed frames are displayed.

5. There are now six HTML pages in this Document window. Each frame is an HTML page, and the frames are inside a frame set, which is also an HTML document. We will save the frame set first.

   a) Select File | Save All. It does not matter what frame you are in when you save the frame set.

   b) Use the browse function to locate the *Learning_Dreamweaver* folder on your hard drive and within it the *ch13* subfolder.

   c) In the File Name field, type *home.html*. Select Save.

   d) While the frame set is selected, let's enter the title for the page. In the Title field at the top of the Document window, type *Bikes R Us*, and then press Enter/Return.

6. Each of the frames is saved as a link to an HTML file. Now we will select each frame one at a time and save them.

   a) Click inside the frame called *leftFrame* in the Document window. Select File Menu | Save. Make sure *Save in* is set to *ch13* in the *Learning_Dreamweaver* folder. In the File Name field, type *menu.html*. Select Save. While this HTML page is selected, let's enter the title for the page. In the Title field at the top of the Document window, type *Menu*, and then press Enter/Return.

   b) Click inside the frame called *topFrame* in the Document window. Select File Menu | Save. Make sure *Save in* is set to *ch13* in the *Learning_Dreamweaver* folder. In the File Name field, type *panel.html*. Select Save. While this HTML page is selected, let's enter the title for the page. In the Title field at the top of the Document window, type *Panel Frame*, and then press Enter/Return.

   c) Click inside the frame called *mainFrame* in the Document window. Select File Menu | Save. Make sure *Save in* is set to *ch13* in the *Learning_Dreamweaver* folder. In the File Name field, type *prodList.html*. Select Save. While this HTML page is selected, let's enter the title for the page. In the Title field at the top of the Document window, type *Product List Frame*, and then press Enter/Return.

   d) Click inside the frame called *miscContent* in the Document window. Select File Menu | Save. Make sure *Save in* is set to *ch13* in the *Learning_Dreamweaver* folder. In the File Name field, type *content.html*. Select Save. While this HTML page is selected, let's enter the title for the page. In the Title field at the top of the Document window, type *Content Frame*, and then press Enter/Return.

   e) Click inside the frame called *extButtons* in the Document window. Select File Menu | Save. Make sure *Save in* is set to *ch13* in the *Learning_Dreamweaver* folder. In the File Name field, type *buttons.html*. Select Save. While this HTML page is selected, let's enter the title for the page. In the Title field at the top of the Document window, type *Extra Buttons*, and then press Enter/Return.

7. To make sure all frames have been saved, select File Menu | Save All. If the Save As dialog window appears, select Cancel. If this is the case, go back to see which frame you did not save. You can do this by clicking in each frame in the Document window and checking the title bar to see if there is a file name (and title). If it seems as though all frames have been saved, select the Window menu and look at the bottom of the menu. If there are any untitled documents listed, open the document and close it without saving it. Then select File | Save All again.

8. Figure 13-19 illustrates the completed Document window. We have labeled each frame with the frame name and file name so that you can check your work. Your document should not display this actual text in the frames.

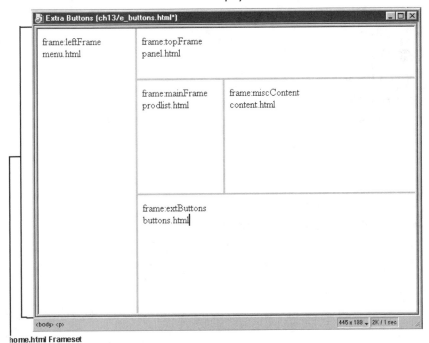

Fig. 13-19. Completed frame (text is for validation purposes only).

9. Preview the file by pressing the F12 key. When the file opens in the browser, it will show up as a blank window because there is no content, borders, or color. Notice that the title of the page is *Bikes R Us*. This comes from the title of the frame set.

10. Close the browser window.

11. Close the Document window for Bikes R Us (home.html).

Practice Exercise 13-2: Linking Content Pages in Frames

Description

In the previous exercise we created the frames and frame set that will make up the home page for *Bikes R Us*. However, there is no content yet. In this exercise we will add a logo in the left frame, a list of bike graphics to choose from in the middle frame, and miscellaneous buttons (such as Home, Contact, and Reference) in the bottom frame. In addition, we will create the interface for the site with background graphics. The following elements are covered in this exercise.

• *Selecting frame set and frames*

• *Creating hyperlinks to frames to change the source of a frame*

• *Inserting an animated GIF*

• *Setting the properties of frames, including the scroll bar*

• *Designing the interface*

• *Using the noFrames content window*

• *Inserting a navigation bar*

• *Inserting tables*

Take a Look

DWComplete Site

CD-ROM

Before beginning the exercise, let's take a look at the exercise in its completed state so you can clearly see what you are about to build.

1. Make sure you are working with the site *DWComplete*. You can confirm this by selecting the site in the Site panel.

2. Find the subfolder *ch13* and locate the file named *dw13ex2.html*. Double click on *dw13ex2.html* to open the file.

3. The file *dw13ex2.html* should now appear in your copy of Dreamweaver MX. Note the following properties of this completed exercise.

   • *There are five frames. If you cannot see the frames, select View Menu | Visual Aids | Frame Borders.*

   • *Bring up the Frames panel if it is not visible, so that you can see the frame names and the frame sets by selecting Window | Frames.*

- *The left frame has a page background image with an image on top of it (the company logo). The top frame has a graphic panel that matches the left frame but is not a background image (the image was inserted).*

- *One of the frames has a scroll bar. When viewed in the browser there is always a vertical scroll bar but never a horizontal scroll bar – no matter how small the window is. This same frame has five bicycle images. Each bicycle image is linked to a URL. Notice that the target for each link is set to a window name, miscContent.*

- *The bottom frame has two buttons with links. The contact button is linked to an e-mail address.*

- *Select Modify | Frameset | Edit NoFrames Content. A similar screen has been created here without frames. If a browser does not support frames, this page will automatically be displayed. We will not put much content in the page, because it is difficult to even test it. But we will add some text in this window.*

Storyboard: On Screen

Figure 13-20 shows you how the finished page will look when viewed through a browser.

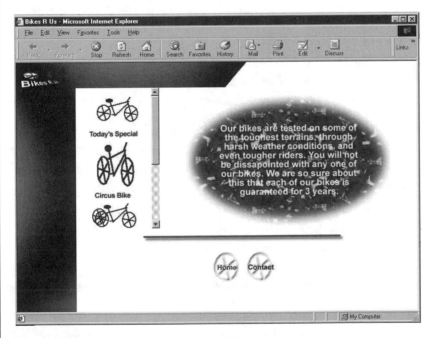

Fig. 13-20. Completed exercise within a browser.

Storyboard: Behind the Scenes

Figure 13-21 shows the HTML source code generated behind the frame set.

```
<frameset rows="*" cols="118,889*" frameborder="NO" border="0" framespacing="0">
  <frame name="leftFrame" scrolling="NO" noresize src="menu.html">
  <frameset rows="50,563*" frameborder="NO" border="0" framespacing="0" cols="*">
   <frame name="topFrame" noresize scrolling="NO" src="panel.html" marginwidth="0">
   <frameset rows="351,209" cols="*">
     <frameset cols="166,720*" rows="*">
      <frame name="mainFrame" src="prodList.html" scrolling="AUTO">
      <frame src="content.html" name="miscContent" scrolling="NO">
     </frameset>
     <frame src="buttons.html" name="extButtons">
   </frameset>
  </frameset>
</frameset>
```

Fig. 13-21. HTML source code for completed frame set.

Step-by-Step Instructions

Go Solo

DWExercises Site

1. Make sure you are working with the site *DWExercises*.

2. We are going to open a frame set created in the previous exercise. If you did not finish the previous practice exercise, you can copy the finished files from *Learning_DWcomplete/ch13/dw13ex1.html* on the companion CD-ROM into the *Learning_Dreamweaver/ch13* folder on your hard drive. Rename the file *home.html*. These files are what you would have created in the previous practice exercise.

   a) Make sure all document windows are closed, including any untitled documents.

   b) Use the Site panel to locate the *ch13* folder and within it the file named *home.html*. Double click on *home.html* to open the file.

   c) The file *home.html* should now appear in your copy of Dreamweaver MX.

3. *home.html* contains five frames. If you cannot see the frames or the frame borders, select View Menu | Visual Aids | Frame Borders.

4. The left frame (which is called *leftFrame*) is going to have a background graphic and a graphic for the company logo.

   a) To insert a background graphic into the frame, we will actually be setting the background graphic for the HTML page linked to this frame. Place the cursor in the left frame and select Modify Menu | Page Properties.

   b) Next to Background Image, click on the Browse button to locate the background graphic image. Use the scroll bar to find the *ch13* folder. Select the file *interface_r1_c1.jpg*.

   c) Click on OK to exit Page Properties.

d) The graphic will automatically be "tiled" in the background of the left frame.

e) Resize the left frame until the graphic does not tile from left to right. The frame should contain only the graphic (approximately 118 pixels).

f) To insert the image for the logo, make sure the cursor is still in the left frame and select Insert Menu | Image. Locate and select the graphic image *brs_logo.gif* in the *ch13* folder.

g) Figure 13-22 displays the page with the content in the left frame.

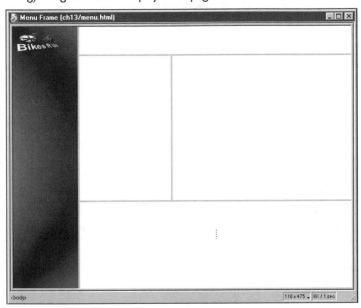

Fig. 13-22. Left frame with background image and logo.

5. The top frame (which is called *topFrame*) is going to have a graphic in it that will continue the interface located in the left frame. We do not want to tile it, so it will not be inserted as a background image.

a) Place the cursor in the top frame and select Insert Menu | Image. Locate and select the graphic image *interface_ r1_c2.jpg* in the *ch13* folder.

b) Notice that the graphic is not flush against the left or top of the frame. This is because frames have a default margin between the frame border and the content in the frame. Let's change this. Select the frame called *topFrame* using the Frames panel (Window | Frames) and type *0* (zero) in the Margin Width field of the Property Inspector. See figure 13-23.

Margin Width

Fig. 13-23. Property Inspector | Frame | Margin Width.

   c)   The height of the frame is still too tall for the graphic we just inserted. Resize the frame called *topFrame* until its height is just tall enough for the interface graphic. The height should be approximately 50 pixels.

6.   Select File Menu | Save All. Then preview your document (F12). There should be a panel on the left and top of the page, with a logo image in the upper left corner. Close the browser.

7.   The frame called *mainFrame* will display images of five bikes. When a bike is clicked on, a description of that bike will appear in the frame called *miscContent*.

   a)   To format the five images of the bikes and have more control over the way they display inside the frame, the images will go into a table. Place the cursor in the frame called *mainFrame* and select Insert Menu | Table. Create a table with five rows, one column, width 100%, and border 0. See figure 13-24.

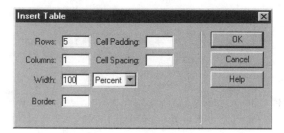

Fig. 13-24. Insert table.

   b)   Each table row will contain a graphic. Insert the following graphics into each table row, starting with the top row. All of these graphics are found in the *ch13* folder.

- *bike1.jpg*
- *bike2.jpg*
- *bike3.jpg*
- *bike4.jpg*
- *bike5.jpg*

c) Resize the width of the table until it surrounds the images.

d) Select the table and set the table alignment to center (Property Inspector | Align | Center), so that the table is in the center of the frame.

e) Select the column of the table and set the Horizontal Alignment setting of the Cell Contents option to Center. The images will display in the horizontal center of each table cell.

f) Select File | Save All.

g) Resize the frame called *mainFrame* until it is just a little larger than the table with the bike graphics – approximately 166 pixels. Do not make it so narrow that a horizontal scroll bar appears.

8. We want the frame with the bikes to have a set size, and the frame to the right of the bike graphics to have a relative size so that it "stretches" with the width of a browser window.

a) To set the frame to relative size, the frame set for the frames needs to be selected. Select the frame *miscContent* in the Frames panel (Window | Frames). Hold down the Ctrl/Option key and press the Up arrow to select its frame set. (You may need to click somewhere in the Document window first, and then repeat this selection process.)

b) In the Property Inspector for the frame set, select the right column in the RowCol Selection diagram. The Units should be set to Relative. This causes the width of the HTML page in this frame to stretch so that the frame set fills the width of the browser window.

9. Select File | Save All. Then preview your document (F12). You should preview in both IE and Netscape to check that the frames and tables are displaying correctly.

10. The right frame called *miscContent* is going to be considered the content for our home page. It will contain a brief introduction to the pages.

a) There will be one image in this frame, and we want it to center in the frame. This is done with a table. Place the cursor in the frame called *miscContent* and select Insert Menu | Table. Create a table with one row, one column, 100%, border 0.

b) Place the cursor inside the table and insert the image called *content1.jpg*, found in the *ch13* folder.

c) Set the alignment of the image to Center, so that it centers in the middle of the table.

d) The image is too high up in the frame because the table height does not fill the frame. Select the table in the frame *miscContent*, set the height to %, and type *90* in the height (H) box. We did not set it to 100% because we want to compensate for the margins, cell padding, and other properties of the table, frame, and browser window. See figure 13-25.

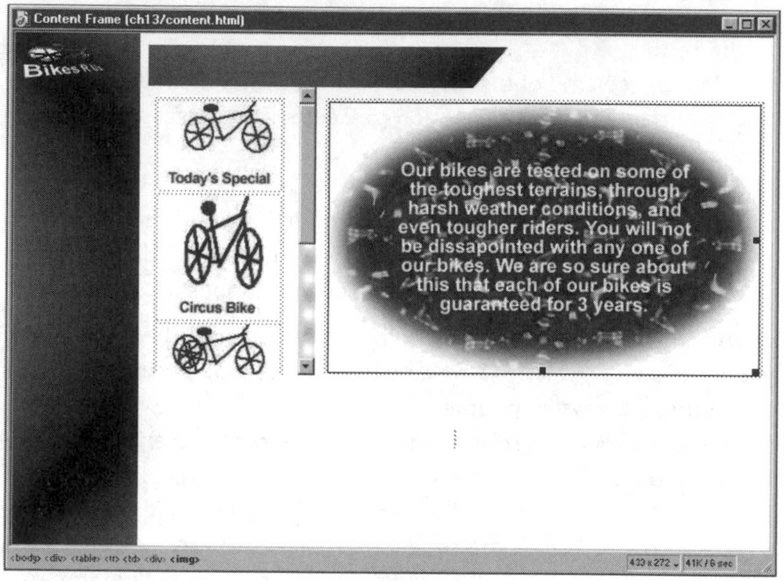

Fig. 13-25. Frame set after completing middle frames.

11. The bottom frame will contain a navigational bar with two buttons: Home and Contact.

a) Place the cursor in the bottom frame, called *extButtons*.

b) Select Insert Menu | Interactive Images | Navigation Bar (or select Insert bar | Common).

c) You are prompted to enter the name of the element (image) for the up state, rollover, down state, and the URL to link the button to.

For Element Name, type in *home*.

For Up Image, browse for *home_f01.jpg* in the *ch13* folder.

For Over Image, browse for *home_f02.jpg* in the *ch13* folder.

For Down Image, browse for *home_f02.jpg* in the *ch13* folder to make the down image the same as the over image. The down image appears when the button is clicked. If nothing is entered here, a blank area appears until the URL link is complete.

For When Clicked, Go To URL, browse for *content.html* in the *ch13* folder.

In the pull-down menu next to the URL, select the window miscContent. This causes the page *content.html* to open in the frame called *miscContent*. This is the middle right frame in the frameset.

We want the navigation bar to be horizontal, so leave Insert/Horizontally and check Use Tables. Figure 13-26 illustrates the completed entries for the Home button.

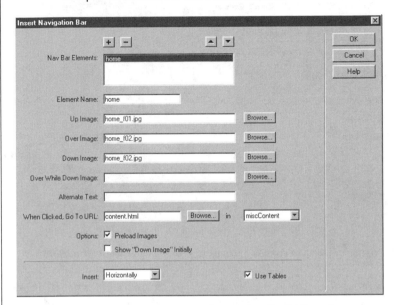

Fig. 13-26. Insert | Interactive Images | Navigation Bar | Home button.

d) While still in the Insert Navigation Bar window, click on the plus (+) key to insert another button in the Navigation bar and enter the following.

For Element Name, type in *contact.*

For Up Image, browse for *contact_f01.jpg* in the *ch13* folder.

For Over Image, browse for *contact _f02.jpg* in the *ch13* folder.

For Down Image, browse for *contact _f02.jpg* in the *ch13* folder to make the down image the same as the over image. The down image appears when the button is clicked. If nothing is entered here, a blank area appears until the URL link is complete.

For *When Clicked, Go To URL*, type in *mailto:sales@ brs.xyz*. Now when the contact button is clicked, the default e-mail software will open, with the *Bikes R Us* e-mail address in the "To" box. Enter your own e-mail address here to actually test the link.

Leave the pull-down menu next to the URL alone. Because we are not opening another HTML page, the Window option does not apply to this button. Figure 13-27 illustrates the completed entries for the Contact button.

CAUTION

At this point in the exercise you are creating an e-mail link for our fictitious web site. As you should when posting any web page with links, be very careful about checking the accuracy of your link addresses. As a precaution here, we are using the *.xyz* extension to keep this exercise clearly within the realm of our fictitious web site.

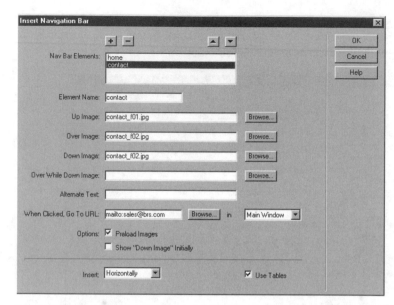

Fig. 13-27. Insert | Interactive Images | Navigation Bar for the Contact button.

e) Click on OK to exit the Navigation Bar dialog box. A table with two buttons (Home and Contact) should be displayed in the bottom frame.

12. The table with the two buttons needs to be in the middle of the frame. Select the table containing the Home and Contact buttons, and then select Align | Center.

13. To finish up this bottom frame, a horizontal line will be placed above the table with the buttons.

   a) Place the cursor to the left side of the table, in the bottom frame, and press the Enter/Return key to insert a new line above the table.

   b) Move the cursor up to the new line above the table and select Insert | Image. Browse and select the file called *vertical_line.jpg* in the *ch13* folder. A horizontal burgundy line appears above the table. Make sure the setting for this horizontal line is Align Center.

14. Select File Menu | Save All. Then preview your document (F12). When the Contact button is selected, an e-mail window opens. When Home is selected, you will not see any change because the page the button is linked to is already displayed in the frame called *miscContent* (the HTML page is *content.html*).

15. Each of the bike graphics now needs to be linked to its own page that will display in the right frame called *miscContent*. The description pages have already been created for you and reside in the *ch13* folder.

a) Select the first bike graphic, called *bike1.jpg*. Using the Property Inspector, select the Browse for File button next to the Link box.

b) Locate the file *btoday.html* in the *ch13* folder within your site. The folder is *Learning_Dreamweaver*. Before selecting the file, make sure that the Relative to option is set to Document.

c) Next to Target, select the window *miscContent*. See figure 13-28.

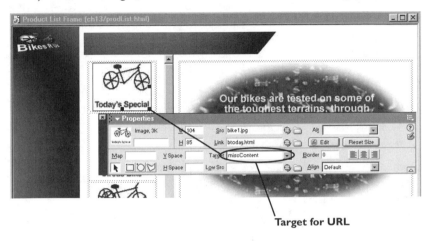

Target for URL

Fig. 13-28. Property Inspector | Target.

d) Link the rest of the bike graphics according to the following list (be sure to select Target | *miscContent* for each of the links).

bike2.jpg links to *bcircus.html*.
bike3.jpg links to *bchild.html*.
bike4.jpg links to *bmountain.html*.
bike5.jpg links to *bunicycles.html*.

16. Select File Menu | Save All. Then preview your document (F12). Be sure to check all of the bike graphic links. If a selected bike's description does not appear in the right frame, but instead replaces the bike's graphic, you probably forgot to set the target to *miscContent*. If you find mistakes, exit the browser and make whatever changes you need to so that the links work correctly.

17. Now let's create a NoFrames page for this frame set (for browsers that do not support frames).

a) Select Modify Menu | Frameset | Edit NoFrames Content. Then type in *This site uses frames. Update your browser or set your preferences so that they will support frames.*

b) To close the NoFrames window, select Modify Menu | Frameset | Edit NoFrames Content again.

·T/P·

When setting links for frames, always make sure the target is set. Otherwise, the link will open the URL and replace the entire page (not just a single frame).

18. To look at the HTML for the frame set, select the outermost frame set in the Frames panel and press the F10 key to open the HTML window. Notice the *frames* tags and the *noFrames* tag.

19. Close the Document window.

Summary

- *Think of frames as a way to divide (visually and functionally) an HTML page into two or more areas. Frames give you the ability to change one or more of these areas within the page without having to redisplay (download) the entire page.*

- *Although most people commonly use the word frame, what they are usually referring to is actually a web page, called a frame set, which consists of two or more separate pages called frames.*

- *A frame set contains two or more frames.*

- *Some browsers do not support frames if they are older than version 3 or are set to text-based only. The NoFrames Content option will display if the browser does not support frames.*

- *Frames can be used for menus, elements of the web site interface, Help, lists, glossary, index, and other features.*

- *Frames can be created either by using predefined frames or using the mouse.*

- *Frames and frame sets have a number of properties that can be changed with the use of the Property Inspector.*

- *In the first guided tour, you took a quick look at creating frames and frame sets, and worked with the Frames panel.*

- *In the first practice exercise, you began the process of creating a frame set and frames. You gained experience selecting frame sets and frames, resizing frames, adding titles to the HTML file linked to the frame, and saving a frame set and frames.*

- *In the second practice exercise, you created hyperlinks to frames, set properties for frames, used the noFrames content window, inserted a navigation bar, and inserted a table.*

C H A P T E R

14

Application Chapter: Using Frames

Introduction

Using frames is a great way to display different areas of information on a page without having to redisplay the entire page. You can change the content in an area (frame) without affecting other frames currently displayed.

Application Exercise Objectives

By the end of this chapter you will have created:

- *A directory of recipes using three frames*
- *Content for each frame, including linkages*

Application Exercise 14-1: Using Frames

Description

In this application chapter, you will create a directory listing for some of the special recipes of *The 21st Century Kitchen*. You will create a page (frame set) with three frame areas. The first frame will be for the banner graphic and the recipe category buttons. The second frame will contain a listing of the various recipes in a category. The third frame will contain the instructions for the recipe selected. A visitor to this site will be able to select any of the four recipe categories. When they select a category, a listing of the available recipes will be displayed. Clicking on any of the recipes (three in this exercise) will reveal the instructions for preparing that particular dish.

Take a Look

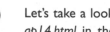

CD-ROM

Let's take a look at how the finished exercise will look. Open the file named *ap14.html* in the *Learning_DWapplication_complete* folder on the companion CD-ROM. Double click on the icon and the file will open in your web browser. Look at the layout of the web page, noticing the graphic and text areas. Take a look at the file and the HTML code in Dreamweaver MX. Note the following properties as you complete this exercise.

- *The graphic banner at the top of the page.*
- *Move the cursor over the buttons (recipe categories) and notice the change in each button's appearance (the Over state).*
- *Click on the Appetizers category and notice how one of the frames changes to a listing of recipes for that category.*
- *Select Entrées, and then select one of the recipe names and see how the frame's content changes.*

You will be using the following Dreamweaver MX concepts in the exercise.

- *Creating and modifying frames*
- *Setting properties of frames and frame sets*
- *Placing content in frames*
- *Using rollover images*
- *Using the Target property to link buttons to new pages*
- *Replacing a frame with a new HTML file when a button is selected*

Storyboard: Browser View

Figure 14-1 shows how the product web page will look in a web browser when the exercise is completed.

Fig. 14-1. Completed exercise within a browser.

Storyboard: Dreamweaver MX View

Figure 14-2 shows how the product web page will look in Dreamweaver MX when the exercise is completed.

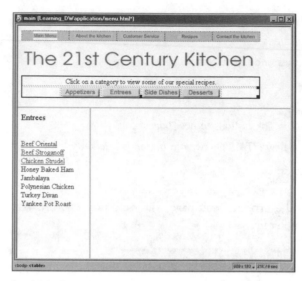

Fig. 14-2. Completed exercise in Dreamweaver MX.

Application Project Steps

**21st Century
KITCHEN SITE**

Complete this exercise on your own, guided by following the general steps. You can always refer back to the completed example you viewed in the "Take a Look" section of this exercise.

NOTE: The following steps are intended as a guide. This is your project, so feel free to make whatever variations you like.

1. Create a new file in Dreamweaver MX.

2. Save the new page as *recipes.html.*

3. From the Frames category of the Insert bar, select Insert Top and Nested Left Frames, the second icon from the right.

4. Select the *<frameset>* tag in the Dreamweaver MX status bar (lower left of the Document window).
   a) Save the frame set and name it *21recip.html* using File Menu | Save Frameset As. Be sure to save it in the folder *Learning_ DWapplication.*
   b) In the Title field, title the frame set *21st Century Kitchen Recipes.*
   c) Make the frame borders visible using View Menu | Visual Aids | Frame Borders. You can also use the View Options icon on the toolbar.

5. Using the Frames panel, click inside the frame called *main*, name it *instructions* in the Frame Name field in the Property Inspector, and save it as *inst.html.*

6. Click inside the frame called *left*, name it *listing* in the Frame Name field, and save it as *list.html.*

7. Click inside the frame called *top*, name it *main* in the Frame Name field, and save as *menu.html*.

8. Place the banner graphic *21ckbnr.jpg* (found in the *ap_media* subfolder) in the frame called *main*. Also above the banner, insert the Library object called *mainNav*.

9. Press Shift + Enter/Return to move the cursor to the next line.

10. Insert a table, two rows, and zero border.
    a) In the first row, type *Click on a category to view some of our special recipes.* Center align the text in the row.
    b) In the second row, split the row into six (6) columns.
    c) In the four (4) middle cells (leave the first and last columns empty), insert rollover images for Appetizers, Entrées, Side Dishes, and Desserts using the graphics *appet.jpg, appeto.jpg, entree.jpg, entreeo.jpg, side.jpg, sideo.jpg, dessert.jpg,* and *desserto.jpg* (found in the *ap_media* subfolder). Place each button in its own cell.
    d) Use the Layout view to place a spacer in the first and last cells (columns) to force the columns to a specific width. Resize the table to fit under the heading. To insert a spacer, select the Table tab at the top of the column and select Add Spacer.

11. If needed, resize the frame called *main* so that the banner, text, and four buttons are visible (drag the bottom border line down to fit).

12. Click in the frame called *listing* and move the cursor over the divider between the *listing* frame and the instruction frame until the cursor changes into a double arrow. Click once on the frame divider. The Property Inspector should now reference the frame set. On the right side of the Property Inspector, select the left column and set the column width value to 160 pixels.

13. Click on the Appetizers button. In the Property Inspector, link the button to the *appet.html* file found in the *Learning_DWapplication* folder, and set the Target option to *listing*. You might have to expand the view of the Property Inspector. If you do not set *listing* in the Target option, your information will appear in the wrong window.

14. Do the same for the Entrées (*entrée.html*), Side Dishes (*side.html*), and Desserts (*dessert.html*) buttons, setting the Target option to *listing*.

15. This might be a good time to use Save All and preview in a browser. If you do not set *listing* in the Target option, your information will appear in the wrong window.

16. Now that we have the frame called *main* (with the banner and the recipe category buttons) and the frame called *listing* (with the listing of each category's recipes) working, we might want to add some of the recipes.

17. Link the three recipe instruction files to the frame called *listing* by placing the cursor in the frame called *listing* and from the File menu selecting Open In Frame to open the *entrée.html* file (in the *Recipes* subfolder).

18. Highlight the words *Beef Oriental*. In the Properties Inspector, link to the *beefor.html* file (in the *Recipes* subfolder) and set the Target option to *instructions*.

19. Do the same for the Beef Stroganoff (*beefst.html*) and Chicken Strudel (*chick.html*) buttons, setting the Target option to *instructions*.

20. Save all frames and preview in a browser. You should be able to see the banner graphic and the four recipe category buttons. Pressing any of the category buttons should reveal the recipe listing for that category. In the Entrée category there are three recipes to view.

To add more structure to the interface for our site, let's change the target for the Main Menu button found in the main navigation bar at the top of the window.

21. Notice the navigation when you click on the Main Menu button. Only the top frame is replaced with the Main Menu page. We want the entire window to be replaced with the Main Menu page.

22. In the Document window, open the Library object called *mainNav* (this is what the Main Menu button is in).

23. Click on the Main Menu button and in the Property Inspector, change the Target option to *_parent*.

24. Click on the Recipes button and in the Property Inspector set the Link option to *21recipes.html*.

25. Save the library and update.

26. In the Document window for the frame set and frames, select File | Save All to incorporate the library changes.

27. Preview the file again and check the Main Menu button to make sure that when it is clicked, the entire browser window is replaced with a new page.

Summary

In this application chapter you have created a directory listing for recipes using frames. You first created a new web page and then added a frame set to it. You named and set the parameters for each of the three frames. You added category information into the *listing* frame for each of four categories. Finally, you added the instructions and linkages for three of the recipes and made them appear in the *instruction* frame.

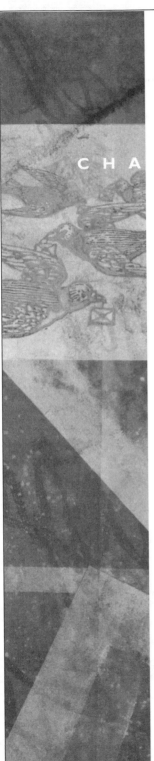

CHAPTER

15

Adding Functionality with Behaviors

Introduction

In previous chapters we touched on the subject of behaviors but never really went into any depth. Previous exercises actually used behaviors that were part of another Dreamweaver MX function. One previous example was with the use of Insert | Interactive Images | Rollover Image. In this example, one image was swapped with the second image, based on a user interaction. The Dreamweaver MX behavior used in conjunction with a rollover image is called a swap image.

Behaviors increase the capabilities of a web document to manipulate content. When a user interacts with a web page, an event occurs (such as clicking on a button). With this event, not only can a link be executed (with HTML code) but we can have a behavior "animate" a button; or, with the use of JavaScript, a pop-up window can appear.

Oh, no! – JavaScript – but I'm not a programmer! Do not worry. Dreamweaver MX creates the JavaScript for you, and there are additional behaviors you can download that are created by third-party developers. By the end of this chapter you will be able to:

- *Describe the structure of a behavior and indicate when it should be used*
- *Use the Behaviors panel*
- *Attach a behavior*
- *Determine the type of event to use*

So What Is a Behavior?

Behaviors are a combination of actions and events. An action takes place in response to an event that occurs. The decision as to when to use a behavior really comes down to determining that HTML by itself cannot accomplish the task you want.

Let's look at an example in the Behaviors panel. Figure 15-1 shows an example of a behavior that has been attached to an image. In this example, when the user clicks the mouse on a button (the event *onMouseDown*), the first image is swapped (the action) with a second image. In addition, when the mouse moves away from the button (the event *onMouseOut*), the button is restored (the action) to its original image.

Fig. 15-1. Behaviors panel.

Shortcut

To open the Behaviors
panel press shift+F3.

Actions

Action is a term used within Dreamweaver MX. Actions are generally named
according to the function they perform. For example, Play Sound plays a
sound, Open Browser Window opens a browser window, and so on. Actions
are a series of HTML and JavaScript commands that are usually inside a
JavaScript function. You are not limited to the actions listed in the Behaviors
panel when Dreamweaver MX was first installed. You can create your own
actions to add to the Dreamweaver list. There are also many third-party
behaviors that can be downloaded from the Internet.

Events (Event Handlers)

An event can be something the user does (such as clicking the mouse or
pressing a key on the keyboard), or something that happens within the
browser window (such as a page loading or closing). Events (or event handlers) have specific names. Events are dynamic and seem to change in both
appearance and structure with the new versions of web browsers.

One of the easiest ways to identify an event in your HTML window is to look
for a word with the prefix *on*, as in *onMouseDown* or *onBlur*. Because JavaScript
is case sensitive, the event name is also case sensitive. If you were to write the
event *onMouseDown* with a lowercase m (i.e., *onmouseDown*), the event would
not work. Events fall into two main categories: Window Modification events
and Interaction events.

Window Modification Events

This type of event affects the browser window or a frame in a page and
includes events such as when a page loads or is closed, or when some attribute of the window is modified. These events usually do not have anything to

do with user interaction. Behaviors associated with these events will normally be placed in the *<body>* tag. Figure 15-2 illustrates possible Window Modification events.

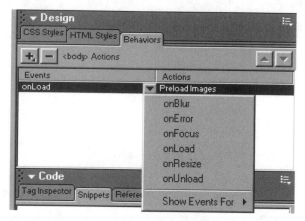

Fig. 15-2. Window Modification events.

Explanations of various events follow.

- onLoad: *When a page or an object loads in the browser. The* onLoad *event is generally attached to the <body> tag to check something (e.g., the browser version) or to change something on the page (a sound that is going to play).*

- onAbort: *When the user interrupts the browser loading a page (e.g., when the user clicks on the Stop button).*

- onResize: *When the user resizes the browser window or a frame.*

- onUnload: *When a page is closed (i.e., when jumping to a new page).*

- onFocus: *When the specified window becomes the focus of the user's interaction (e.g., clicking inside a window).*

- onBlur: *When the focus of the user is no longer on the specified window (e.g., when the user clicks the mouse outside the current active window). This is the opposite event of* onFocus.

Interaction Events

This type of event includes keyboard and mouse events. These events occur when the user interacts with an element on the page. Behaviors with these events will normally go in the link *<a>* tag for the element. Figure 15-3 shows some Interaction events. Notice that *onBlur* and *onFocus* are listed here as well as being listed as Window events. The difference is that in Window events the events are based on the window, and Interaction events are based on an object.

Fig. 15-3. Interaction events.

Explanations of interaction events follow. See figure 15-4.

- **onMouseDown:** *When the user first presses the mouse button. This is generally used to activate a sound or animation – something to occur as soon as the mouse is clicked.*

- **onMouseUp:** *When the user lets up (releases) the mouse button (after it has been down). This is generally used to jump (link) to a URL because it gives the user a chance to change his mind by moving the mouse out of the area before releasing the mouse button.*

- **onMouseOut:** *When the cursor (pointer) moves away (out of the bounding box of an image) from the specified object.*

- **onMouseOver:** *When the cursor (pointer) first moves over the bounding box of a specified object (without clicking on it). This differs from onMouseWithin, which "matches" as long as the mouse is over the object. onMouseWithin is only available with IE4 and above.*

- **onBlur:** *When the focus of the user is no longer on the specified object. An example would be when the user clicks outside a text field that was the original focus. (This is the opposite event of onFocus.)*

- **onFocus:** *When the specified object becomes the focus of the user's interaction. An example would be clicking inside a text field. (This is the opposite event of onBlur.)*

- **onClick:** *When the cursor is clicked on the specified object. The mouse must be released before the action occurs. (Use onMouseDown to make something occur immediately.)*

·T/P·

(onMouseDown) vs. onMouseDown: events with parentheses occur before events without parentheses. Events with parentheses can only be attached to a link. The following shows the chronological order with (onMouseDown) vs. onMouseDown.

Example 1:

*(onMouseOut)
(onMouseOver)
onMouseDown*

Example 2:

*(onMouseDown)
(onMouseOut)
(onMouseOver)*

Also, if an event with parentheses is attached to an object, a null link (the text *javascript:;*) is inserted into the Link field. This gives the object a cursor (the hand) when the pointer is rolled over the image. Another way to get the cursor (and make an object look like it is "hot") is to enter a # sign in the Link field.

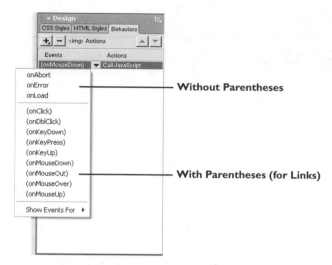

Fig. 15-4. Behaviors panel showing differences in events.

Using Behaviors: The Relationship Between Actions and Events

Probably the most difficult part of working with behaviors is determining where or what to attach the behavior to. To help with this, try to determine *when* you want an action to occur, which should help you determine *where* in the document the behavior (and event) should be inserted.

When selecting a behavior, Dreamweaver MX looks at *what* the behavior is being attached to (object, text, window, and so on), and then displays only those behaviors available for that element (all behaviors are not available for all elements). When a behavior is selected, Dreamweaver MX selects a default event for that behavior (again, based on the element it is being attached to). You can then select a different event if you need to.

Primary Steps for Attaching a Behavior

The following is a list of steps to be used in attaching a behavior to an element in your page.

- *Select an object, text, or HTML tag.*
- *In the Behaviors panel, click on the plus (+) button. A list of available behaviors will appear. The available behaviors depend on the type of media you have selected, such as text, image, body of the page, and so on.*

- *Fill in the appropriate selections for the behavior.*
- *In the Behaviors panel, the action for the behavior will be listed with the event. Select another event for the action, if necessary.*
- *To select a different event, select the Event/Action combination. The Down arrow appears next to the event. Selecting the arrow (it is a menu) will display a list of available events based on the browser version. At the bottom of the list is the option to show events for a different browser version.*
- *If you want to make sure your page works in older browser versions, make sure you select Show Events For | 3.0 and Later Browsers. Each browser supports some events that are not in the other browsers or that work a little differently. If you know what browser everyone will use (or are limiting users to a particular browser), specifically show the events for that browser.*

The following are some examples of when you might want to use behaviors. Some of these are included with Dreamweaver MX, and others you can find from third-party sources. Use a behavior to:

- *Open a new browser window to display an index or glossary*
- *Control the animation in a timeline*
- *Change the text displayed in the browser window's Status bar to tell the user where a button will link (instead of just displaying the URL for the link)*
- *Control Flash and Shockwave*
- *Play a sound in the background or when a button is clicked*
- *Call custom JavaScript that you or a third party has developed*

Working with Behaviors

Modifying a Behavior

If the action and/or the event for a behavior needs to be changed, select the element (object, text, or tag) to which the behavior is attached. Then in the Behaviors panel (shown in figure 15-5) double click on the action to modify it.

To change the event, select the behavior in the Behaviors panel. Select the Down arrow that appears between the event and the action. Select the event from the displayed list. To make sure the event works with the browser version you are targeting, select Show Events For at the bottom of the list of events.

*T*I*P*

The Snippets panel (Window | Snippets) has some predefined snippets (code) that will check the browser type and version. Look under the folder JavaScript | Browser Functions within the Snippets panel. Double clicking one of the snippets will insert a JavaScript function into your document. This lets you redirect the browser to a different page.

Fig. 15-5. Behaviors panel showing more than one action available for the same event.

Deleting a Behavior

To delete a behavior, select the element (object, text, or tag) to which the behavior is attached. Then in the Behaviors panel select the behavior and click on the Minus (–) button at the top of the panel (or press the Delete key on your keyboard).

Characteristics of Behaviors

- *More than one behavior can be attached to a single element.*

- *An event can have more than one action. For example, the onMouseDown event may trigger a sound and a link to a URL. You can also specify the order in which the actions occur.*

- *Not all behaviors can be attached to any HTML tag. For example, the onLoad event cannot be attached to a link (<a>) tag. The Behaviors panel will only list the events you can use with a specific tag.*

- *All behaviors (events and/or actions) do not work in all browsers or browser versions.*

- *Behaviors cannot be selected while in a Library object.*

- *Behaviors can be attached while in a template. However, behaviors cannot be attached to a page linked to a template unless the JavaScript function it is calling already exists in the attached template. For example, if the template already has a function to swap images, a page attached to that template is simply calling that function. The reason behaviors cannot be attached to pages with templates is that behaviors insert code in the <Head> tag and this is locked, except for the page title.*

Guided Tour 15A: Behaviors Panel

Before we actually begin attaching behaviors to a page, take a little time to experiment with the Behaviors panel.

1. Open a new HTML document using File Menu | New and General | Basic Page | HTML.

2. Type in *go next.*

3. Check to see if the Behaviors panel is visible by selecting Windows Menu | Behaviors.

4. Make sure the phrase *go next* is selected. From the Behaviors panel, select the Plus (+) button.

5. Notice the actions that are available for the highlighted text item. Select one of the actions and fill in any information that is requested.

6. After the action has been selected, the action and event are displayed in the Behaviors panel. Select the behavior, and the Down arrow next to the event. Notice the events that could be selected.

7. At the bottom of the Events list, select Show Events For and select a different browser version. See the change in the events. Make sure you select Show Events For | 4.0 and Later Browsers before you are finished.

8. Select the *<body>* tag in the Status bar at the bottom of the Document window. Look at the behaviors that are available.

9. Preview the page to see how the behaviors you have selected affect the page.

Practice Exercise 15-1: Opening and Closing Browser Windows

Description

Generally, web site developers want to keep viewers within their site as long as possible while still providing the ability to link to related sites, open additional windows, and open support files. We can perform this balancing act by using a behavior that will open a new window, while the current window stays open. The user can view the new page while the original page remains present, minimizing the possibilities of the user straying away or getting lost. The new window can be set to open at a specific size, and with or without toolbars, Status bar, or scrolling options. When the user is finished with this new window, she simply closes it and returns to the original page that is still open.

We actually first used this behavior in Chapter 9, but now will add more detail concerning available parameters. In this exercise, selecting the Glossary button opens a new window of terms. The user can then select the Close button to close the Glossary window. The following elements are covered in this exercise.

- *Attaching a behavior to an image*
- *Opening a new browser window at a set size and with properties turned on/off*
- *Closing the browser window with a behavior*
- *Changing the event for a behavior*
- *Swapping image on rollover*

Take a Look

DWComplete Site

CD-ROM

Before beginning the exercise, let's take a look at the exercise in its completed state so that you can clearly see what you are about to build.

1. Select the *DWComplete* site.

2. Locate the *ch15* folder and within it, and the file named *dw15ex1.html*. Double click on *dw15ex1.html* to open the file.

3. The file *dw15ex1.html* should now appear in your copy of Dreamweaver MX. Note the following properties of this completed exercise.

    a) Open the Behaviors panel (Window | Behaviors). Select the graphic with the text *Glossary of events*. Notice in the Behaviors panel that there is the behavior Open Browser Window, based on the event *onClick*. Double click on this behavior to see the properties that have been set.

    b) While the *Glossary* graphic is still selected, look in the Property Inspector. The Link box contains *javascript:;* (there is a colon and a semicolon after *javascript*).

    c) Notice some additional formatting on the page: the use of a table to position the graphics on the page, the table is not centered, and the table is confined to a set width (pixels).

4. Close *dw15ex1.html*.

5. Locate the *ch15* folder and within it the file named *glossary.html*. Double click on *glossary.html* to open the file.

6. This is the page that will open when selecting *Glossary of events* from the previous document. Select the graphic *Close*. In the Behaviors panel is the behavior Call JavaScript.

7. Look in the Property Inspector for the graphic *Close*, and in the Link box for the JavaScript that is executed.

8. Notice the use of a table to separate the glossary terms and images.

Storyboard: On Screen

Figures 15-6 and 15-7 show you how the finished pages will look when viewed through a browser.

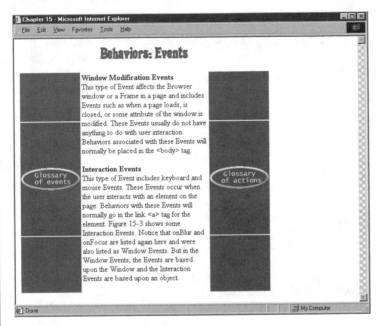

Fig. 15-6. Completed exercise within a browser.

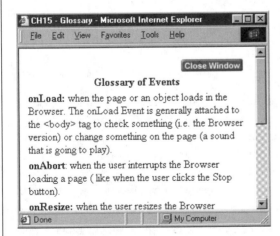

Fig. 15-7. Completed exercise showing the Glossary window.

Storyboard: Behind the Scenes

Figure 15-8 shows the HTML code created behind the behaviors in this exercise. Highlighted is the JavaScript function and the behavior attached to the Glossary of Events button.

Fig. 15-8. HTML window for completed exercise.

Unlike text, when attaching a behavior to an image, the image does not need to already have an anchor tag around it. Multiple behaviors are available in the Behaviors panel at the beginning. Text, on the other hand, must have an anchor tag before any behaviors are available for selection in the Behaviors panel.

Step-by-Step Instructions

1. We are going to open an existing document that was copied to your hard drive when you installed the chapter exercises in Chapter 1.
   a) Change to the *DWExercises* site. Use the Site panel to locate the *ch15* folder and within it the file named *main.html*. Double click on *main.html* to open the file.
   b) The file *main.html* should now appear in the Document window of Dreamweaver MX.

2. When the button Glossary of Events is clicked, it should open a new browser window with some glossary words.
   a) Click on the Glossary of Events button, and then select Window Menu | Behaviors. The Behaviors panel is now displayed.

b) Select the Plus (+) button in the top left of the window to view the Behaviors pull-down menu.

c) Locate and select Open Browser Window.

d) The Open Browser Window dialog box is now open. See figure 15-9. Insert the following information in the dialog box fields.

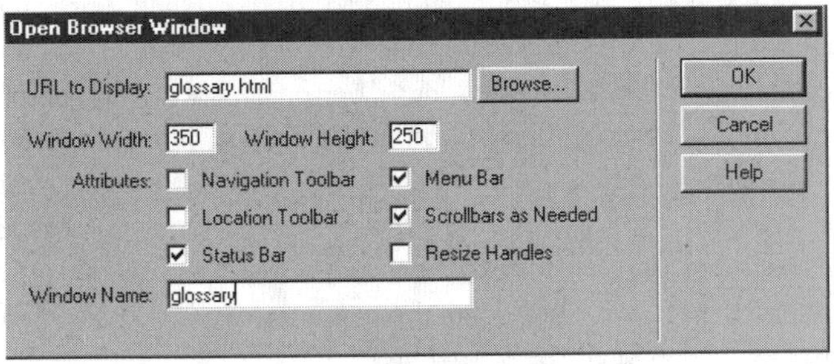

Fig. 15-9. Behaviors | Open Browser Window.

- URL to Display: *Browse for the file glossary.html in the ch15 folder. Before selecting the file, make sure that Select File from File System is selected and that Relative to is set to Document. The URL is the page that will be opened in the new browser window.*

- Window Width (W) and Height (H): *W should be set to 350, and H set to 250. This width and height is in pixels and will give the Glossary page enough room to open without a horizontal scroll bar being displayed.*

- Attributes: *We will want a Status bar and a Menu bar to be displayed. With the Menu bar displayed, the user can print the page and use any of the other browser options. The Status bar will allow us to display some message as a link is being selected. The Scroll bar must be selected if the new window is opened at a smaller size than the content in the page. If the Scroll bar were not selected, the user would not be able to scroll down (or horizontally) to view additional areas of a page.*

  Menu Bar: Check it.

  Scrollbars as Needed: Check it.

  Status Bar: Check it.

e) The following are other attribute options (which we will leave unchecked).

- Navigation Toolbar: *Displays the browser's navigational buttons, such as Back and Next.*

- Location Toolbar: *Displays the Address bar in the browser window.*

- Resize Handles: *Allows the user to resize the window. If this is not checked, the size of the browser window is locked.*

• Window Name: *Used for JavaScript and links for referencing the new window. This can be used to close or modify the window from another window. As with other names, do not include spaces or other special characters in the name.*

f) Click on OK.

g) There may be some modifications needed to make the link work the way we want it to. Listed in the Behaviors panel you should see an event beginning with *on*, such as *onMouseOver* or *onClick*. Which event you see at this point may depend on whether you have used the behaviors before in Dreamweaver MX. To the right of the event, you will see a Down arrow and then the behavior Open Browser Window. We want the browser to open when we click on the text and let up on the mouse. Therefore, the event we want is *onClick*. To change the event, perform the following.

Click on the Down arrow. A list of available events for the browser version is now listed. Select Show Events For. We are going to want our site's visitors to be able to use the browser version 4.0 or above, so select 4.0 and Later Browsers.

Click on the Down arrow again and the events available for browser version 4.0 and above are listed. Select (onClick).

h) Save the file.

i) Preview the page to see how the behavior opens a new browser window when the Glossary of Events button is clicked, and to see the size of the window as it opens.

j) Close both browser windows and return to Dreamweaver MX.

3. Let's look at the HTML code and the JavaScript that was generated when we selected Open Browser Window. Remember that we are still in the file *main.html*. Refer to figure 15-10 as we look at the HTML explanation.

a) To see both the Design window and the HTML source code, select the Show Code and Design Views button in the Dreamweaver MX toolbar.

b) Select the graphic *Glossary of Events*.

c) Looking at the HTML source code in Code view, the *<img src>* tag is highlighted because you have the image selected in the Document window.

• *Now look above the <img src> tag and look for the anchor (<a>) tag. The anchor tag (<a>) surrounds the <img src> tag. The anchor tag is required if an object links to a URL or anchor, or has a behavior. The HREF attribute in the <a> tag must at a minimum contain a URL (or, if this is not a link, a pound sign or the text* javascript::;*). The Property Inspector will display the value of the HREF attribute in the Link field.*

·T/P·

The difference between *onMouseDown* and *onClick* is that *onMouseDown* happens immediately when the mouse button is pressed. The user cannot change her mind and move the mouse away from the object. On the other hand, in order for the *onClick* event to execute, the cursor must remain over the object as the mouse is clicked and released.

- *Within the anchor tag is the source code for the behavior (onClick).*

- *At the top of the HTML source code is the JavaScript function (MM_openBrWindow) that was generated by the Dreamweaver MX behavior.*

```
"Glossary of events" image src tag:
<a href="javascript:;"    onClick="MM_openBrWindow('glossary.html',",'status=yes,
menubar=yes, scrollbars=yes,width=350,height=250')">

JavaScript function for MM_openBrWindow:
function MM_openBrWindow(theURL,winName,features) {
  window.open(theURL,winName,features);
}
```

Fig. 15-10. HTML source code for Open Browser Window behavior.

d) Let's take a closer look at the behavior.

- *When the user clicks on the image, the function MM_openBrWindow is called, as follows.*

  ```
  onClick="MM_openBrWindow( )
  ```

- *Three parameters are passed to the function, as follows. They follow the name of the function and are enclosed by parentheses. These are the options we selected when the Open Browser Window dialog box opened for the behavior.*

  ```
  "MM_openBrWindow('glossary.html','','status=yes,
  menubar=yes,scrollbars=yes,width=350,height=250')"
  ```

- *The first parameter is glossary.html. This is the URL to display.*

- *The second parameter is glossary. This is the window name.*

- *The third parameter includes all attributes we selected and their values: Status bar, Menu bar, Scroll bars, Width, and Height.*

e) Scroll to the top of the source code and you will see the JavaScript section (<script>) in the <head> tag. Within the <script> tag is the function *MM_openBrWindow*.

- *Remember that we are passing three parameters to the function: the URL, the window name, and the attributes for the window. The function accepts these parameters by including holders on the function line after the name of the function. The order of the parameters matches the order in which they were passed from the onClick, as follows.*

  ```
  function MM_openBrWindow(theURL,winName,features)
  ```

  theURL: *Will accept the value glossary.html*

  winName: *Will accept the value glossary*

  features: *Will accept the values:*

·TIP·

To set the anchor (<a>) tag without actually setting a link, type a pound sign (#) or the text, *javascript:;* (there is a colon and semicolon after *javascript*) in the Link box for the text. The text will then be underlined and colored, like a link. The null link (*javascript:;*) is preferable.

 HTML

·TIP·

Appendix C, found on the companion CD-ROM, will give you more detail about the syntax of JavaScript.

```
'status=yes,menubar=yes,scrollbars=yes,
 width=350,height=250'
```

- *The JavaScript follows the function line and will open the new window with the parameters we passed, as follows.*

```
window.open(theURL,winName,features)
```

- *With the parameters added, this is also the same as the following.*

```
window.open('glossary.html','glossary',
 'status=yes,menubar=yes,scrollbars=yes,
  width=350,height=250')
```

4. We will add a button on the Glossary page to close the new window.

   a) In the Site panel, locate the *ch15* folder and within it the file named *glossary.html*. Double click on *glossary.html* to open the file.

   b) Select the button image containing the text *Close Window*. When functional, this button will close the current window when the button is clicked. This button will also need to change images (from the Up state to the Down state) when the button is clicked.

   c) In the Behaviors panel, select Swap Image. When the dialog window is opened, the current image, called *closeWindow*, is automatically selected.

   d) Select the Browse button and in the *ch15* folder select the file *close_down.jpg*. Back in the Swap Image dialog window, the checkboxes to Reload Images and Restore Images onMouseOut are already selected. This will preload the *close_down.jpg* and set an *onMouseOut* event to set the file source of the image back to its original location and image. Click on OK.

   e) Let's review the changes in the Behaviors panel when the Swap Image behavior was attached. With the Close Window button selected, refer to the Behaviors panel. See figure 15-11.

·T/P·

Adding this "close button" is not absolutely necessary, because a visitor can use the close button in the Title bar of the window or use the File menu to close the window. However, many web designers include additional buttons like this so that the user will always have navigational control within the application and not have to rely on the browser window tools.

Fig. 15-11. Behaviors panel with Swap Image and Swap Image Restore.

- *There are now two new behaviors, as follows.*

  (onMouseOut) – Swap Image Restore: *Will return the button appearance back to its original image when the mouse rolls away from the button. This was created because the Restore Images onMouseOut checkbox was selected.*

  (onMouseOver) – Swap Image: *This will swap the image (closeWindow) when the mouse/cursor rolls over the image.*

- *Another behavior was also attached to the body of the tag. In the Status bar, click on the <body> tag. In the Behaviors panel is the behavior onLoad – Preload Images. Double click on the behavior and see that the close_down.jpg file will be preloaded into memory when the page loads. This behavior was attached to the page when the Preload Images checkbox was selected in the Swap Image behavior.*

- *Look at the HTML code. The Swap Image and Swap Image Restore both call JavaScript functions. These functions have been added to the <script> tag in the <head> of the document.*

5. To have the Close Window button actually close the current browser window, we will need to call JavaScript.

   a) Select the image *Close Window*.

   b) In the Behaviors panel, select the behavior Call JavaScript. See figure 15-12.

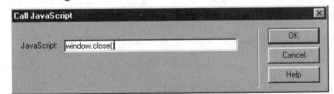

Fig. 15-12. Call JavaScript behavior.

   c) Type in *window.close()*. There aren't any spaces between the parentheses or between the words. This JavaScript will close the current window.

   d) Click on OK.

   e) The event *onMouseDown* is the default event for this action when 4.0 and Later Browser is selected. You might remember from an earlier discussion in this chapter that if an event is surrounded by parentheses, links (in the Link box) will also be activated. Because we do not have any links, it does not matter whether we use *onMouseDown* with or without parentheses. But to stay consistent with the other events, we will use *onMouseDown* with parentheses. Click on the Down arrow next to *onMouseDown*, and then select *(onMouseDown)*.

299

Selecting an event with parentheses – in this case, *(onMouseDown)* – inserts the null link *javascript:;* in the Link field if it is empty.

f) Look at the HTML source code for the *Close Window* image. When the Call JavaScript behavior is used, the *<a>* tag calls the function *MM_callJS()*. The following line shows the function call. It sends the JavaScript you typed in (*window.close()*) to the function.

```
onMouseDown="MM_callJS('window.close()')"
```

·T/P·

An alternative to using the Call JavaScript behavior is to type the JavaScript directly into the Link box of the Property Inspector.

g) Figure 15-13 shows the use of typing the JavaScript *window.close()* into the Link field instead of using the behavior Call JavaScript.

JavaScript

Fig. 15-13. JavaScript in the Link box.

6. Save the file.

7. To test the Close Window behavior, preview *main.html* from the Site panel (select the file and press F12 while in the Site panel). Now select the Glossary button and the Glossary page opens in its own window. Finally, select the Close Window button and the Glossary window closes.

8. Close the browser window to return to Dreamweaver MX.

9. Close the file *glossary.html*.

·T/P·

If you use *window.close()* to close a browser window that has not been opened by another browser window, you will receive the prompt box illustrated in figure 15-14. There is no way to get around this, so you may want to just instruct the user to use the browser's menu to close a window if you do not want her to receive this prompt.

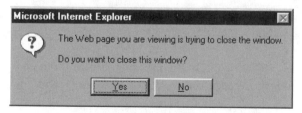

Fig. 15-14. Prompt message used in a browser window.

Dreamweaver MX Extensions: Third-party Behaviors

The Macromedia Extension Manager provides the means to "extend" the functionality and capabilities of Dreamweaver MX. (There are also extensions for Flash.) These extensions can add items to menus and behaviors, and items to the Insert bar. The Extension Manager has to be downloaded and installed before adding extensions. Within the Commands menu in Dreamweaver is the submenu Get Commands.

This menu option links to the Macromedia site from which you can download the Extension Manager. It also includes a list of Macromedia and third-party extensions that can be installed on your computer. These extensions include behaviors not included in Dreamweaver MX or that will enhance the existing Dreamweaver MX behaviors. The following are some of the extensions you may find.

- *Using history to go back or forward to a page that was previously loaded*
- *Inserting plugins*
- *Playing sounds*
- *Checking form data*

Once the Extension Manager is installed, an additional menu option (Manage Extensions) is added to the Commands menu. Figure 15-15 illustrates the window for the Extension Manager. To install extensions using the Extension Manager window, select File Menu | Add Extension from the menu bar in the Extension Manager window. Find and select the extension file you downloaded. The extension should then be listed in the Extension Manager window.

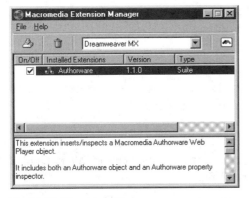

Fig. 15-15. Extension Manager.

Most extensions will display a description and a note on how to use the extension. Highlight the extension in the Extension Manager and the description displays in the bottom half of the window.

When you download Dreamweaver MX extensions, we suggest placing them all in the same folder so that you can easily find and install them from the Extension Manager.

The extensions for the Extension Manager can also be linked from the Behaviors panel. At the bottom of the Behaviors list (in the Behaviors panel) is Get More Behaviors.

Practice Exercise 15-2: Pop-up Messages

Description

When you want to display additional information on a web page based on a specified action of the user, you could display a layer (we will do this in the chapter on layers), swap an image with an image, or jump to a new page. Pop-up messages (displayed in a new page) are very useful when you do not have the screen "real estate" on your page for more information and do not want to limit the viewer access by inserting layers in your page (they only work with browsers of version 4 and above). Pop-up messages can be used for many things, including the following.

- *Warnings*
- *Feedback for a test question*
- *Description of an image*
- *Instructions on using a tool*

The following elements are covered in this exercise.

- *Attaching a behavior to text*
- *Using the Pop-up Message behavior*
- *Modifying an event to use for a behavior*

Take a Look

Before beginning the exercise, let's take a look at the exercise in its completed state so you can clearly see what you are about to build.

1. Select the *DWComplete* site.

2. Locate the *ch15* folder and within it the file named *dw15ex2.html*. Double click on *dw15ex2.html* to open the file.

3. The file *dw15ex2.html* should now appear in the Dreamweaver MX Document window. This is the glossary file we used in the previous exercise. We are going to add another behavior to it. Note the following properties of this completed exercise.

    a) Open the Behaviors panel (Window | Behaviors). Select the blue underlined text *onLoad* in the Document window. Notice in the Behaviors panel that there is the behavior Pop-up Message, based on the event *onMouseOver*. Double click on the behavior to see the message that will be displayed.

    b) While the text *onLoad* is still selected, look in the Property Inspector. The Link box contains *javascript:;*.

DWComplete Site

CD-ROM

4. Close *dw15ex2.html*.

Storyboard: On Screen

Figure 15-16 shows you what the finished page will look like when viewed through a browser.

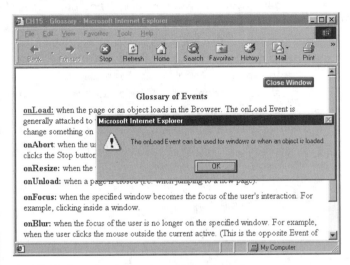

Fig. 15-16. Completed exercise within a browser.

Storyboard: Behind the Scenes

Figure 15-17 shows the HTML code created behind the behavior Pop-up Message, used in this exercise.

```
Anchor tag around the text "onLoad":
<a href="javascript:; " onMouseOver="MM_popupMsg('The
onLoad Event can be used for windows or when an object is
loaded.   ')">onLoad:</a>

The JavaScript function for the Popup Message:
function MM_popupMsg(msg)
{   alert(msg);
}
```

Fig. 15-17. HTML source code for the completed exercise.

Step-by-Step Instructions

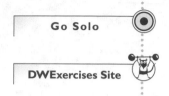
1. Make sure you are in the *DWExercises* site. Use the Site panel to locate the *ch15* folder and within it the file *glossary.html*. Select this file, which can be used even if you did not complete the previous exercise.

2. When the mouse is rolled over the word *onLoad*, a pop-up message will appear.

   a) Select the word *onLoad* on the left side of the screen. Using the Behaviors panel, select the Plus (+) button. We want to select the behavior Pop-up Message, but it is not available. There has to be a link or text in the Link box to attach a behavior to text. Click on a white area in the Behaviors window to deselect the Behaviors pull-down menu.

   b) With the word *onLoad* still highlighted, type *javascript:;* in the Link box in the Property Inspector. Press Enter/Return to set the text in the Link box. See figure 15-18.

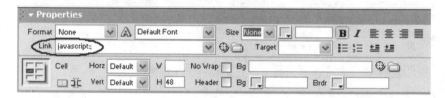

Fig. 15-18. javascript:; in Link box for image.

   c) Select the Behaviors panel again and you should be able to select Pop-up Message. You may have to click away from the word *onLoad* and then click back on it before selecting the behavior.

   d) Type the following in the Message box.

   The onLoad Event can be used for windows or when an object is loaded.

   e) Click on OK. See figure 15-19.

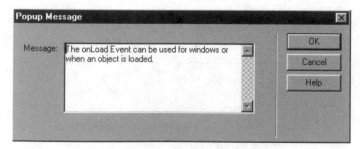

Fig. 15-19. Message window for Pop-up Message behavior.

3. The pop-up message should appear when the mouse rolls over the word *onLoad*. Now we need to change the event from *onClick* to *onMouseOver*.

    a) Click on the Down arrow (between the events and the actions). A list of available events for the browser version is now listed.

    b) Select *onMouseOver*.

4. Save the file.

5. Preview in a browser. Roll the mouse over the word *onLoad* and the pop-up message appears.

6. Close the browser.

Summary

*   *Behaviors expand the functionality of a web page. They can help web pages become more dynamic by changing elements based on user interaction, controlling the way a web page loads, and waiting for conditions to occur before executing commands.*

*   *Behaviors are primarily precoded JavaScript that give your HTML pages more functionality.*

*   *A Dreamweaver MX behavior is a combination of an event and an action. Specific events may vary across browsers and browser versions.*

*   *Actions are usually named according to the function they perform. Actions are a series of HTML and JavaScript commands that are usually contained inside a JavaScript function.*

*   *Events can be something the user does or something that happens within the browser window. Events (or event handlers) have predefined names. Events fall into two main categories: Window Modification events and Interaction events.*

*   *Probably the most difficult part of working with behaviors is determining where or what to attach the behavior to. To help with this, try to determine when you want an action to occur, which should help you determine where in the document the behavior (and event) should be inserted.*

*   *A behavior can be attached to a page to be executed when the page loads or unloads, or when there is an error.*

*   *Attach a behavior to an object to enhance interaction with a user.*

*   *Most behaviors will generate JavaScript and JavaScript functions. The functions are inserted in the <head> tag of the page.*

*   *To attach a behavior to text, the text must already have a link, or have a pound (#) sign or the text javascript:; in the Link box. This is part of the link (<a>) tag. The javascript:; is called a null link and is automatically inserted in the Link field if an event with parentheses, such as (onMouseDown), is used.*

*   *In the first guided tour, we took a quick look at the Behaviors panel.*

·T/P·

If you cannot see the Down arrow in the Behaviors panel (allowing you to select a new event), click on the behavior (action) in the Behaviors Panel.

- In the first practice exercise, you attached a behavior to an image, opened a browser window using specific properties, closed a browser window with a behavior, changed the event for a behavior, and swapped an image on rollover.

- The Macromedia Extension Manager provides the means to "extend" the functionality and capabilities of Dreamweaver MX. These extensions can add items to menus and behaviors, and items to the Insert bar. The Extension Manager has to be downloaded and installed before adding extensions.

- In the second practice exercise, you attached a behavior to text, used the Pop-up Message behavior, and modified an event to use for a behavior.

CHAPTER

16

Application

Chapter:

Adding

a Behavior

Introduction

Behaviors offer added functionality beyond what typical HTML code can provide. As you work with more and more behaviors, you should find it easier to determine what Dreamweaver MX behavior should be used and where. In this application chapter we will attach a behavior to the body of the page so that when the page loads (begins to display on the screen), an action will occur. Our action will be to route the browser to a different web page, based on a condition: whether the browser is at least version 4.0 or older.

Application Exercise Objectives

By the end of this chapter you will have created an index page for *The 21st Century Kitchen* Web site that includes :

• *A behavior to check the user's browser version.*

• *If the behavior identifies a web browser version of 4.0 or higher, the web site will load its normal home page.*

• *If the behavior does not identify a web browser of 4.0 or higher, a warning page will be displayed, informing the visitor that she will not be able to view this web site because the web site uses functions her browser does not support (such as frames).*

Application Exercise 16-1: Adding a Behavior

Description

In this application chapter we will create an index page for *The 21st Century Kitchen* web site that includes a behavior that will check the version of the browser on the viewer's computer. We will also create an alternate web page with a warning about the browser version and what functions will not be able to be viewed.

Take a Look

CD-ROM

Let's take a look at the finished exercise. Open Dreamweaver MX and use File Menu | Open to locate the companion CD-ROM. Locate the folder *Learning_DWapplication_complete* and select the file *ap16.html*. Look at the layout of the web page, noticing the text and graphic areas. Take a look at the file and the HTML code in Dreamweaver MX. You will be using the following Dreamweaver MX concepts in the exercise.

• *Attaching behaviors to <body> tags*

• *Text and formatting*

Storyboard: Browser View

Figure 16-1 shows how the browser warning page will look in a web browser when the exercise is completed.

Fig. 16-1. Completed exercise viewed within a browser.

Storyboard: Dreamweaver MX View

Figure 16-2 shows the Check Browser dialog box when the exercise is completed.

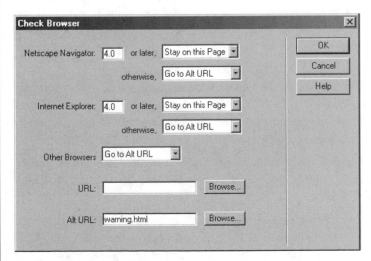

Fig. 16-2. Completed exercise showing Check Browser dialog box.

Application Project Steps

Complete this exercise on your own, guided by the following general steps. You can always refer back to the completed example you viewed in the "Take a Look" section of this exercise.

NOTE: The following steps are intended as a guide. This is your project, so feel free to make whatever variations you like.

21st Century
KITCHEN SITE

1. Create a new file in Dreamweaver MX.

2. Title the page *The 21st Century Kitchen Browser Warning*. Go ahead and set the background color to match the other pages in the site (#FFFFCC).

3. Save the new page as *warning.html* in the *Learning_DWapplication* folder.

4. Insert the banner graphic at the top of the page *21ckbnr.jpg* found in the *ap_media* subfolder.

5. Add an extra line under the banner graphic and type in *The features of this Web site require a browser version of 4.0 or better*. (You might want to use a larger text font to make sure the message is noticed.)

6. Save the *warning.html* file.

7. Open the file *home.html* found in the *Learning_DWapplication* folder. This page was created in an earlier chapter.

8. You now need to assign a behavior to this page. Bring up the Behaviors panel (Shift + F3), and select the Plus (+) button to display the list of available behaviors.

9. The Check Browser behavior might not be available. Behaviors always have to be attached to a tag. You can either select an object (which is really selecting the tag for the object) or, if the behavior applies to an entire page, select the *<body>* tag.

10. You will want to apply the Check Browser behavior to the entire page using the *<body>* tag. To do this, select the *<body>* tag in the Status bar found in the lower left corner of the Dreamweaver MX Design Document window. Just one mouse click is needed to select the *<body>* tag.

11. Go back to the list of available behaviors using the Plus (+) button on the Behaviors panel. You should now be able to select the Check Browser behavior.

12. In the Check Browser window, set both browsers to 4.0 or Later and change the setting in both of the pull-down menus from Go to URL to Stay on this Page. Remember to do this for both browsers.

13. For the Otherwise pull-down menus, select Go To Alt URL.

14. The Other Browsers pull-down menu should also be set to Go To Alt URL.

15. In the bottom of the Check Browser window, leave the URL box empty but add the *warning.html* page in the box for the Alt URL. See figure 16-2 for the completed settings.

16. Save your work, and preview in a variety of browsers if possible.

Summary

In this application chapter you have added a behavior to the first page of The 21st Century Kitchen web site. You have also created a warning page that will inform the visitor that the browser he is using is not at least a 4.0 level, which means that it will not be able to display some of the features of this web site. When the browser opens this page (the new first page), it will run the behavior. If the browser is a 4.0 level or above, it will stay on the *home.html* page. If the browser is less than level 4.0, the browser will open the *warning.html* page.

C H A P T E R

17

Broaden Links with Anchors and Image Maps

Introduction

In Chapter 10, we discussed the use of linking HTML pages by creating a hot link using a word, phrase, or single graphic element. In this chapter, we will extend the use of links by discovering how to make only a portion of a graphic "hot" through the use of image maps. We will also see how to jump (link) to a specific area in a page using anchors instead of just jumping to the top of a page. By the end of the chapter you will be able to:

- *Create anchors to jump to a certain area in a page*
- *Describe the use of image maps*
- *Create image maps*
- *Manage and troubleshoot links*

Anchors

As you continue to set up the structure of your web pages, one thing you will want to think about is the relationship between the pages and how much content should go on each page. Ask yourself questions such as the following.

- *How many individual pages do I want to have?*
- *Should a page be no longer than what can fit on a single screen (on the average)?*
- *Should each page be limited to one subject area, or will a page contain many topics and categories that can be separated by headings?*

If you decide that specific pages should contain a lot of information, it may be appropriate to create a navigation menu within that page. For example, look at the HTML page in figure 17-1. It has been broken down into five separate areas of information. Instead of having the user scroll and search for an item, the user can select the item from the menu. Selecting this menu item causes the display of that page to instantly jump to the location of that item. This is especially useful for lengthy pages that would otherwise require a lot of scrolling.

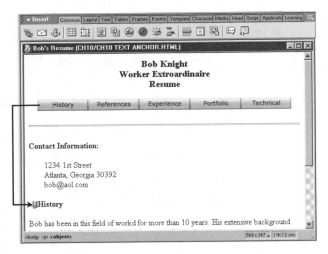

Fig. 17-1. HTML page with menu linked to an anchor.

When you want to link to a specific location in an HTML document, you will link to what is called an anchor. This is also sometimes called a "fragment." Normally a browser will display a page starting at the top (or beginning) of that page. However, with the use of anchors, we can configure a page to display starting at any point in the page we designate – wherever we place an anchor.

Setting Up an Anchor in the Current Page

There are two parts to using anchors in your pages: creating the anchor itself, and setting the link to the anchor. To create an anchor, you would perform the following steps.

1. Open the page you want to add an anchor to. Position the cursor just before the content you want to link to. This content will appear at the top of the browser window when the user selects the link.

2. Select Insert Menu | Named Anchor, or select Named Anchor from the Common tab (third from the left) in the Insert bar.

3. Type in the name of the anchor. Use a name that provides some meaning relating to the content or the position in the page. Anchor names cannot contain special characters or spaces. However, you can use the under-score (_) in the name. Each anchor needs a unique name.

To create the link to the anchor, you would perform the following steps.

1. Highlight (select) the text or graphic to link from.

2. Create the link to the anchor by selecting the Property Inspector and typing in the pound (#) sign followed by the anchor name (e.g., *#section1*),

·T/P·

When naming anchors, do not use spaces or special characters. If you have created a link to an anchor and it does not work, check the name of the anchor and make sure you have not added a space in the middle of the name or at the end. Also, be sure to match uppercase and lowercase in the names. Anchors are case sensitive.

or by selecting the Property Inspector and dragging the Point to File icon to the Anchor icon. See figure 17-2. The Anchor icon looks like a boat anchor inside a yellow emblem. If you cannot see the Anchor icon, select View | Visual Aids | Invisible Elements.

Fig. 17-2. Anchor icon.

Notice that when you use the Point to File icon, a pound sign (#) and the name of the anchor appear in the Link field of the Property Inspector. See figure 17-3.

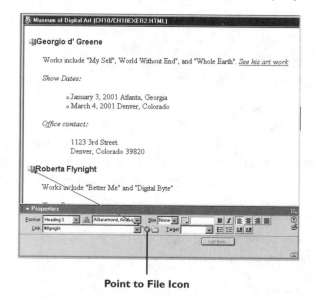

Point to File Icon

Fig. 17-3. Using the Point to File icon (in the Property Inspector) to link to an anchor.

Linking to an Anchor on Another Page

In addition to using anchors on the same page, you can link to an anchor on a new page. When the new page opens, it will open at the location of the anchor and not at the top of the page, as it would have done without the use of an anchor. To accomplish this, you will use the same steps you use for creating an anchor in the current page, but in addition you will include the name of the new document in front of the anchor name. For example, to link to an anchor called *glossary* in the document called *page1.html*, the Link field would contain the following.

```
page1.html#glossary
```

There are no spaces around the pound (#) sign, and the names of the page and the anchor are case sensitive. To link to an anchor on another page that is not in the current site, you would write the following.

```
www.NameOfNewSite.xyz/page1.html#glossary
```

Practice Exercise 17-1: Linking to a Fragment of a Page Using Anchors

Description

In this exercise we are going to create a web site for a fictitious organization, The Museum of Digital Art. On its web site, the museum wants to list the artists they feature, along with show dates and the contact information for each artist. They also want to link this page to another page that lists the artists, along with their works of art. The following elements are covered in this exercise.

- *Creating an anchor*
- *Linking to a point (anchor) on the current page*
- *Linking to a point (anchor) on a different page*
- *Using the Point to File icon to create a link*
- *Using View |/ Visual Aids | Invisible Elements to see anchors*
- *Using HTML related to anchors*

Take a Look

Before beginning the exercise, let's take a look at the exercise in its completed state so that you can clearly see what it is you are about to build.

 DWComplete Site

 CD-ROM

1. Make sure you are working with the *DWComplete* site. You can confirm this by selecting the *DWComplete* site from the Site panel.

2. Locate the *ch17* folder and within it the file named *dw17ex1.html*. Double click on *dw17ex1.html* to open the file.

3. The file *dw17ex1.html* should now appear in your copy of Dreamweaver.

4. To make sure you can see the anchors on the page, select View | Visual Aids | Invisible Elements (it should be checked).
   a) Select the text *Georgio d' Greene*. Look in the Property Inspector at the link. The pound (#) sign in front (at the beginning) of the link indicates the text is linked to an anchor within the current document. The anchor is called *greene*.

b) Scroll down the page and find the entry for *Georgio d' Greene*. It lists the show date and office contacts. In front of *Georgio d' Greene* is an anchor. Select the anchor and the Property Inspector displays its name, *greene*. Changing the name will not automatically change reference (link) names to the anchor.

c) Scroll down the page to listing about Georgio d' Greene. Select the underlined text "See his artwork". It is linked to the file *artwork1.html*. At the end of the link is the text *#greene* indicating that the link is to an anchor (called *greene*) on the *artwork1.html* page.

d) Notice the anchors next to each of the artist listings. Each artist at the top of the page is linked to an anchor within the page displaying the show dates and office contacts.

e) Notice the following further properties of this page.

- *The font of the text of each artist's name is set to AGaramond, Arial, sans serif. The text will display in the first available font in this list or the default font.*

- *The first paragraph is indented.*

- *The bulleted list is indented.*

- *The horizontal line across the page was created using the Horizontal Rule object under Insert bar | Common.*

5. Close *dw17ex1.html*.

6. Locate the *ch17* folder and within it the file named *artwork1.html*. Double click on *artwork1.html* to open the file.

7. This is the page that will open when accessing this artist's work from the previous document. Note the following properties of this completed exercise.

- *Next to* Georgio d' Greene *is an anchor named* greene. *In the previous document, there was a link* (artwork1.html#greene) *that points to this anchor.*

- *There are links for all of Georgio d' Greene's works.*

Storyboard: On Screen

Figure 17-4 shows you what the finished page will look like when viewed through a browser.

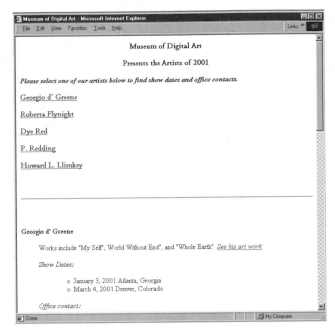

Fig. 17-4. Completed exercise viewed within a browser.

Storyboard: Behind the Scenes

Figure 17-5 shows the key HTML code for anchors.

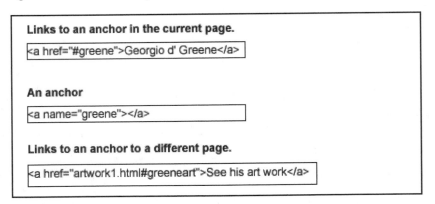

Fig. 17-5. HTML source code for the completed exercise.

Step-by-Step Instructions

Go Solo

DWExercises Site

1. We are going to open an existing document that has been copied to your hard drive when you installed the chapter exercises in Chapter 1.

   a) Change to the *DWExercises* site. Use the Site panel to locate the *ch17* folder and within it the file named *artists.html*. Double click on *artists.html* to open the file.

   b) The file *artists.html* should now appear in the Document window.

2. Each of the artists at the top of the page will link to a point (anchor) in the current page, with information about that artist. See figure 17-6. The first thing we need is an anchor.

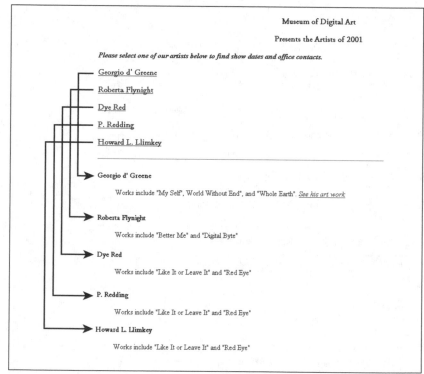

Fig. 17-6. You will create these links.

   a) Below the horizontal rule, find and place your cursor in front of the text *Georgio d' Greene*. Select Insert Menu | Named Anchor, or use Named Anchor on the Common tab in the Insert bar. See figure 17-7.

Named Anchor

Fig. 17-7. Insert bar | Common | Named Anchor.

b) You will be prompted for the name of the anchor. Type in *greene*. This references the name of the artist we are pointing to. Press the Enter/Return key. The Anchor icon is displayed next to the text *Georgio d' Greene*.

c) To link to this anchor, highlight the text *Georgio d' Greene* at the top of the page (it is at the top of the list with the other artists).

d) To link to the anchor called *greene*, in the Property Inspector Link field, type *#greene*. (It is case sensitive and space sensitive. Do not enter any spaces.)

e) Save the file.

f) Preview the page in a browser to test the link. When you select *Georgio d' Greene*, the page scrolls down to place the listing for *Georgio d' Greene* at the top of the page.

g) Close the browser window.

3. Now let's create another anchor for the next artist. This time we will use the Point to File icon to link to the anchor.

a) Below the horizontal rule, find and place your cursor in front of the text *Roberta Flynight*. Insert another named anchor just before the text *Roberta*.

b) You will be prompted for the name of the anchor. Type in *flynight*. Press the Enter/Return key. An anchor icon is displayed next to the text *Roberta Flynight*.

c) To link to this anchor, highlight the text *Roberta Flynight* at the top of the page. Make sure the Property Inspector is open. While *Roberta Flynight* is still selected, scroll down the page until you find the anchor you inserted next to the *Roberta Flynight* listing.

d) In the Property Inspector, drag the Point to File icon to the anchor next to *Roberta Flynight* (hold down the mouse while you drag). Do not let go of your mouse until you see *#flynight* appear in the Link field of the Property Inspector. See figure 17-8.

·T/P·

You can also use the Point to File feature to link to an anchor. You will do this in step 3.

·T/P·

The keyboard shortcut for Insert Named Anchor is:

Ctrl+Alt+A (Windows)

Cmd+Opt+A (Macintosh)

Highlighted Text Referenced in the Property Inspector

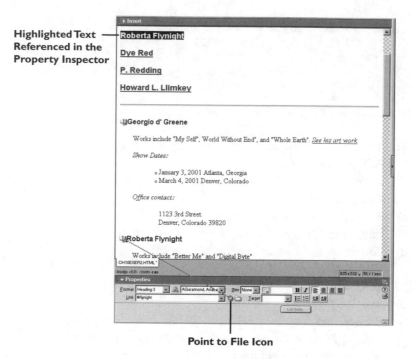

Point to File Icon

Fig. 17-8. Using the Point to File icon to link to an anchor.

    e)   Save the file.

    f)   Preview the page in a browser to test the link. When you select *Roberta Flynight*, the page scrolls down to place the listing for *Roberta Flynight* at the top of the page.

    g)   Close the browser window to return to Dreamweaver MX.

4.   Using what you have learned in steps 2 and 3, create an anchor next to (in front of) the *Dye Red* and *P. Redding* listings under the horizontal rule. Then create a link from the artist names at the top of the page to these new anchors. Refer to figure 17-6 to make sure you have the link-to-anchor pairs we are looking for. Preview the page in the browser to test the links.

5.   Save the file.

6.   There is another page that has a listing of the artwork for *Georgio d' Greene* and *Roberta Flynight*. We want the user to be able to jump from the page that lists the artists (*artists.html*) to the page that lists the artwork, and to display this artwork page at a specific point for the artist selected.

    a)   In the previous steps, we created the anchor first, then linked to that anchor. You can also go ahead and create the link to an anchor and then create the anchor. Just be very careful that you remember how you spelled the anchor.

b) At the *Georgio d' Greene* listing, place your cursor at the end of the lines of text *Without End* and *Whole Earth*. Type in *see his artwork*. Set the text style to italic.

c) With the text *see his artwork* selected, in the Property Inspector Link field, select the Browse button and locate the file *artwork1.html* in the *ch17* folder.

d) In the Link field, after the file name *artwork1.html*, we will type the name of the anchor we are going to create in that file. Type in *#greeneart*. Even though this anchor does not yet exist in the file *artwork1.html*, Dreamweaver MX does not check it until you preview the file in the browser.

e) Save and close the file *artists.html*.

f) Back in the Site panel, locate and open the file *artwork1.html* in the *ch17* folder.

g) To create an anchor for the *Georgio d' Greene* work, locate the artwork listed for *Georgio d' Greene*. Place your cursor next to *Georgio d' Greene* and insert a named anchor. When prompted for the anchor name, type in *greeneart*. See figure 17-9.

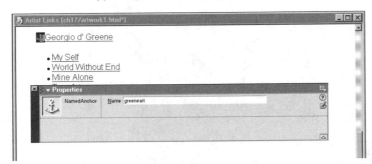

Fig. 17-9. Anchor in artwork1.html.

h) Save the file and close the document.

i) We will use the Site panel to preview the page. Select the file *artists.html* in *ch17*.

j) Press the F12 key on your keyboard to preview the file in the default browser. You can also right mouse click (Mac, Opt + click) on the file and select Preview in Browser. Test the links to the anchors. Select *Georgio d' Greene*, and the window scrolls down the page to the *Greene* listing. Click on the text *see his artwork*. The *artwork1.html* file is displayed in the browser window.

k) Close the browser window and return to Dreamweaver MX.

·TIP·

Image Maps

Macromedia Fireworks includes a tool for creating image maps. You can create/ modify/open an image in Fireworks, create an image map (including links), and export the required HTML directly from Fireworks. You can then import the image and its HTML to your Dreamweaver MX page.

As you continue developing web sites, you will probably soon run into a situation where you have an image (whether it is an elaborate line drawing, graphic, or photograph) in which you want to make individual sections of the image interactive. You may find that the image cannot be easily broken into smaller images that will redisplay properly as one image. The solution to this type of problem can be found by using an image map.

An image map creates invisible hot (clickable) areas over your image. The "hot areas" or "hot spots" are defined by pixel coordinates and can be in the shape of an oval, rectangle, or polygon. The user will never see the "hot areas" because they are invisible. The user will only see the image beneath.

Image maps are a regular HTML feature. Dreamweaver MX uses the Property Inspector to create and modify image maps. Figure 17-10 shows an example of how an image map might look when viewed in Dreamweaver MX.

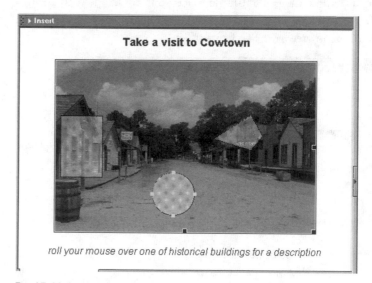

Fig. 17-10. Image map in Dreamweaver MX.

The following are the basic steps for creating an image map.

1. Insert an image.

2. Bring up the Property Inspector and select the image to be used for the image map.

3. Use the Image Map tools (in the bottom left of the Property Inspector) to draw hot areas over the image in the form of a circle or rectangle, or trace (using the Polygon tool) the area you want to include.

4. Name the image map using the Property Inspector while the original image or a hot spot is selected. All hot spots will be linked to the same image map. Use the common naming conventions: do not include spaces or special characters, and stick to lowercase.

5. If you want a new page to be displayed when clicking on a hot spot, insert a URL in the Link window in the Property Inspector for each applicable hot spot. See figure 17-11.

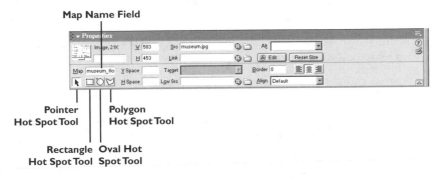

Map Name Field

Pointer Hot Spot Tool

Polygon Hot Spot Tool

Rectangle Hot Spot Tool **Oval Hot Spot Tool**

Fig. 17-11. Property Inspector showing Image Map tools.

The following are tips for creating an image map.

- *It is generally better not to overlap hot spots. But if you need to, the hot spot that is drawn last (on top of the previous one) will control any overlapping hot areas. You can change which hot spot is on top by selecting Modify | Arrange | Send To Back or Bring To Front.*

- *To draw a perfect square or circle hot spot, hold down the Shift key as you draw the hot spot.*

- *The following are notes on the polygon hot spot.*

  - *To draw a polygon, select the Polygon tool. Using this tool, each time you click on the image a corner point is created for the polygon. You will begin to see a shape when at least two points are created.*

  - *To modify the points on a polygon, use the (image map) Pointer tool to drag a point on the polygon. You first must select (click inside) the polygon to see the points. Points cannot be deleted.*

  - *To add a point to a polygon, select an existing polygon (hot spot) with the Pointer tool. Then select the Polygon tool. While the polygon is still selected, click on the image with the mouse. A new point is created on the existing polygon as long as the polygon is selected.*

- *Using the <Alt> tag with image maps is very inconsistent. Some browsers will not display them correctly, whereas other browsers will show them intermittently. Do not rely on the <Alt> tag when using image maps.*

·T*i*P·

An alternative to using image maps is "slicing" images into small pieces and placing them in tables within an HTML page. Many packages, including Macromedia Fireworks, can "slice" a large image into smaller images. This is sometimes preferable to image maps, as it provides more flexibility (swapping the area under the hot spot with another image). In addition, the individual pieces of a "sliced" image, in some cases, will download faster than a single large image.

HTML for Image Maps

There are three main parts to the HTML for an image map, as follows.

1.   The image the hot spots relate to, the tag for which is as follows.

```
<img src="cowtown.jpg">
```

2.   The map and the coordinates of the hot spots, the tag for which is as follows, where the name of the map is *cowtown*.

```
<map name="cowtownmap">
```

In the following, the hot spot shape (*<area>* tag) is a rectangle, and links to a page called *grocery.html*.

```
<area shape="rect" coords="48,188,156,296"
href="grocery.html">
```

In the following, the hot spot shape is circular, the coordinates are referenced by x, y, radius (347, 289, 59), and links to a page called *pharmacist.html*.

```
<area shape="circle" coords="347,289,59"
href="pharmacist.html">
```

In the following, the hot spot shape is a polygon, each point (x, y of four points) on the polygon is in the coords parameter, and links to a page called *hats.html*.

```
<area shape="poly" coords="330,156,423,89,509,214,348,242"
href="hats.html">
```

3.   Use the *<usemap>* attribute within the image tag to reference the image map to use, as follows, where *usemap* references the image map called *cowtownmap*.

```
<img src="cowtown_graphic.jpg" width="585" height="437"
usemap="#cowtownmap" border="0">
```

Practice Exercise 17-2: Creating an Image Map

Description

Image maps are useful for creating interactive group pictures — such as a family tree, high school graduation picture, or company organizational chart. The director of our fictitious Museum of Digital Art wants an interactive diagram of the museum floor showing the various types of art displayed there. The plan is that when the user rolls the mouse over a room, a brief description of the room will be displayed. When the user clicks on a room, a new page is displayed, describing the works of art in that room. The following elements are covered in this exercise.

- *Creating and modifying image maps*
- *Linking to a page*
- *Using the <Alt> tag*
- *HTML for an image map*

Take a Look

Before beginning the exercise, let's take a look at the exercise in its completed state so you can clearly see what you are about to build.

DWComplete Site

CD-ROM

1. Make sure you are working with the site *DWComplete*. You can confirm this by selecting the *DWComplete* site from the Site panel.

2. Locate the *ch17* folder and within it the file named *dw17ex2.html*. Double click on *dw17ex2.html* to open the file.

3. The file *dw17ex2.html* should now appear in your copy of Dreamweaver. Note the following properties of this completed exercise.

    • *The light green boxes and green polygon over the graphic image are hot spots in the image map.*

    • *Select one of the hot spots. Look in the Property Inspector and it will show you the link, <Alt> tag, and image map the hot spot is associated with.*

Storyboard: On Screen

Figure 17-12 shows you what the finished page will look like when viewed through a browser.

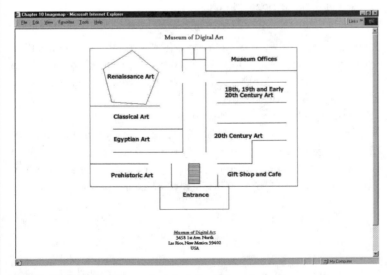

Fig. 17-12. Completed exercise viewed within a browser.

Storyboard: Behind the Scenes

Figure 17-13 shows the HTML code created behind the image map and the image graphic it is associated with. The following are the primary tags to look at.

- <img> *and the attribute* usemap *point to the graphic image and the image map associated with it.*

- <map> *and the attribute* name *start the tag for the image map.*

- <area> *and the attribute* shape *are within the* <map> *tag and define the coordinates of the hot spots.*

```
<img src="museum.jpg" width="583" height="453" usemap="#museum_floor" border="0">
   <map name="museum_floor">
      <area shape="rect" coords="325,1,581,65" href="#" alt="Museum Offices" title="Museum Offices">
      <area shape="rect" coords="1,325,228,388" href="#" alt="Prehistoric Art" title="Prehistoric Art">
      <area shape="rect" coords="1,162,260,227" href="#" alt="Classical Art" title="Classical Art">
      <area shape="rect" coords="1,227,259,291" href="#" alt="Egyptian Art" title="Egyptian Art">
      <area shape="rect" coords="326,97,583,154" href="century.html" alt="18th, 19th and Early 20th Century Art" title=
"18th, 19th and Early 20th Century Art">
      <area shape="rect" coords="325,211,581,261" href="#" alt="20th Century Art" title="20th Century Art">
      <area shape="rect" coords="357,324,582,388" href="giftShop.html" alt="Gift Shop and Cafe" title="Gift Shop and Cafe">
      <area shape="poly" coords="40,59,117,11,188,68,156,153,63,148" href="renArt.html" alt="Renaissance Art" title=
"Renaissance Art">
   </map>
```

Fig. 17-13. HTML code for completed exercise.

Step-by-Step Instructions

Go Solo

DWExercises Site

1. We are going to open an existing document that was copied to your hard drive when you installed the chapter exercises in Chapter 1.
    a) Change to the *DWExercises* site. Use the Site panel to locate the *ch17* folder and within it the file named *diagram.html*. Double click on *diagram.html* to open the file.
    b) The file *diagram.html* should now appear in the Document window.

2. The page contains a diagram of the rooms in the museum. Hot spots are to be placed over each room in the museum. When the user clicks on a hot spot, a page will be displayed in the browser window describing the content or function of the room.
    a) Select the graphic image of the museum.
    b) The Property Inspector displays attribute options for the image, including the image map. The name of the image map is used by JavaScript to execute the hot spots. To name the image map, type *museum_floor* in the Map field in the Property Inspector. See figure 17-14.

Map Name Field

Fig. 17-14. Property Inspector | Image Map Name.

3. We will need a polygon hot spot to outline the Renaissance Art room.
   a) While the graphic image is still selected, select the Polygon Hot Spot tool in the Property Inspector.
   b) To draw the polygon, move the cursor over one of the points of the Renaissance Art room and click the mouse. Move the cursor to draw a line to the next point on the room and click the mouse. A figure will start to form. Try to draw the polygon just inside the room itself. See figure 17-15. You will see why we want to stay inside the room when it is previewed in the browser.

Fig. 17-15. Creating a polygon hot spot in an image map.

   c) Type *Renaissance Art* in the Alt box.
   d) Link the hot spot to the file called *renArt.html* in the same folder (*ch17*). (Use the Browse button next to the Link field.)
   e) Save the file.
   f) Preview the page in a browser to test the hot spot. When you move the cursor over the Renaissance Room, you may see the tool tip (from the *<Alt>* tag) appear under your cursor. Note that the *<Alt>* tag is inconsistent with image maps, especially in different browsers (that is, they do not always display). Click on the hot spot to link to the page containing information about the Renaissance Room.
   g) Close the browser window.
4. The Gift Shop area will be our next hot spot, but it will be rectangular to match the shape of the room.
   a) While the *museum* graphic image is selected, select the Rectangular Hot Spot tool in the Property Inspector.

b) To draw the rectangular hot spot, move the cursor to an upper corner of the Gift Shop and drag the mouse to the opposite lower corner. See figure 17-16.

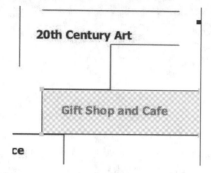

Fig. 17-16. Creating a rectangular hot spot over an image.

c) Type *Gift Shop* in the Alt box.
d) Link the hot spot to the file called *giftShop.html* in the *ch17* folder.
e) Save the file.
f) Preview the page in a browser to test the hot spot. When you move the cursor over the Gift Shop, you may see the tool tip (from the *<Alt>* tag) appear under your cursor. Click on the hot spot to link to the page containing information about the Gift Shop.
g) Close the browser window.

5. Using the previous steps as a guide, create a hot spot over the 18th Century room and link to *century.html*. Preview the page in the browser to test the links.

6. Save your work.

Instead of linking to a new page as you roll over or click on a hot spot, some alternative uses of the image map include displaying a new graphic or an animation on the page. Each time a hot spot is selected, the image changes. We will do this in a later chapter when we work with layers.

Troubleshooting Links

As you continue to develop more of your web site, the number of links between pages and to anchors on pages may become quite extensive. You will probably not only have links within your own site but also links to references outside your site.

Chances are that somewhere along the way a link is not going to work. It will be broken because a site or page no longer exists, a page name has changed, or the structure of your site has changed and some links did not "update" correctly. Dreamweaver MX provides some handy tools for checking and fixing these broken links.

Checking for Broken and Other Problem Links

Dreamweaver MX will check your site for links that may cause problems when viewed on the Web. To start the checking process, select Check Links Sitewide from the Site menu of the Site panel, or use Control + F8. This menu option is available in the Document and Site panels.

The Link Checker panel (in the Results panel group) will appear. This panel contains the results of various operations you can run within Dreamweaver. When you run a search, check validation, check for target browsers, run site reports, view an FTP log, or view server debugging information, the results will be displayed in the Results panel. For now, we will look at the Link Checker function.

The Check Links Sitewide dialog window includes a pull-down menu in the Show field. The following describe the options found here. See figure 17-17.

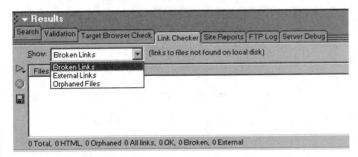

Fig. 17-17. Link Checker panel.

Broken Links: Is a list indicating when a linked file does not exist or does not reside in the location or path as defined in the link destination.

External Links: Lists files located outside your site. As you first begin to work with Dreamweaver MX, you may find numerous files listed here as external links – when they really should not be. Remember that your site root folder defines the location of all files in your site, and their relationship to one another.

Files listed in External Links should commonly be linked to another full web address, such as http://*www.macromedia.com*. If the link contains a valid address, this listing is not a problem link. However, if files are listed here without a full and valid web address, you know these links will need to be corrected.

The media files listed here will include graphics, video, sounds, and so on. If you are intentionally linking to another site to get the media, and the link contains a full and valid web address, files will be listed as correct links. On the other hand, it is a common mistake to see media listed here with a path to a hard drive name, which will cause a problem. For example, the following is a file listed in External Links that would cause a problem.

```
file:///C:/peanuts.html
```

While still in the Link Checker panel, you can actually correct the location or name of a link. Just click on a file in either the broken links or external links. The name and path to the file can now be edited. If the file is listed more than once, Dreamweaver MX will change all links to that file.

When posted on the Web, this code will result in the user's browser trying to load a file called *peanuts.html* from the user's local C drive. Most of the time, media files should be located within your site. The following are reasons many files mistakenly become external links.

- *When linking to an HTML file or importing a media element, the original file existed outside the current site root folder and you did not select Yes when prompted to copy the file into the site root folder.*

- *The HTML file with the external link was copied from another computer and may now reside in a different folder name.*

Orphaned Files: Indicates files that are not linked from any other file in the site. This list would usually tell you that a file is not being used within your site and you could delete it. Be very careful about deleting any files until you make sure that the link to this file simply has not been added, or that the link is not typed correctly. As a suggestion, you may want to move orphaned files to a backup folder created outside your site folder — just in case you want to use this file later.

Changing a Link to a File Sitewide

If you want to change a link so that it links to a different file and this link exists in multiple places, you can select Change Link Sitewide from Site Panel | Site Menu. See figure 17-18. You will be prompted to enter the old file that is already linked, and then the new file to which to link. If you use the Site panel to select the old file first, that file will be the file to change. You may want to use this option after you have added a new contact page and want all Contact Us buttons pointing to the new home page.

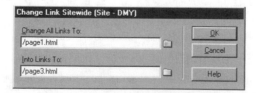

Fig. 17-18. Change Link Sitewide option.

Menu Options

There are many menu and pop-up menu options in the Site panel for adding, modifying, and deleting links. Note that these options are only available if a file is selected in the site map. See figure 17-19.

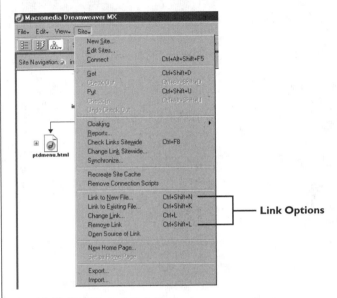

Fig. 17-19. Site Menu | Link Options.

Link to New File: This option will create a link to a new file. Dreamweaver MX will prompt you for the name of the new file, the page title, and the text for the link. See figure 17-20.

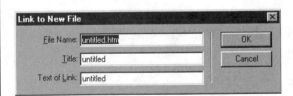

Fig. 17-20. Link to New File option.

Link to Existing File: This option will create a text link to a file that already exists. Dreamweaver MX will prompt you to search for the existing file. The name of the file, without its extension, will be inserted for the Text of Link parameter.

Change Link: This option is only available when a linked file is selected. This option switches the current linked file with a (selected) new linked file. You cannot undo this option.

Remove Link: This option is only available when a linked file is selected. This option removes the link to the current file from the preceding file in the file map. You cannot undo this option.

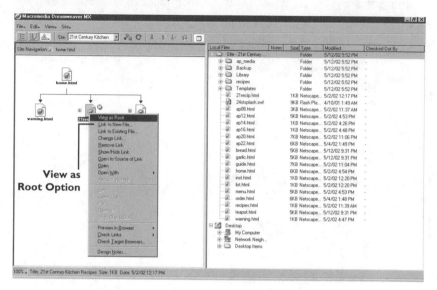

Fig. 17-21. Pop-up menu | Link Options.

View as Root: This option is available in the pop-up menu when a file in the site map is right clicked (PC) or Control-clicked (Macintosh). See figure 17-21. It will display the current file at the top of the site map. The site navigation from home page to current page is displayed at the top of the site map. Using your mouse, you can select any file in the Site Navigation option to set as the root. See figure 17-22.

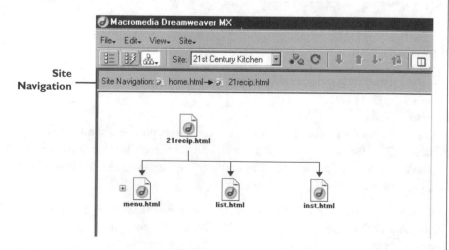

Fig. 17-22. View as Root | Site Navigation.

Before you get ready to reveal your site to the general public, be sure to use the tools we have just discussed to check for any problem areas. One of the biggest turn-offs to a user is to click on a link in a web site and get the message "Page does not exist."

Summary

- When you want to link to a specific location in an HTML document, you will link to what is called an anchor. This is also sometimes called a "fragment." Normally, a browser will display a page starting at the top (or beginning) of the page. However, with the use of anchors, we can configure a page to display starting at any point in the page we designate – by placing and linking to an anchor.

- There are two parts to using anchors in your pages: creating the anchor itself, and setting the link to the anchor.

- In addition to linking to anchors on the same page, you can link to an anchor on a new page. When the new page opens, it will open at the location of the anchor and not at the top of the page, as it would have normally done without the use of an anchor.

- In the first practice exercise you created an anchor, linked to an anchor in a current page, linked to an anchor in a different page, used the Point to File feature to create a link, used View | Visual Aids | Invisible Elements to see anchors, and viewed the HTML related to anchors.

- An image map creates invisible hot (clickable) areas over your image. The "hot areas" (or "hot spots") are defined by pixel coordinates and can be in the shape of an oval, rectangle, or polygon. The user will never see the hot spots because they are invisible.

- In the second practice exercise you created and modified image maps, created links from these image maps to pages, used the <Alt> tag, and viewed the HTML for an image map.

- Dreamweaver MX will check your site for links that may cause problems when viewed on the Web. To start the checking process, select Site Menu | Check Links Sitewide. This menu option is available in the Document and Site panels.

- If you want to change a link so that it links to a different file and this link exists in multiple places, you can select Site Menu | Change Link Sitewide while in the Site panel.

- There are many menu and pop-up menu options in the Site panel for adding, modifying, and deleting links.

CHAPTER

18

Working with Layers

Introduction

At some point in your web page development you are going to think something like "Wouldn't it be nice if I could put this picture here and have it overlap this other picture here." Or maybe, "I'd like to let the viewer design a living space by dragging and positioning graphics of furniture." Enter layers.

Layers allow you to position one or more elements (graphic images, video, animation, or simple text) anywhere on a page without interfering with what is already in that location on the page. Layers can be positioned on top of each other and can be dragged around the screen. Layers can contain animation that has been created using the Dreamweaver MX timeline feature. We will work with timelines in the animation chapter.

The main problem with layers is that they are not supported in some of the older web browsers. Internet Explorer 4 (and above) and Netscape Navigator 4 (and above) support layers. However, even under these programs, the way layers behave is not consistent among browsers. If you are going to use layers, you will need to thoroughly test your application in a variety of browsers, browser versions, and computer platforms to make sure layers align properly and do not shift when viewed. By the end of this chapter you will be able to:

- *Describe why and when to use layers*
- *List the basic steps for creating layers*
- *Use Dreamweaver MX tools for creating and modifying layers*
- *Recognize the HTML code associated with layers*
- *Use behaviors to change layers*

An Overview of Layers

Think of a layer as a special type of window that lies on top of the document and has its own HTML content, properties, background color, and background image. In figure 18-1, each piece of furniture is in its own layer so that it can be moved around by the viewer independently of the other pieces of furniture – all on top of the room diagram. Layers allow the viewer to move the furniture around on screen as though rearranging the room. An interaction could also be added for each piece of furniture to allow the viewer to exchange each element for a different piece of furniture. A rug could even be placed on the diagram, providing the viewer the ability to change its color.

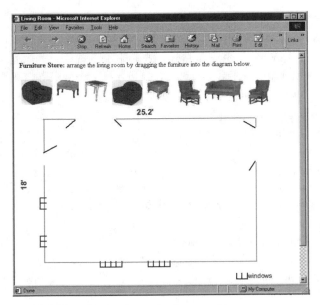

Fig. 18-1. Movable furniture via the use of layers.

Some of the key points about layers are that they can:

- *Be nested inside each other.*
- *Be moved/dragged around the screen by the viewer.*
- *Be animated.*
- *Be arranged on top and behind other layers.*
- *Contain their own background color and graphics – separate from the page.*
- *Be visible or invisible. Behaviors can be attached to a layer to change its visibility based on some action or condition.*

The main thing to remember about layers is that they do not work in older browsers (before version 4.0) and do not work consistently across all browsers. If you think many of your users may not have the required browser level, you are not completely out of luck. There is a workaround of sorts.

If you are not sure your typical user's browser will support layers, you can still create a page with layers, using the flexibility of placing objects anywhere on the page and converting the layers to tables. Dreamweaver MX has a menu option (Modify Menu | Convert | Layers to Tables) that performs this task very easily. One limitation with this approach is that the tables cannot be created if any layers overlap each other. To keep the same spacing between the original layers, a bottom row or right column is created with transparent GIFs (spacers), so that the objects stay in the same position as when they were in a layer.

Suggestions for Using Layers

If the design of a page requires objects to be on top of each other and you cannot get around it by combining the graphics into a single graphic (outside Dreamweaver MX) or by using tables, layers may be the way to go. The following are some examples of when you might want to use layers.

- Quizzes and information gathering: *Place the feedback in an invisible layer. When the user answers the question, use a behavior to make the layer visible, displaying the feedback.*

- Animation: *Simulate some process where many objects move along different paths on the screen. You could also use Flash for the animation, but this would require a plugin, whereas animating within Dreamweaver MX layers does not.*

- Menu tabs: *When the user selects a menu option, its tab appears at the front of the menu and the previous tab goes to the back.*

- Pointing: *A map of the United States is displayed, and when the user rolls the cursor over a city, the name and demographics are displayed. When the cursor rolls away from the city, the information disappears.*

Before Working with Layers

Later in this chapter you will start with some hands-on experience in working with layers. Before we begin, let's take a look at some general information about layers. The following are the basic steps for establishing a layer.

1. Create the layer using Insert bar | Common tab | Draw Layer, or Insert Menu | Layer. A layer marker will appear in the document representing the location of the layer in the HTML code.

2. Name the layer using the Property Inspector or Layers panel (Window | Others | Layers).

3. Once the layer is created, reposition the layer where you want it located on the page.

4. Insert the element or elements in the layer.

5. Resize the layer to "shrink" around its content.

6. Set the background color and graphic for the layer, if applicable.

7. Test the page in multiple browsers (4.0 and above).

8. Additionally, set the initial visibility of each layer once it has been positioned, its content entered, and its size adjusted. Then create any behaviors pertaining to the layer.

Layer Terminology

- Z index: *Stacking order of layers. A layer with a lower-numbered Z index is behind a layer with a higher-numbered Z index.*

- Stacking order: *Another name for Z index.*

- Parent: *Layer outside another layer when layers are nested.*

- Child: *Layer nested within another layer. A child can inherit the visibility of its parent, and layers always move with a parent.*

Layers Panel

The Layers panel (Window | Others | Layers) lists all layers in the page, the visibility, and the Z index for each layer. It also illustrates nested layers by showing a branching line. In figure 18-2, layer 1 is nested within layer 3.

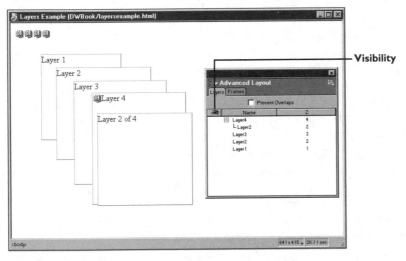

Fig. 18-2. Layers panel.

Note the following regarding the Layers panel.

- *The name of the layer can be changed by double clicking on the name in the Layers panel and typing the new (unique) name.*

- *The stacking order (Z index) of layers can be modified in the Layers panel by double clicking on the Z index and typing a new number, or dragging a layer up or down in the list. When a layer's Z index is changed, all other layers are renumbered to accommodate the moved layer.*

- *The visibility can also be changed. The Eye icon reflects the visibility options: an open eye means the layer is visible, a closed eye represents a hidden layer, and nothing in the visibility columns is for inherit (or default). Inherit makes a nested layer inherit the visibility of its parent.*

Shortcut

To open the Layers panel, press F2.

• The Layers panel contains the option Prevent Overlaps. This prevents you from inadvertently creating nested layers or layers that overlap each other. This is useful if there is a possibility that layers are going to be converted to tables because overlapping layers cannot be converted. This option is also available by selecting Modify | Arrange | Prevent Layer Overlaps. This does not automatically fix layers that already overlap or are nested.

Property Inspector for Layers

The following key properties (options) for layers are found in the Property Inspector. See figure 18-3.

Fig. 18-3. Property Inspector | Layers.

The position of layers is set according to the top left corner of the document, no matter the size of the browser window. If you are aligning layers with objects that are inside tables (e.g., for use as pop-ups when the image is selected), remember that tables can be set relative to the size of the browser window (by setting them to center align or setting the width/height as a percentage).

• Layer ID: *Name of the layer. It is very important to enter a name here, as the name is used in the Layers panel and in scripting. The name can only contain letters and numbers and cannot start with a number. Do not include special characters in the name, and do not include spaces. Every layer name must be unique.*

• L (Left) and T (Top): *Position of the layer relative to the top left corner of the page (which is 0,0). For this reason, if you are using layers to link to the position of an object in a table, you will want to force the table to display at a specific location and not grow or shrink with the browser window. You can accomplish this through the use of spacers (spacer.gif) in a column or row that will force the table (or column/row) to a specific size.*

• W (Width) and H (Height): *Size of the layer in pixels. The size of the layer cannot be smaller than the content in the layer. This size will be overridden by the size of the layer content.*

• Z-index: *Stacking order of the layer. Lower Z-index (number) layers are behind higher-numbered Z-index layers.*

• Vis (Visibility): *The default is usually the same as inherit. The options are Inherit, Visible, and Hidden.*

Inherit makes a nested layer inherit the visibility of its parent (the layer it is nested in).

• Tag: *HTML tags for layers. The recommended tags for layers are <div> and <span>. The other two tags, <layer> and <ilayer>, only make layers visible in Netscape.*

• Overflow: *Determines what happens if the content of a layer is larger than the layer. The options are Visible, Hidden, Scroll, and Auto.*

- *Visible will make the layer large enough to show all of its content.*

- *Hidden will hide content that does not fit in the layer size.*

- *Scroll always displays scroll bars whether the content is larger than the size of the layer or not.*

- *Auto displays scroll bars only if the content size exceeds the size of the layer.*

- Clip: *Determines what part of the content will be clipped if the content size exceeds the size of the layer. This is set in pixel distance from the layer's boundaries.*

- A/B: *Specifies the stacking order relative to other layers. This option is only available when the <layer> and <ilayer> tags are used. A specifies the layer above the current layer. B specifies the layer below the current layer.*

HTML for Layers

The following is the HTML code for defining layers.

```
<div id="Layer1" style="position:absolute; left:79px;
top:63px; width:237px; height:166px; z-index:1; background-
color: #003300; layer-background-color: #003300; border: 1px
none #000000; visibility: visible">Words in the layer.</div>
```

The *<div>* tag defines the layer. Everything after *style* is in quotes.

When two layers are nested, the inside layer is inside the *<div>* tag of the nesting layer.

Behaviors to Use With Layers

The following behaviors, which come with Dreamweaver MX, are very useful when used with layers.

- Change Property: *Changes any of the layer properties found in the Property Inspector. This is especially useful for hiding and showing layers (visibility). The Z index can also be changed, for instance, if multiple objects are animating on the screen.*

- Drag Layer: *This behavior allows a layer to be moved (constrained or unconstrained) by the user. A target can be set so that when the user lets go of the layer (drops it), its position is checked against the target position. This behavior is used for drag-and-drop interactions in the Macromedia CourseBuilder extension.*

- Show/Hide Layers: *This can hide or make visible more than one layer at a time. For instance, when the user answers a multiple-choice question, the distracters (wrong answers) could be hidden while the feedback is made visible.*

- Set Text: *Changes the text of the layer to the new specified layer. This is great for tips, feedback, news, and so on. The formatting of the text can also be inserted through the use of HTML source code.*

Practice Exercise 18-1: Layering Graphics and Text

Description

Bozeman Grammar School is creating an online quiz for the fourth-grade Geography class. Each multiple-choice quiz question has four possible answers. Feedback will be given for each answer. The user will not be able to go to the next question until the current question has been answered correctly. The following elements are covered in this exercise.

- *Creating layers*
- *Using behaviors to show/hide layers*
- *Setting the properties of layers*
- *Inserting images into layers*
- *Using the Layers panel*

Take a Look

Before beginning the exercise, let's take a look at the exercise in its completed state so that you can clearly see what it is you are about to build.

DWComplete Site

CD-ROM

1. Open the *DWComplete* site.

2. Locate the *ch18* folder and within it the file named *dw18ex1.html*. Double click on *dw18ex1.html* to open the file.

3. Preview in a browser.
   a) The only thing displayed on the screen when the page is first loaded is a question with four distracters (buttons A through D).
   b) Click on answer A. The button depresses and feedback is displayed underneath the question.
   c) Click on answer C. The button for answer A returns to its normal (Up) state and the feedback changes to refer to answer C. This also happens when D is selected.

d) Click on answer B. The button depresses, with A, C, and D returning to their normal states. The feedback tells you that B is the correct answer.

e) Click on the Next button. The button depresses and a new question is displayed.

f) The feedback for incorrect answers is displayed on a red background, whereas the correct answer feedback is displayed on a yellow background.

g) Exit the browser. In the Document window, there are no layers displayed. Open the Layers panel (Window | Others | Layers) and notice there are five layers. All five layers are hidden.

Storyboard: On Screen

Figure 18-4 shows you what the finished page will look like when viewed through a browser.

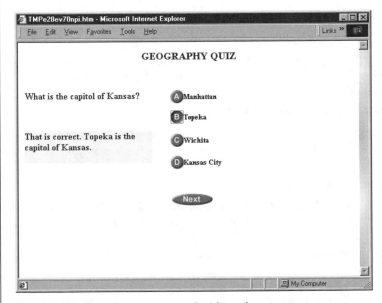

Fig. 18-4. Completed exercise viewed within a browser.

Storyboard: Behind the Scenes

Figure 18-5 shows the HTML code created behind the layers.

```
<div id="answera" style="position:absolute; width:226px; height:34px; z-index:1; left:
11px; top: 156px; visibility: hidden; background-color: #FF0000;
layer-background-color: #FF0000; border: 1px none #000000">
    <h4>No. But Kansas State University is in Manhattan. Try again.</h4>
</div>


<div id="next" style="position:absolute; left:271px; top:268px; width:63px; height:21px;
z-index:2; visibility: hidden">
<a href="dwexer1a.html"
onMouseOut="MM_swapImgRestore()">

<img name="Image5" border="0" src="next_f01.jpg" width="71" height="20"
onMouseDown="MM_swapImage('Image5',",'next_f02.jpg',1)"></a>

</div>
```

Fig. 18-5. HTML source code for completed exercise.

Step-by-Step Instructions

Go Solo

DWExercises Site

1.   Make sure you are working with the *DWExercises* site. You can confirm this by selecting Site Menu | Site panel | *DWExercises*.

2.   We are going to open an existing document.
     a)   Use the Site panel to locate the *ch18* folder and within it the file named *quiz1.html*.
     c)   Double click on *quiz1.html* to open the file.

3.   We will create the layers first. There is already one layer created that contains the feedback for answer A. Because the feedback is all going to have the same format and location, we will just copy the *answera* layer for the other feedback. See figure 18-6.

Marker Icon
for Layer
"answera"

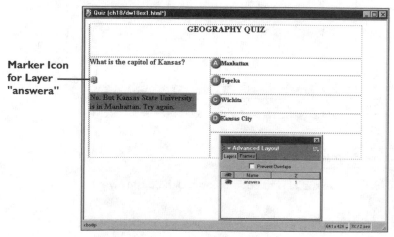

Fig. 18-6. Layer answera.

a) Notice that the marker icon for the layer (the icon has a C in it) is in the cell under the question stem. (If you do not see the marker icons (yellow icons), select View | Visual Aids | Invisible Elements.) As we copy the layer, try to have all marker icons next to each other in this cell. This makes it easier to select the layers and see where they fall in the natural flow of the document. You can also select layers by selecting their marker icon.

b) Select the layer called *answera* by both clicking inside the layer (with the feedback) and selecting its selection handle, or select the layer called *answera* in the Layers panel. Notice that the marker icon for the layer is behind the layer.

c) Copy the layer (Edit | Copy), click next to the marker icon for Layer *answera*, and paste (Edit | Paste).

d) In the Property Inspector or Layers panel, name the new layer *answerb*. Make the following changes to layer *answerb*.

• *Change the background color to yellow. B is the correct answer, so this feedback will be positive feedback.*

• *Change the feedback to read* Yes, Topeka is the capital of Kansas. *See figure 18-7.*

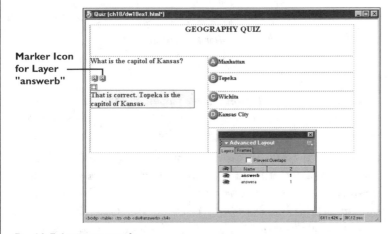

Marker Icon for Layer "answerb"

Fig. 18-7. Layer **answerb**.

e) Copy the layer called *answera* (Edit | Copy), click next to the marker icon for layer *answerb*, and paste (Edit | Paste).

f) In the Property Inspector or Layers panel, name the new layer *answerc*. Make the following changes to layer *answerc*.

• *Change the feedback to read* No, Wichita is not the capital. Try again.

g) Copy the layer called *answera* (Edit / Copy), click next to the marker icon for layer *answerc*, and paste (Edit | Paste).

h) In the Property Inspector or Layers panel, name the new layer *answerd*. Make the following changes to layer *answerd*.

    • *Change the feedback to read* No, Kansas City is not the capital. Try again.

i) The Layers panel should look like that shown in figure 18-8. The Z index (stacking order) of the layers does not matter for this exercise because only one feedback layer will be visible at a time.

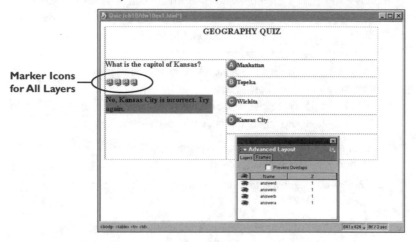

Fig. 18-8. Layers panel and marker icons after feedback is added.

4. Save the file.

5. When an answer is selected, three things happen: all other buttons return to their original Up state, the button selected goes to a Down state, and the feedback for the current answer is displayed.

6. To force all other buttons to their normal Up state, the behavior Swap Image will be used. Select button A. Look in the Behaviors panel (within the Design Panel group) and notice that there is already a behavior there for Swap Image. This was created by inserting the button using Insert | Interactive Images | Rollover Image. The *onClick* event causes the A button to swap images when it is clicked and the mouse is let up.

a) Double click on the action Swap Image for the object *a_button* (the graphic for A). First notice that the Restore Images on MouseOut option is not checked. We do not want the image to return to its initial state until we tell it to (when another answer is selected).

b) While still in the Swap Images dialog box, select the image *b_button*. Browse for and select the file *b_f01.jpg*. This is the B button in the normal (Up) state. An asterisk should appear next to the image *b_button* to indicate that it is being swapped.

c) Select the image *c_button*. Browse for and select the file *c_f01.jpg*.

d) Select the image *d_button*. Browse for and select the file *d_f01.jpg*.

e) The Swap Image dialog box should look like that shown in figure 18-9, with all images having asterisks next to them. Click on OK.

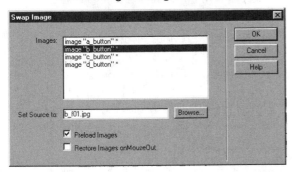

Fig. 18-9. Swap Image dialog box after each button image has been selected.

f) We just completed the behavior for answer A. When A is selected, all other buttons (B, C, and D) will be forced (swapped) to display in their Up states.

7. Buttons B, C, and D also need to have the Swap Image behavior changed so that all unselected buttons return to the Up state.

a) Select the B button (*b_button*) graphic. Double click on the Swap Image behavior for B. The following swap images should be selected for each button image.

  • *A (a_f01.jpg)*

  • *C (c_f01.jpg)*

  • *D (d_f01.jpg)*

b) Select the C button (*c_button*) graphic. Double click on the Swap Image behavior for C. The following swap images should be selected for each button image.

  • *A (a_f01.jpg)*

  • *B (b_f01.jpg)*

  • *D (d_f01.jpg)*

c) Select the D button (*d_button*) graphic. Double click on the Swap Image behavior for D. The following swap images should be selected for each button image.

  • *A (a_f01.jpg)*

  • *B (b_f01.jpg)*

  • *C (c_f01.jpg)*

8. Save the file.

9. Preview in a browser. Select each button. As you select a button, it goes down (selected state), and all other buttons that were previously selected go back up (unselected state). Exit the browser.

10. Now for the feedback. When a button (A, B, C, or D) is selected, its corresponding feedback is displayed. Any previous feedback is hidden.

   a) Select the graphic for button A. In the Behaviors panel (within the Design Panel group), click on the Plus (+) button, and then select Show/Hide Layers.

   b) All layers are listed. Change the following by selecting a layer name and then selecting either Show or Hide (as indicated). See figure 18-10.

   • answera   (Show)
   • answerb   (Hide)
   • answerc   (Hide)
   • answerd   (Hide)

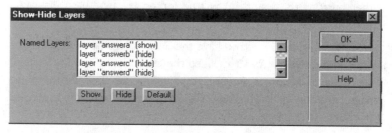

Fig. 18-10. Show/Hide Layers for a button A behavior.

   c) Select the graphic for button B. In the Behaviors panel, click on the Plus (+) button and select Show/Hide Layers. Change the following.

   • answera (Hide)
   • answerb (Show)
   • answerc (Hide)
   • answerd (Hide)

   d) Select the graphic for button C. In the Behaviors panel, click on the Plus (+) button and select Show/Hide Layers. Change the following.

   • answera (Hide)
   • answerb (Hide)
   • answerc (Show)
   • answerd (Hide)

e) Select the graphic for button D. In the Behaviors panel, click on the Plus (+) button and select Show/Hide Layers. Change the following.

- answera *(Hide)*
- answerb *(Hide)*
- answerc *(Hide)*
- answerd *(Show)*

11. Before testing, the layers should be hidden when the page first loads. Using the Behaviors panel, change the visibility of *answera*, *answerb*, *answerc*, and *answerd* to hidden (closed eye). Alternatively, you can use the Property Inspector for each layer. See figure 18-11.

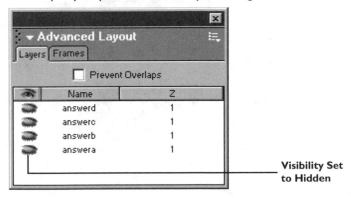

Visibility Set to Hidden

Fig. 18-11. Layers panel | Hidden Layers.

Shortcut

To change the visibility of all layers at one time, click on the top (heading) of the visibility column in the Layers panel.

12. Save the file.

13. Preview in a browser. Select each button. As you select a button, it goes down (selected state) and its feedback is displayed. Only one feedback should appear at any one time. If you see overlapping layers, go back and check the Show/Hide Layers behavior for the corresponding buttons (see step 10). B is the correct answer. Exit the browser.

14. The last tasks are for button B – the correct answer. A Next button should appear when B is selected.

a) Place the cursor in the cell under the answers (row 5, column 2). Insert a layer by selecting Insert Menu | Layer, or by selecting Insert bar | Common | Draw Layer.

b) Name the new layer *next*.

c) Insert an image in this layer. Select Insert | Image and browse for the image called *next_f01.jpg* in the *ch18* folder.

d) In the Property Inspector, name this image *next*.

e) This image will swap with another image (the button's Down state) when the button is selected. In the Behaviors panel, click on the Plus (+) button and select the Swap Image behavior.

- *The image has an asterisk (*) next to it to indicate that this is the image to be swapped. Browse and select the file next_f02.jpg. Click on OK.*

- *The event needs to be* onMouseDown *so that the button changes to the new image as soon as the mouse clicks down on the button. Select the Event pull-down menu, and then select* onMouseDown. *If this option is not available, make sure Show Events For is for browser versions 4.0 and above. See figure 18-12.*

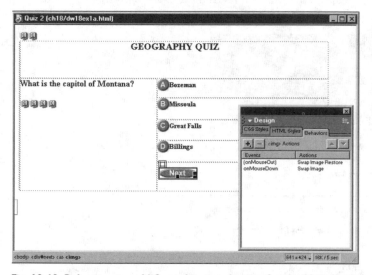

Fig. 18-12. Behaviors panel | Swap Image selection for the Next button.

f) The button will link to a new page with the second quiz question in it. With the image for the Next button selected (not the layer), click on the Link Browse button and browse for the file *quiz2.html* in the *ch18* folder. This file was copied from the companion CD-ROM.

g) Save and preview in a browser. The Next button is on screen when the image for the page is loaded. Click on the button. The button depresses and a new question is displayed. Close the browser.

15. The Next button should not appear until the correct answer is selected.

a) Select the B button. Double click on the behavior Show/Hide Layers, which is already attached to this button. We have already set up this distracter's layer to Show/Hide.

b) Select the layer called *next*. Click on the Show button. Click on OK to exit the dialog box.

c) The layer called *next* should be hidden when the page is loaded. In the Layers panel, set the layer called *next* to Hidden.

d) Save and preview in a browser. Click on the A button. Its feedback appears. Click on the B button. Its feedback appears, as does the Next button. Click on the Next button and you are taken to the next question. Exit the browser.

> • *Check all the other buttons as well to make sure the Down states are showing, as well as their feedback.*

16. Figure 18-13 shows the final Behaviors panel. The Z index for each layer may differ from yours. That does not matter, because the feedback layers are never on screen at the same time and the other layers do not overlap each other.

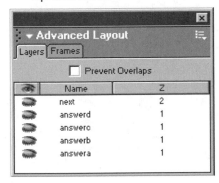

Fig. 18-13. Layers panel when the exercise is completed.

17. Close the Document window.

18. Open and preview *quiz2.html* from the *ch18* folder. Notice the feature that has been added. When B is selected (the correct answer), an animation appears. Look at the layers and behaviors to see how this was created. We will look at this type of animation (using timelines) in Chapter 19.

Guidelines for Developing Layers

Nested Layers

A nested layer is a layer that exists inside another layer, like a subset. The nested layer does not have to be totally enclosed by its parent; it can actually be larger than the parent or overlap it. The characteristics of a nested layer include the fact that it moves with the parent layer and that it can inherit the visibility of the parent layer. Animations make use of nested layers so that two items can move together in the same path. A nested layer will show up as an indented layer in the Layers panel.

Shortcut

Nested layers can also be created using the Layers panel. Hold down the Control/Command key and drag a layer name to the layer it should be nested in. Let go of the mouse when a box appears around the nested layer.

Preferences

As you are drawing layers, they can be drawn on top of each other and can be drawn to any size. Setting the Dreamweaver MX preferences for layers (Edit Menu | Preferences) can force a layer to be nested inside another layer when one layer is drawn to overlap another layer. Once a layer has been created, use the Layers panel and Property Inspector to make modifications to the layer. See figure 18-14.

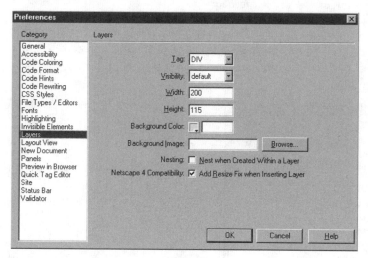

Fig. 18-14. Preferences | Layers.

Z-index and Stacking Order

Each layer has what is called a Z index. This defines the stacking order of the layers on the page. The lower the Z index, the more in the background a layer is. For example, a layer with a Z index of 1 will be behind a layer with a Z index of 2. To change the stacking order (to force a layer behind or in front of another layer), you can change the Z index in the Layers panel or in the Property Inspector.

Using the Layers panel, you can also drag a layer up or down in the list of layers to change its stacking order. If two layers have the same index, the listing order in the Layers panel determines the stacking order. The layers at the top of the Layers panel are in the foreground. The layers at the bottom of the Layers panel list are in the background. See figure 18-15.

Z-Index

Fig. 18-15. Layers panel showing Z-index and stacking order.

Creating, Selecting, Resizing, Moving, and Modifying Layers

To create a layer, perform one of the following.

• *Place the cursor on the page where you want the layer and then select Insert Menu | Layer. The layer is created with the default layer size set via Edit | Preferences | Layers. The default size is 200 by 115 pixels.*

• *Draw a layer by selecting the Draw Layer icon under Insert bar | Common tab. This option lets you draw a layer at any size and anywhere on the page. You can also drag the Draw Layer icon from the Insert bar to the page, which inserts a layer at the default size.*

A layer is selected when the selection handle and resize handles are visible. To select a layer, perform one of the following.

• *Select the name of the layer in the Layers panel.*

• *Place the cursor inside the layer. A selection handle appears in the upper left corner of the layer. Click on the selection handle, which selects the entire layer. The Property Inspector will now reference the layer.*

• *Click on the layer's border. The selection handle and the resize handles appear.*

• *Shift-click inside a layer. Note that this will allow multiple layers to be selected, one at a time.*

• *Click on the layer marker in the Document window.*

• *Select the <layer> tag in the Status bar at the bottom of the Document window.*

The layer must be selected before it can be resized. To resize a layer, perform the following.

• *Select the layer and then drag the resize handles.*

Alternatively, you can perform one of the following.

- *You can also type the new coordinates of the layer in the Property Inspector for a particular layer.*

- *To resize a layer one pixel at a time, press the Control key (Windows and Macintosh) and simultaneously press one of the Arrow keys.*

- *Multiple layers can be resized at the same time. Select the appropriate layers and then select Modify | Align | Make Same Width or Make Same Height. The layers will all be set to the last layer selected (this layer will be highlighted in black). See figure 18-16.*

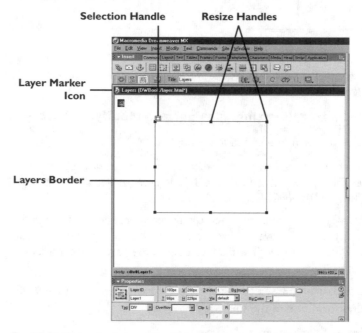

Fig. 18-16. *View of a layer element in Dreamweaver MX and the Property Inspector.*

To move a layer, perform one of the following.

- *Select the layer and then drag the selection handle at the top left corner of the layer.*

- *Drag the layer border.*

- *Change the coordinates (L, left; T, top) in the Property Inspector. These are the left and top positions from the left corner of the page. The left corner has the coordinates 0,0.*

You can also move the layer one pixel at a time by selecting the layer and then using the Arrow keys.

Layer Tips

The following are suggestions you may find useful when working with layers.

- *To convert layers to tables, select Modify Menu | Convert | Layers to Tables.*

- *To convert tables to layers, select Modify Menu | Convert | Tables to Layers.*

- *Name each layer. These names will be needed to attach behaviors to the layers. These names will also be useful when looking at the list of layers in the Layers panel so that you will know what each layer is, instead of just seeing the generic names, such as layer 1, layer 2, and so on.*

- *To select multiple layers, hold down the Shift key as you click inside each layer you want, within the page or from the Layers panel.*

- *To draw multiple layers (one after another), hold down the Ctrl/Cmd key as you draw a layer. This keeps the Insert Layer button selected in the Insert bar.*

- *Remember that the position of the layer is relative to the top left corner of the page. The top left corner of the page has the coordinates 0,0.*

- *To get the context menu for a layer, first select a layer. Then, when the resize handles are visible, right-click (Control-click on the Macintosh) the selection handle.*

- *To align two or more layers, select the layers, and then select Modify | Align.*

- *To change layers from front to back, or vice versa, select the appropriate layer and then select Modify | Arrange | Send To Back or Bring To Front. You can also change the Z-index option to change the stacking order.*

- *To stack layers relative to another layer, use the Layers panel, and type in the Z-index number.*

- *To resize multiple layers at the same time, select two or more layers and then use the Property Inspector to change the size, or select Modify | Align | Make Same Width or Make Same Height.*

- *To align and resize layers more consistently, select View | Grid | Show Grid, and View | Grid | Snap to Grid.*

Summary

- *Layers allow you to position one or more elements (graphic images, video, animation, or simple text) anywhere on a page without interfering with what is already in that location on the page. Layers can be positioned on top of each other, dragged around the screen, or made to contain animation that has been created using the Dreamweaver MX timeline feature.*

- *The only problem with layers is that they are not supported in some of the older web browsers. Only Internet Explorer 4 and Netscape Navigator 4 (and above) support layers, and even in these browsers the way layers behave is not consistent.*

- *Think of a layer as a special type of window that lies on top of the document and has its own HTML content, properties, background color, and background image.*

- *Basic steps in using layers are: create the layer, name the layer, insert the element(s) in the layer, resize the layer, set the background color and graphic, test the page in multiple browsers, set the initial visibility of each layer, and create any behaviors pertaining to the layer.*

- *There are some behaviors that come with Dreamweaver MX that are very useful when used with layers: Change Property, Drag Layer, Show/Hide Layers, and Set Text.*

- *In the practice exercise you created layers, used behaviors to show/hide layers, set properties for layers, inserted images into layers, and used the Layers panel.*

- *A nested layer is a layer that exists inside another layer, like a subset. The nested layer does not have to be totally enclosed by its parent; it can actually be larger than the parent or overlap it. The characteristics of a nested layer include that it moves with the parent layer and that it can inherit the visibility of the parent layer.*

C H A P T E R

19

Creating Animation with Dreamweaver MX

Introduction

In this chapter we will see how Dreamweaver MX can animate objects using its own capabilities, without using imported animation created in other programs, such as Flash. Yes, Dreamweaver MX can play these other types of animation (Flash movies and animated GIFs), but there are advantages to using Dreamweaver MX's built-in animation capability. We will explore using Flash movies a little later in this chapter.

However, before beginning this chapter, you should first have a basic understanding of working with layers, because creating animation in Dreamweaver MX involves the use of layers. If you need to, you may want to review Chapter 18.

In this chapter we are going to take an object and move it within an HTML page. We can even give the user control over the animation, providing the ability to stop or play the animation by adding one or more behaviors. By the end of this chapter you will be able to:

- *Create animation using timelines*
- *Use Dreamweaver MX tools for creating and modifying layers*
- *Recognize the HTML code associated with timelines*
- *Use behaviors to change timelines*
- *Import Flash objects*

Animation with a Timeline

With the use of layers, you can create animations that do not require plugins, ActiveX controls, or Java applets. You can accomplish this with the use of timelines. Timelines are created with dynamic HTML (DHTML). DHTML enables objects to change position and/or style with the use of a scripting language. Timelines use the JavaScript scripting language to change the size, position, visibility, and/or stacking order of layers, over time. Timelines can also be used to change the source of images over time, such as for a slide show. If you have ever worked with Macromedia's Director or Flash, you will find the Dreamweaver MX timeline very familiar. See figure 19-1.

Pop-up Menu   **Playback Head Channel**

Behavior Channel

Animation Channels

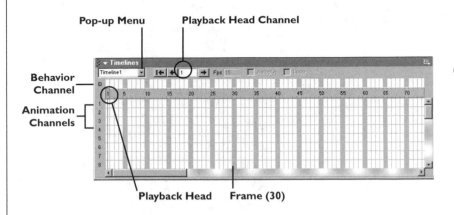

Playback Head   **Frame (30)**

Fig. 19-1. Timeline panel.

·T/P·

To open the Timeline panel, select Window | Others | Timelines or use the shortcut Alt/Opt + F9.

The timeline consists of frames (columns) and channels (rows). A frame represents a single point in the timeline. Frames are numbered sequentially, starting with the number 1 on the far left and continuing to the right, for as many frames as exist within the timeline.

The playback head (playhead) is the red square with a red vertical line underneath. The playhead moves from left to right, "playing" all content in each frame (across all channels) as it enters each frame. The frame number currently being "played" appears in the Playback Head channel. The playhead continues to move across the timeline until it displays the last frame with a layer in it, or until it encounters a behavior that directs it to do something else.

Channels are the horizontal rows in the timeline. The topmost channel (B) is called the Behavior channel, where behaviors are inserted. When the playhead encounters a behavior within a frame in this channel, it is immediately executed. Behaviors may contain an action that instructs the playhead to go to a specific frame, change the stacking order of layers in the frames, or even change the size of a layer. The channels below the Behavior channel are called animation channels, and are where layers will be placed for animation.

Creating an Animation

Probably the main thing to remember when creating animation using the timeline is that you are animating a layer, which includes all content in that layer. To create an animation, perform one of the following. See figure 19-2.

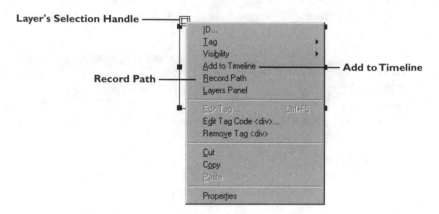

Layer's Selection Handle ————

ID...
Tag ▶
Visibility ▶
Add to Timeline ————— **Add to Timeline**
Record Path ————— Record Path
Layers Panel

Edit Tag...   Ctrl+F5
Edit Tag Code <div>...
Remove Tag <div>

Cut
Copy
Paste

Properties

Fig. 19-2. Context menu for a layer.

- *Select the layer's selection handle and select Record Path from the context menu (right-click or Modify | Timeline | Record Path of Layer). Drag the selection handle around the screen to create the animation path. Let up the mouse button to end the path. The timeline will now contain an animation bar for controlling the animated layer.*

- *Select the layer and select Modify | Timeline | Add Object to Timeline, or right-click on the layer's selection handle, and select Add to Timeline or drag the layer into the Timelines panel.*

  - *A keyframe (small circle in the Animation bar) automatically appears at the first and last frame of the animation.*

  - *Select the last frame with the keyframe. Drag the layer's selection handle to move the layer to a new position on the screen. The layer will animate from its original position to this new position.*

  - *To add positions along the path, a keyframe must be added for each change in position. Click on the Animation bar in the frame where a new keyframe should be located. Control-click (Windows) or Command-click (Macintosh) on the frame in the Animation bar to insert a keyframe. Keyframes can be moved to a new frame by dragging the keyframe inside the Timelines panel. See figure 19-3.*

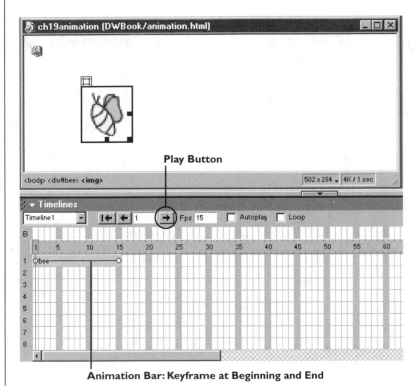

Animation Bar: Keyframe at Beginning and End

Fig. 19-3. Timeline with simple animation.

Hold down the Play button in the Timelines panel to preview the animation on the page.

Keyframes

A keyframe is a special frame, designating where the layer changes any of its properties, such as position, size, visibility, and so on. A keyframe is required whenever there is a new or changed setting for the properties of a layer. For example, in regard to movement, whenever a layer changes the direction of its position (when it turns), a keyframe is required. If a layer is changing its visibility (or size) between frames 9 and 10, a keyframe must be created in frame 10 – the frame in which the change will be displayed. Keyframes are identified as circles on the Animation bar in the Timelines panel. Figure 19-4 shows an example of two animations in the timeline.

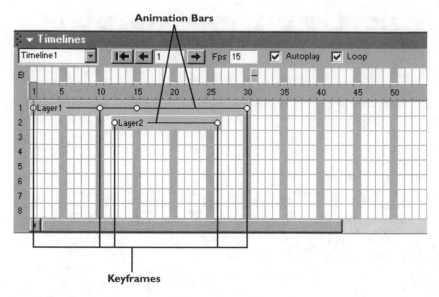

Fig. 19-4. Animation bars with keyframes.

Adding a Keyframe

To add a keyframe, select the Animation bar in the Timelines panel. Control-click (Windows) or Command-click (Macintosh) on the frame in the Animation bar. Alternatively, select the Animation bar. Then right-click on a frame in the Animation bar and select Add Keyframe from the context menu.

Deleting a Keyframe

Right-click on the keyframe on the Animation bar in the Timelines panel and select Remove Keyframe from the context menu. See figure 19-5.

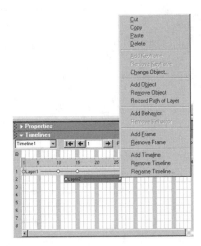

Fig. 19-5. Context menu for timeline.

To add an object to a timeline or modify an existing timeline, you can select Modify Menu | Timeline. See figure 19-6.

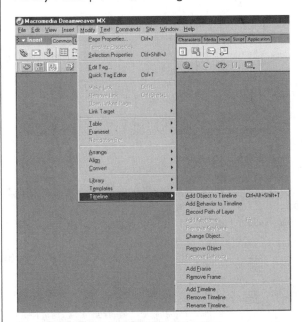

Fig. 19-6. Menu option Modify | Timeline.

Tips for Working with Timelines

Later in this chapter you will take a guided tour to actually look at a document that contains a timeline. But first, review the following key points and terminology regarding timelines. Refer to figure 19-7.

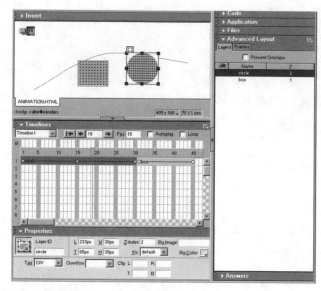

Fig. 19-7. Animation example.

- Timelines contain only layers and behaviors. If an object or text is to be animated, it must first be inserted into a layer.

- A frame is a single point in time.

- Animation channels display bars for animating layers. Only one object (layer) can be in a channel at a specific point in time (frame). But a channel can change to a new object in a new frame. For example, a circle may animate in Channel 1, from frames 1 – through 30, but then a square animates in Channel 1, from frames 31 through 45.

- Animation bars show the duration of each object's animation.

- To create animation using a timeline, you need to have one or more layers already created in the document. The fastest way to then animate the layer is to use the context menu option Record Path.

- The playback head (playhead) displays the content of each frame in the timeline as it passes through each frame.

- The duration of an animation is defined by the number of frames the object (layer) spans in the timeline. In the example, the duration of the box is 15 frames. The duration can be changed by dragging the last keyframe to a higher frame number (to make the duration longer) or to a lower numbered keyframe (to make it shorter). All keyframes are adjusted accordingly.

- The speed at which an object animates is expressed in terms of frames per second (fps). The default is 15 fps. Browsers always play every frame of the timeline, even if they cannot keep up with the specified rate (fps). The multiple objects animating at a single point in time, combined with other activities going on in the document simultaneously, will affect the rate at which the animation will play.

- Behaviors reside in the Behaviors channel (B) — the top channel in the timeline. They execute as the playhead enters the frame in which the behavior resides.

- There can be more than one timeline in a document. There is a pull-down menu on the timeline from which you can select (switch) each timeline. Use different timelines if a behavior in one timeline interferes with the animation of an object. For example, if one object is just looping around in a circle for 10 frames, its timeline will be only 10 frames in length. Any objects that will take up more than 10 frames should be placed in another timeline.

- Timelines do not automatically start playing when a page is loaded. Select the Autoplay checkbox on the timeline to insert a JavaScript command to start the timeline when the page is loaded.

- By default, when the playhead reaches the timeline's last frame that has an object (layer) in it, the timeline will stop executing. Select the Loop checkbox in the timeline to have the playhead jump back to frame 1 and start the timeline over. Loop always places a behavior in the frame immediately after the last frame containing a layer.

- To insert a behavior in the timeline, determine at what point in the timeline the behavior should be executed and then click on the frame in the Behaviors channel. Using the Behaviors panel (Window | Behaviors), click on the Plus (+) button to select from a list of available behaviors. The behaviors will only be executed when the playhead encounters the specific frame with the behavior in it. Behaviors in timelines do not only have to do with layers, but can be used to jump to a new URL at a specific frame, to play sound, to swap images, and so on.

- To move the entire animation path of a layer, select the Animation bar in the Timelines panel and then drag the layer to a new position.

- Animation for the same object cannot overlap; that is, the same object cannot have two Animation bars that reside in the same frames of a timeline (or multiple timelines).

- An animation can be applied to a different object (layer) by selecting the Animation bar and Modify | Timeline | Change Object. You will be prompted to select the new object (by name). This is useful if you want to animate more than one object along the same path as another object. Copy the animation sequence (Animation bar in the Timelines panel), paste into a new channel (or frame), and select Change Object.

HTML for Timelines

If you look inside the HTML timeline source code, you will see a JavaScript function called *MM_initTimelines*. Dreamweaver MX created this function's name. You can change the name of the function, but every occurrence of a call to the function name would also have to be changed. When a timeline is first

·T/P·

Show/Hide Layers: Timelines allow you to switch images in a layer. This can slow down the animation, however, because the new image must be downloaded and this will take time. Images that are already in a timeline are downloaded before the animation begins. As an alternative to switching images in a single layer, try hiding a second layer with the new image. The second layer begins its animation in the frame immediately after the end of the first layer.

 HTML

used in a document, Dreamweaver MX inserts this function at the beginning of the HTML code within the *<head>* tag. This function is called from within the *<body>* tag, wherever the timeline has been inserted. See figure 19-8.

```
function MM_initTimelines() { //v4.0
    //MM_initTimelines() Copyright 1997 Macromedia, Inc. All rights reserved.
    var ns = navigator.appName == "Netscape";
    var ns4 = (ns && parseInt(navigator.appVersion) == 4);
    var ns5 = ......
    }
}


function MM_timelinePlay(tmLnName, myID) { //v1.2
    //Copyright 1997 Macromedia, Inc. All rights reserved.
    var i,j,tmLn,props,keyFrm,sprite,numKeyFr,first
    ........
    } }
}


</head>

<body bgcolor="#FFFFFF" text="#000000" onLoad="MM_timelinePlay('Timeline1')">
```

Fig. 19-8. HTML for timelines.

Figure 19-8 shows part of the JavaScript function *MM_initTimelines*. The example also shows another function, called *MM_timelinePlay*. Dreamweaver MX inserts this function when the Autoplay checkbox is selected on the Timeline panel. The first command in the *<body>* tag calls this function as soon as the page is loading (*onLoad*).

Behaviors to Use in Timelines

The same behaviors that are used with layers (Change Property, Drag Layer, and Show-Hide Layers) can also be inserted into timelines. However, the following behaviors can also be used with timelines.

Go to Timeline Frame: Tells the playhead to jump to a specified frame in a selected timeline. If the timeline is not already playing, the timeline will not automatically start playing. Add another behavior, Play Timeline, to play the timeline.

There is also the option to cause the timeline to loop, but the loop option can only be applied to a behavior inserted into the Timeline Behavior channel (not attached to an object, such as a button outside the timeline). When a number is typed in the Loop field of the behavior (i.e., Go to Timeline Frame behavior), the playhead will execute the behavior that number of (loop) times. For instance, if a Go To Timeline Frame behavior is inserted at frame 15, and is told to go to frame 10, loop 3, when the playhead reaches frame 15 it will play frame 15, jump back to frame 10, play forward to frame 15, jump back to frame

10, and so forth — executing the loop three times. After the third loop, it will continue to play forward after frame 15.

Play Timeline: Starts playing a specified timeline. Timelines do not automatically start playing unless the Autoplay box is selected in the Timelines panel. This behavior could be attached to text or a button for the user to control the timeline.

Stop Timeline: Stops the animation for a specified timeline.

Guided Tour 19A: Timelines

This guided tour will show you an example of a document that uses a timeline for animation. In fact, it uses two timelines. You will have a chance to look at the way the animation was created, modify the animation, and look at some behaviors used in conjunction with the layers and the timeline.

CD-ROM

1. Select File Menu | Open and locate on the companion CD-ROM the *Learning_DWcomplete* folder and the subfolder *ch19*. Locate the file named *dw19tour.html*. Double click on *dw19tour.html* to open the file.

2. The file *dw19tour.html* should now appear in your copy of Dreamweaver MX.

3. Preview in a browser to see the animation in this document. Notice that there are two objects animating on the screen. Select the button Go to Timeline 2. The animation stops and a different animation begins. Select the button Go to Timeline 1. The animation stops and the original animation starts up again. Close the browser.

4. Let's look more closely at these animations.
    a) Select Window Menu | Others | Timelines. There are actually two timelines in this document. Select *Timeline1* in the Timeline pop-up menu. See figure 19-9.

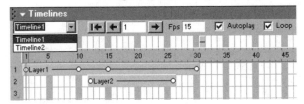

Fig. 19-9. Multiple timelines and the Timeline pop-up menu.

    b) Channel 1 contains an animation for the layer called *Layer1*. The animation has a duration of 30 frames. There are keyframes in frame 10 and in frame 15.

c) Channel 2 contains an animation for the layer called *Layer2*. This animation does not start until frame 12, and only continues to frame 26. There are no keyframes in the middle of the animation.

d) Click somewhere on the Animation bar for *Layer1*. Notice the animation path on the screen for the layer. Each time the layer changes direction, a keyframe is needed (in this case, frames 10 and 15). See figure 19-10.

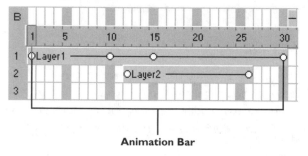

Animation Bar

Fig. 19-10. Animation bar with keyframes.

e) Hold down the Play button to see the animation in this timeline. Watch *Layer1* follow the animation path. See figure 19-11.

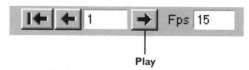

Play

Fig. 19-11. Timelines panel showing Play button.

f) Select the Animation bar for *Layer2* and play the timeline to see the *Layer2* animation path.

5. We will change the animation for *Layer2*.
   a) Click on frame 20 in the Animation bar for *Layer2*.
   b) To insert a keyframe in frame 20, select Modify Menu | Timeline | Add Keyframe, or press the F6 key.
   c) Drag the layer to a new position on the screen. The animation path will now go from the position of the keyframe in frame 12, to the keyframe in frame 20, to the keyframe in frame 26.

6. To move the entire animation for *Layer2* to the right side of the screen, perform the following.
   a) Select the Animation bar for *Layer2*. Do not select the Animation bar where a keyframe resides, as that will only select that frame.

b) Drag the layer (on the screen) more toward the right side of the screen. The animation path follows the layer. The Animation bar in the timeline does not change.

7. Notice that the Loop and Autoplay boxes are selected for *Timeline1*. This makes the timeline start to play as soon as the page is loaded and forces it to loop (play) as long as the page is loaded or until the timeline is stopped.

a) To see the JavaScript and behaviors used for the Autoplay and the Loop, select Window | Behaviors to display the Behaviors panel.

b) Select the *<body>* tag down in the Status bar at the bottom of the Document window.

c) The Behaviors panel should show the event *onLoad* and the action Play Timeline. Double click on Play Timeline. The dialog shows that *Timeline1* will be played (*onLoad*). Close the dialog box. See figure 19-12.

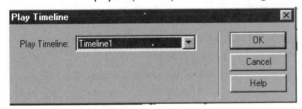

Fig. 19-12. Play Timeline in the Behavior dialog box.

d) Press F10 to see the HTML source code in the Code Inspector. Find the *<body>* tag. The *onLoad* event is calling the function *MM_timelinePlay* and passing it a parameter – the name of the time-line to play (*Timeline1*) when the page loads. See figure 19-13.

```
<body bgcolor="#FFFFFF" text="#000000" onLoad="MM_timelinePlay('Timeline1')">
```

Fig. 19-13. HTML to call JavaScript function MM_timelinePlay.

e) Scroll upward in the HTML code and you will find the functions *MM_timelinePlay*, *MM_initTimelines()*, *MM_timelineStop*, and *MM_time-line Goto*. Each of these functions is created (and inserted) by Dreamweaver MX when a timeline is first created, when it is set to Autoplay, and when a behavior (such as Stop Timeline, Play Timeline, or Go To Timeline Frame) is selected to control the timeline.

f) Press F10 to close the Code Inspector.

8. When the timeline was set to Loop, a behavior was inserted in the Behavior channel in the frame after the last frame in the timeline.

a) In frame 31 of the Behavior channel, notice the dash, which means there is a behavior in that frame. Single click on the behavior (the dash) in frame 31.

b) The Behaviors panel shows the event *onFrame31* and the action Go To Timeline Frame.

c) Double click on the action Go To Timeline Frame. The dialog shows that upon entering frame 31 (the event), the playhead will jump (go to) frame 1 and continue playing. Close the dialog box. See figure 19-14.

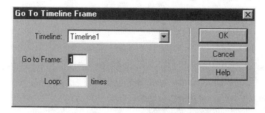

Fig. 19-14. Go To Timeline Frame behavior in the Behavior dialog box.

9. Change the speed and smoothness of the animation for layer 1 by dragging the keyframe in frame 15 to frame 20. Play the timeline to see the difference.

10. Change the timeline to *Timeline2* by selecting *Timeline2* in the pop-up menu in the Timelines panel. Play *Timeline2*. The animation starts off screen and animates across to the middle of the screen.

a) Lengthen the duration of the animation by dragging the last keyframe (frame 15) to frame 30.

b) Add one or more keyframes and change the animation path (add the keyframe and then drag the layer).

c) Check the Loop checkbox to make *Timeline2* loop continuously. Play the timeline.

11. Let's have the text in the layer change over time. It already changes in frame 5. To look at the behavior, single click on frame 5 in the Behaviors channel, and then double click on the action Set Text of Layer. Notice the *<font>* tag, to set the color of the text. If the color is not set (in this case, to red), when the text is changed in the layer it goes back to the default color of the text for the page (in this page, black).

a) In *Timeline2*, select frame 10 in the Behaviors channel.

b) Click on the Plus (+) button in the Behaviors panel, and then select Set Text | Set Text of Layer.

c) Select *Layer3* in the Layer box.

d) In the HTML box, type *This is third text line*. See figure 19-15.

e) Preview in a browser to see the text change.

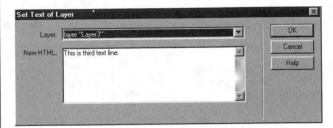

Fig. 19-15. Set Text of Layer option in the Behavior dialog box.

12. Look at the behaviors attached to the button Go to Timeline2.

    a) Click on the button Go to Timeline2.

    b) In the Behaviors panel are two behaviors to execute for the event onMouseDown (when the button is clicked).

    c) Double click on the action Stop Timeline. When the button is clicked, it will stop Timeline1. Click on OK.

    d) Double click on the action Play Timeline. When the button is clicked, it will also play *Timeline2*.

13. Look at the behaviors attached to the button Go to Timeline1. They are just the opposite of the *Timeline2* button.

14. Change the name of *Timeline1* to *animate1* by single clicking on the name in the Timelines panel pop-up menu.

15. Change the stacking order of *Layer1* so that it displays above *Layer2* when it crosses its path. In the Layers panel (Window | Others | Layers), drag *Layer1* above *Layer2*. Watch the Z-index option change for the layers.

16. The button Go to Timeline1 should disappear (become invisible) when the button Go to Timeline1 is clicked.

    a) Click on the button Go to Timeline1.

    b) In the Behaviors panel, click on the Plus (+) button and select Show-Hide Layers.

    c) Select the layer *goto1* in the Layers panel.

    d) Click on the Hide button.

    e) To make sure the Go to Timeline1 button stays/becomes visible, select the layer *goto2* and then click on the Show button. Click on OK. See figure 19-16.

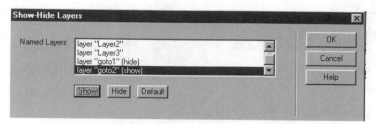

Fig. 19-16. Show-Hide Layers option in the Behaviors panel.

f) There should now be three actions for the *onMouseDown* event. See figure 19-17.

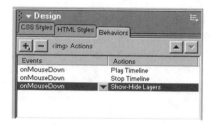

*Fig. 19-17. Behaviors panel showing **onMouseDown** event.*

17. The button Go to Timeline2 should disappear (become invisible) when the button Go to Timeline2 is clicked.
    a) Click on the button Go to Timeline2.
    b) In the Behaviors channel, click on the Plus (+) button and then select Show-Hide Layers.
    c) Select the layer *goto2* in the Layers panel.
    d) Click on the Hide button.
    e) To make sure the Go to Timeline1 button stays/becomes visible, select the layer *goto1* and click on the Show button. Click on OK.
    f) If the event for Show-Hide Layers is not *onMouseDown*, single click on the event and from the pull-down menu (Down arrow) select *onMouseDown*.

18. The button Go to Timeline1 should be invisible when the page loads.

    a) In the Layers panel, select the layer *goto1*.
    b) Click under the Visibility column until the closed-eye icon appears, or in the Property Inspector select Hidden for the Vis setting.

19. Preview in a browser. Select the buttons to switch between the timelines.

Dreamweaver and Flash

Macromedia Flash is quickly becoming the standard for creating interactive web animations. Flash allows you to combine vector and bitmapped graphics with audio to create interactive animations. Flash also uses scripting to interact with HTML, other multimedia applications (such as Director), and external programs such as XML and JSP. See figure 19-18.

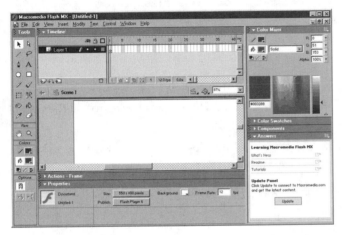

Fig. 19-18. Flash MX interface.

A great use of Flash in HTML documents is for sound. Sound is not an easy element to control in HTML documents because it needs a player, and a user may have a number of different players installed, including QuickTime, RealPlayer, Windows Media Player, and others. Each of these players reacts to HTML and JavaScript differently, so that you almost have to find a way to check the type of software installed on a user's machine before playing a sound. To get around this, and primarily ensure your sounds will play, create a sound-only Flash file, shock it, and insert it as a sound to play as background music, narration, or sound effects. This will require the user's browser to have the Flash Shockwave plugin installed. This plugin comes with a newer version of most browsers.

To insert a Flash file into a web page, perform the following steps.

1. Open and save a new web page.

2. From the Insert bar, Common tab, click on the Insert Flash icon and locate the Flash SWF file you want to import. You can also select Insert Menu | Media | Flash.

3. Dreamweaver will insert the following code, where *flash.swf* is the name of the calling Flash animation file. Note that this is for a Flash MX file (the player is version 6).

```
<object classid="clsid:D27CDB6E-AE6D-11cf-96B8-
444553540000" codebase="http://download.macromedia.com/
pub/shockwave/cabs/flash/swflash.cab#version=6,0,29,0"
width="550" height="400">
 <param name="movie" value="flash.swf">
 <param name="quality" value="high">
 <embed src="flash.swf" quality="high" pluginspage=
 "http://www.macromedia.com/go/getflashplayer"
 type="application/x-shockwave-flash" width="550"
 height="400">
 </embed>
</object>
```

4. Check to make sure the *param name src* and the *embed src* are both set to the name of your Flash SWF file. These are required to call the appropriate ActiveX controls and plugins.

5. You can modify the settings of how the Flash file displays by using the Property Inspector. See figure 19-19.

Fig. 19-19. Property Inspector showing Flash MX object.

Summary

- *With the use of layers, you can create animation that does not require plugins, ActiveX controls, or Java applets. You can accomplish this with the use of timelines.*

- *Timelines are created with dynamic HTML (DHTML). DHTML enables objects to change position and/or style with the use of a scripting language. Timelines use the JavaScript scripting language to change the size, position, visibility, and/or stacking order of layers, over time.*

- *The timeline consists of frames (columns) and channels (rows).*

- *A frame represents a single point in the timeline. Frames are numbered sequentially, starting with the number 1 on the far left and continuing to the right, for as many frames as exist within the timeline.*

- *Channels are the horizontal rows in the timeline. The topmost channel is called the Behavior channel, where behaviors are inserted, to be executed in a specific frame or frames.*

- *The playback head (playhead) is the red square with a red vertical line underneath. The playhead moves from left to right, "playing" all content in each frame (across all channels) as it enters each frame.*

- *A keyframe is a special frame, designating where the layer changes any of its properties, such as position, size, visibility, and so on. A keyframe is required whenever there is a new or changed setting for the properties of a layer.*

- *There are some additional behaviors that can be used with timelines: Go to Timeline Frame, Play Timeline, and Stop Timeline.*

- *In the guided tour you worked with a document that contained two timelines. You looked at how it was created, modified the animation, and looked at some behaviors used in conjunction with layers and the timeline.*

20

Application Chapter: Working with Layers

Introduction

As you are developing web pages, you will encounter situations in which you will want to control how objects are placed on the screen. That is, you will want to specify the exact placement of objects. When objects overlap, you will want to specify which object appears to be on top. The use of layers is an effective way to handle these types of situations. Just like many graphic software programs, Dreamweaver MX allows you to control objects through the use of layers.

Application Exercise Objectives

By the end of this chapter you will have:

- *Created a page using layers to display information about types of products* The 21st Century Kitchen *web site offers*
- *Created an image map*
- *Used behaviors to add functionality to the page*

Application Exercise 20-1: Working with Layers

Description

In this application chapter, you will create a quick guide for visitors by providing an overview of what products are available at *The 21st Century Kitchen*. The visitor will be presented with a page containing four icons representing the four product categories of our online store. When the visitor selects any of the four icons, a pop-up window will appear that lists the various types of products available in that category. You will also create an image map from a graphic and add behaviors to this image map and to the layers. The type of image map we will create uses a technique commonly known as "disjointed rollovers."

Take a Look

CD-ROM

Let's take a look at what the finished exercise will look like. Open Dreamweaver MX and use File Menu | Open to locate the companion CD-ROM. Locate the folder *Learning_DWapplication_complete* and select and open the file *ap20.html*. Look at the layout of the web page, noticing the graphic and text areas. Take a look at the file and the HTML code in Dreamweaver MX. You will be using the following Dreamweaver MX concepts in the exercise.

- *Creating layers and using the Layers panel*
- *Using image maps for linking items*

- *Alt image*
- *Property Inspector*
- *Using behaviors to show-hide layers*
- *Displaying text based on user interaction*

Storyboard: Browser View

Figure 20-1 shows how the product web page will look in a web browser when the exercise is completed.

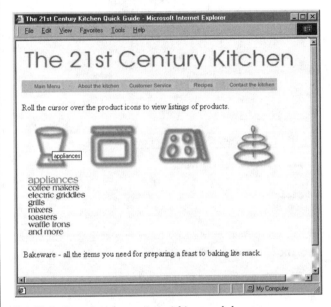

Fig. 20-1. Completed exercise within a web browser.

Storyboard: Dreamweaver MX View

Figure 20-2 shows how the product web page will look in Dreamweaver MX when the exercise is completed.

Fig. 20-2. Completed exercise in Dreamweaver MX.

Application Project Steps

Complete this exercise on your own, guided by following the general steps. You can always refer to the completed example you viewed in the "Take a Look" section of this exercise.

NOTE: The following steps are intended as a guide. This is your project, so feel free to make whatever variations you like.

1. Create a new HTML document in Dreamweaver MX.

2. Title the page *The 21st Century Kitchen Quick Guide*. Set the background color to #FFFFCC.

3. Save the new page as *guide.html* in the folder *Learning_DWapplication*.

4. Insert the banner graphic *21ckbnr.jpg* (from the *ap_media* subfolder) in the current document (*guide.html*). Under the banner graphic, insert the Library object called *mainNav*.

5. Underneath the navigation bar (*mainNav*), type *Roll the cursor over the product icons to view listings of products*.

6. Underneath the text, place the kitchen graphic called *kicons.jpg* (found in the *ap_media* subfolder).

7. In the Property Inspector, in the Map Name field for the image *kicons.jpg*, type *kicon.*

8. Using the Rectangular Hot Spot tool (from the Property Inspector), create a hot spot around each of the four icon symbols.

9. In the Alt Entry field for each hot spot, type the following for the corresponding hot spot: *appliances, bakeware, cookware,* and *specialty items.* See figure 20-3.

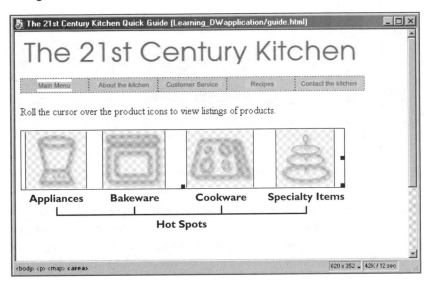

Fig. 20-3. Image map with four hot spots.

10. We are going to insert the product listing for each item in the image map. Make sure Dreamweaver MX is in Standard view (Insert bar | Layout, or Control + Shift + F6) and that the Layers panel is showing. Press Enter/Return to insert about four lines under the icon image. This will help to align the product listings and still see the marker icons for the layers.

11. Create a new layer using Insert | Layer. A marker icon for the layer and the layer outline should appear.

12. Insert the graphic *layerap.gif* into the layer. Name the layer *ap.* The cursor must be positioned inside the layer before importing the graphic image. Then use the position handle (upper left corner) to move the layer to under the left edge of the icon image (under the picture for appliances). Resize the layer to shrink around the image. See figure 20-4.

Layer Marker Icon   **Product Listing for Appliances**

Fig. 20-4. First layer, with product listing for Appliances.

13. Create new layers for the other three hot spots using the graphic files *layerbw.gif*, *layercw.gif*, and *layersi.gif* (found in the *ap_media* subfolder). Remember to name each layer (*bw*, *cw*, and *si*): *bw* stands for *bakeware*, *cw* stands for *cookware*, and *si* stands for *specialty items*. See figure 20-5.

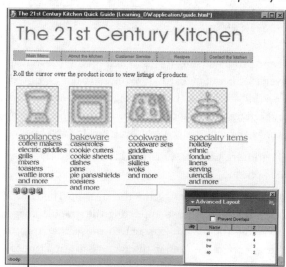

Marker Icons for All Layers

Fig. 20-5. All four layers with product listings.

14. Add one more layer just after the other four product listing layers, and name it *directions*. You may want to use Insert bar | Common to create this layer, so that you can draw it below the other layers. Inside this new layer, type the text *Roll the cursor over a product family name to view a description.*

15. The Z-index column in the Layers panel controls the order of the layers. The higher the number, the closer to the front of the screen.

16. When the page first loads, only the directions should be visible, not the four product layers. Using the Layers panel, make the four product layers invisible by clicking to "close the eye." Now when the page first loads, all layers will be invisible except the layer directions.

17. A behavior needs to be attached to each of the product graphic hot spots to show or hide the layers. Click to select the *appliances* graphic hot spot (the *blender* graphic). Open the Behaviors panel and click on the Plus (+) button to call up the Behaviors list.

18. Select Show-Hide Layers. In the Show-Hide Layers window, set layer *ap* to show (by selecting the *ap* layer and clicking on the Show button). Set the other three layers to hide. The layer description should always be marked Show (or not set at all). Do not forget to scroll down and set the layer *si* to Hide. Click on OK to save the settings. Notice that the event defaults to *onMouseOver*, which is the event we want.

19. Set the behaviors for the other three product families: *bakeware*, *cookware*, and *specialty items*. Make sure the layer description is always set to Show. Table 20-1 outlines the various layers set to Show-Hide for each hot spot behavior.

Table 20-1: Hot Spot Behavior Settings for Various Layers

'ap' hot spot	'bw' hot spot	'cw' hot spot	'si' hot spot
ap - Show	ap-Hide	ap-Hide	ap-Hide
bw-Hide	bw-Show	bw-Hide	bw-Hide
cw-Hide	cw-Hide	cw-Show	cw-Hide
si-Hide	si-Hide	si-Hide	si-Show

20. This might be a good time to save and test your page in a browser.

21. Let's add four more layers for descriptions of the product families. The viewer will be able to read these descriptions when they roll the cursor over the product listings. Go to the Layers panel and "open the eyes of" (make visible) the four product listing layers.

22. Click on the *Appliances* product listing graphic to select it. In the Behaviors panel, click on the Plus (+) button to call up the Behaviors list. Select Set Text | Set Text of Layer and in the New HTML field, type: *Appliances – all the appliances that you will need from breakfast preparation to after dinner coffee.* Make sure the layer in the Layer box is the layer description. Click on OK.

23. Add the following description text for the *Bakeware* product listing graphic: *Bakeware – all the items you need for preparing a feast to baking a lite snack.*

24. Add in the following description text for the *Cookware* product listing graphic: *Cookware – all the items you need for preparing blueberry pancakes to shrimp stirfry.*

25. Add in the following description text for the *Specialty Items* product listing graphic: *Specialty Items – looking for those special items to add to your culinary arsenal, from preparation to presentation.*

26. In the View column of the Layers panel, set the *ap*, *bw*, *cw*, and *si* layers to invisible (closed eye).

27. Update the Library object *navBar* with links for the Appliances, Bakeware, Cookware, and Specialty Items buttons. Because we do not have pages for these topics yet, link all four of them to the *guide.html* page.

28. Save your work and preview in a browser. You should be able to see the product family listing when the cursor rolls over the graphic images. When the cursor rolls over the family listing, the directions should change into a description of the product family.

Summary

In this application chapter you created a quick guide for viewing the different types of products *The 21st Century Kitchen* offers. You have created an image map from a menu graphic. You created five layers (the four product family listings and a description field). You used behaviors to display the product family *listing* layer when the user rolls the cursor over the product graphic. Finally, you added another set of behaviors to provide description text for each of the four product families.

May I Take Your Order? — Forms

Introduction

Usually web sites provide some type of information to the visitor. On the other hand, sometimes web site owners want to obtain information from the web visitors. Forms can be used to request topic-specific information, to obtain suggestions to improve the web site, to request contact information, or to take orders for products. In addition, forms are also used for online testing, in that forms provide such a variety of interactive methods. By the end of this chapter you will be able to:

- *Describe common uses of a form*
- *Use the various Form objects*
- *Recognize the basic HTML behind forms*
- *Describe different methods to process form information*

Forms in Brief

Anytime you see a checkbox, radio button, fill-in-the-blank, or pull-down menu in a web site, a form is probably being used. Forms can be a primary factor in making an e-commerce site possible, by providing the means for accepting passwords and ordering information. The following are some of the common uses of forms.

- *Quizzes with multiple-choice or fill-in-the-blank questions*
- *Surveys*
- *Enrollment in online training/learning*
- *Subscribing*
- *Downloading files (where the user can select specific files through the use of pull-down menus and checkboxes)*
- *Letting the user make preferences (options to determine the path through a web site)*

Now think of some reasons you might want to obtain information about a visitor, such as the following.

- *Selling magazines? What magazines do they currently read? Do they travel? What hobbies are they interested in?*
- *Want to sell your company's services? Ask your visitor you can help them. What is their business? How many employees?*
- *Want to give information to visitors on travel in your area? Have them sign a guest book and fill out a survey on what other information they would like to see.*

Form Objects

A form can contain multiple Form objects, and a page can contain more than one form. The following are the available Form objects. See figure 21-1.

- Form: *Adds a form area to a document*
- Text Field: *Fill in the blank, notes, fixed or variable length*
- Hidden Field: *Stores user data that is hidden from the user, such as information that was entered the last time the user visited the site*
- Checkbox: *Multiple selections allowed in a group of buttons*
- Radio Button: *Only one selection allowed in a group of buttons*
- Radio Group: *A collection of radio buttons*
- List/Menus: *Pull-down menus, list of items to scroll through, multiple or single selections in the list*
- Jump Menu: *A list or pop-up menu of selections for a user, with each selection linking to a URL*
- Image Field: *Image used as input, such as for a graphical button or a collage of graphics to pick from*
- File Field: *Text field with a browser button to search for a file on the user's hard drive for uploading to a server*
- Button: *Usually used to submit the form data*
- Label: *To associate a label with a specific field*
- Field Set: *Tag that contains a grouping of form elements*

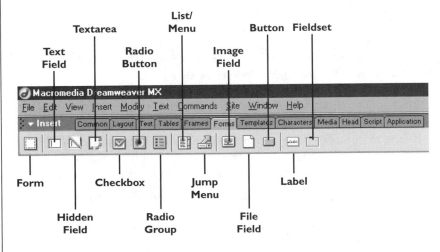

Fig. 21-1. Insert bar | Forms.

All Form objects have a field name that should be used to define the type of information being collected. This name plays a vital part in the functionality of some of the Form objects.

Creating a Form

Think of the form as a shell surrounding multiple input fields called Form objects. A form has the following three components (see figure 21-2).

- *The form itself. The form is designated by the <form> tag.*

- *The Form objects that accept input from the user. All of the Form objects related to a form must be between the opening and closing <form> tags.*

- *The Submit button, which sends the data input to the server via a scripting program. We will talk about processing the data later in the chapter.*

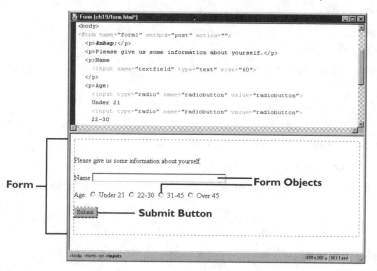

Fig. 21-2. Example of a form and HTML source code.

Note also the following regarding forms:

- *Be sure to label each field in a form. This lets the application processing the form know the purpose of the input information (name, date, address, and so on). The labels should be unique (within a form) and only one word. Do not include spaces or special characters in the name. Underscore (_) can be used in labels.*

- *To select the form, select the <form> tag in the Status bar or click on the red dotted area of the form.*

- *The dynamic text and database functions of Dreamweaver MX provide the means for processing form data. Dynamic text and database functions are discussed in Chapter 24.*

Forms are really so simple to use that we will jump right in and create one in this next practice exercise.

Practice Exercise 21-1: Setting up a Radio Button and Text Field

Description

A radio button lets a visitor make one selection from a group of radio buttons. Because only one selection can be made, if the user changes his mind and selects another radio button in the group, the previous radio button is unchecked (or cleared). For this exercise, we will be working with a fictitious real estate web site. We will be asking the user to indicate what price range should be used to begin looking for houses. The following elements are covered in this exercise.

- *Setting up a form*
- *Inserting a radio button Form object*
- *Inserting a text field Form object*
- *Setting the properties for the radio button*
- *Working with the HTML for the radio button*

Take a Look

Before beginning the exercise, let's take a look at the exercise in its completed state so that you can clearly see what it is you are about to build.

 DWComplete Site

1. Make sure you are working with the site *DWComplete*. You can confirm this by selecting *DWComplete* from the Site panel.

 CD-ROM

2. Locate the *ch21* folder and within it the file named *dw21ex1.html*. Double click on *dw21ex1.html* to open the file.

3. The file *dw21ex1.html* should now appear in your copy of Dreamweaver MX. Note the following properties of this completed exercise.

   - *Notice the red dotted line on the page. This delineates the form (<form>) tag.*

   - *Select each of the radio buttons and notice in the Property Inspector that they all have the same name but different values.*

   - *Select one of the text fields. The width of the text field is set by the Char Width option.*

   - *Select the form by clicking on the red dotted line. The Property Inspector shows a Method to an e-mail address.*

Storyboard: On Screen

Figure 21-3 shows you how the finished page will look when viewed through a browser.

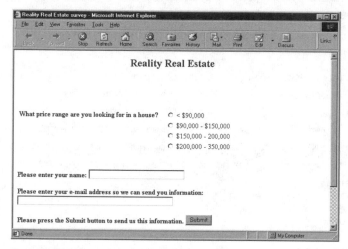

Fig. 21-3. Completed exercise within a browser.

Storyboard: Behind the Scenes

Figure 21-4 shows the HTML code created behind the form and Form objects in this exercise.

```
<form action="mailto:me@mymail.com?subject=Price Houses" method="post" enctype="text/plain" name="survey" id="survey">
  <p> </p>
  <table width="610" border="0">
    <tr>
      <td width="336" valign="top"><strong>What price range are you looking for in a house?</strong></td>
      <td width="264"><table width="200">
        <tr>
          <td><label>
            <input type="radio" name="pricerange" value="1">
            <$90,000</label></td>
        </tr>
        <tr>
          <td><label>
            <input type="radio" name="pricerange" value="2">
            $90,000 - 150,000</label></td>
        </tr>
        <tr>
          <td><label>
            <input type="radio" name="pricerange" value="3">
            $150,000 - 200,000</label></td>
        </tr>
        <tr>
          <td><label>
            <input type="radio" name="pricerange" value="4">
            $200,000 - 350,000</label></td>
        </tr>
      </table></td>
    </tr>
  </table>
  <p><strong>Please enter your name:
    <input name="name" type="text" id="name">
    <br>
    <br>
    Please enter you e-mail address so we can send you information:<br>
    <input name="email" type="text" id="email" size="50">
    </strong></p>
  <p><strong>Please press the Submit button to send us this information.
    <input type="submit" name="Submit" value="Submit">
    </strong></p>
  <p> </p>
</form>
```

Fig. 21-4. HTML source code for completed exercise.

Step-by-Step Instructions

1. Make sure you are working with the site *DWExercises*. You can confirm this by selecting *DWExercises* from the Site panel.

2. Let's create a new file in the *ch21* folder.
   a) In the Site panel, select the *ch21* folder.
   b) Create a new file in this folder by selecting File Menu | New File from the Site panel.
   c) Name the file *realq.html* and press Enter/Return.
   d) Now open the file you just created, *realq.html*.

3. Because this is a new file, set the page title to *Reality Real Estate Survey*.

4. Enter a text title at the top of the page. Type in *Reality Real Estate* and set the paragraph to Heading 2, center alignment.

5. Enter some extra lines between the heading and the next line.

6. On approximately the third line, insert the form by selecting Insert Menu | Form, or Insert bar | Forms | Form (leftmost icon). A red dotted line will appear in the page. This sets the bounding area of the form. In the Property Inspector, name the form *survey*.

7. The rest of the content in this exercise will go inside this form. You know you are inside the form if the Status bar is showing the *<form>* tag along with the name of the form.

8. Inside the form, press Enter/Return a few times to create some blank lines.

9. Inside the form on the second line, type in the following.

   What price range are you looking for in a house?

10. Set the style of the question to Bold, Left Alignment.

11. Because we would like the radio buttons to align on the right side of the question, we will use a table to format the radio buttons. The question should also go in the table.
    a) Insert a table above the question with 1 row and 2 columns, width 500 pixels, border 0.
    b) Select and drag the questions text to the top row and the first column. Resize the left column so it is just wide enough to fit the question text. See figure 21-5.

Go Solo

DWExercises Site

·T*i*P·

To select a form, either click on the red dotted line of the form or select the *<form>* tag in the Status bar at the bottom of the window. The Status bar will display the name of the form within the *<form>* tag (i.e., *<form#survey>*).

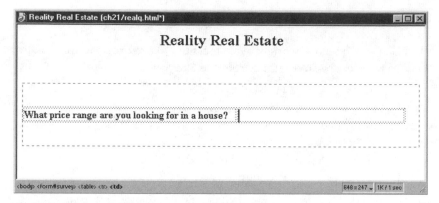

Fig. 21-5. Question label for radio button inserted into a table.

12. There are going to be four radio buttons. The value of each radio button will be a single number (1 to 4) representing each of the price ranges. When the form is processed, the values (1 to 4) will be sent, not the labels. The price ranges are as follows.

1	< $90,000
2	$90,000 to 150,000
3	$150,000 to 200,000
4	$200,000 to 350,000

Each radio button will have a label corresponding to the value of the radio button. The radio buttons will go in the second column, each in its own row.

a) Place the cursor in the first row, second column, of the table.

b) From the Insert bar, select the Forms tab.

c) Select Insert Radio Group. You could also select Insert Menu | Form Objects | Radio Group. A dialog box will appear for the Radio group.

d) In the dialog box, name the Radio group *pricerange*.

e) Double click on the first line under the Label column and change *Radio* to *<90,000*.

f) Double click on the first line under the Value column and change *radio* to *1*. See figure 21-6.

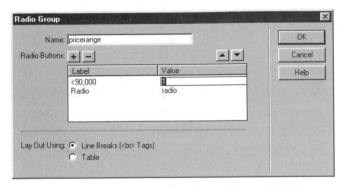

Fig. 21-6. Radio Group dialog box with first button defined.

13. For the second radio button, replace the label and value on the second line to the following.

    a)   Label (90,000 – 150,000)

    b)   Value (2)

14. For the rest of the radio buttons, click on the Plus (+) button to create a new button, and change the value and label according to the following.

    a)   Label ($150,000 – 200,000), Value (3)

    b)   Label ($200,000 – 350,000), Value (4)

15. At the bottom of the dialog box, click the Table radio button next to Lay Out Using. See figure 21-7.

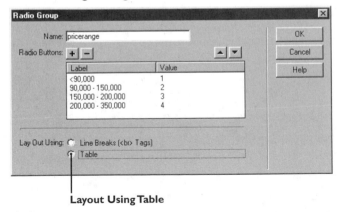

Layout Using Table

Fig. 21-7. Radio Group dialog box showing four radio buttons.

16. Click OK to close the dialog box. Notice that when you select each of the radio buttons, the name is always *pricerange*. Remember that radio buttons should allow the user to select only one item out of the group.

·T/P·

If you want the user to be able to select only *one* radio button within a group of buttons, each of the radio buttons must have the same name. In the example here, all radio buttons are called *pricerange*.

To make this happen, the radio buttons must all have the same name. In this group, the name is *pricerange*.

17. Add dollar signs ($) to the front of the price ranges (e.g., <$90,000) by selecting the text in the Design window.

18. To make the question display at the top of the table cell, place the cursor in the cell with the question *What price . . .* and in the Property Inspector, change the vertical alignment (Vert) to Middle.

19. Save the file and preview it in a browser. You should be able to select only one radio button. Exit the browser.

20. Now we want to ask the user for her name.

    a) Press Enter/Return after the table, with the radio buttons in it, to enter two (2) more blank lines. You should still be inside the form.

    b) For the name prompt, type in *Please enter your name:*.

    c) Change the style to Bold.

    d) From Insert bar | Forms, select Insert Text Field.

    e) In the Text field Name box, type *name*.

    f) To allow enough room for someone to enter first and last name, enter *30* in the Char Width option. See figure 21-8.

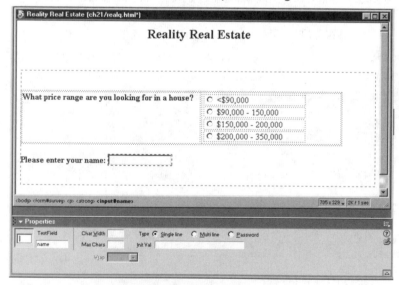

Fig. 21-8. Text field showing name entry.

21. Save the file and preview it in a browser. You should be able to enter your name, as well as select an option from the radio buttons. Exit the browser.

22. Let's now create one more text field to ask for the user's e-mail address, so that we can send the information requested.

a) Press Shift + Enter/Return after the Name field to insert a line break after the Name field.

b) For the e-mail prompt, type in *Please enter your e-mail address so we can send you information:.*

c) Change the style to Bold.

d) Add a single line break after the e-mail request text.

e) From Insert bar | Forms, select Insert Text Field.

f) In the Text field Name box, type *email*.

g) Enter *50* in the Char Width option. See figure 21-9.

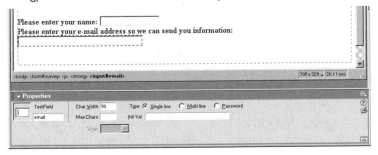

Fig. 21-9. Text field showing email entry.

23. We now need to add a Submit button to the form. When the user selects the Submit button, the form data will be sent to your e-mail address.

a) Press Enter/Return after the E-mail field to go to a new line.

b) For the button prompt, type in *Please press the Submit button to send us this information.*

c) Change the style to Bold.

d) From Insert bar | Forms, select Button.

e) We will not change any of the properties for the button. The action is a Submit Form action. See figure 21-10.

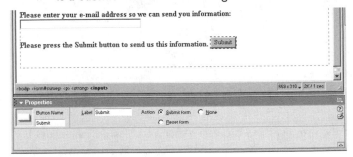

Fig. 21-10. Submit button.

24. To send the form information via e-mail, the Method for the form must be set.

CAUTION

At this point in the exercise you are working with an e-mail function for our fictitious web site. We are using the *.xyz* extension and suggesting you use your own e-mail address to keep this exercise clearly within the realm of our fictitious web site and to avoid accidentally bombarding someone with a lot of unwanted e-mail.

Our caution here is especially noteworthy in situations for which you may have an "always on" Internet connection.

·T/P·

When *enctype* =
"text/plain" is inserted
within the form tag
and the action is set
to e-mail, the form
data will be inserted
in the message of the
e-mail. If this special
code is not added,
the data will be sent
as an attachment to
the e-mail.

CAUTION ⚠️

When submitting form
data via e-mail, the
type of e-mail commu-
nications program the
user is using (Outlook,
Netscape, AOL, etc.)
will affect the way
the data is sent. Some
software will send the
e-mail without opening
the e-mail window,
whereas other soft-
ware will open the e-
mail window in which
the user will have to
press a Send button.

If you do not know or
cannot specify the type
of e-mail software the
user will be using, you
may find that you will
have more control
with the submission of
form data by using a
CGI script. We provide
some additional infor-
mation about CGI
scripts a little later
in this chapter.

a) Select the form by clicking on the *<form#survey>* tag in the Status bar at the bottom of the window, or by clicking on the red dotted out-line for the form.

b) Set the Method to POST in the Property Inspector.

c) In the Property Inspector Action box, type in the following information. Substitute your own e-mail address for *me@YourEMailGoesHere.xyz*. See figure 21-11.

```
mailto:me@YourEMailGoesHere.xyz?subject=Price Houses
```

Fig. 21-11. POST via e-mail.

25. To insert the form data inside the e-mail instead of as an attachment, the *enctype* code needs to be added to the *<form>* tag. Type *text/plain* into the Property Inspector Enctype box. See figure 21-12 to view the correct entry in the Enctype box.

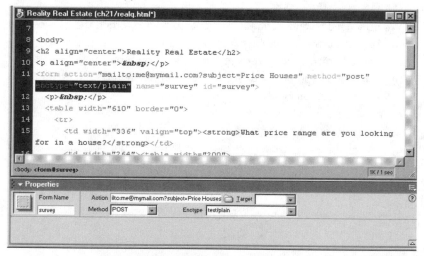

Fig. 21-12. Form tag with enctype code.

26. Save the file and preview it in a browser. When you click on the Submit but-ton, Dreamweaver MX will want to connect to the Internet if you are not already online, so that the e-mail can be sent. (See the previous Caution.)

27. Close the browser and the file *realq.html*.

Detailed Overview of Forms

Now that you have some practice with forms, let's summarize the primary steps needed to create a form, and look at the form in more detail.

Summary: Primary Steps in Creating a Form

1. Place the cursor on the page where you want the form.

2. Select Insert Menu | Form, or Insert bar | Forms tab | Form. This will insert a red dotted area on the page, which represents the form area but is not visible when the page is viewed in a browser. All Form objects (radio boxes, buttons, and text areas) must go inside the form area. By default, a form will take up 100% of the page width, whereas the height of the form is set by the content placed within the *<form>* tag. See figure 21-13.

·T/P·

The Snippets panel has some pre-defined code for forms including drop down menus.

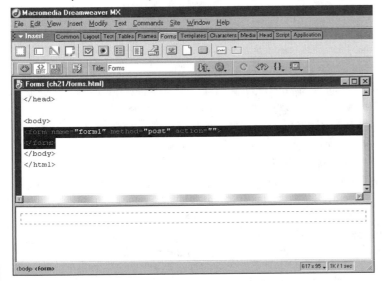

Fig. 21-13. Form area on a page, and the <form> tag.

3. Name the form in the Property Inspector. If the Property Inspector does not reference the form, select the form by selecting the *<form>* tag in the Status bar or clicking on the red dotted line around the form. See figure 21-14.

Fig. 21-14. Property Inspector for a form.

4. Use Insert | Form Object or the Forms tab on the Insert bar to insert a Form object. If you insert a Form object before inserting the form, or insert the object outside a form area, you will be asked whether you want to insert a *<form>* tag. If you select No, any data input to the Form object will not be processed with the form. If you select Yes, the information entered in the object will be processed with the form.

5. Type any labels next to Form objects. Radio buttons and checkboxes will need a label (i.e., Yes and No). Text fields should also have some type of label referencing them.

Form Objects

Forms consist of form fields called Form objects in Dreamweaver MX. Let's look in more detail at some of the unique settings for each of the Form objects.

Input | Text Field:

Text fields are text boxes on the page where the user can type in information. These are used for passwords, personal information, notes, and so on. The following options are available for text fields.

• Single or multi-line input: *A multi-line text field will have a vertical scroll bar and is actually called a text area. A multi-line text field also uses the <textarea> tag instead of the <input> tag (as does the single-line text field).*

• *Set the text field as a password field. The input will be displayed as asterisks (*) as the user types data into the field.*

• *Char Width will set the maximum number of characters that can be displayed in the field. The default is around 20 characters for a multi-line field if a character width is not entered (24 characters for a single-line text field).*

• *Text fields can be preset with an initial value. For instance, in a survey, the most common or popular answer can be present in the text field.*

Single-line and password text fields:

• *Max Chars sets the maximum number of characters that can be entered into the field. Leaving the field blank lets users enter as much text as they want. If the number of characters exceeds the Char Width setting, the text field will scroll. See figure 21-15.*

·T/P·

Text fields cannot be selected and resized with the cursor. Char Width sets the size of the field. The field will *not* resize if more characters are entered than the width, but a scroll bar will display.

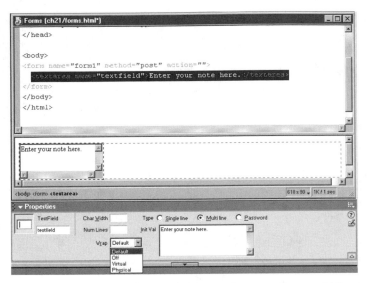

Fig. 21-15. Text field in a form and Property Inspector for a multi-line text field.

Multi-line text fields:

- *Char Width: sets the maximum number of characters that can be displayed in the field. Leaving the field blank lets users enter as much text as they want. If the number of characters exceeds the Char Width setting, the text field will scroll.*

- *Num Lines defines the number of lines to display at any one time. This sets the height of the field. If the field is left blank, two lines will be displayed. If the user types in more than will fit, the field will scroll as the user's additional information is entered.*

- *Wrap defines how text will wrap. The available options are Default (No), Virtual (word wrap in text area), and Physical (word wrap in the text area and when data is sent for processing).*

Input | Hidden Field

The hidden field (or hidden entry) is used to send information (in string format) with a form, along with data input by the user, which provides additional information not seen by the user. This may include information from a cookie or some type of label for the current site. Some CGI scripts (which handle the form data) require some type of hidden fields. Uses here include current date and time, name of the URL, and user ID. See figure 21-16.

·T/P·

Using JavaScript, the value of the Hidden field can be set to information passed to the HTML page, values of variables, or some other value captured in the page. The JavaScript is the same as that used to change the value of text fields, as follows. In this example, the name of the Hidden field is *timeSubmit* in the first form on the page.

```
currDate = new Date(
)//get the current
date and store in
variable currDate
```

```
//changes the value
to the current time
in milliseconds
```

```
document.forms[0]
.timeSubmit.value =
currDate.getTime()
```

Because the value of a Hidden field set by JavaScript can be cleared out if the user refreshes a page, do not set the value until the form is being submitted (using the *onSubmit* event).

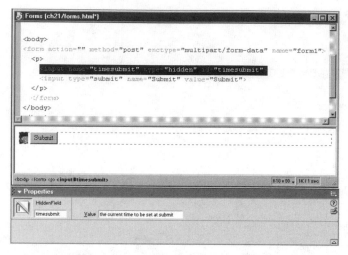

Fig. 21-16. Hidden field Form object and Property Inspector.

Options for a hidden field:

Only the value of the hidden field is entered. This can be changed with JavaScript.

Input | Textarea

The Textarea option allows you to add a multi-line text area. The Textarea Properties panel and options are the same as with the Text Field option. Within the HTML code, you will notice that the Textarea field inserts the tag *<textarea>* as opposed to a text field, which inserts the *<input>* tag.

Input | Checkbox

A checkbox lets the user select one or more options from a group. Use checkboxes to let users select from more than one selection such as different music styles. See figure 21-17.

·T/P·

When creating checkbox group, create one checkbox, name it, and then copy the checkbox to create the other selections in the group. When the checkbox is copied, Dreamweaver automatically adds a number at the end of the name to make it unique. Music becomes *music1*, *music2*, and so on. Then you just have to change the value.

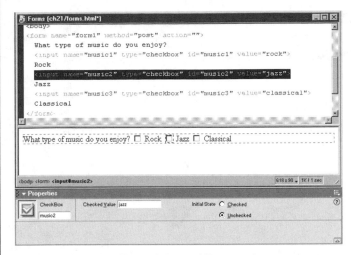

Fig. 21-17. Checkbox Form object and Property Inspector.

Options for checkbox:

- *The Checkbox Name field must have a unique name in the form. This is a description of the checkbox. For example, if asking the user what his favorite music is, the name fields for the group may all be* music, *with a number after each, such as* music1, music2, *and so on.*

- *Checked Value contains the value of the checkbox. Be sure to enter a value here that represents the user's answer. For example, the checked value might be* jazz *or a number (1) corresponding to music type (1). The checked value lets the processing application know what the user's answer is.*

- *For Initial State (*Checked *or* Unchecked*), select* Checked *for those options you believe the user will most often select, or want the visitor to select. For instance, if asking the visitor "Who is interested in joining?": Self, family, neighbors,* Self *would be checked at the beginning.*

Input | Radio Button

A radio button lets the user select only one option from a group. Uses here include a Yes/No response, salary range, and rating of 1 to 4. See figure 21-18.

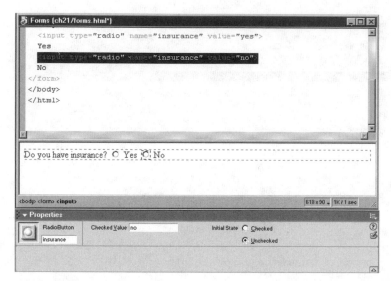

Fig. 21-18. Radio button Form object and Property Inspector.

By giving a group of radio buttons the same name, only one of the buttons can be checked at any one time. If you will have multiple radio buttons in a specific section of a form, use the Radio Group option.

If there is more than one group of radio buttons in a single form, each group must have its own unique name. For example, if the groups for gender and age both have the same name (*moreInfo*), checking Female would turn off the selections for age as well.

Options for a radio button:

• *The Radio Button Name field should contain the same name for all buttons in the group. This ensures that only one selection can be made. This should be a descriptive name for the button choices (the button group).*

• *Checked Value contains the value of the radio button. Be sure to enter a value that represents the user's answer. If using a yes/no checkbox, the check value should be yes or no. The check value lets the processing application know what the user's answer is.*

• *For Initial State (Checked or Unchecked), select Checked for those options you believe the user will most often select, or want the visitor to select. For instance, if asking the visitor "Do you want to receive our newsletter?" Yes/No, Yes would be Checked at the beginning, because you usually want visitors to keep hearing about you.*

Input | Radio Group

Whereas a radio button allows the user to select only one response from a group, the Radio Group is a shortcut to create more than one radio button in a group. All radio buttons created within a Radio Group are already associated. The Radio Group Name option (top entry box) ensures that only one selection can be made from the list. The Plus and Minus buttons allow you to add or remove items from the list. The Move Up and Move Down buttons allow you to modify the order in which the buttons and their labels appear in the list. Uses here include selecting one (only one) item from a list and selecting (for example) your departure city from a list of four cities.

NOTE: See the previous practice exercise for an example of the Radio group.

Options for a Radio group:

Once you create a Radio group, the options for each button are the same as those for individual radio buttons.

Input | List/Menu

A list and a menu are defined in HTML by the *<select>* tag. The difference between the two is the way in which they are displayed to the user. A menu is a pull-down (drop-down) menu that always displays just one item until the user employs the scroll bar. Only one item may be selected at a time. By default, the first item in the menu displays when the form loads in a browser window. A list is considered a scrolling menu. It has options a menu does not, as follows.

- *More than one item in the list can be displayed when the form loads in the browser window. This is the Height option and is set in terms of the number of lines to display at any one time. If a height greater than 1 is entered, the list does not drop down, as a menu does. The list would initially display as a list (and would not drop down).*

- *Allow Multiple lets the user select more than one item from the list by holding the Control/Command key down while selecting an item. See figure 21-19.*

·T/P·

In a list, if a height greater than 1 (one) is entered, or *Allow Multiple* is checked, the list does not drop down but the scroll bar becomes a stepping scroll that only displays one selection at a time. See figure 21-19.

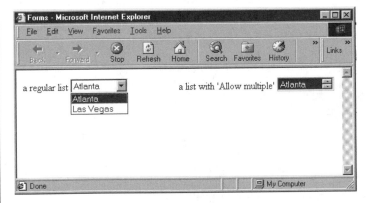

Fig. 21-19. Two lists, one with Allow Multiple checked.

Uses of a menu include such things as state/country selections, and salary range selections. Uses of a list include such things as choices of interests (places to travel, music, magazines), and hardware or software the user owns. See figure 21-20.

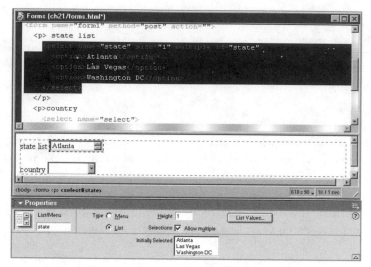

Fig. 21-20. List/Menu Form object and Property Inspector.

Options for menus and lists:

The List Values button is used to enter the names of list/menu items that appear to the user. You would also enter the values of each menu item. The value is used to know what item the user selected when the form is processed. Usually the value is the same as the menu item, although if it is feasible we suggest abbreviating so that the value will not have any spaces and will not have too many characters. See figure 21-21.

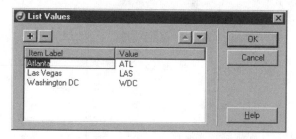

Fig. 21-21. List Values option for a List/Menu field object.

Input | Jump Menu

A jump menu is a combination of a list/menu form object and a button object. In addition, a behavior is added to both the list/menu and the button that "jumps" the user to the specified item. The menu item can be a URL, external document, e-mail, image, text file, or any other file that can open in a browser.

Jump menus can be added to a page by selecting Insert bar | Forms tab | Jump Menu, or Insert Menu | Form Objects | Jump Menu. When the insertion is made, a dialog box appears asking for the name of the menu (this is the name of the menu Form object) and the items within the menu. It also asks for the URL of each menu item. Once the menu items are entered, back in the Property Inspector for the menu form object that was created, the menu can be changed to a list so that the visitor can see all options in the list (Height option) or select more than one list item at a time. See figure 21-22.

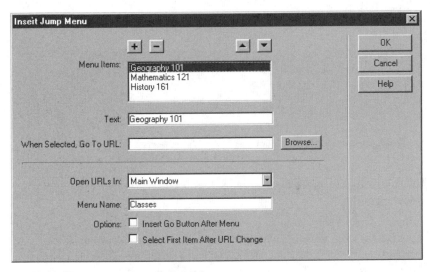

Fig. 21-22. "Insert jump menu" dialog box.

Uses of the jump menu include jumping to a URL in the current site or another site, and selecting from a list of PDF or other external document files that will open from the server.

·T/P·

The difference
between a jump
menu and a list/menu
is that the jump menu
will have a behavior
attached to it with
the action called
Jump Menu.

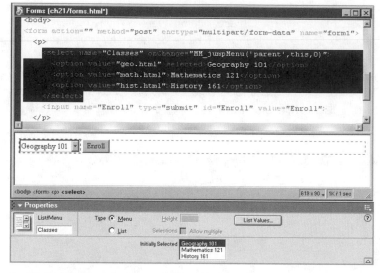

Fig. 21-23. Jump menu Form object and Property Inspector.

The following are options for a jump menu within the "Insert jump
menu" prompt.

- *Menu items are the individual names in the menu. These can be descriptions of
  the URL to jump to, or the URL itself. There are Move Up/Down buttons to
  change the order of the menu items. The Plus (+) button adds a new menu
  item, and the Minus (-) button deletes a selected menu item.*

- *URL to jump to when the menu item is selected (highlighted).*

- *Open URLs indicates where to open the URL. This would normally only be
  changed when working with frames or if the URL should open in its own
  browser window.*

·T/P·

When using a jump
menu, do not confuse
the visitor by placing a
Go button when it is
not going to be used.

- *Insert Go Button After Menu inserts a button (like a gray Submit button) next to
  the menu.*

- *Select First Item After URL Change jumps to the selected URL as soon as one is
  selected (highlighted). It does not wait for the Go button to be selected.*

To change the options once a jump menu has been inserted, double click on
the behavior attached to the jump menu form object (onChange | Jump Menu),
or select Modify Menu | Jump Menu. This allows you to change the menu items,
URLs to jump (link) to, and all other options for jump menus. If only the menu
items need to be changed, in the Property Inspector for the jump menu form
object, click on the button *List values* and enter/change the menu items and
their values. By default, the value is the same as the menu item.

Input | Image Field

An image field is also called an image button. It is like a custom button and can be used in place of the (gray) Submit button. Uses here include selecting a product picture for purposes of purchase, and sending information (custom button). See figure 21-24.

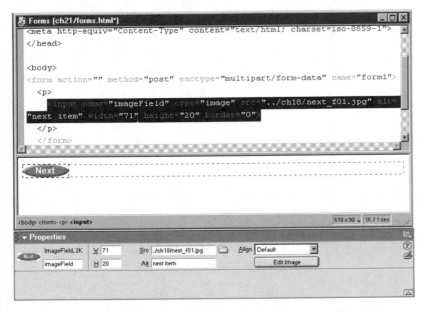

Fig. 21-24. Image field Form object and Property Inspector.

Options for an image field:

When an image field is inserted, a dialog box will appear asking you to select the image source (just like the prompt you get when inserting a regular image object). The options for an image field are the basic options for an image object: *src*, *alt*, *align*, *width*, and *height*.

Input | File Field

A file field, also called a file selection, lets a user enter a file name into a text field, or to select a Browse button to search for a file on the user's hard drive. When the Submit button is clicked, the file is uploaded with the rest of the form information. For example, let's say you are in a site that will accept and post your resume for you. By selecting the Browse button, you can search your hard drive for your resume file and then upload it to the site (as part of the form).

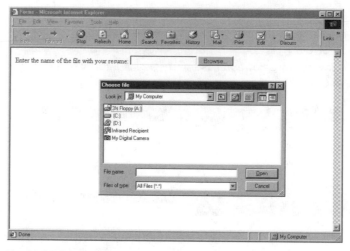

Fig. 21-25. File field example using the Browse button.

Uses here include such things as doctor's notes posted to a central transcription site, and changes to product information for a web master.

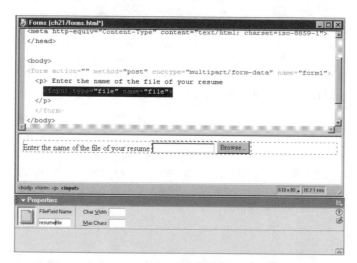

Fig. 21-26. File field Form object and Property Inspector.

The options for a file field are Char Width (maximum characters to display) and Max Chars (maximum characters in the field). See figure 21-26.

Input | Button

Form buttons are always gray and are typically used to submit form information or reset the form to the initial values of the fields. Uses here include submitting or resetting form information, and creating button distracters in quizzes.

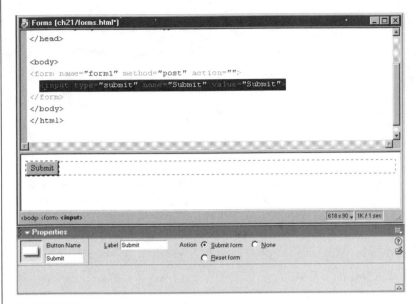

Fig. 21-27. Button Form object and Property Inspector.

Options for the button Form object (see figure 21-27):

- *Custom label or Reset/Submit selection*

- *Reset sets all fields in the form back to their original state (usually blank or with preset values).*

- *Submit sends the form information to a CGI script on the server.*

Input | Label

The Label object allows you to associate a label with a specific field.

Input | Fieldset

The Fieldset object allows you to group multiple form fields.

HTML Source Code for Forms

Form objects are also called input items. The HTML *<input>* tag defines most of the Form objects. See figure 21-28. The *<form>* tag, as follows, surrounds the Form objects and sets the manner of processing the form data through the Method (*POST* or *GET*) and the action to be taken. The action could be an e-mail, CGI script, or other program that will process the data from the form and send it to the server.

```
<form name="survey" method="post" enctype="text/plain"
action="mailto:me@mymail.xyz?subject=Price Houses">
```

 HTML

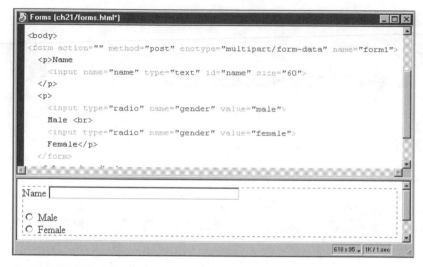

```
Forms (ch21/forms.html*)                                    _ □ ×
<body>
<form action="" method="post" enctype="multipart/form-data" name="form1">
  <p>Name
    <input name="name" type="text" id="name" size="60">
  </p>
  <p>
    <input type="radio" name="gender" value="male">
    Male <br>
    <input type="radio" name="gender" value="female">
    Female</p>
  </form>
```

Name [   ]

○ Male
○ Female

618 x 95 ▾   1K / 1 sec

Fig. 21-28. HTML for a form.

The *<input>* tag, as follows, defines the type of input the user will make. In the following example, the input type is a radio button. Each name/value pair in a form is sent via the *action* attribute.

```
<input type="radio" name="pricerange" value="1">
```

The following is the end tag for a form.

```
</form>
```

Behaviors Associated with Forms

Although many behaviors can be used with a page containing forms, there are some behaviors that are only to be used with forms. These are discussed in the following.

Validate Form: Checks the data entered in the form to make sure it is valid, whether this means the field has been selected or filled or a specific value has been selected or entered. To attach this behavior, the form must contain a button form field (usually submit) and at least one object that can be validated, such as a text field. The Validate Form behavior is then attached to the button so that the validation is performed when the button is pressed. See figure 21-29.

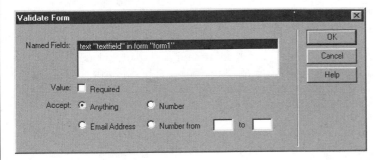

Fig. 21-29. Validate Form behavior.

Set Text of Text Field: Places a text string in a specified text field. This can be used for setting the initial value of the field, and replacing the text value after a certain amount of time (as in a test to give the user a hint). To attach this behavior, first select a text field in the form.

Notice in figure 21-30 that the default event is *onBlur* when the mouse is focused on the text field (*onFocus*) or not focused (*onBlur*) and another part of the screen has been clicked on. The text field could also be changed when the text field is changed (*onChange*), or when a key on the keyboard has been pressed (*onKeyDown*, *onKeyUp*, *onKeyPress*).

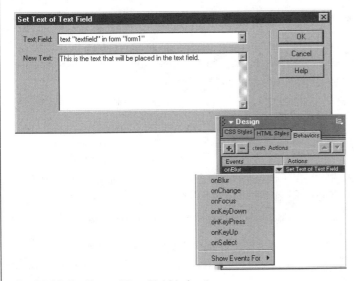

Fig. 21-30. Set Text of Text Field behavior.

Processing Form Information

We have discussed the various ways to interact with a user using the Form objects. But what happens to the information the user has entered or selected? This is where the form itself comes in. The *<form>* tag contains an action parameter that defines what will happen to the form information when the form's Submit button is selected.

- POST: *Will send the form information to a specified CGI script, e-mail, or other processing application in the body of the message.*
- GET: *Will send the form information to the server as form values appended to the specified URL. The URL address is limited to 8,192 characters, so do not use the GET method if the form data is too long. GET is also not a secure form of passing information, so do not use this with credit card information and other sensitive data.*

You can use JavaScript or VBScript on the client side (user's computer) to display pop-up messages based on the user's input. You can also send the information via e-mail.

E-mail

To send form information via e-mail, you would perform the following.

1. Insert a Submit button in the form. Make sure the action is set to *submit*.

2. Select the form by either selecting the *<form>* tag in the Status bar or clicking the red dotted line for the form. When the form is selected, the Property Inspector will reference the form.

3. Set the method to *POST*.

4. In the Property Inspector Action box, type in the following.

   ```
   mailto:me@emailAddress.xyz
   ```

There are no spaces in the *mailto* line. You can also send a subject with the e-mail by adding a *subject=* parameter after the e-mail address, as follows.

   ```
   mailto:me@emailAddress.xyz?subject=User Info
   ```

Again, there are no spaces in the line except in the string for the subject. See figure 21-31.

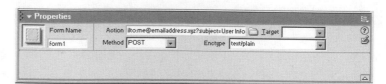

Fig. 21-31. Sending form information via e-mail.

When sending form information via e-mail, by default the form information will be sent as an attachment to an e-mail with the name/value pairs separated by an ampersand (&). To embed the form data inside the body of the e-mail, add the *enctype* parameter to the *<form>* tag, by typing text/plain in the Enctype field for the Properties for the form. The following HTML code is generated for the enctype.

```
<form name="form1" method="post" action=""
enctype="text/plain">
```

You cannot save or send form information without using scripting on the server side. ASP programs, XML, ColdFusion, and CGI scripts can perform this data processing.

CGI Scripts

CGI (Common Gateway Interface) programs are those that allow two software applications (and really two computers) to communicate with each other. A CGI script acts like a middleman. CGI scripts are usually written in Perl, C++, or Visual Basic, but there are some prewritten CGI scripts out there that can be downloaded from the Internet, and others that come with software applications. However, if you have specific information you want to gather, you will probably want to get a programmer to create a custom CGI script for you.

CGI scripts generally are placed in a folder called *cgi_bin*. Many servers provide standard CGI scripts you can use. Note that not all servers provide access to CGI scripts, and not all servers allow you to upload your own CGI scripts. Contact your Internet service provider for more information. The file name for the CGI script goes in the Action box of the form's Property Inspector.

Practice Exercise 21-2: Insert a Jump Menu

Description

In this next exercise we will create an online resource page. It contains many links to sites on the Web, and to external documents within the current site. From a pull-down menu, the user can select a file to link to. The following elements are covered in this exercise.

- *Inserting forms*
- *The jump menu*
- *The menu Form object*
- *The button Form object*
- *Behaviors for a jump menu*

Take a Look

Before beginning the exercise, let's take a look at the exercise in its completed state so that you can clearly see what it is you are about to build.

1. Make sure you are working with the site *DWComplete*. You can confirm this by selecting *DWComplete* from the Site panel.

2. Locate the *ch21* folder and within it the file named *dw21ex2.html*. Double click on *dw21ex2.html* to open the file.

3. The file *dw21ex2.html* should now appear in your copy of Dreamweaver MX. Preview in your web browser, testing the menu listing and the links to other files. Select the file *Get Information* to jump to a file in the current folder. This is the information form created in the previous exercise. Note the following properties of this completed exercise.

   • *You can only select one file at a time.*

   • *Clicking the Go button opens the new file.*

Storyboard: On Screen

Figure 21-32 shows you what the finished page will look like when viewed through a browser.

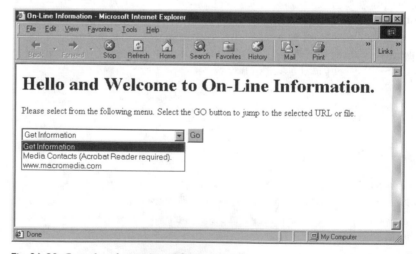

Fig. 21-32. Completed exercise within a browser.

Storyboard: Behind the Scenes

Figure 21-33 shows the HTML code behind the jump menu created in this exercise. Two JavaScript functions were generated by Dreamweaver MX when the jump menu was inserted. One is attached to the button, and the other one is attached to the menu form object.

```
HTML source code for form tag
<form name="form1">
  <select name="menu1" onChange="MM_jumpMenu('parent',this,0)">
    <option value="realq.html" selected>Get Information</option>
    <option value="mediacontacts.pdf">Media Contacts (Acrobat Reader required).</option>
    <option value="www.macromedia.com">www.macromedia.com</option>
  </select>
  <input type="button" name="Button2" value="Go" onClick="MM_jumpMenuGo('menu1','parent',0)">
</form>
```

Fig. 21-33. HTML source code for completed exercise.

Step-by-Step Instructions

1. Make sure you are working with the site *DWExercises*. You can confirm this by selecting *DWExercises* from the Site panel.

2. We will select an existing file in the *ch21* folder.
   a) In the Site panel, find and select the file *online.html* in the *ch21* folder.
   b) There is a heading line and a prompt in the page.
   c) Place the cursor under the prompt sentence.

3. The jump menu is a Form object.
   a) From the Insert bar | Forms tab, select Jump Menu. See figure 21-34.

Jump Menu

Fig. 21-34. Insert bar | Forms | Jump Menu.

   b) The Jump Menu dialog box appears, asking for details about the menu items to include in the menu. In the text box, type *Get Information*.
   c) With Go To URL selected, type in *realq.html*, or use the Browse button and find *realq.html* in the *ch21* folder. (We created this file in a previous exercise.)

Go Solo

DWExercises Site

d) Check the button Insert Go Button After Menu. The name of the menu will stay as *menu1*. This names the entire menu form object, not each of the menu items. See figure 21-35.

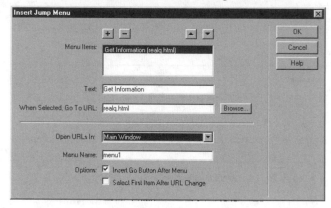

Fig. 21-35. Jump menu with one menu item and Go button selected.

e) To add another menu item, click on the Plus (+) button.

f) In the Go To URL box, type *www.macromedia.com*. Click inside the Text box. The text will now equal the information in the URL box. See figure 21-36.

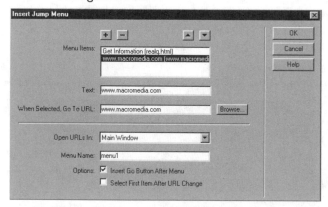

Fig. 21-36. Jump menu with second menu item linking to an external web site.

g) Add another menu item by clicking on the Plus (+) button.

h) In the Text box, type *Media Contacts (Acrobat Reader required)*.

i) With Go To URL selected, use the Browse button to find the file *mediacontacts.pdf* in the *ch21* folder. The user will need Adobe Acrobat Reader to open this file.

j) Click on the Up arrow button to move *Media Contacts* above *www.macromedia.com* in the menu. See figure 21-37.

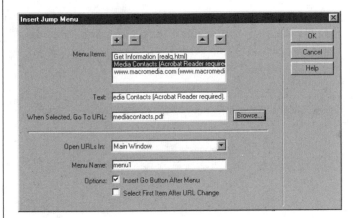

Fig. 21-37. Jump menu with item moved up in the menu.

4. Make sure the Insert Go Button After Menu button is checked. Click on OK to exit the Jump Menu window. On your page is now a menu form object.

5. Save the file. See figure 21-38.

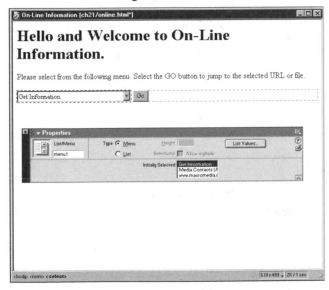

Fig. 21-38. Completed jump menu with the Property Inspector.

6. Select the menu form object. In the Property Inspector notice that the name of the field is *menu1* and that there are three list values. If the values of the menu items needed to be changed, click on the List Values button.

7. Pull up the Behaviors panel (Windows Menu | Behaviors), and with the menu form object still selected, notice the behavior: *onChange* | Jump

Menu. The event *onChange* is triggered when a change, or selection, is made by the user. Double click on the action Jump Menu. The Jump Menu dialog box is displayed again. This is an easier and faster way to modify the values and menu items. Close the dialog box. See figure 21-39.

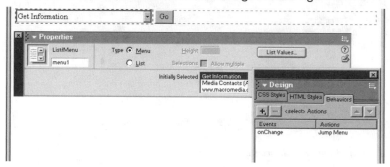

Fig. 21-39. Jump Menu behavior attached to menu item.

8. Let's look at the HTML code for the menu form object.
    a) Select View | Code and Design, or select the Show Code and Design Views button just below the toolbar.
    b) Notice the behavior attached to the menu, as follows. It is using the *onChange* event and will call the JavaScript function *MM_jumpMenu*. It is also sending some parameters to the function.

```
<select name="menu1"
onChange="MM_jumpMenu('parent',this,0)">
```

    c) Scroll to the top of the Code view and note the *<script>* tag. Somewhere within that *<script>* tag you will find the function *MM_jumpMenu*.

9. In the Design View window, click on the Go button.
    a) Notice in the Behaviors panel that a behavior was attached to this button, as well as the menu form object. See figure 21-40.

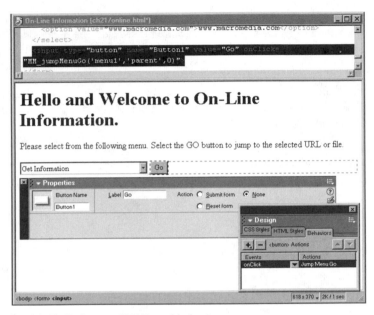

Fig. 21-40. Go button HTML and behavior.

    b) This time the event is *onClick* and the action is *JumpMenuGo*. Looking at the HTML source code, this is also a JavaScript function called *MM_jumpMenuGo* in the *<script>* tag.

10. Preview in a browser. Select Media Contacts, and a PDF file will open as long as you have Adobe Acrobat Reader loaded on your computer.

Summary

- *Anytime in a web page you see a checkbox, radio button, fill-in-the-blank, or pull-down menu, a form is probably being used.*

- *Some of the common uses of forms include quizzes, surveys, enrollment in online training, subscribing, downloading files, and making purchases.*

- *A form can contain multiple Form objects, and a page can contain more than one form. The available Form objects are Text Field, Hidden Field, Checkbox, Radio Button, Radio Group, List/Menu, Jump Menu, Image Field, File Field, Button, Label, and Fieldset.*

- *In the first practice exercise you set up a form, inserted a radio button Form object, set the properties for the radio button, and worked with the HTML for the radio button.*

- *Although many behaviors can be used with a page containing forms, there are some behaviors that are only to be used with forms, such as Validate Form and Set Text of Text Field.*

- *The <form> tag contains an action parameter that defines what will happen to the form information when the form's Submit button is selected. The options are* POST *and* GET.

- *You can also send form information via e-mail.*

- *CGI (Common Gateway Interface) scripts are programs that allow two software applications (and really, two computers) to communicate with each other. CGI scripts are frequently used in conjunction with processing form data.*

- *In the second practice exercise you inserted forms (Jump Menu, Menu Form Object, Button Form Object) and worked with behaviors for jump menus.*

CHAPTER

22

Application

Chapter:

Adding a Form

Introduction

Using forms gives you the ability to interact with visitors to your web site. Forms on your web site can be used for a variety of reasons. For example, you can obtain information (such as mailing address, phone numbers, and so on) from site visitors. Forms can also be used to help your visitors place orders for products or services. They also can provide the means to allow your visitors to request information from you.

Application Exercise Objectives

By the end of this chapter you will:

- *Create a form to gather information from a user*
- *Use the various types of Form objects, including buttons, fields, and menus*

Application Exercise 22-1: Adding a Form

Description

In this application chapter you will create a visitor-information and order form for *The 21st Century Kitchen* web site. The order form will collect two types of information: information about the person ordering and what the person is ordering. This order form will primarily use text fields, but we will also use checkboxes, radio buttons, and a submit button.

Take a Look

CD-ROM

Let's take a look at what the finished exercise will look like. Open Dreamweaver MX and use File Menu | Open to locate the companion CD-ROM. Locate the folder *Learning_DWapplication_complete*. Select and open the file *ap22.html*. Look at the layout of the web page, noticing the graphic and text areas. Take a look at the file and the HTML code in Dreamweaver MX. You will be using the following Dreamweaver MX concepts in the exercise.

- *Creating forms and Form objects*
- *Setting the properties of the Form object*
- *Sending form data via e-mail*
- *Inserting a horizontal rule*

Storyboard: Browser View

Figure 22-1 shows how the web page will look in a web browser when the exercise is completed.

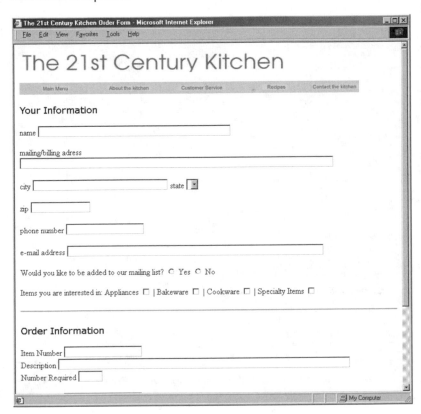

Fig. 22-1. Completed exercise within a browser.

Storyboard: Dreamweaver MX View

Figure 22-2 shows the HTML source code behind the form.

The 21st Century Kitchen Order Form [Learning_DWapplication/order.html]

```
<form name="form1" method="post" action=
"mailto:youremail@yourcompany.xyz">
  <p><font size="4" face="Verdana, Arial, Helvetica, sans-serif">Your
Information</font></p>
  <p>name
    <input name="textfield" type="text" size="52" maxlength="48">
  </p>
  <p>mailing/billing adress
    <input name="textfield2" type="text" size="86" maxlength="72">
  </p>
  <p>city
    <input name="textfield3" type="text" size="36" maxlength="24">
    state
    <select name="select">
    </select>
  </p>
  <p>zip
    <input name="textfield4" type="text" size="15" maxlength="10">
  </p>
  <p>phone number
    <input name="textfield5" type="text" size="20" maxlength="12">
  </p>
  <p>e-mail address
    <input name="textfield6" type="text" size="70" maxlength="60">
  </p>
  <p>Would you like to be added to our mailing list?
    <input type="radio" name="radiobutton" value="radiobutton">
```

`<body> <p>`   1K / 1 sec

Fig. 22-2. Completed exercise showing HTML source code.

Application Project Steps

Complete this exercise on your own, guided by following the general steps. You can always refer to the completed example you viewed in the "Take a Look" section of this exercise.

NOTE: The following steps are intended as a guide. This is your project, so feel free to make whatever variations you like.

1. Create a new page in Dreamweaver MX.

**21st Century
KITCHEN SITE**

2. Save the page as *order.html* in the folder *Learning_DWapplication*.

3. Title the page *21st Century Kitchen Order Form*.

4. For consistency, insert the *21st Century Kitchen* banner graphic at the top of the page (*21ckbnr.jpg* found in *ap_media*) and the Library object *mainNav*.

5. Insert a form using the Insert Form icon from Insert bar | Forms. As you are creating the order form, refer to figure 22-2 for layout suggestions.

6. Insert text fields for name, mailing/billing address, city, zip, phone number, and e-mail address. You can set the character widths and maximum char-

acters of each text field. We suggest something like: name 52/48, address 86/72, city 36/24, zip 15/10, phone number 20/12, and e-mail address70/60. Remember to name each field in the Property window.

7. Add a List/Menu field for the state next to the City field.

8. Add a line asking if the visitor would like to be on the mailing list. Use radio buttons for the Yes and No responses.

9. Add a line asking what type of products they are interested in (Appliances, Bakeware, Cookware, Specialty Items). Use checkboxes.

10. Add a horizontal rule to visually divide the form at this point.

11. Add three additional text fields for Item Number, Description, and Number Required. Our suggestions for character widths and maximum characters: Item Number 20/12, Description 80/160, and Number Required 5/3.

12. Copy the three order fields you just created and paste one or more times to fill out your order form.

13. Finish your form by adding a Submit button at the bottom of the page. Use the Insert Button feature on the Forms tab.

14. Select the form and enter the following e-mail information in the link box:

    mailto:youremail@CompanyName.xyz (enter your own e-mail
    address here)

15. Type *text/plain* in the Enctype field of the Forms Property Inspector.

16. Save each page and preview your work in a web browser.

17. Update the Library object called *navBar* so that the Place Order button links to this file (*order.html*).

Summary

In this application chapter you have created a form that gathers information about a user to send as an e-mail attachment. The form includes the typical types of Form objects: radio buttons, checkboxes, and text fields. The Submit button sends the information in the form as an attachment.

CHAPTER 23

Managing, Testing, and Publishing Your Site

Introduction

Hopefully, before you have finished creating an entire site, you have thought about checking for possible problem areas. Problem areas can be anything from broken links because you have accidentally deleted a file, to JavaScript that does not work properly on different browsers. Dreamweaver MX provides many tools to help you prevent these problems before you publish your site to the Internet and users catch the errors before you do. How embarrassing! This chapter focuses on the Site panel and managing your site. By the end of this chapter you will know how to:

- *Check the compatibility of HTML and scripts across browsers*
- *Check and fix broken links*
- *Remove unused files*
- *Use the Site Reporting feature to clean up your site*
- *Publish your site to the Web*

Guided Tour 23A: Managing Your Site

The Site panel has many features that help you manage the files and links of your web site. The following guided tour will point out the features you will probably use most often. The tour will also cover those features that will help minimize bugs and errors in your web site.

1. We are going to work primarily in the Site panel, so expand the panel so that the window is split into two sides; the site map and remote site on the left, and the site files on the right.

2. Open the site *DWExercises* from the Site panel. (This site was created in Chapter 4.)

3. Select the *ch23* folder. Let's look at some of the tools that help to manage the files and their properties.

4. Using the site files on the right side of the Site panel, right click (Windows) or Control + click (MAC) on the file *index23.html*. This brings up a context menu for the file.

Notice the many options that affect the file. See figure 23-1. Note the following in particular.

- Turn off Read Only: *This is useful when you have downloaded a file from the web site using the Get command that can leave the file locked. We recommend, however, that you always Check Out a file if you are working on a team (instead of unlocking the file using Turn off Read Only).*

- Set Home Page: *This will reset the home page to the current selected file.*

- Design Notes: *Make notes about the progress of a file's development, what media is missing, and so on.*

- Preview in Browser: *You do not need to open a file in order to preview it in a browser. Just select the file in the Site panel and press F12 to preview it.*

- Cloaking: *Cloaking excludes files and folders from any operations that you specify, such as Get, Put, and Check In/Out. This is useful if you want to upload your entire site but have a folder that is used just for testing, which should not go on the site. You can also set cloaking to exclude files from template update. To turn cloaking on, select the folders or files and select Cloaking from the file's context menu (right mouse click). You can also set the preferences to always cloak a specific file type, such as JSP files.*

- Rename: *If you need to rename a file in Dreamweaver MX (HTML, image, sounds, or anything referenced in a page), be sure to rename it in Dreamweaver MX, not in the Windows Explorer or in a file list outside Dreamweaver MX. When it is renamed in Dreamweaver MX, all links (and references) to that file are updated accordingly. Note that if a file is on your remote site, but not on the local site, Dreamweaver MX will not know that the file exists and cannot update it.*

When you delete or move a file in your local site while outside Dreamweaver (Windows Explorer or Macintosh Finder), the links are not automatically fixed. When you delete or move files while in Dreamweaver, files are relinked and warnings are given when links will be broken.

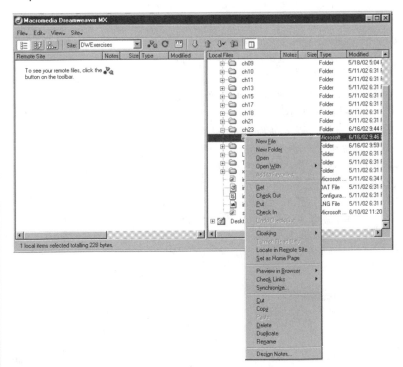

Fig. 23-1. Site panel showing context menu.

Shortcut

Site Map: Alt/Opt+F8

5. Click on the Site Map button in the far left side of the toolbar, or select View Menu | Site Map. See figure 23-2.

Fig. 23-2. Site Panel showing Site Map button in toolbar.

6. The reason the file *index.html* is displayed at the top of the map is that the file was defined as our home page when we first defined the *DWExercises* site. Select *index.html* in the site map on the left side of the Site panel. Right click (Windows) or Control + click (Mac) on *index.html* to display the context menu in the site map. Notice again the many options. Some of these are different from the options seen while in Site File view. See figure 23-3.

    • Link to New File: *A very quick way to create a link to a file and create the file at the same time. It will even set the title of the new file.*

    • Link to Existing File: *To create multiple links one right after the other. Then you can open the file to edit the look and format of text links.*

    • Change Link: *To switch the link to a different file or media element (select the file in the site map that should no longer be linked and select a new file from the pop-up menu).*

    • Remove Link: *A very quick way to remove the link from a file. It does not remove the text or media element the link is attached to − it just removes the HTML tag for the link.*

    • View as Root: *Does not set the current file as the home page but will display it at the top of the site map as though it were the home page. This will force the site map to display this file at the top of the tree. This can be useful if you want to see just the relationships (links) between a few files instead of the entire site.*

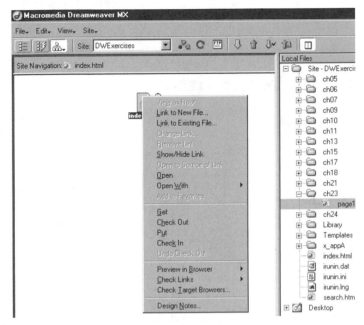

Fig. 23-3. Site Map view showing context menu.

7. Select *index23.html* (in the *ch23* folder) and from the context menu select Set as Home Page. Notice in the site map that *index23.html* is now at the top of the map and indicates that it is linked to three files (*page1*, *page2*, and *page3*).

8. Select *page1.html* in the site map and from the context menu select View as Root. Notice just under the toolbar that the home page (*index23.html*) is listed as the first file in the site navigation. To get *index23.html* back as the root, click on *index.html* at the top of the site map, where it says *Site Navigation*. See figure 23-4.

Site
Navigation —
Line

Fig. 23-4. Site Map view showing Site Navigation area.

9. To modify the settings for a site, select Site Menu | Edit Sites, or from the Toolbar pull-down menu select Edit Sites. To change the current site, double click on the name of the site in the Toolbar pull-down menu. See figure 23-5.

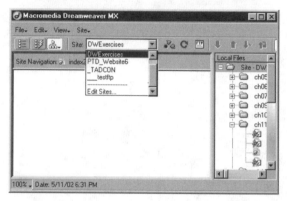

Fig. 23-5. Site panel showing Toolbar pull-down menu.

10. A new feature in Dreamweaver MX is the ability to import or export site settings. This is very useful when you want to share the settings with another team member or just copy the settings to another computer. The settings are all the settings you see in the Site Definition window. To export or import the site settings, in the Site panel, select Site Menu | Import/Export. See figure 23-6.

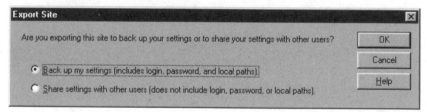

Fig. 23-6. Site panel showing Export settings.

Guided Tour 23B: Browser Compatibility

For this guided tour we will use the web pages created in Chapter 13. Those pages have some features supported only by browsers version 4 and above and contain behaviors. The Browser Compatibility option will be used to check if the HTML in one or more files is compatible with a given browser.

1. Open the *DWComplete* site by selecting the site in the Site panel.

2. In Windows, collapse the Site panel so that you have access to the Window menu.

3. From the Site panel, select the *ch13* folder. We will check all files for Chapter 13.

4. Select Window Menu | Results | Target Browser Check.
   a) Look at the left side of the Results panel and locate a small, green, right-hand arrow.
   b) Click on the arrow and then select Check Target Browsers for Selected Files/Folders in Site.

5. A dialog box appears asking which browser to check. You can only check one browser at a time. Select Internet Explorer 6.0 and click on the Check button. See figure 23-7.

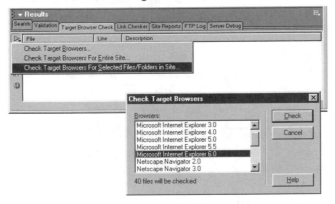

Fig. 23-7. Results panel showing Check Target Browser option.

6. A Target Browser Check report is displayed. You can save the report by clicking on the Save Report button. You can also view the report in a browser window by clicking on the Browse Report button (looks like the WWW icon). See figure 23-8.

Save Report ———
Browse Report ———

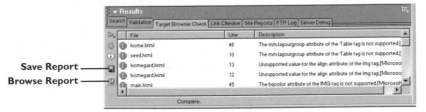

Fig. 23-8. Results panel showing Target Browser Check report.

7. Any files that have possible errors when viewed in the target browser are listed. Warnings will appear with a red explanation next to the file name.

8. Scroll down the page to see any errors, or double click on any file listed to open the file at the point in the file where the warning or error was found.

·T/P·

The Check Target Browsers feature is also available for a single file. Open an HTML file and select File | Check Page | Check Target Browsers. Only the specific file selected will be checked for errors.

Guided Tour 23C: Check and Fix Broken Links

For this guided tour, we will use the files from Chapter 23. We have intentionally left a few broken links in the files to show how the Check Links feature works.

1. Open the *DWComplete* site from the Site panel.

2. Select the *ch23* folder. We will check all files for Chapter 23.

3. Select Window Menu | Results.
   a) Select the tab called Link Checker.
   b) At the top left corner of the Results panel, select the green arrow and select Check Links for Selected Files | Folders in Site.

Shortcut

Right mouse click
(Ctrl+click: Mac) on a
folder or file and select
Check Links.

4. The first window that will appear will list any files with broken links. Both *page1.html* and *page2.html* have broken links to the same file – *page4.html*. The problem is that there is no file called *pag4.html* in the site, but there is a file called *page3.html*. See figure 23-9.

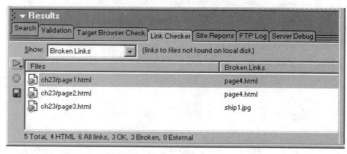

Fig. 23-9. Results panel showing Broken Links.

5. To fix the link, single click on the broken link (*page4.html*) and change the name to *page3.html*. You could also use the Browse Folder button, but because we know the exact name we will type in the change.

6. Press Enter/Return to make the change. You will then be asked "Do you want to fix the remaining broken references to this file?" Select Yes. See figure 23-10.

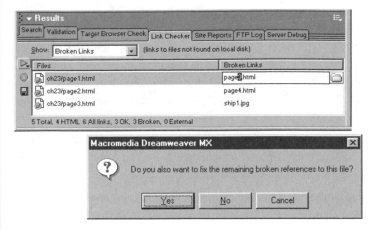

Fig. 23-10. Using Results panel | Link Checker to make a change to a broken link.

7. Because both files that were listed (*page1* and *page2*) had the same broken link, when you selected Yes to fix all links to this file, both files were fixed, saved, and removed from the broken links list.

8. The option Save at the bottom of the Check Links box does not save your changes. It saves a report of all broken links found in the specified files (or site).

9. The last broken link is a link to an image. *page3.html* should really be linked to *ship.jpg* (not *ship1.jpg*). Again, either change the name to *ship.jpg* or browse for *ship.jpg* in the *ch23* folder. Press Enter/Return to make the change to the link.

10. While still in Results panel | Link Checker, from the pull-down menu, select External Links. See figure 23-11.

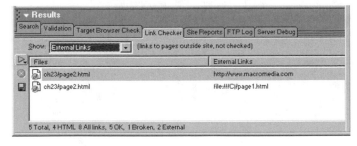

Fig. 23-11. Results panel showing External Links.

11. External links will list all links to URLs outside the local site. This includes full URLs (such as *http://www.macromedia.com*) and documents (PDFs, images, and so on). It also lists all empty JavaScript references (*javascript:;*). These were inserted for hypertext that did not have an actual link or

used behaviors to link to files. You should not need to worry about files that are listed with *javascript:;*. You should check out any external URLs to make sure they still exist. The most important external links to check (and fix), however, are those that link to specific files on your hard drive. That usually means that the link will not work once it is posted to the remote site. In this example (see figure 23-11), *page2.html* is linking to a file on the C drive.

This should put up a big warning sign, as it is very unlikely a user will have the correct file on his C drive. The external files need to be copied to the root or other folder within your local site.

12. Use the Save Report button in External Links to save a report of all external links. You can then print the report to check on each of the links.

13. Change links in the External Links window just like we did in the Broken Links window. Type the correction or use the Browse button to find the correct external file.

14. There is another feature, similar to Check Links, that will check the entire site. While in the Site panel, select Site | Check Links Sitewide.

Checking links in the entire site will show a third category of links, which is orphaned files. These are files Dreamweaver MX does not find any reference to and are probably not being used. However, be careful that the files are not just being referenced. You can delete orphaned files directly from this list by just selecting the file and pressing the Delete key.

·T/P·

The Snippets panel includes code to insert Accessible features such as navigation and Form objects. Select Window | Snippets (shift + F9) and find the Accessible folder.

15. You can also check the accessibility of a file. The document is checked against Section 508 accessibility guidelines of the 1998 Rehabilitation Act. Select the file or folder you want to check and select File Menu | Check page | Check Accessibility. The report will be displayed under the Site Reports tab in the Results panel. See figure 23-12.

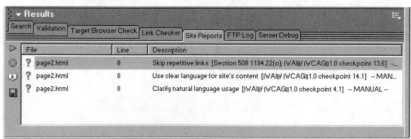

Fig. 23-12. Results panel showing accessibility report.

Guided Tour 23D: Design Notes

We have included design notes in this chapter because it is a method of documenting changes, problems, and any other notes to yourself or other team members about a particular file. You may find that an error appears as you are developing pages, or that the Check Browser report identifies an error you are unable to fix at that time. By using design notes, you can make a note to yourself or to the other members of the team to fix the error. We will create a new file for this guided tour.

1. Open the Site panel for the *DWExercises* site by selecting Site Menu | Open Site | *DWExercises*.

2. We will create a file in the *ch23* folder. Select the *ch23* folder in the *DWExercises* site. From the Site panel's File menu, select New File. For the name of the file, type in *usenotes.html*, and then press Enter/Return.

3. Without even opening the file (because we are not going to actually put anything in it), while *usenotes.html* is selected, select File Menu | Design Notes, or right mouse click on the file and select Design Notes from the context menu.

4. Click on the Calendar icon in the upper right corner of the dialog box to enter the date of this note.

5. You can select notes from multiple categories. See figure 23-13. Because we want to draw attention to a problem, on the Basic Info tab, Status pulldown menu, select *needs attention*.

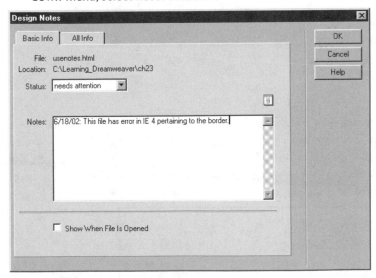

Fig. 23-13. Design Notes | Basic Info.

6. In the Notes box, type *This file has error in IE 4 pertaining to the border.*

7. Select the All Info tab. The note you just entered is listed.

8. Using the Plus (+) button, add another note about this file, or go back to the Basic Info window and select a category to enter a new note. When it asks you for the name, this is a unique name. If you enter a name already being used, it replaces the value of the name with the new value you enter. For instance, the notes already contain a line with the name *notes*. That is the line you entered for the notes. Do not use that name again unless you want to change the note. You could enter the name *notes2* for another line of notes, or just add to the *notes* line already in the design notes. See figure 23-14.

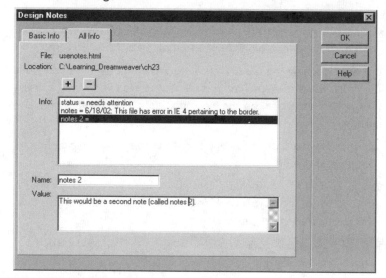

Fig. 23-14. Design Notes.

9. Click on OK to exit the design notes.

10. The file will now have a small icon next to it, indicating that the file has a design note on it (see figure 23-15). When the file is posted to the remote site and the Design Notes feature is turned on (Define Sites option), the same icon will appear next to the file to let other members on the team know that the file has a note. They can open the note and add to it.

Fig. 23-15. File with a design note.

11. Every file has its own *Design Note* file that is kept in a folder called *_notes*. This folder resides in each folder of the site.

12. To turn off the Design Notes feature so that the *_notes* folder is not automatically created (and you do not have to keep deleting the folder so that it does not get posted), go into Edit Sites (Site menu) and turn off Design Notes. There is also an option to clean up notes that are not linked to a file (the file has been deleted).

Guided Tour 23E: Site Reports

There are so many little things in HTML that you may forget to set while working in Dreamweaver MX, even with all the panels and windows that Dreamweaver MX provides. Site reports can help you find these forgotten items without opening up every single file. We will use the files in *ch23* for the tour.

1. Open the *DWExercises* site from the Site panel.

2. Select the *ch23* folder.

3. From the Site menu, select Reports. See figure 23-16.

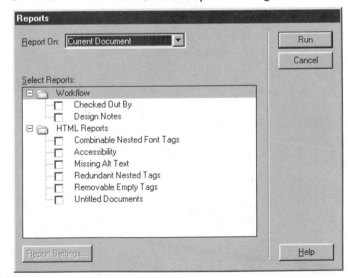

Fig. 23-16. Reports.

4. You can print a report based on a selected file or files, the entire site, or a folder. Select Entire Current Local Site.

5. Under HTML reports, select Missing Alt Text (and any other options you would like to check).

6. Click on the Run button.

7. The report will be displayed in the Results panel group under Site Reports.

8. Select the green arrow in the Results panel. This will bring the Reports dialog box back up so that you can select another report.

9. Click on the Save Report button to save the report so that you can print it.

Setting Up a Remote Site

Throughout the exercises in this book we have set up sites but never defined the remote site on the Internet server. When you are ready to copy your files from your hard drive to a server, Dreamweaver MX will need to know how and where you want to place those files. This is set up in Site Menu | Edit Sites | Remote Info. Remote Info provides specific information about your remote site that Dreamweaver MX will need when you are ready to copy or upload the files from your local computer (defined in Local Info) to the remote site or web server. Let's look at details of the information contained on the Remote Info page. See figure 23-17.

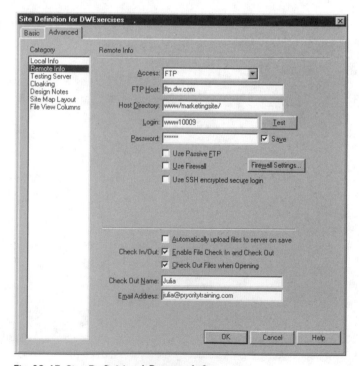

Fig. 23-17. Site Definition | Remote Info.

Remote Info: Access

This pull-down menu is used to define how you are going to access the remote site on the web server (or network server).

- None: *Means you will not be connecting to the Web using Dreamweaver MX. For those of you who are not always connected to the Internet, use None to keep Dreamweaver MX from trying to "check out" files when you open a file. (See Check In/Check Out.)*

- FTP (File Transfer Protocol): *Means you are going to send and receive files from the Web via FTP using the Server Access feature of Dreamweaver MX.*

- Local/Network: *Means you are using a local server on a network or NFS server (Macintosh), with AppleTalk, for your remote site.*

There are three other protocols to select for the server access: RDS (Remote Development Services), SourceSafe Database, and WebDAV (Web-based Distributed Authoring and Versioning protocol). See the Dreamweaver MX Help for more information on these servers. See figure 23-18.

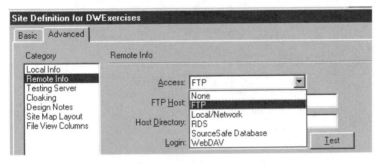

Fig. 23-18. Site Definition | Remote Info | Server Access.

We will look at two of the server access types in more detail: FTP and Local/Network.

Server Access: FTP

You will need the following information if you select FTP as the server access type. Refer to figure 23-18.

- *FTP Host: This is the network or organization that will be hosting your web site. An example might be* ftp.mindspring.com.

- *Host Directory: This is the location where all of your web site files will reside on the remote site. An example might be* www *or* www/marketingsite. *You can leave this field blank and it will assume you are accessing the root directory on the FTP site.*

• Login: *This is your log-in name. This field is required and must match the log-in name you are given by the web administrator. If this field is incorrect, an error message will appear when you try to connect to the remote site.*

- Password: *This is a unique password that is required along with your log-in name. If this field is incorrect, an error message will appear when you try to connect to the remote site.*

- Test: *Once you have entered the host, log-in, and password, click on the Test button to test the connection to the site.*

Local/Network Server Access

You will need the *Remote* folder if you select Local/Network as the server access type. This is the folder where your site files are loaded on the server. See figure 23-19.

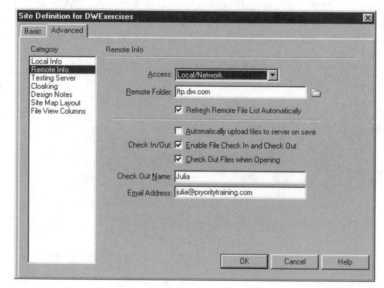

Fig. 23-19. Site Definition | Remote Info | Local/Network Server Access.

Remote Info: Enable File Check In and Check Out

Another option in the Remote Site window is Enable File Check In and Check Out. When you are working on a team where more than one person may be working on files for the same site, you will want to use the Check In/Out feature. When this option is checked, each time someone opens a file on the remote or local site, Dreamweaver MX will set a flag at the remote site, indicating that the file is in use, and will display the name of the person who has the file checked out.

We recommend that you do not check the Save box next to the password if you are not working on a secure computer. With the password saved, anyone using your computer could connect to the Web and make changes to the site.

Under Server Access, if you select FTP or Local/Network and you have enabled File Check In/Check Out, each time you open a file on the local site Dreamweaver will try to connect to the server to check out the file. If you are not connected to the Internet while working in Dreamweaver, you may want to set Server Access to None until you are ready to put files on the remote site. Otherwise, you will experience distractions as Dreamweaver tries to "connect" when no connection is currently available.

This feature will prevent two or more people from accessing the same file at the same time. This feature can also be useful even if only one person is working on a file, but working from multiple computers such as at home and at work. The following options are available for Check In/Out.

- **Check Out Files When Opening:** *This option will check out the file if the file is opened from the Site window. It does not check out the file if it is opened with File | Open File.*

- **Check Out Name:** *You use this field to type in the name that will be displayed next to any files that are opened, as long as the Enable File Check In/Out and Check Out Files options are checked. If you are working on the same files from different computers, use different check-out names for each computer. This information is kept on the local hard drive of the current computer.*

- **E-mail Address:** *Enter your e-mail address here so that other team members can send you e-mail if they need to contact you (for example, if you have checked out a file and they need it). The e-mail address will display with your name when a file is checked out from the remote site. See figure 23-20.*

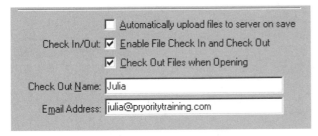

Fig. 23-20. Site Definition | Remote Info | Enable File Check In and Check Out.

Summary

- *Dreamweaver MX provides many tools and features to check for possible errors in your site. This includes checking for broken links, possible problems in external links, and errors in HTML and JavaScript across browsers.*

- *Use design notes to document development in your files. They are especially useful to remind yourself to look at a possible problem area in a file. You can also warn other team members about an error or how it was fixed.*

- *Use the Reports feature to document and clean up files in your site.*

- *When many people are working on the same group of pages on a site, they should use the Check In/Check Out feature found under Site Definition.*

- *You can wait to set up the Remote Site Info feature until you are actually ready to post files to the server. If you are working on a team, placing files on the server may be one of the easiest and fastest ways for everyone to have access to the most current files.*

·T/P·

If a file is opened outside Dreamweaver, the Check In/Out feature is not in effect. The Check In/Out feature only works while working inside Dreamweaver.

·T/P·

Use the menu option Edit | Select Checked Out Files (in the Site panel) to quickly highlight all files on the local site that you have checked out.

·T/P·

You definitely do *not* want two people to be working on the same file at the same time! At a minimum, you will lose the changes from one person after he has saved his changes, as the second person saves her changes, overwriting the first person's changes. Dreamweaver's Check In/Out feature helps prevent this.

C H A P T E R

24

Dynamic Pages

Introduction

In your development of web pages, you may have had a need to store data externally to your web pages. If you need to see an example of data that is external to a web page, just go to almost any online catalog or travel agency. This is an example of linked web pages pulling data in from another source at runtime when a user is viewing the web page.

This is where dynamic data comes in. Dynamic data can be as simple as the current time or today's stock quote, or as vast as all products in an online catalog. In this chapter we are just going to introduce you to the concepts of adding dynamic data to a web page. Throughout this chapter are examples to give you a feel for dynamic content. We have chosen one server technology software (ColdFusion) to process our dynamic content. Most of the steps will be transferable to the server technology you decide to use. By the end of this chapter you will be able to:

- *Describe the steps needed to create a web application*
- *Understand the steps in Dreamweaver MX to connect to a database*
- *Add dynamic data to a page*
- *Add a dynamic form to a page that will be used to update a database*

Overview

Dreamweaver MX gives you the tools you need to create dynamic web sites. What is meant by "dynamic" is the way content is placed within a web page. The content does not have to be typed in manually (hardcoded), otherwise known as static data. Web pages can contain information that is "dynamically" placed on the page as the user is viewing the page.

For example, think of yourself as a web site developer for a business that provides hundreds of products. Management wants a web site containing information for every product. Think about how long it would take to create a page containing the product name, number, description, and photograph for every product. Luckily, the folks in marketing have all the product information in a database (computerized listing of products with all necessary information). All you need to do is copy and paste the information into the pages of your web site. Even though you do not need to locate the content, this still takes a very long time.

Now think about how quickly you could create a site with a single product page – a product page containing special links called bindings. These "bindings" automatically copy and paste specific product information from the database and place it into the correct area of the web page as a person views the page.

Let's also add the ability to search the product listing and only show products that match the criteria the user specifies. Examine figures 24-1 through 24-3. Then we will review common terms used in this environment.

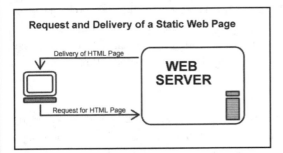

Fig. 24-1. Processing a static page.

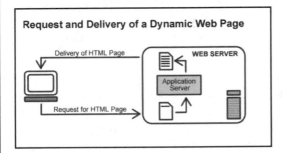

Fig. 24-2. Processing a dynamic page.

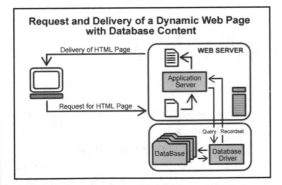

Fig. 24-3. Processing a dynamic page with database content.

Terms

There are a few terms you should become familiar with in order to understand and work with dynamic pages.

Web Application

A web application is a collection of regular (static) and dynamic web pages. A static page is one that always loads in a browser with the same content – the same text, graphics, sound, and so on. A dynamic web page is a page that changes over time, per a user request, or because of some condition. The final content of a dynamic web page is not complete until the user actually requests the page to be displayed in a browser and the page is sent to the user's browser.

Web Server

A web server is sometimes referred to as an HTTP server. A web server is the software that processes web pages to pass to a browser. When creating regular (non-dynamic pages), your browser interprets the HTML code without a server. But dynamic pages have additional code that is not HTML. This code must first be processed and translated into HTML (by the web server) before sending it to the user's browser. You can install web servers on your local machine to test your dynamic pages (discussed further later in this chapter).

Application Server

To run web applications, your web server needs to work with an application server. An application server is software that works with a web server to process the special server-side scripts and tags (e.g., JSP script) in a web page. When such a page is requested, the web server sends the page to the application server for processing before sending the page to the browser.

Common application servers include Macromedia ColdFusion MX, Macromedia JRun, Microsoft .NET Framework, PHP, IBM WebSphere, Jakarta Tomcat, and ASP application servers. The application server is typically installed on the same system that runs the web server.

Document Type

Used in the database environment, a document type in its simplest sense is the type of software technology you will use to communicate with a database or other external data. The different document types (or technologies) include ColdFusion, ASP, JSP, and PHP. The document type is matched with the application server to process dynamic pages. The document type must be set before connecting to a database.

Database

A database is a collection of data formatted into records, fields, and tables. Each record (typically a row of data) contains specific pieces of information, also known as fields (typically columns of data). For example, in a database of the members of an organization, each person would have one record (their information), and each record would have various fields of information (first and last names, addresses, phone numbers, and so on).

Database Query

A database query extracts information from specific fields and records from a specific database. The search criteria is specified in terms of a database language called SQL. Dreamweaver can generate most of the SQL you will need to communicate with databases.

Dreamweaver MX Features and Tools to Use with Dynamic Content

In addition to the general tools used to create and format HTML pages, there are some specific tools that are used only with dynamic pages. The Application panel group contains panels to create and update dynamic pages. See figure 24-4.

- Databases panel: *Defines the data sources (databases) for the current page.*

- Bindings panel: *Displays the specified fields (recordSet) of the database and allows you to drag and drop links for displaying content in a page.*

- Server Behaviors panel: *Used to add server-side script to a dynamic page. The script sets the functions to process the dynamic content, such as updating a database.*

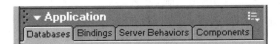

Fig. 24-4. Application Panel group.

The Insert bar has an Application tab (category), which lets you add dynamic content and server behaviors to your page. See figure 24-5.

Fig. 24-5. Insert bar showing Application tab.

Depending on the document type you are using, additional tabs appear in the Insert bar. For instance, if you are using ColdFusion MX, the Insert bar has three categories just for ColdFusion MX: CFML Basic, CFML Flow, and CFML Advanced. (CFML stands for ColdFusion Markup Language.)

One of the tools you will use with dynamic pages is the Live Data view, which is found on the Dreamweaver toolbar and also in the View menu. This view will show the actual database content you have bound to the web page –

comparable to what it will look like when displayed in a browser. You can also preview all of your dynamic pages in a browser. The web server and application server will handle the processing of the dynamic content. There are three primary phases involved in creating dynamic pages.

1. Set up a web application. Configure the system to have both a web server and application server.

2. Set up the Dreamweaver site.

3. Connect to a database.

We will examine these phases and then look at some ways to create and modify dynamic pages using a live example. Let's start with the first step – setting up the web application, including the web server and application server.

Phase I: Setting Up a Web Application

A web application needs both a web server and an application server. These servers refer to software, not hardware, when referencing the web application.

Windows: For development purposes in Windows, the software can be installed on the same computer as Dreamweaver or on a network for other team members to access. Possible web servers are the Microsoft Personal Web Server (PWS) or Internet Information Server (IIS). PWS and IIS are installed to the folder called *\Inetpub* on your root drive. Check for the existence of the folder to see if a web server has already been installed.

Macintosh: On the Macintosh, the server software can be installed on a web hosting service or on a remote computer. MacOS X and above allows the servers to be installed locally, using the Apache web server and PHP application server.

Web Application I: Setting Up a Testing Server

The first step is to install a web server, via one of the following.

Microsoft Personal Web Server (PWS), Windows 98 and NT Workstation: The PWS installation program can be found on the Windows (98 or NT) CD, or you can download the program from the Microsoft web site.

Internet Information Server (IIS), NT server, Windows 2000, or Windows XP: To install IIS, select Add/Remove programs from Control Panel | Settings and select Window Components | IIS.

Apache web server, MacOS X: Visit the Apache web site for instructions on installation at *http://httpd.apache.org/*.

The first step in setting up a web application is to install and setup the testing server.

Our example: We installed Personal Web Server to *C:\Inetpub\wwwroot* (which is the default install location). Restart the computer after installation. The PWS can now be accessed by selecting the icon in the System Tray (Window task bar) or from Start menu | Programs | Accessories | Internet Tools. The Personal Web Manager will appear, showing the home directory and home page of the web server. See figure 24-6.

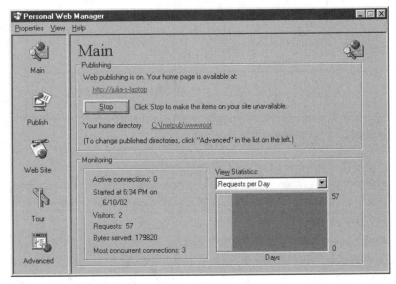

Fig. 24-6. Personal Web Server (PWS) Manager.

Web Application 2: Installing an Application Server

Before you can start using and setting up parameters for a dynamic page, you will need to install the application server that can process your special scripts and codes. Figure 24-7 lists the various application servers you can use. Many factors influence the application server (and document type) you choose to develop: ease of use, accessibility and features of the software (including price), and whether the web server supports the type of technology you have chosen. For example, not all web servers support ColdFusion, and .NET Framework only works with IIS 5 or higher.

·**T/P**·

The second step in setting up a web application is to install an application server.

Server Technology	Application server	Advantages
ColdFusion	Macromedia ColdFusion MX	Supported by Dreamweaver, ease of use
ASP.NET	Microsoft IIS 5 with .NET Framework	
ASP	Microsoft IIS or PWS Sun Chili! Soft ASP	
JSP	Macromedia JRun IBM WebSphere Apache Tomcat BEA WebLogic	
PHP	PHP server	Free server and can work on most web servers

Fig. 24-7. Types of application servers.

The examples in this book use ColdFusion. ColdFusion is quickly becoming a standard application server technology. It is not too difficult to understand, and a developer's version of the software is available on the Dreamweaver MX CD and at the Macromedia web site.

The ColdFusion application server is available for Windows, Linux, Solaris, and HP-UX systems, and can be installed on your local computer for testing and development purposes. After installing ColdFusion, the ColdFusion administrator can be accessed from the Window Start menu. To stop ColdFusion MX (and the JRUN MS DOS window that appears), select Stop ColdFusion MX from the Start menu.

Our example: ColdFusion was installed to *C:\CfusionMX*. A password was entered, and the checkbox, labeled *RSLogin same as above*, was activated. Restart the computer after installation.

Windows: ColdFusion can be stopped or started by selecting Macromedia ColdFusion MX from the Start menu. The ColdFusion administrator provides access to data sources and passwords, among other things.

·TIP·

Step 3 in setting up a web application is to create a root folder. This folder is needed for defining the test server in Dreamweaver MX.

Web Application 3: Creating a Root Folder

The root folder you create in this step will be referenced in the testing server section of your site definition (in Dreamweaver MX). The testing server for ColdFusion is the root folder of the application server (where ColdFusion MX was installed). ColdFusion was installed to *C:\CFusionMX\wwwroot*.

Our example: We have created a folder called *dynamicData* in the *C:\CFusionMX\wwwroot* folder.

Web Application 4: Create an ODBC Data Source

This is optional at this point. Create an ODBC Data Source. While we are working outside Dreamweaver, you should go ahead and create the data source name (DSN) needed for the Microsoft Access database that is going to be used in this example.

The fourth step in setting up a web application, is to create an ODBC data source.

Our example: Using Windows, perform the following.

1. From the Control panel (Windows Start Menu | Settings | Control Panel), select ODBC Data Sources.

2. Select the System DSN tab.

3. Select the driver for the data source. We selected the Microsoft Access Driver.

4. Define the data source.
    a) The Data Source Name is an alias that is used to reference the actual database file. Type *studentDSN* in the Data Source Name field.
    b) Click on the Select button.
    c) Browse for the database file. The database file that we will use in this chapter is found in *Learning_Dreamweaver/ch24/students.mdb*.
    d) Click on the OK button.
    e) You should now see your data source name listed in the System Data Sources.

5. Exit the ODBC Data Source Administrator.

Phase 2: Setting Up Dreamweaver MX

Now that the web application servers have been set up, we can configure a site in Dreamweaver MX to access dynamic data. The required steps are listed in the Application panel group. As each step is completed to use dynamic data, the step is checked off in the Application panel. See figure 24-8. The three main steps are as follows.

*   *Create a site.*
*   *Choose a document type.*
*   *Set up the testing server.*

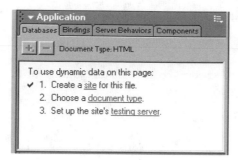

Fig. 24-8. Application panel group and steps for using dynamic data.

1. Create a site. We suggest that you start with a new site, because the Site Definition wizard will default to the correct settings needed for dynamic data. If you start with an existing site, you will need to enter the correct paths and data needed for the settings.

    a) Select Site Menu / New Site. Do not enter the wizard yet, but stay in the Advanced tab.

    b) In the Local Info category we only need to enter the site name and local root folder. For our example, establish the following.

    Site name: *dynamicdata*
    Local Root Folder: *C:\dynamicData*

    c) Select the Remote Info category. Note that the remote folder will be used as the default location for the testing server (see step 4). For our example, establish the following.

    Access: *Local/Network*
    Remote Folder: *C:\CFusionMX\wwwroot\ dynamicData*

    d) Click on OK. You should notice in the Databases panel that *Create a site* is checked. Note that you could go ahead and setup the Testing server at this point (see step 4).

2. The next step is to select a document type. See figure 24-9 for the various document types available. The document type reflects the application server you are using.

    a) From the Application panel group (Window | Databases), click on step 2. Choose a document type.

    b) For our example, we selected ColdFusion as the document type.

TIP

The first step in configuring Dreamweaver MX to access dynamic data, is to define a site to link to the application servers.

TIP

The folder to share your files is the remote folder. This is the same folder that was created in previous step 3 for setting up the web application.

TIP

The second step in configuring Dreamweaver MX is to choose the document type. We will choose ColdFusion.

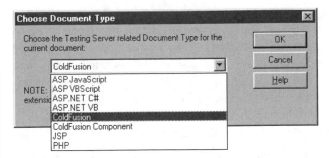

Fig. 24-9. Selecting a document type.

3. Set up a testing server for the site. The testing server defines where the dynamic pages you create will be processed (where you will save your pages). The location of the testing server will default to the remote location if one was selected. In this example, we are going to use ColdFusion and test on the same computer Dreamweaver was installed on.

The third step in configuring Dreamweaver MX is to define the site's testing server (Site Menu | Edit Sites).

   a) From the Databases panel, select *step 3. Set up the site's testing server* (or select the site to edit in the Site panel).

   b) Select the Testing Server category. See figure 24-10. For our example, establish the following.

   Server model: *ColdFusion*
   Access: *Local/Network*
   Testing Server Model: *C:\CFusionMX\wwwroot\dynamicData* (This defaults to the remote server folder.)
   URL Prefix: *http://localhost:8500/dynamicData/* (The 8500 is the port address of the application server. This shows up each time you access the ColdFusion Administrator.)

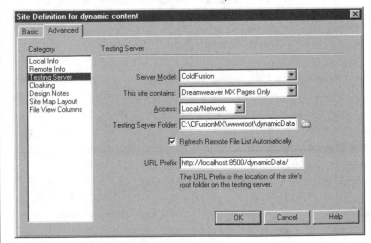

Fig. 24-10. Site Definition | Testing Server.

The URL prefix is used to display data and connect to databases while you design and develop in Dreamweaver. The URL prefix consists of the domain name (for the testing server) and a web site's home directory or virtual directory. *LocalHost* can be used in place of your domain name when Dreamweaver is loaded on the same system as your server. The domain is the root of your server (in our case *C:\CFusionMX\wwwroot*) and the home directory we have selected is *dynamicData*.

To start ColdFusion, select ColdFusion MX. Start from Start Menu | Macromedia ColdFusion MX. Wait for the JRUN window to finish. It will say something like "Server default ready."

Note that the ColdFusion application requires an RDS log-in (remote development services), but you may not need to enter this, depending on the type of application server you have installed.

4. The URL prefix acts like your domain name – what would be entered in a browser to access your pages. Dreamweaver bases the domain name on the remote folder location. *localHost* references the root folder (or home directory) when Dreamweaver runs on the same system as the web server (in our example, PWS). You can open the PWS or IIS administrator to locate and change the domain name (called the home directory). In our example, the domain is *C:\Inetpub\wwwroot* (referenced by *localhost*), and the home directory is *dynamicData*.

5. To test the URL prefix, while in the Testing Server category, select the Basic tab to go back into the wizard. Using the next and prev buttons, go to the screen (called *Testing Files, Part 2*) where there is a button called *Test URL*. Click on the Test URL button. If the test is not successful, check the following.

- *A basic problem you may have is that either the web server (in our case, PWS) is not running or the application server (in our case, ColdFusion) is not running.*

- *Sometimes the testing server folder gets modified by Dreamweaver (especially if you select not to enter the remote folder). Go back to the Advanced tab to check all settings.*

- *Check the URL prefix again. If Dreamweaver and your server are on the system, does the URL prefix have the port number after localhost? Check the spelling of the host directory and whether the directory actually exits in the server.*

Your web application is now set up and you are ready to connect to a database.

Phase 3: Connecting to a Database

Before you can connect to your database with Dreamweaver MX, you must make sure you have installed a web server and an application server and have created a site in Dreamweaver with a testing server defined (follow the previous steps).

In this example, we are going to connect to a Microsoft Access database that has been copied to your computer into *Learning_Dreamweaver/ch24*. To use this file in our example, copy the file called *catalog.mdb* from the *ch24* folder (or from the companion CD-ROM) to the folder we defined as our local site: *C:\dynamicData*. We are now ready to connect to that database.

1. In order to communicate with ColdFusion from Dreamweaver (and create our connection to a database), you must first log in with the RDS log-in. In the Application panel group (we are using the Database panel), select *RDS login*. Type in the log-in you entered when installing ColdFusion MX.

2. The first step to actually connect to a database is to create the ColdFusion data source. Select Data Source from the Application panel. (You do not need to repeat this step if you have already created a data source in ColdFusion MX.)

3. The ColdFusion MX data source screen will open (you may need to enter the log-in for the administrator first). See figure 24-11. For our example, perform the following.

   a) Data Source Name: *connStudents*

   b) Driver: JDBC-ODBC Bridge (this is the driver to connect to Access databases)

   c) Click on the Add button.

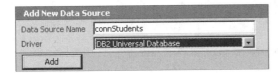

Fig. 24-11. ColdFusion | Data Source (screen 1).

4. In the JDBC-ODBC bridge screen, from the ODBC DSN drop-down menu, select *studentsDSN*. (This is the ODBC data source we created outside Dreamweaver while setting up our web application.) See figure 24-12. Click on the Submit button.

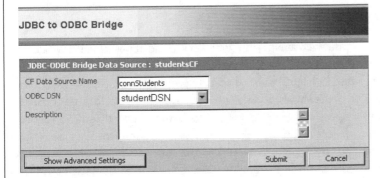

Fig. 24-12. ColdFusion | Data Source (screen 2).

5. Your new data source (*connStudents*) should be listed under Connected Data Sources. The status will show OK if the connection was made. You

·T/P·

If you have already created a ColdFusion data source, click on the Modify Data Sources button in the Database panel in Dreamweaver MX. This will load ColdFusion MX and the data source screen. You can also set up all data sources by opening the ColdFusion MS administrator and selecting the Data Source option.

·T/P·

Use the ColdFusion MX administrator to edit or delete an existing data source. Make sure if you are connecting to a data source in Dreamweaver that has been deleted or renamed that each record set referencing the old data source is updated. Double click on the record set and select the new data source.

·T/P·

When viewing the structure of a database in the Database panel, right click on a table name and select View Data to see the data in that table. (If you get an error, make sure the application server is running).

·T/P·

The Bindings panel lets you define and select the sources of dynamic content for your page. The options can also be found via the Insert bar | Application tab.

can also click on the Verify All Connections button if a status is not shown. If you have an error, check the driver (the driver should be JDBC-ODBC) and that you selected the correct DSN. Also make sure that the testing server is pointing to the root folder of ColdFusion (the application server). See figure 24-13.

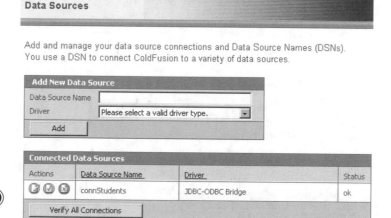

Fig. 24-13. ColdFusion | Data Source connection verification.

a) Close the window to return to Dreamweaver MX.
b) View the database structure in Dreamweaver. In the Databases panel, your data source name should be displayed. Click on the Plus (+) button to expand the list and see the structure of the database. Notice that the primary key (represented by a yellow key next to a data type) is displayed where applicable.

Adding Dynamic Data to a Page

You have created the web application (web server and application server), created a site, and connected to a database (data source). Now we can link data to a dynamic page. To begin, we need to retrieve fields from the database so that we can display the values or fields on the page. This is performed through what is called a query and is performed by creating a record set. The record set stores the content of the database and acts as the intermediary between the database and the application server (in our example, that will be ColdFusion). A record set is a listing of specific fields in a database. Each listing has a record set name.

1. Create a new page. Select File Menu | New | Dynamic page and select the type of application you are using for your dynamic pages (in our example we select ColdFusion).

2. Save the file and name it *studentList*. Note that if you are using ColdFusion, the page will inherit a *.cfm* extension.

3. To perform a database query, the following steps should be taken.
   a) Select the Bindings panel (Window Menu | Bindings or Ctrl/Cmd + F10).
   b) Click on the Plus (+) button, and then *RecordSet(Query)*. (This option is also found in the Server Behaviors panel.)

4. Look at the RecordSet dialog box. See figure 24-14.
   a) Name the record set. The name is like a group or family name that represents the field or fields within the record set. For our example, name the record set *rsStudents*.
   b) From the Data Source drop-down menu, select *connStudents*. This was created earlier in the application server. If you get an error, check that the database file you are connecting to is still in the same location on the hard drive.
   c) Select the fields. We want to get just the last and first name. Select the radio button labeled *Selected* next to the Columns option. Then highlight *last_name* and *first_name* (use the Ctrl key to select more than one field).
   d) Sort the fields. To list the name in last-name order, set the sort to *last_name*.
   e) Test the record set. Click on the Test button. A list of all records in the database is displayed, with only the fields you selected.

·T/P·

If you get an error with the database, check that the ColdFusion MX connection has not stopped. You can tell it has stopped if the JRUN dialog box says "Finished" in the title bar. Just close the dialog box and restart ColdFusion MX.

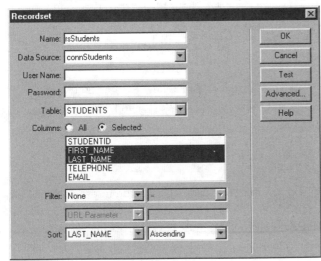

Fig. 24-14. RecordSet dialog box.

   f) Look at the SQL. Click on the Advanced button. You can see the SQL code that has been generated to extract just the fields you selected.

·T/P·

Structure Query Language (SQL) is used by an application server to extract and save data to a database.

This (advanced) screen is where you can enter additional SQL and modify what Dreamweaver has created. Select Simple to go back to the original RecordSet dialog box.

g)   Click on OK to save the record set. The record set *rsStudents* should now be listed in the Bindings panel. Expand the record set to see the field listed that you selected for the record set. See figure 24-15.

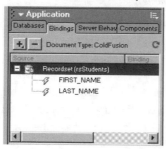

Fig. 24-15. Bindings panel with record set expanded.

h)   Select Code view to see the code that has been generated in your file. You should see the same SQL script you saw in the RecordSet dialog box. If you are using ColdFusion, the *<cfquery>* tag surrounds the record set query you just performed.

Displaying the Fields on a Page

If you are going to display more than one record (i.e., more than one name in our example), it is better in most cases to have some type of formatting for the fields. One of the best ways to do this is with a table so that each column corresponds to a field.

1.   Insert a table in your HTML page (either a new page or an existing page within your site). We will use a one-row, two-column table.

2.   From the Bindings panel, drag the field called *last_name* to the first column.

3.   From the Bindings panel, drag the field called *first_name* to the second column. See figure 24-16.

4.   To test the page, click on the Live Data View button in the toolbar (see figure 24-16), or select View Menu | Live Data. To deselect Live Data, deselect the Live Data View button. You must have the testing server defined before you can view live data.

·T/P·

Note that the record set is linked to the page, not to Dreamweaver. To have the same record set for another page, copy the record set from the Bindings panel (right-click/copy). Open the page to copy to the record set to. Right click on the title bar of the Binding or Server Behaviors panel and select Paste.

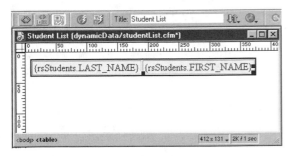

Fig. 24-16. Dynamic data added to a page.

5. Enter Code view and see the tag and the scripting around the fields that are being displayed. ColdFusion uses the *<cfoutput>* tag to display the results of a query (or other operation).

Displaying More than One Database Record

1. Select the first row of your table.

2. Select the Server Behaviors panel (Window | Server Behaviors).

3. Click on the Plus (+) button, and then select Repeat Region from the pop-up menu.

4. Define how many records you want to display. For our example, select All Records.

5. Notice that your table now has a tag above it. For ColdFusion, notice that our *<cfoutput>* tag is above the table. In Code view, note that the *<cfoutput>* tag surrounds all fields instead of being connected to just one field at a time.

6. Test the page by clicking on the Live Data button. All records of the database should now be displayed.

A Shortcut for Displaying All Records of a Record Set in a Table

1. Select Insert bar | Application category.

2. Place your cursor in the page where you want to display the database values. Select Dynamic Table from the Insert bar. See figure 24-17.

Fig. 24-17. Insert bar | Dynamic Table button.

·T*i*P·

The option to display only a certain number of records is useful for a results page. A results page provides detail about records based on search criteria by a user, such as looking for a product that costs less than $10.00.

3. Select the data source to use, make your selection of the number of records to display, and click OK.

4. A table is created with column titles and a repeat region for all fields in the data source. You can then modify the titles and add additional columns if you want.

5. Note that the disadvantage of creating your display in this manner is that all fields of the record set are automatically displayed, each in its own column. Of course, the table can always be modified.

Dynamic Images: Binding Images to a Page

Displaying dynamic images is just like displaying other dynamic content except that only the name of the image file is located in the database file. The name is then used to link the image located outside the database and the dynamic page. It is essential that the location of the images stay the same in relation to the working (local) page, including when the page is loaded on the server. Be sure to transfer all images to the server when you are ready to publish the page.

1. From the Bindings panel, double click on your record set to open it. Note that the record set must first be created by selecting the Plus (+) button from the Bindings panel and then selecting RecordSet(Query).

2. From the Columns option, select the field for the image. The value in the field is just the name of the image file name. Close the RecordSet dialog box.

3. Create a new column in your table.

4. From the Bindings panel, expand the record set. Drag the Image field to the new table column, or in the Property Inspector click on the image Src Browse icon (the folder). From the Select File dialog box, at the top of the window, select Select File Name From: Data Source. Select the Image field. (Notice the Format option in this window.)

5. Select View | Live Data.

Server Behaviors

Server behaviors are tasks that allow you to interact with the data in a database. This includes adding records to a database, deleting records, and updating a record. The dynamic pages that have these functions are referenced by task and will appear in most of the Dreamweaver Help pages that deal with active pages.

• Results page: *Displays the results of records in a database query. The user determines what displays on this page by specifying some type of search criteria.*

- Detail page: *Displays all records and fields in a database. This page also has Update/Delete/Insert options but usually only with administrator privileges.*

- Update page: *Displays all fields in a record as form elements on a page.*

- Insert page: *Displays a blank form for inserting a new record.*

- Delete page: *Displays a record that can be deleted. This page can be combined with an Update page.*

Dreamweaver comes with some predesigned server behaviors for these active pages. You can also download server behaviors and create your own. There are also what are called "live objects" – objects built around server behaviors.

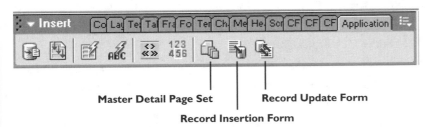

Fig. 24-18. Insert bar | Application showing Live Objects

The following live objects are found in the Insert bar under Application. See figure 24-18.

- Master/Detail Page Set: *A master page lists database records and has links to see more detail about the record. The links have a goto to link to a detail page. For instance, the master page could have a list of all catalog objects and a part number. Clicking on the link from part number takes the user to a detail page about the specific product.*

    - *The Master/Detail Page Set object will create a detail page and add dynamic content and server behaviors to both master and detail page. You begin to use this object by first creating a master page and displaying the results of a record set with a Repeat Region behavior.*

- Record Insertion Form: *This adds an HTML form and an Insert Record server behavior to the page. The result is an insert page with a blank form inside a table and a Submit button.*

- Record Update Form: *This adds an HTML form and an Update Record server behavior to the page. The result is an update page with an existing record's field in a form and a Delete button and Submit button.*

The following section will show you how to build a form with dynamic content (data from a database) and allow the user to update the database. You might want to use this to create a user database file or allow someone to remotely update a catalog list.

Binding Form Elements to a Dynamic Page and Updating a Database

This example uses a database called *catalog.mdb* in the *Learning_Dreamweaver/ ch24* folder. Connect to this database.

First, create a results page to show all records in the database.

1. Create a new data source called *CatalogDSN* (in the Windows Control Panel | ODBC data sources) and select the Access database called *catalog.mdb*, found in *Learning_Dreamweaver/ch24*.

2. Connect to the database (data source) in the application server (ColdFusion MX in our example). Call the data source *connCatalog*.

3. Select File Menu | New | Dynamic Page. We are continuing to use ColdFusion, so select ColdFusion MX dynamic page.

4. Save the file as *catalogPage*.

5. Create a record set for this page (Bindings panel | Plus (+) button). Name it *rsCatalog*, and select all records from the data source called *connCatalog*.

6. We will use a live object to insert a form to display the catalog records. From Insert bar | Application, select Record Insertion Form (third icon from the right on the bar).

7. In the Record Insertion Form dialog box, select the data source *connCatalog* and select to display 10 records. Click OK.

8. A table has been created with all fields of the database in individual columns. Insert a new line under Product Name, and move the placeholder for Product Description to under Product Name. Delete the column labeled Product Description. Rename the second column *Product Name/Description*.

9. Click on the Live Data button to see all records of the database. Look in the Server Behaviors panel to see all behaviors that were created when you selected Live Object | Record Insertion Form.

10. We want to display the price of the products as a currency number. In the Server Behaviors panel, select Dynamic Text and select the field UnitPrice. Change the format to one of the currency formats. We selected Currency | International Format. View the live data again to see the new format.

11. Save the file. We are done with the results page. See figures 24-19 and 24-20. Now we will create the update page.

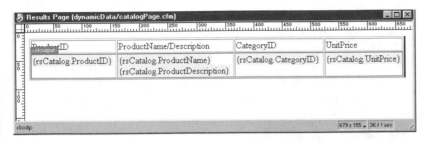

Fig. 24-19. Results Page | Design View.

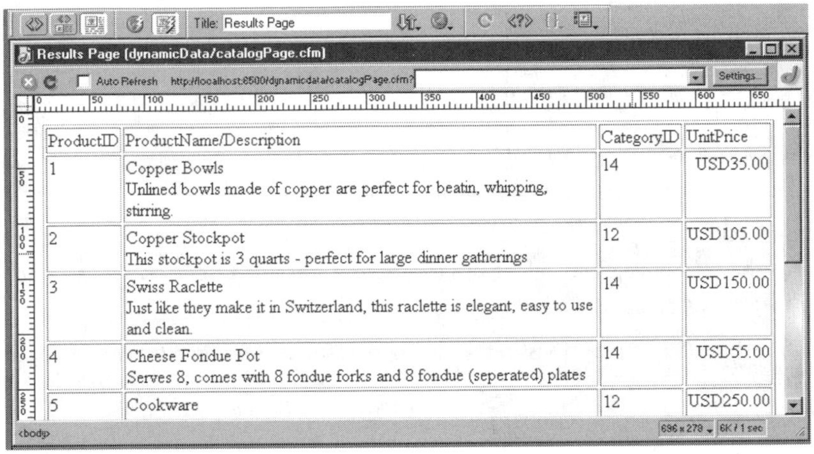

Fig. 24-20. Results Page | Live Data View.

Second, create an update page with a blank form to insert a new record in the database.

1. Select File Menu | New | Dynamic Page. We are continuing to use ColdFusion, so select ColdFusion MX dynamic page.

2. Save the file as *formPage*.

3. Copy the record set called *rsCatalog* from the page called *catalogPage* that we just created (this record set has all records from the *connCatalog* data source).

   a) To copy the record set, after opening the page called *catalogPage*, right mouse click (Control + click: Mac) on the record set *rsCatalog* in the Bindings panel and select Copy.

   b) Return to the page called *formPage*, right mouse click on the title bar of the Bindings panel, and select Paste.

4. Because we are going to insert a new product record into our catalog, it would help to know what the available categories are. There is a table in

·T/P·

There can be more than one record set on a page and bound to a single form.

our database called *categories* that has the ID and descriptions. We can select from a list of these categories as we create our new record. We need a record set for this table in order to do that.

a) Create a new record set and name it *rsCategories*. Link to the data source *connCatalog* and the table called *categories*. Sort the record set by category. See figure 24-21.

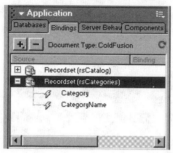

Fig. 24-21. Record set linked to categories table.

·T/P·

When using the Record Insert Form option, do *not* press Enter or click OK until you are sure you have set everything. You cannot come back into this dialog box to reset parameters.

5. In the file *catalogPage*, select the live object Record Insertion Form under Insert bar | Application.

6. Set the following options in the dialog box for the Record Insertion Form (see figure 24-23).

a) *Data Source: connCatalog*

b) *Table:* Products

c) *After Inserting, Go To:* browse for the *catalogPage* file. When you click on the Insert button, the browser will jump to the results page.

d) Delete any fields that will not be inserted manually. The ProductID field is an auto-number field and should not be entered manually. Delete the ProductID column.

e) Select the column called CategoryID.
   • *Change the label to Category.*

   • *The category will be selected from a list of available categories from the categories table, so select* Display As: Menu. *Click on the Menu Properties button. See figure 24-23.*

   • *Menu Properties: We are going to populate the pop-up menu with the available categories from the categories table. We want to display the descriptions of the categories but only save the category ID in the products table. Establish the following.*

   RecordSet: *rsCategories*

   Get Labels From: *CategoryName*

   Get Value From: *Category*

Select Value Equal To: *Click on the lightening bolt icon to see a list of available fields. Select Category from the rsCategories record set.*

8. Click on OK.

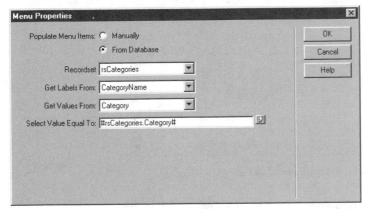

Fig. 24-22. Menu properties for Category field.

   f)   Click OK in the Record Insertion Form. See figure 24-23.

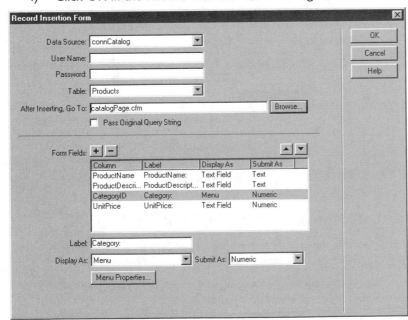

Fig. 24-23. Record Insertion Form dialog box completed.

Preview in the browser (F12) to test this. Type the information for a new product. Notice the selection of category descriptions from the pop-menu button. When you click on the Insert button, the new page (*catalogPage*) is displayed in the browser, with your new product listed in the catalog. See figures 24-24 and 24-25.

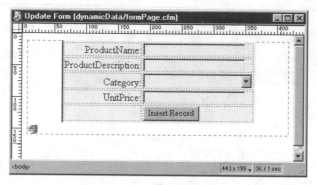

Fig. 24-24. Update Form page in Design view.

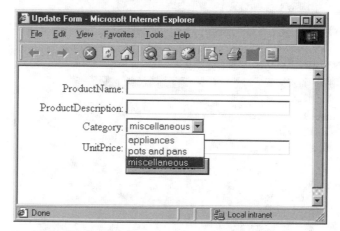

Fig. 24-25. Update Form page as previewed in a browser.

Additional Notes on Dynamic Content

- *Dynamic content can replace existing text or can be added to the existing text on a page. The Bindings panel displays the available record sets and selected fields.*

- *Placeholders represent the dynamic content (when not in Live Data view) and take the form {recordSet.columnName}.*

- *Dynamic content can be formatted with CSS styles, just like any other content on a page.*

- *Dynamic content can also be formatted with predefined data formats that come with Dreamweaver (numbers, currency, and so on). Select the dynamic content on the page, and from the Bindings panel select the Format column (you may need to widen the panel to see this column).*

Summary

In this chapter we have given you the steps needed to begin working with dynamic content using Dreamweaver MX. In summary, remember the following points to create dynamic pages.

- *A web server and an application server must be installed, configured properly, and available in order to create dynamic pages.*

- *Connecting to a database involves creating a data source to the database both within the application server and in the ODBC data sources.*

- *To access database content from a dynamic page, create a record set in Dreamweaver MX to the data source and select the fields you want to use.*

- *To automatically place data in a web page, drag a field from the Bindings panel to its proper location on the web page. Use tables, layers, and forms for positioning and formatting the layout of the data you are "binding" to the page.*

- *Use the Live Data view feature to see the results of a record set within a dynamic page.*

- *Preview the dynamic page in a browser to work with forms and insert/update dynamic content.*

- *Be sure to include all databases, dependent content, and all dynamic pages with your web site when you are uploading your site to the Web.*

INDEX